THE MARINER'S DICTIONARY

THE
MARINER'S DICTIONARY

BY GERSHOM BRADFORD

BARRE PUBLISHERS, BARRE, MASSACHUSETTS

1972

To the late Felix Riesenbergs—Father and Son

Copyright © 1972 Barre Publishers

Library of Congress Catalog Card Number 72-77971

International Standard Book Number 0-8271-7214-1

Manufactured in the United States of America

INTRODUCTION

The inception of this book in 1918 occurred in the cabin of the U.S.S. (schoolship) NEWPORT. Captain Felix Riesenberg felt there was a need of a nautical dictionary and suggested that I take on the task. For many years sea terms had interested me, so I proceeded to build a manuscript. Every seaman who crossed my track, whatever craft he served in, and those in related activities ashore where button-holed and questioned for words and meanings—always hoping for fresh definitions and new terms. To those helpful men of the sea and shore, I make my acknowledgements. Older dictionaries have also contributed extensively.

In 1926 I had a manuscript but no publisher. Shortly there came a break. Captain Riesenberg, at a banquet, was seated beside the late and revered editor of *Yachting*, Herbert Stone. In the course of conversation the editor mentioned that his magazine was planning to get out a useful book a year. The Captain asked if he had ever thought of a nautical dictionary. Mr. Stone liked the idea. I shipped the manuscript. It was turned over to Alfred Loomis and we began to exchange letters relative to various terms. *The Glossary of Sea Terms* came out in 1927.

In 1940 *Yachting* gave up its books and the *Glossary* went into the hands of Dodd, Mead and Company. It was out of print and Mr. Edward Dodd expressed a desire to republish. I revised and the second edition came out in 1942. In 1954 Mr. Dodd negotiated an agreement with Cassell of London for an English edition.

Yachting has never lost its interest in the glossary and after again revising the book, I had the much appreciated benefit of having the valuable suggestions of the talented and experienced associate editors, Alfred F. Loomis and William H. Taylor. Those two friendly cooperators have most regrettably and prematurely reached the bank of the Deep River and have crossed over to Jordan side.   G.B.

PREFACE

A distinctive language of the sea prevails along all the littorals of the world. Wherever the sea-fog penetrates the land, men—and even women and children—understand the peculiarities of speech which form the lingo of their sailormen. And it dates back to those early times when men first sailed from sight of land.

It is a rich type of expression if measured by the adventure and romance it has brought us; from oars to sail, and sail to power, term has been added to term, phrase built upon phrase; from out of that dimness of time explorers, man-of-warsmen, privateers, buccaneers, slavers, whalers, and deep-sea traders mean and grand have left the marks of their personalities upon it.

It is the vernacular of a hard life—a life of great demands, of grand traditions—and its terms are correspondingly rugged, terse, picturesque and romantic. It is sharply concise where the necessity of emergencies demands; it is apt and comprehensive, as in the term, "under goose-winged topsails"—just showing to a gale a bit of canvas the shape of a goose's wing; and where there is a touch of poetry it is poetic, as in "rolling down to St. Helena."

The language of the sea has become extensive in consequence of the interminable parts of a vessel, its intricate rigging, the many types of craft, various maneuvers, and the precise way of doing things.

Some terms have many meanings, some have different interpretations in different localities, and some are vague at best. Even such commonplace terms as "a fair wind" or "catching a crab" will often start a controversial discussion. The attempt has been made here to give the best sea usage.

This work has been compiled from the viewpoint of the seaman for the information and pleasure of all those interested in the sea, ships, navigation and sea routine. It does not cover the engineer's important part in seafaring—that would make another book. It has been the compiler's endeavor to fill its pages with live terms and also those semi-obsolete names that one is liable to run across in our nautical histories and sea stories.

It is natural that, owing to Britain's insular situation and America's long littorals, the seamen's terms should become a robust part of the English language. With sea connections afloat and ashore we became interested in the preservation of these words. Our collection of selected terms became the first manuscript in 1926 and over the years the second edition went out of print, but the manuscript received continuing revision and updating. Now Barre Publishers makes this edition available.

G.B.

ABBREVIATIONS

A, Amplitude
a, Altitude difference
alt, Altitude
aλ, Assumed longitude
Bn, Beacon
CB, Compass bearing
CC, Compass course
CE, Compass error
CE, Chronometer error
Cn, course
Cpgc, Course per gyro compass
CZn, Compass azimuth
D, Deviation
d, Declination
dec, Declination
dev, Deviation
diff, Difference
dist, Distance
DLo, Difference of longitude
DR, Dead reckoning
dλ, Difference of longitude
EqT, Equation of time
ETA, Estimated time of arrival
f, Latitude factor
g, Acceleration of gravity
GAT, Greenwich apparent time
GHA, Greenwich hour angle
GMT, Greenwich mean time
GST, Greenwich sidereal time
h, Altitude of celestial body

Hc, Computed altitude
HE, Height of eye
HHW, Higher high water
HLW, Higher low water
Ho, Observed altitude
HP, Horizontal parallax
hs, Sextant altitude
ht, Tabulated altitude
HW, High water
I, Magnetic dip
IC, Index correction
Kn, Knot
L, Latitude
l, Difference of latitude
LAN, Local apparent noon
LAT, Local apparent time
lat, Latitude
LHA, Local hour angle
LHW, Lower high water
LL, Lower limb
LLW, Lower low water
Lm, Middle latitude
LMT, Local mean time
long, Longitude
LST, Local sidereal time
LW, Low water
M, Heavenly body
m, Meridional difference
mag, Magnetic
MB, Magnetic bearing

mb, Millibar
MC, Magnetic course
MHHW, Mean higher high water
MHW, Mean high water
MHWN, Mean high water neaps
MHWS, Mean high water springs
mi, Mile or miles
MLLW, Mean lower low water
MLW, Mean low water
MLWN, Mean low water neaps
MLWS, Mean low water springs
MSL, Mean sea level
MZn, Magnetic azimuth
p, Polar distance; departure
pgc, per gyro compass
Pn, North pole
Ps, South pole
psc, per standard compass

pstgc, per steering compass
RAR, Radio acoustic ranging
Rbn, Radio beacon
RDF, Radio direction finder
RF, Radio frequency
SD, Semi-diameter
SH, Ship's head
SHA, Sidereal hour angle
TB, True bearing
TC, True course
Tg, Ground wave reading
Tgs, Ground wave—sky wave
TH, True heading
Ts, Sky wave reading
Tsg, Sky wave-ground wave
TZn, True azimuth
Var, Variation
W, Watch time

ILLUSTRATIONS

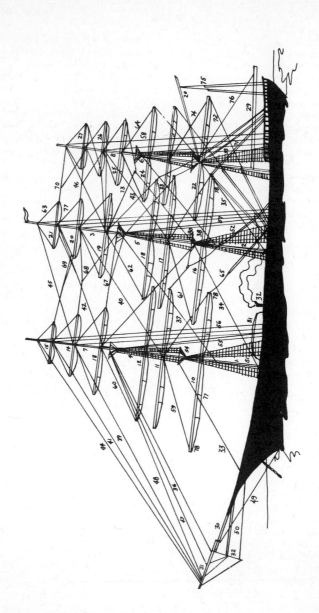

SPAR AND RIGGING DIAGRAM OF A FULL-RIGGED SHIP

(See following page for key)

SPARS

1. Fore-mast
2. Main-mast
3. Mizzen-mast
4. Fore-topmast
5. Main-topmast
6. Mizen-topmast
7. Fore-topgallant-mast
8. Main-topgallant-mast
9. Mizzen-topgallant-mast
10. Fore yard
11. Fore lower topsail yard
12. Fore upper topsail yard
13. Fore topgallant yard
14. Fore royal yard
15. Fore skysail yard
16. Main yard
17. Main lower topsail yard
18. Main upper topsail yard
19. Main topgallant yard
20. Main royal yard
21. Main skysail yard
22. Crossjack yard
23. Mizzen lower topsail yard
24. Mizzen upper topsail yard
25. Mizzen topgallant yard
26. Mizzen royal yard
27. Mizzen skysail yard
28. Spanker gaff
29. Spanker boom
30. Bowsprit
31. Jib-boom
32. Martingale-boom.

RIGGING

33. Fore stay
34. Main stay
35. Mizzen stay
36. Fore topmast stay
37. Main topmast stay
38. Mizzen topmast stay
39. Fore topgallant stay
40. Main topgallant stay
41. Fore royal stay
42. Main royal stay
43. Mizzen royal stay
44. Royal skysail stay
45. Main skysail stay
46. Mizzen skysail stay
47. Jib stay
48. Flying jib stay
49. Bobstay
50. Martingale stays
51. Fore rigging
52. Main rigging
53. Mizzen rigging
54. Futtock shrouds
55. Fort topmast backstays
56. Fore topgallant, royal, and skysail backstays
57. Main backstays
58. Mizzen skysail backstay
59. Starboard fore lift
60. Starboard fore topsail lift
61. Starboard main lift
62. Starboard main topsail lift
63. Port skysail lift
64. Mizzen topsail lift
65. Port fore brace
66. Port fore lower topsail brace
67. Port fore topgallant brace
68. Port fore royal brace
69. Port fore skysail brace
70. Port main skysail brace
71. Port main brace
72. Port crossjack brace
73. Port mizzen topgallant brace
74. Port crossjack lift
75. Spanker vangs
76. Spanker boom topping-lifts
77. Foot ropes
78. Flemish horse
79. Fore topmast cross-trees
80. Main top
81. Long boat
82. Galley smoke pipe

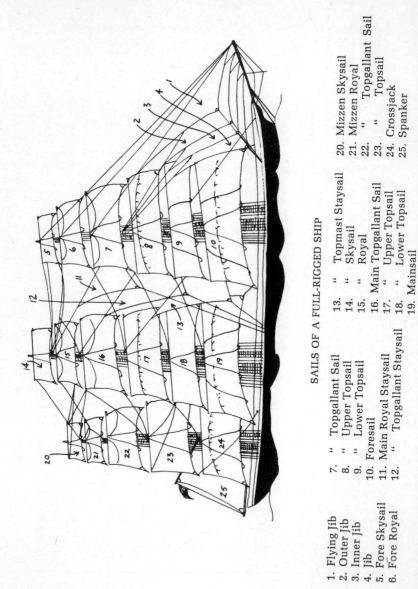

SAILS OF A FULL-RIGGED SHIP

1. Flying Jib
2. Outer Jib
3. Inner Jib
4. Jib
5. Fore Skysail
6. Fore Royal

7. " Topgallant Sail
8. " Upper Topsail
9. " Lower Topsail
10. Foresail
11. Main Royal Staysail
12. " Topgallant Staysail

13. " Topmast Staysail
14. " Skysail
15. " Royal
16. Main Topgallant Sail
17. " Upper Topsail
18. " Lower Topsail
19. Mainsail

20. Mizzen Skysail
21. Mizzen Royal
22. " Topgallant Sail
23. " Topsail
24. Crossjack
25. Spanker

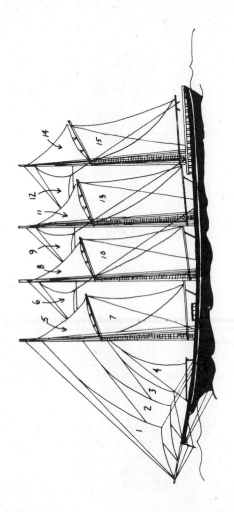

SAILS OF A FOUR-MASTED SCHOONER

1. Flying Jib
2. Outer Jib
3. Inner Jib
4. Fore Staysail

5. Fore Topsail
6. Main Topmast Staysail
7. Foresail
8. Main Topsail

9. Mizzen Topmast
   Staysail
10. Mainsail
11. Mizzen Topsail

12. Spanker Topmast Staysail
13. Mizzen Sail
14. Spanker Topsail
15. Spanker

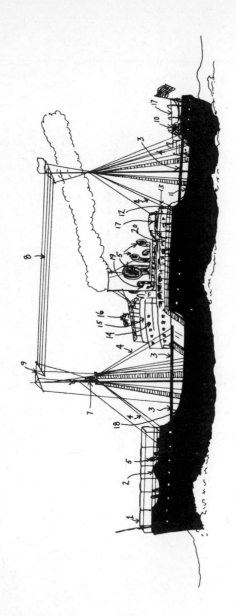

CARGO STEAMER

1. Forecastle
2. Windlass
3. Cargo Booms
4. Boom Topping Lifts
5. Ventilators

6. Funnel
7. Masts
8. Aerials
9. Signal Yards
10. Poop

11. After Well Deck
12. Bridge Deck
13. Boat Deck
14. Captain's Bridge
15. Navigating Bridge

16. Standard Compass
17. Boats
18. For'd Well Deck
19. Fiddley
20. Officers' Rooms, Galley, etc.

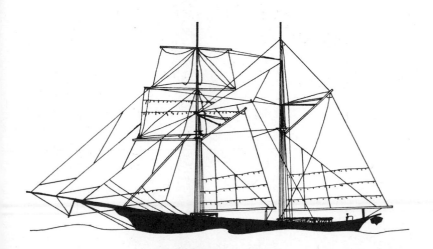

TOPSAIL SCHOONER

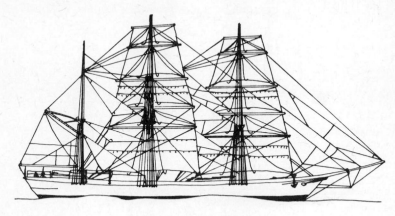

BARK (OR BARQUE)

BARKENTINE

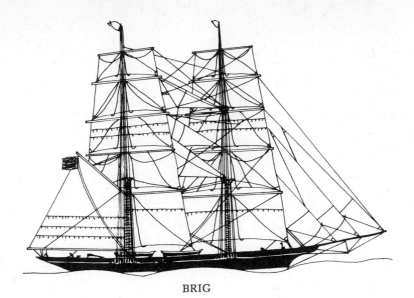

BRIG

HERMAPHRODITE BRIG (See Brigantine)

THE MARINER'S DICTIONARY

A

A1, the highest classification given to a vessel by Lloyds and other insurance organizations.

A.B., an abbreviation for an able-bodied seaman; a man who should be able to do all work required of a seaman. See Ordinary Seaman.

ABACK, a term applied to a vessel whose yards are so trimmed that the wind is on their forward side and tending to drive her astern. Laying the "topsails to the mast" is done deliberately in maneuvering ship, but when by accident, either through a shift of wind or careless steering, the ship is said to be "taken aback." Being taken aback has accounted for the loss of many ships. A fore-and-aft rigged vessel caught aback with boom tackles set may be in trouble.

ABAFT, towards the stern.

ABAFT THE BEAM, any direction between the beam and the stern.

ABEAM or **OFF THE BEAM,** the direction at right angles to the line of the keel.

ABERRATION, a slight apparent change in the position of a heavenly body, or the movement of the earth during the interval of the passage of light from a heavenly body to the observer.

ABOARD, on or in a vessel. Close aboard is to be in close proximity to a ship or obstruction. *With starboard tacks aboard,* a phrase which signifies that the yards of a sailing vessel are braced up so that the starboard lower corner, the tack, is to windward and forward, being hove down to the *tack bumpkin.* The vessel is then sailing close-hauled on the starboard tack.

ABOUT SHIP, to tack ship.

ABOVEBOARD, above decks; also, without concealment or deceit.

ABOX, the head yards and after yards being braced on opposite tacks. Square-rigged ships formerly used to lie this way when it was desired to maintain a proximate position for gamming or awaiting a pilot.

ABREAST, opposite or at right angles to.

ABSENT FLAG, a small square blue signal flown from a yacht's starboard spreader to signify that the owner is not aboard.

ABURTON, casks stowed end to end athwartship.

ACCELERATION, the increasing motion of a body. It is also the correction necessary to be applied to mean time to change it into terms of sidereal time.

ACCOMMODATION LADDER, a flight of steps leading down a ship's side by which small boats may be entered or the vessel boarded.

ACCOUNT, TO GO ON THE, the term used when a sailor turned pirate.

ACOCKBILL, the position of an anchor when it hangs by the chain over the bow.

ACOUSTIC CLOUDS, areas of atmosphere through which sound is impeded, deflected or stopped. Such a condition accounts for the occasional erratic reception of fog signals and a steamer's whistle.

ACT OF MAN, the action of the master of a vessel in sacrificing spars, cargo or furnishings for the preservation of the remainder. Under such circumstances all parties interested in the ship and cargo stand their proportionate share of loss. It becomes a case of *General Average.*

ACT OF PROVIDENCE or **GOD,** an accident to spars, vessel or cargo occurring through the action of wind and weather over which the master has no control. Under such circumstances the insurance is adjusted by particular average, where each loss is separately settled.

AD VALOREM, proportionate to value.

ADIABATIC (Meteorology), variations in volume or pressure not accompanied by gain or loss of heat.

ADJUSTMENT OF A COMPASS, the method of placing magnets and iron masses about a compass so as to oppose the magnetism existing in the ship and her fittings, with the purpose of compensating the deviation as nearly as possible.

ADJUSTMENT OF THE SEXTANT, the process of testing and rectifying the position of the glasses of the instrument in their relation to the frame and each other. See Sextant.

ADMEASUREMENT, the work of measuring the various dimensions, capacities and tonnage of a ship for official registration.

ADMIRAL, the commanding officer of a naval fleet. There are four grades—Fleet Admiral, Admiral, Vice-Admiral and Rear Admiral. The largest size of wooden fid is called an *admiral.*

ADMIRALTY LAW, that branch which deals with cases connected with the duties and rights of shipping. In the United States all such cases differ from common law in that they are tried only in United States courts.

ADRIFT, without being fast to a stationary object.

ADVANCE, the amount a vessel moves in the direction of her original course after the helm has been put over and until she has turned through 90°. Also, money paid to a seaman upon "signing on" for a voyage. It was usually a month's pay. The advance was deducted from his future wages—a practice now illegal in the United States. Money advanced to sailors in intermediate ports of a voyage on account of a final settlement. In the United States a seaman is entitled to one-half the wages due in any port.

ADVENTURE, small consignments of goods sent abroad in a ship to be sold by the master, or bartered, for foreign merchandise. In former days the shipmaster acted as an agent for his relatives and friends, even his children, who desired to indulge in a little speculation.

AERIAL, a fine wire, or set of wires, used to propagate and receive the radio waves. The aerial is usually rigged between trucks.

AFFREIGHTMENT, a contract for chartering a vessel in whole or in part for the transportation of merchandise.

AFLOAT, the condition of resting buoyantly upon the water, the upward pressure being equal to that of gravity.

A-FRAME DERRICK, a type in which the mast is formed by two timbers crossed by a ground timber at the foot; the foot of the boom is stepped in the ground timber; two additional ground timbers also form an A and serve as a foundation.

AFT, towards the stern.

AFTER BODY, the stern section of a vessel.

AFTER GUARD, the men detailed to tend the gear at the after part of a vessel. Also, the officers, who have their quarters aft; the owner of a yacht and his guests.

AFTER PEAK, a compartment in the very stern; the after peak bulkhead forms the forward side of the after peak and protects the vessel in case of an accident to the propeller (tail) shaft or stern bearings.

AFTER PERPENDICULAR, a verti-

cal line at the after edge of the sternpost.

AFTER YARDS, those abaft the foremast.

AGAINST THE SUN, a term applied to a rotary motion that is opposite to the hands of a watch.

AGONIC LINE, one of no variation.

AGROUND, on the bottom.

AGULHAS CURRENT, a branch of the South Indian Equatorial Current which flows down through the Mozambique Channel along the eastern coast of Africa. Upon arriving off the Agulhas Bank it is deflected to the southward and later to the eastward.

AHOY, a customary hail to a boat or vessel.

A-HULL, a term applied to a vessel hove-to under bare poles with helm alee.

AIR, a term meaning a movement of air, as, a *light air.*

AIR ALMANAC, published at four-month intervals, is primarily for aviators, but through the facility of its use has favor with surface navigators. It furnishes data at ten-minute intervals and to 1′ of arc, which navigators find of sufficient accuracy for their ordinary needs.

AIR FUNNEL, one of the air courses for ventilation between the frames, ceiling and planking of a wooden ship.

AIR PORT, a round opening, which is usually closed, with a heavy glass hinged cover.

AIR STRAKES, ducts for ventilating the holds.

AIRPLANE, a platform upon which is loaded a draft of cargo—is hoisted by a bridle attached to a cargo hook. It is a pallet.

ALBATROSS, the largest sea-fowl, is found chiefly in the Southern Hemisphere. They have a wing spread that sometimes reaches 13 feet. They are capable of the most remarkable long sustained flights. There was formerly a superstition that the soul of a departed sailor animated the albatross and for this reason seamen were reluctant to kill them.

ALEE, away from the direction of the wind, usually referring to the helm.

ALIDADE, an instrument for taking bearings.

ALL HANDS, the whole ship's company.

ALL IN THE WIND, every sail shaking.

ALL NIGHT IN, a night's sleep with no watch.

ALL STANDING, to be fully equipped; to be quickly brought to a stop is said to be *brought up all standing. To turn in all standing* is to retire with one's clothes on.

ALL-A-TAUNT-O, all gear hauled taut; ship-shape.

ALLIGATOR NAVY, the force consisting of amphibious craft.

ALMACANTARS, circles parallel with the rational horizon on the celestial sphere.

ALOFT, above the decks; overhead.

ALOFT THERE!, the customary hail to men aloft.

ALONGSHOREMEN, the handlers of cargoes.

ALONGSIDE, by the side of a pier or of a vessel.

ALOW, low, near the decks; sometimes meaning below decks.

ALOW and **ALOFT,** a term used when a vessel is carrying all sails—including stunsails.

ALPHABET FLAGS of the International Code: Alfa, Bravo, Charlie, Delta, Echo, Foxtrot, Golf, Hotel, India, Juliet, Kilo, Lima, Mike, November, Oscar, Papa, Quebec, Romeo, Sierra, Tango, Uniform, Victor, Whiskey, Xray, Yankee, Zulu.

For complete information see Publication 102, International Code of Signals, of the U.S. Naval Oceanographic Office.

ALTITUDE (Alt.), the height of a body above the horizon. The altitude as measured with a sextant is the *observed altitude* and in the case of the sun needs correction for dip, refraction, semi-diameter, parallax and index error (see individually) in order to obtain the true altitude.

ALTITUDE AZIMUTH, a method of obtaining the bearing of the sun or a star by solving the astronomical triangle for the azimuth, or angle at the zenith. The altitude gives zenith distance; the declination the polar distance; the latitude by dead reckoning the co-latitude.

ALTITUDE DIFFERENCE, the amount the computed altitude differs from the true altitude of a body in the determination of position lines. The true attitude being that measured by the sextant. If the true altitude is the larger, the altitude difference is measured from the assumed position of the ship towards the body, otherwise away from it.

ALTO-CUMULUS (A-Cu.), clouds are partially shaded white or grayish, composed of large globular masses, which often become confused.

ALTO-STRATUS (A-S.), clouds form a thick veil of a deep gray color through which the sun or moon can be easily seen.

AMAIN, all at once, on the run.

AMBERGRIS, a light grayish substance used in the preparation of perfumery where its singular blending quality is of great value. It comes from an intestinal secretion in a sperm whale.

AMIDSHIPS, usually in the line of the keel, but sometimes midway between bow and stern; usually corrupted to 'midships.

AMPLITUDE, the angle at the zenith between the prime vertical and the vertical circle passing through the observed body. It is sometimes considered as the arc of the horizon from the true East or West point to the body at rising or setting. An amplitude should be observed when the sun is about one apparent diameter above the horizon. The bearing is taken by compass and compared with the calculated or true amplitude. The difference is the error of the compass. The true amplitude is found by using Tables 27 and 28 Bowditch or by adding the secant of the

latitude and the sine of the declination, which gives the sine of the true amplitude.

ANCHOR, a device of iron so shaped as to grip the bottom and hold a vessel by the chain or rope attached. Anchors are of many types, some for the same purpose, others for different uses. The largest or heaviest anchor of a vessel is known as the street anchor;

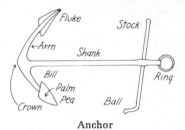

Anchor

those in ordinary use are called *bowers; stream anchors* for light work and easy handling; *kedges* for running warps. They are lighter than stream anchors. There are also *grapnels,* bearing many flukes for dragging purposes and mooring small boats. Some anchors have movable flukes and some are stockless. The latter are the most used owing to the ease of stowage, being merely hove up in the hawse pipe and made fast. Another division is made in the kinds of anchors: A *solid anchor* is one where the shank and flukes are forged together, while a *portable anchor* is capable of being taken to pieces. An anchor is said to be *acockbill* when it hangs by the chain over the bow, and *apeak* when the chain is hove short and the anchor is ready to break out. An anchor is said to *bite* when it takes a good hold in the bottom, but *comes home* when it begins to drag, while to *bring home* an anchor is to heave the ship up to it. To *shoe an anchor* is to bolt planks to the flukes in order to enlarge their area for use on a soft bottom. Modern anchors of light weight and high tensile strength are popular for vessels of small tonnage; especially yachts. There are also sea anchors.

ANCHOR BRACKET. Instead of resting on a ship's rail and billboard, anchors often are made fast on brackets on the bows, hence the name.

ANCHOR CHAIN, heavy studlinked chain attached to an anchor for mooring or anchoring purposes.

ANCHOR DECK, a very short forecastle for the stowing of the anchor.

ANCHOR HOY, a lighter equipped with derrick for the handling of heavy anchors.

ANCHOR LIGHT, a white light visible all round the horizon shown from the forward part of a vessel at anchor. On vessels 150 feet or more in length a similar light is also shown aft, but 15 feet lower than the forward light. Also called *riding light.* Vessels of less than 65 feet may anchor without lights in Special Anchorage Areas shown on the charts.

ANCHOR LINING, a number of strips of wood or iron to protect the ship against injury from the bill of the anchor.

ANCHOR or **MOORING POLE,** is often used by a small vessel or boat when obliged to anchor in an exposed position. The cable from the anchor is shackled to the lower end of the pole and the cable or pendant from the bow is shackled to the upper end of the pole. This arrangement tends to absorb the shock on the anchor.

ANCHOR POCKET, a recess at the hawse pipe into which the anchor flukes are hove, giving the vessel a clear flush bow for maneuvering around the docks.

ANCHOR WATCH, a detail of the crew keeping watch while a vessel is at anchor.

ANCHORAGE, an area set apart for anchored vessels; a suitable place for anchoring. *Prohibited anchorage,* a section of a harbor kept free of anchored vessels.

ANCHOR'S AWEIGH, when it is off the bottom.

ANEMOMETER, an instrument which turns by the strength of the wind in a horizontal plane. The impulse is given to cups set vertically on horizontal arms. The velocity is recorded by the revolutions of the vertical shaft on an indicator by means of gears.

ANEROID BAROMETER, like the mercurial, an instrument for measuring the pressure of the atmosphere. It resembles a clock in shape and appearance. The dial is graduated into isobars and into inches, tenths and hundredths, upon which a hand indicates the atmospheric pressure. The variations of pressure are exerted upon a metallic box from which most of the air has been exhausted, and a combination of levers sensitively adjusted communicates the movements of contraction and expansion to the index on the face.

ANGARY, RIGHT OF, is given a belligerent under stress of necessity to seize the ships of a neutral for its own use.

ANGLE COLLAR, a circle formed with an angle iron.

ANGLE IRON or **FRAME,** a bar of iron bent longitudinally, so that it shows an angle in cross section.

ANGLE OF REPOSE, the greatest angle at which a bulk cargo will rest without shifting.

ANNIE OAKLEY, a ventilated spinnaker with several stabilizing holes.

ANNUAL VARIATION, the amount the magnetic compass changes in a year, due to changes in the earth's lines of force. It varies in different localities, and is not a consistent change.

ANNULAR, pertaining to or having the form of a ring. An annular eclipse exists when the moon covers the middle portion of the sun but leaves a ring of light overlapping it.

ANOMALY, the angle at the sun between the line drawn from the sun to perihelion and the radius vector, reckoned in the direction of the earth's motion.

ANSWERING PENNANT, a red and white vertically striped pennant flown when answering a signal.

ANTARCTIC CIRCLE, the northern margin of the Antarctic zone, which is in 66° 32′ S. Lat.

ANTENNA, an arrangement of conductors, usually aloft, for the reception and sending of radio waves.

ANTI-CORROSIVE PAINT, applied as a first coat to steel in order to prevent corrosion of the plates.

ANTICYCLONIC, a condition where the winds blow out from a center of high pressure. The direction is opposite to the cyclonic movement and is of an outward spiral nature. It is associated with atmospheric high pressure with clockwise winds in the Northern Hemisphere and counterclockwise in the Southern Hemisphere.

ANTI-FOULING COMPOSITION, a paint for vessels' bottoms containing copper, mercury, or other chemicals for the destruction of marine growth.

ANTIPODEAN DAY, the day gained in crossing the meridian of 180° when sailing eastward. That is, there may be, for instance, two Mondays, May 14th.

ANTIPODES, the point or country on the side of the world diametrically opposite; New Zealand and Australia are often referred to as the Antipodes by English people.

ANTISCORBUTIC, a food which has a counteracting effect on scurvy, such as onions, potatoes and lime juice.

APEAK, the position of an anchor when hove short and about to be broken out.

APHELION, is the point in the

earth's orbit that is farthest from the sun.

APOGEE, the point in the moon's orbit that is farthest from the earth.

APRON, an inner stem of a vessel fayed on the after side of the main stem for its reenforcement.

APSIDES, LINE OF, connects the perihelion and aphelion of the earth's orbit.

AQUARIUS, the eleventh sign of the zodiac.

ARCH CONSTRUCTION, a system in which the deck beams are of unusual size and strength, relieving the necessity for lower beams and allowing a clear interior for bulk cargoes.

ARCH PIECE, the member of a ship's structure forming the arch over the propeller.

ARCHED SQUALL, one whose advancing front is higher in the middle than at the sides.

ARCTIC CIRCLE, the southern limit of the Arctic Zone, which is in lat. 66°32′ N.

ARCTIC CURRENT (Labrador C), a cold flow of water to the southward along the Labrador and Newfoundland coasts. It encounters the Gulf Stream off the Grand Banks. The ice in various forms met on the steamer lanes is brought down from Greenland's waters by this current.

ARETMON MAST, an ancient spar serving as a foremast and raking somewhat forward. The sail served the same purpose as jibs of modern vessels in keeping the bow off.

The modern bowsprit grew out of the artemon mast with a gradually diminishing "steeve" or angle from the horizontal.

ARIES, the first sign of the zodiac. See First Point of Aries.

ARM, the part of an anchor between the crown and the flukes. See also Yardarm.

ARMING, the process of filling the cavity in the bottom of a lead with tallow by which specimens of the bottom are obtained, which aids the mariner is locating the position of the ship.

ARREST. The detention of a vessel in the custody of the law until a claim or judgment is satisfied.

ARTICLES, the contract signed by a seaman upon joining a merchant vessel.

ARTIFICIAL HORIZON, a device by the use of which the altitude of a heavenly body above the horizon can be obtained on land. It consists of a small basin of mercury protected from disturbance by the wind. The actual reading of the sextant is *twice* the altitude of the body; if the lower edge of the sun's image is used then the semidiameter is additive; there is no dip correction. Molasses or any other viscous fluid may be used instead of mercury.

ARTIST, a mariner of former days who was versed in navigation when the practice of the science was considered an accomplishment.

ASH BREEZE, progress made with oars in a calm. (Sometimes a *White Ash Breeze.*)

ASHORE, on the bottom or on the shore; aground.

ASSUMED POSITION. In the establishment of a position line by celestial observation a point is taken in the vicinity of the D.R. position. The altitude of a body is computed, or taken from the tables, for this position. When the computed altitude is compared with the measured altitude of the body by sextant, the difference between them is the altitude difference. (q.v.)

ASTERN, backwards; behind the vessel.

ASTROLABE, an old-fashioned instrument for taking altitudes of heavenly bodies.

ASTRONOMICAL DAY, 24 hours of solar time reckoned from noon to noon.

ASTRONOMICAL LATITUDE, the angular distance from the equator to the zenith; as shown by the plumb line or apparent zenith.

ASTRONOMICAL TIME, starts at noon (0 hours) and runs to the succeeding noon, through 24 hours. It is thus 12 hours behind civil time.

ASTRONOMICAL TRIANGLE, a spherical triangle on the celestial sphere, one of whose angles is at the pole, one at the body observed, and the other at the zenith of the observer. The sides are *Polar Distance* (90° ± d), *Zenith Distance* (90°-Alt.) and *Colatitude* (90°-Lat.). The angle at the pole is the *Hour Angle* and the angle at the zenith is the *Azimuth*. The North Pole is used in north latitude and the South Pole in south latitude.

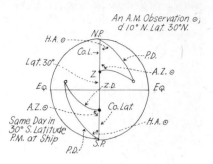

Astronomical Triangle

ATHWART, at right angles to the fore and aft line of a vessel. Also *Athwartships*. *Athwart the tide,* applies to a vessel lying across the current.

ATHWART HAWSE, across a vessel's bow or anchor chain.

ATLANTIC RANGE, the coast of the United States bordering the Atlantic Ocean.

ATLANTIS, LOST. In early times, references were made to a large and opulent land in the Atlantic which is supposed to have settled and is now referred to as the Lost Atlantis.

ATOLL, a circular islet nearly or entirely enclosing a lagoon; usually of coral formation.

ATRIP, when the anchor is broken out and leaving the bottom.

AUGMENTATION (Aug.), the apparent increase of the semi-diameter of a celestial body as it approaches the zenith. Used in navigation particularly in reference to the moon's semi-diameter. When the moon is directly overhead, the observer is occupying the part of the earth that is nearest the body, but when the moon is on the horizon, the observer is the same distance from the body as the center of the earth, hence one half of the earth's diameter farther away than when the body is overhead. So it follows that when the body is in the horizon the apparent semi-diameter is less, and increases towards the zenith because it is getting nearer.

AURORA AUSTRALIS and **BOREALIS,** southern and northern lights. A luminous phenomenon supposed to be electrical in its origin which illuminates the polar skies at times with scintillating beams of light, often in color. They move from the horizon towards the zenith. See also Merry Dancers.

AUSTRAL, pertaining to southern regions.

AUTOMATED SHIP, one in which the steamer's power is controlled and operated from the bridge, thereby reducing the personnel of the engineers' department.

AUTUMNAL EQUINOX, the moment (about September 22nd) that the sun crosses the Equator, bound south. It is also applied to the position of the sun at the intersection of the equinoctial and the ecliptic.

AUXILIARIES, small engines for winches, pumps, dynamos, etc.

AUXILIARY, a vessel propelled both by sails and by mechanical power.

AUXILIARY ANGLE, a subsidiary angle which facilitates the process of a calculation.

AVAST, an order to stop, to cease hauling.

AVERAGE, there are two kinds of average—Particular and General Average. Each is a process of arriving at an adjustment of insurance for loss at sea.

AVERAGE BOND, given by the owners of merchandise, in a case of General Average, pledging that they will pay their share and not detain the vessel or delivery of the cargo.

AWASH, the condition when the seas wash over a wreck or shoal, or when a vessel is so low that water is constantly washing aboard in quantities.

AWAY, an order to shove off—"Away boats." To lower a boat or draft of cargo—"Lower away."

AWEATHER, towards the direction of the wind, to windward.

AWEIGH, the position of an anchor which has been broken out and is off the bottom.

AWNING, a canvas protection from the sun, taking name according to its location, as, forecastle awning, bridge awning, etc.

AWNING-DECKED VESSEL, a type having a continuous upper deck of light construction, and the sides wholly enclosed above the main deck.

AXIS, the line around which a body revolves. The axis of a channel is a line through its center.

AYE AYE, SIR, a term used by a subordinate to his superior in acknowledgement of an order.

AZIMUTH. This element is so important to the navigator that great familiarity with it is desirable. An azimuth is a bearing of a heavenly body; it is measured from the elevated pole, that is, in north latitude from the north point of the horizon through 360°. An azimuth may also be expressed as the angle at the zenith lying between the meridian of the observer and the vertical circle passing through the body. The true azimuth may either be computed (see Altitude and Time Azimuths) or taken from tables, or from a diagram. Azimuth is used by engineers where seamen use the word "bearing."

AZIMUTH CIRCLE (Bearing Finder), a metallic circle made to fit on a compass for the purpose of taking azimuths. There is a revolving mirror on one side by which the reflection of the sun is caught and thrown into a prism situated directly opposite, also on the rim of the circle. The rays, here thrown downward in a thread of light upon the rim of the compass card, indicate the sun's bearing. There are also sight vanes for use in taking bearings of landmarks.

AZIMUTH CIRCLE, a vertical circle originating at the zenith, and intersecting the horizon at right angles.

AZIMUTH DIAGRAM, a convenient device by which the azimuth may be obtained graphically without troublesome interpolation.

B

B.P., between perpendiculars, q.v.

B.T.U., British Thermal Unit.

BABY JIB TOPSAIL, the smallest of the jibs usually carried by yachts, and is set well aloft on one of the outer stays.

BACK; to back an anchor, is to send an extra anchor to the bottom with its shank made fast along the cable to assist the first anchor, or to shackle the extra anchor to the chain near the lower one before letting go. The wind *backs* when it changes against the hands of a watch, but *veers* if it changes with them. Square sails are *backed* or *aback* when the wind is on their forward side throwing them against the mast. If this occurs through a shift of wind or a careless helmsman, a ship is said to be *taken aback. To back water* with oars is to push instead of pull. *To back* any piece of gear is to set up a preventer.

BACK SIGHT, to bring a body to the point of the horizon directly opposite that point used in a fore or ordinary sight. It is used as a test for excessive refraction, or when intervening land or a fog bank obstructs the fore sight. Due to the mechanical limitations of the instrument it can be taken only when the celestial body is in high altitude. A back sight sextant reading should be subtracted from 180 degrees.

BACK SPLICE, a method of finishing the end of a rope by tucking the strands back from the end which is crowned.

BACK WASH, the water thrust aft by the action of the screw or paddle wheels. Waves running out through a prevailing sea after striking a cliff or sea wall.

BACK WATER, to push on the oars, making sternway.

BACK WIND, the flow of air from sail against another on the wrong side. In a yacht an improperly set head sail may so interfere with the efficiency of the mainsail.

BACK A YARD, is to brace it in such a way as to bring the wind on the forward side of a sail.

BACKBOARD, a rest board set athwartships in the stern of a small boat.

BACKBONE, the ridge rope of an awning; into it are turned the parts of the crows-foot for tricing it up.

BACK-HAND ROPE, left-handed rope.

BACKING, winds changing against the hands of a watch in the northern hemisphere; changing clockwise in southern hemisphere. See *Veering.*

BACKING AND FILLING, a sailing ship working up a river on a flood tide with a head wind, fills or backs her sails, sets or takes in the jib and spanker, as necessary to maintain a position clear of the banks. This is known as *backing and filling.* It was extensively practiced on the Chinese rivers in early days. The process of working latitude and longitude alternately forward and backward is called *backing and filling.*

BACKLASH, shocks caused by play in steering gear or other mechanical devices.

BACKROPES, stay the dolphin striker from aft; they lead in to the bows.

BACKSTAYS, part of the standing rigging of a ship. They lead from the topmast, t'gallant and royal mastheads to the chains abaft the rigging to support the mast from aft. When carrying a heavy press of sail in strong winds extra or *preventer backstays* may be set up temporarily. In some small fore-and-aft-rigged vessels backstays are set up on each tack and the lee ones cast off to allow a freer swing to the boom. These are called *shifting backstays* or *runners.* Single-masted yachts with inboard rig use *permanent* or *standing backstays.* The forward backstays in a ship are called *breast backstays.*

BACKSTRAPPED, a term applied to a vessel underway and unable to stem the current; or sometimes to one becalmed under high land.

BAFFLE (BAFFAL) PLATES, are set vertically in tanks to prevent the violent shifting of liquids from side to side.

BAFFLING WINDS, are frequently shifting winds and light airs.

BAG, sails with leeches taut and canvas slack are said to *bag*.

BAGGALA, an Arab vessel of the Indian Ocean. It has two masts and is a swift sailer.

BAGGY WRINKLE, a form of chafing gear made by hitching a great number of short rope yarns around two lengths of small stuff, so that the ends come out between them. It is wound in close contact round a stay, giving a bushy appearance, and saves wear on a sail at the point of chafe.

BAG-PIPE, to shift the sheet of a sail in such a way as to bring the sail aback.

BAG-REEF, a term applied to a single reef in a fore-and-aft or square sail.

BAGUIO, a typhoon in the Philippines.

BAIL, to dip water out.

BAILER, a device of many shapes used to remove water from a boat.

BALANCE LUG, a small boat rig. The sail sets from a small yard and carries a boom which projects forward of the mast.

BALANCE REEF-BAND, runs from the jaws of the gaff of a fore-and-aft sail about parallel with the boom, making a triangular sail when *balance reefed*.

BALANCED RUDDER, one that has a certain amount of its area (weight) forward of the pivoting point.

BALANCING RING or **BAND,** a ring fitted with a link at a point on the shank of an anchor, where, when hoisted, it will balance the anchor. The anchor is stowed by hooking the fish fall into this ring and hoisting it on deck.

BALANDRA, a coastal craft of western South America. It is of crude workmanship, rather high-sided, and rigged as a sloop or schooner.

BALDHEADED SCHOONER, one without topmasts.

BALE, alternate form of *Bail*.

BALE-BAND, is found (sometimes) at the mast-head supported by the cap, into which the flying jib stay is made fast.

BALEEN, whalebone. A horny sieve hanging from the the upper jaw of a right whale like a fringe. It is by means of this baleen that the whale strains its food from a mouthful of sea water.

BALLAHOU, a West Indian schooner whose masts are raked at different angles, usually the foremast forward and the mainmast aft. Although fast-sailing they were not trim in appearance; hence the term has now come to be used for old and lubberly appearing vessels.

BALLAST, a quantity of iron, stone, gravel or other weighty substance placed in the lower hold of a vessel, or in some cases metal bolted to the keel, to increase stability by lowering the center of gravity. Spaces used for water ballast such as double bottoms, peak tanks, deep tanks and cofferdams are not included in net tonnage. A vessel sails *in ballast* when she carries no cargo. Water, sometimes oil, in ballast tanks is the most common method of ballasting a large vessel.

BALLAST LOGS, are lashed alongside to prevent capsizing.

BALLAST PASSAGE, one made in ballast, but especially referring to the empty passage of a tank steamer.

BALLAST TANKS, are in the lower holds of vessels for carrying water ballast, also called *Double Bottoms.* They can be pumped out and flooded at will and used to trim ship.

BALLINGER, an obsolete vessel of about 100 tons having a small freeboard but good length, and adapted for sail and oars. The type originated on the shores of the Bay of Biscay in the 14th century.

BALLOON JIB, a very large head sail of light material used on yachts and fishermen in light and moderate weather.

BALLOW, deep water inside a bar.

BALSA, a raft or catamaran used in the coastal trade of South America; also a very light, buoyant wood used in the manufacture of life rafts.

BANK, a large shoal with a sufficient depth of water to prevent the sea breaking and is usually navigable. Dangerous reefs and shoals may exist on banks. *To double bank the oars* is to place two men at an oar. A boat is double banked if two men are pulling on one thwart. Fires are *banked* when kept partially smothered by coal or ashes. The *right bank* of a river is the right side when headed downstream.

BANKER, a large fishing vessel which frequents the offshore fishing banks.

BAR, a shoal usually of sand or mud opposite a river mouth or harbor entrance.

BAR BOUND, held in port by heavy seas on the bar.

BAR LATTICE BOOM, is constructed of latticework steel and serves as a cargo or derrick boom.

BARBAR, a strong cutting wind of the Gulf of St. Lawrence which is filled with particles of ice.

BARBETTE, a bulging placement for a secondary battery in the side of a naval vessel.

BARDEN, the method of installing *grain fittings* as described under that heading.

BARE POLE CHARTER, one in which the bare ship is chartered with no crew. Sometimes called a *bare hull* and even *bare boat* charter. The charterer for a stipulated sum takes over the vessel with a minimum of restrictions.

BARE POLES, a term given when a vessel underway is without sail set. A vessel is sometimes *hove to under bare poles* when no canvas will stand.

BARGE, a general name given to a large pulling boat. It is often given to flat-bottom craft, but more particularly to vessels built for towage purposes, to carry bulk cargoes, as *sand barge, coal barge,* etc. Formerly the term was applied to the elegantly fitted boats or vessels of state, and we still have the *admiral's barge,* which is a fine fast motorboat for this officer's use. There is a type of work boat in England called a *barge.* The so-called *Thames barge* is of the ketch or yawl rig with a large loose-footed (no boom) mainsail, the peak of which is supported by a sprit. It is fitted with brails and usually a topsail is carried; if it has only pole masts it is called a *stumpy.*

BARGING, is a maneuver used at a starting line by a yacht contending for a windward position. She tries to force her way between other yachts and the windward end of the line, all being on the same tack. By gaining an overlap, after the starting gun, such a barging boat would shout for "room," destroying a well-planned start of the yachts to leeward. This practice is now eliminated by the "anti-barging rule." A leeward boat approaching a starting line, after the gun, is not now obliged to give way to an overlapping yacht shouting for room. The leeward boat must not head above the course for the first mark, nor luff to interfere with a yacht to windward.

BARK (BARQUE), a three-masted vessel square-rigged on the fore and main but fore-and-aft on the mizzen. A four-masted bark is square-rigged on the fore, main, and mizzen, but fore-and-aft on the after mast, according to most common usage, although this rig by some authorities is called a ship, and even a *shipentine.* The term

"bark" was first applied to a small type of galley, early in the history of ships.

BARKALONGA, a Spanish type of vessel having two or three masts lug rigged. It was used in the Mediterranean and occasionally came to the West Indies in early days.

BARKENTINE (Barquentine), a three-or-more-masted vessel square-rigged on the fore, and fore-and-aft on the main and mizzen or any additional masts.

BARNACLES, small shellfish which attach themselves to the sides of vessels, piers, and driftwood.

BAROGRAPH, an instrument which automatically registers barometric pressure. It consists of a cylinder driven by clock gear, around which is secured a sheet of cross-section paper. A self-inking pen actuated by an aneroid barometer is brought in contact with the revolving paper and leaves a record.

BAROMETER, is an instrument for measuring the barometric pressure. There are two types, Aneroid and Mercurial Barometers.

BARQUE, alternate spelling for Bark.

BARRATRY, the wilful casting away of a ship by her master; also any breach of trust on his part.

BARREL, a receptacle for liquids which has different capacities for various uses. As a barrel of crude oil is 42 gallons; in whaling days a barrel was 31½ gallons.

BARREL-BOWED, applies where the bow is nearly circular at the deckline gradually assuming sharper lines to a finer entrance at the waterline.

BARRIER REEF, a protecting reef that skirts a coast, taking the force of the sea. Very often small vessels can navigate in comparatively smooth water inside a barrier reef. Notable among barrier reefs is the Great Barrier Reef off the eastern coast of Australia.

BASS ROPE, coir rope.

BATHYMETRIC CHARTS, are those that emphasize the curves of equal depths; they facilitate contour navigation.

BATHYSPHERE, a pressure resisting vessel, in which scientists are lowered to great depths where through windows they can study marine life and collect oceanographic data. The most advanced device for this work is the navy's *Trieste,* cyclindrical in shape, capable of moving slowly over the bottom and has reached extreme depths.

BATTEN CLEATS, right-angled brackets welded to a hatch coaming into which the battens are dropped and drawn firmly against the tarpaulins by wedges.

BATTEN POCKETS, are sewed into sails to hold the battens at desired angles.

BATTENS, strips of iron that fit over brackets welded to the sides of a hatch coaming and secure the hatch-covering tarpaulins. When securely wedged the hatches are said to be battened down. Wooden or plastic battens are long slender strips placed in sails to support and hold their form, especially to flatten the leaches of racing sails. Battens are placed about the rigging to save the gear from chafing. *Cargo battens* are long planks in the holds and 'tween decks along the ship's side to protect cargo from sweat and rust.

BATTLE PORTS, are dead lights, that is, no light—the covers of solid metal for air ports.

BAULK, a heavy squared piece of timber.

BAWLEY, a small English sloop which carries a gaff topsail and whose mainsail has no boom, brailling to the mast.

BAYAMO, a violent squall on the south coast of Cuba.

BAYOU, an inlet from a bay or river; a term commonly used in the Southern States.

BEACH, the sandy shore washed by the surf; to *beach* a vessel is to run her ashore for a purpose. A seaman unemployed is "on the beach."

BEACHCOMBER, a derelict seaman not anxious for employment, but living off the country and the bounty of visiting ships' cooks. They are seemingly entranced with the port they are in—usually in a foreign country.

BEACON, an aid to navigation, usually unlighted. Beacons take various forms to be conspicuous and characteristic. They usually carry either cages, bells, diamonds, or cones as topmarks. See Radio Beacon.

BEAK or **BEAK-HEAD,** first used in the days of the galleys when much dependence in attack was placed on a ram forward, known as the beak. Later a platform raised on the forward part of the upper deck of medieval ships (probably to facilitate the actions of the fighting men) was called the beak-head. In our own early sailing ship days the term lost its romantic atmosphere and the term "head" was applied to a space for the crew's latrines between the figurehead and the forecastle bulwarks.

BEAM, a thwartship timber or member of a vessel upon which the decks are laid. The depth of a beam is called the *moulding,* its breadth the *siding.* The greatest breadth of a vessel. A vessel may be referred to as a *five beam vessel,* meaning that her length is five times her beam. A clipper ship was from five to six times her beam in length.

BEAM ENDS. A vessel is on her *beam ends* when listed to an angle where her beams are almost perpendicular, and her righting power gone so that she does not return to her normal upright condition. This occurs usually through shifting of the cargo or ballast; it may be caused in a sailing craft by a sudden squall or by a heavy sea inducing too deep rolling.

BEAM FILLING, cargo in small packages convenient for filling the space between the beams.

BEAM KNEE, the enlarged end of a beam (for separate right-angled piece) by which it is attached to a frame.

BEAM LINE, the line of the tops of beams, indicating the intersection with the frames.

BEAM TRAWL. See Otter trawl.

BEAM WIND, one that blows athward a vessel's fore and aft line, at right angles with the keel.

BEAMY, having an unusual breadth of beam in proportion to the length.

BEAR, a hydraulic machine for punching holes in the structure of a vessel. *Deck bear* a heavy mat loaded with sand, stones or grate bars hauled back and forth on the deck, by ropes, for scouring purposes. To *bear down* is to approach from windward. To *bear up* is to come up to the wind, or to an object. To *bear off the land* is to stand offshore. To *bear off* is to push, fend or breast a boat off a wharf, float or a vessel's side. *Bear away* is to steer away from anything, especially from the direction of the wind.

BEAR A HAND, to hurry work; to lend help.

BEARDING, the forward part of a rudder; the reduction of surface in a timber from a given line, as is seen in the stem of a vessel.

BEARDING ANGLE, the angle the stem takes with the keel plates.

BEARDING LINE, the trace of the inner surface of the ship's skin on the keel, stem or stern post. It is closely associated with the rabbet of the keel.

BEARING, the direction of an object expressed in terms of compass points or degrees.

BEARING AND SOUNDING. When only one known object is in sight and there is no opportunity to use a four point bearing, or two bearings and the run between, a single bearing may be laid down on the chart and by taking a sounding an approximate position may be obtained, provided the soundings are characteristic and that there are not several positions where the depths are the same.

BEARINGS OF A VESSEL, the widest part at the water line when in trim. The buoyant support of a vessel forward.

BEATING, working to windward by successive tacks.

BEATING THE BOOBY, swinging the arms from side to side to accelerate the blood's circulation.

BEAUFORT SCALE, indicates the wind's velocity and is tabulated as follows:

Force Wind	Velocity (approx.) Knots
0. Calm	Less than 1
1. Light air	1 to 3
2. Light breeze	4 to 6
3. Gentle breeze	7 to 10
4. Moderate breeze .	11 to 16
5. Fresh breeze	17 to 21
6. Strong breeze	22 to 27
7. Moderate gale	25 to 33
8. Fresh gale	34 to 40
9. Strong gale	41 to 47
10. Whole gale	48 to 55
11. Storm	56 to 65
12. Hurricane	over 65

Hurricanes are numbered 12 to 17 according to velocity, 15 being for winds of 90–99 and 17 for those of 109–118 knots.

BECALM, to blanket a sail or vessel by intercepting the wind with other sails or with another vessel. A vessel unable to make progress through the lack of wind is *becalmed.*

BECKET, a small piece of rope made into a circle for various uses. Also a small piece of rope with an eye in each end to hold the foot of a sprit at the mast of a small boat, or sometimes to hold an oar. The term is often applied to any simple eye which receives the hook of a block.

BECKET BEND (Sheet Bend), an efficient bend used for the purpose of uniting two ends of rope or a rope's end to an eye. It jams with the strain, will not slip and is easily cast loose.

BECUEING, a method of securing the rope to a small anchor for use on rocky ground, by which a sharp jerk, breaking the light seizing, shifts the pull on the line from the ring to the crown of the anchor and effects its release when caught among the rocks.

BED, is the general term given to the foundation of an engine, boiler or any other object of weight.

BEES, pieces of wood attached to the sides of the bowsprit through which pass the fore-topmast stays, thence in to the bows where they are set up with lanyards.

BEFORE THE MAST. Men living in the forecastle are said to be before the mast.

BEFORE THE WIND, having the wind coming from astern.

BELAY, to make fast; to cease.

BELAYING PIN, a device of brass, iron or wood which is set in the pin or fife rails for securing the running rigging.

BELL BUOY, a floating (usually unlighted) beacon equipped with a bell so installed as to ring by the motion of the waves.

BELL PULL, a wire connection from the deck to the engine-room by which a gong is sounded, giving signals to the engineer.

BELL ROPE, a short piece of rope made fast to the clapper of the ship's bell by which it is rung.

BELL'S PURCHASE, comprises four single blocks of which two are movable and two are fixed. A bight of the fall is fast to one moving block.

BELLY, the swelling of a sail.

BELLY BAND, a strengthening cloth of canvas below the lower reef band.

BELLY STRAP, a rope around a small boat from which an anchor is suspended when carrying out a kedge.

BELOW, beneath the deck.

BEND, a combination of turns and tucks by which one rope is fastened to another, or to a spar. As a verb—to secure a sail to a yard or other spar. To shackle the chain to the anchor.

BENDING SHACKLE, connects the chain to the anchor. It is heavier than the shackles between the different shots of chain.

BENDS, the thick planks of a vessel, strakes of which extend from the main deck to the turn of the bilge or the waterline. *Caisson disease* is known as the bends.

BENDY RIG, is used on small racing craft. The shape and composition of the mast lends itself to flexibility; a careful adjustment of headstay, shrouds and backstays controls the bend of the mast, contributing the efficiency of the mainsail.

BENEAPED. The spring tides being the highest high water oblige a vessel, so unfortunate as to ground at this time, to wait two weeks for the next spring tide to release her. Such a vessel is said to be *beneaped.*

BENT, a section or span of a bridge.

BENTINCKS, triangular courses. The *Bentink boom* is a spar across the foot of a square foresail, sometimes formerly used by whalers.

BERI-BERI, a disease of the nerves which causes paralysis, swelling of the legs and a condition of dropsy. It occasionally appears on vessels trading in the East.

BERM, a small shoal spot in the delta country of California.

BERMUDIAN ('MUDIAN) RIG. A vessel sparred and rigged for mutton leg sails, it having reached a high state of efficiency in those islands. This rig has largely supplanted the conventional gaff rig.

BERTH, a place to sleep aboard ship; a position for a vessel to tie up or to anchor; a position of employment aboard ship. A margin of safety in passing a dangerous obstruction, as, to give a rock a *wide berth.*

BESET, enclosed by drifting ice.

BEST BOWER, the heavier of the two anchors carried on the bow.

BETWEEN DECKS ('Tween Decks), the space between any two decks, but especially that in a cargo vessel below the main deck.

BETWEEN WIND AND WATER, the part of a vessel along the waterline.

BIBBS, heavy wooden solid brackets bolted to the hounds to support the trestletrees.

BIDARRA, a light staunch boat used in Bering Sea. Its framework is of light strong wood secured by thongs and covered with waterproof canvas. They can carry 5 or 6 tons of cargo. They are called Skin Boats locally.

BIGHT, any part of a rope within the ends, a bend. Also a cove or indentation in the coastline.

BILANDER, a two-masted sailing vessel once seen in European waters with large trapezoidal mainsail set from a lateen yard. The vessel was otherwise square-rigged.

BILGE, the turn of the hull below the waterline; when the curve is sharp the craft is said to have *hard* or *sharp* bilges; if the curve is slow, she has *easy* or *slack* bilges; that part of the inside hull about the keelson where bilge water collects is called the *bilges*. The part of a cask having the greatest diameter is the bilge.

BILGE BLOCKS, are hauled under a vessel's bilge in dry dock before the water is pumped out to support the vessel somewhat as on a cradle.

The *bilge block chains* pass from the inner end of the bilge blocks to the opposite side of the dry dock and are used to haul the blocks close under the hull as she settles on the keel blocks. Similar supports are used when a vessel is hauled on a marine railway.

BILGE AND CANTLINE, a method of stowing casks where the lower tier is arranged *chine and chine* (or bilge and bilge) and the next tier lies in between the lower rows. The lower tier is the *ground tier;* those above the *riders.*

BILGE FREE, the bilge of a cask being clear of the deck by resting on skids.

BILGE KEELS (BILGE CHOCKS), keels at the turn of the bilge to offer resistance to the rolling motion of a vessel. Also called *rolling chocks.*

BILGE SHORE, a timber placed at the bilge of a vessel in dock, or on the ways, to keep her upright.

BILGE STRAKES, the extra heavy planking or plating at the bilge, either outside or the ceiling inside.

BILGE STRINGER, a fore and aft stringer placed across the frames at the bilge to give strength. The English call this a *bilge Keelson.*

BILGE WATER, collects by seepage or leakage into the bilges.

BILGED, a vessel stove at or near the bilge. To fail an examination and be dropped from an institution.

BILGEWAYS, timbers laid beneath a vessel under construction, parallel with the keel and inclined towards the water.

BILL, the tip of an anchor. Also called the *pea.*

BILL-BOARD, an inclined steel or iron plate at the rail of a vessel by the cathead to receive the fluke of the anchor when secured.

BILL OF HEALTH, a document asserting that the health of a crew is good upon leaving port. The document further shows the number of contagious diseases existing in the port of departure. It is obtained from the health officer or American consul, and is visaed by the consul of the country of destination. It is presented to a similar officer or other authority upon arrival.

BILL OF LADING, a document in which the master acknowledges the receipt of goods aboard. It is a description of the goods shipped and an agreement to deliver them in good condition, except for the dangers of the sea and foreign enemies.

BILLET, an assigned place to sleep.

BILLET-HEAD, a small scroll used in place of the more pretentious figurehead. Sometimes applied to the loggerhead of a whaleboat.

BILLY BOY, a type of ketch in England.

BILOXI MEAN GULF LEVEL, is a datum 0.78 ft. above the mean level of Mississippi River mouth.

BINNACLE, a box or non-magnetic metallic container for the compass. It is fitted with lamps, both oil and electric for night work. When provided with attachments and receptacles for magnets used in the compensation of magnetism, it is known as a *compensating binnacle.*

BINNACLE LIST, a sicklist—the names of those excused from duty by the doctor.

BINOCULARS, a double telescope arranged for both eyes. There are two kinds, the *Galilean,* which embodies the old principle of simple lenses, and the *prismatic,* which gives a wider field by use of an arrangement of prisms. The Galilean type is used for night glasses.

BIRD'S NEST, a defect of distended strands in wire rope caused by a kink.

BIREME, an ancient vessel propelled with two banks of oars. See Trireme.

BISCUIT TIN, an airtight tin or galvanized iron receptacle for the life boats' emergency ration.

BISHOP'S RING, a ring around the sun usually with its outer edge of reddish color. It is probably due to particles of dust in the air as it is seen after all great volcanic eruptions.

BITT A CABLE, to make fast to the bitts by a turn under the thwartship piece and again round the bitt head; to *double* or *weather bitt* a cable an extra turn is taken.

BITT HEADS, the upper parts of the bitts.

BITTER END, the last end of a rope or cable that is doing important work. The bitter end of an anchor chain is made fast in the bottom or side of the chain locker.

BITTS, a pair of iron or wooden heads set vertically to which mooring or towing lines are made fast. In small craft a bitt is a single vertical timber head, forward or aft, with a thwartship pin through it, around which mooring and towing lines are secured.

BITUMASTIC CEMENT, an anticorrosive paint for tanks.

BLACK BOOK, a name often given to Lloyd's Record of Losses.

BLACK GANG, the coal firing force.

BLACK SEA MOORING, is 240 feet in length consisting of 180 feet of ten inch (circumference) manila; one end spliced into a special hand-wrought thimble. This thimble takes the end of a 60 ft. length of 1¾ inch (diameter) galvanized plow steel wire rope. In the end of the wire is a 5-foot eye splice.

BLACK STREAM. See Kuroshio.

BLACKWALL HITCH, a turn of a line around the hook of a block in such a way that the line binds itself. A double turn makes a *double blackwall hitch.* If made around the bill and shank of the hook it is a bill blackwall hitch.

BLADE, a wing of a propeller or a wing of a patent log. The flat part of an oar. The edge that cuts the water is the leading edge and the after side the trailing edge; the forward side of a blade is the suction side. The part of the arm of an anchor located back of the palm.

BLANKET. When a sailing vessel gets to windward of another, taking wind from the other's sails, the latter is said to be blanketed. *Blanket pieces,* in whaling, refer to

strips of blubber taken from a whale.

BLANKET LEE, a snug berth.

BLEEDERS, plugs in the bottom of oil tanks.

BLINDERS, a sharp mounting swell over a submerged rock that does not break except in heavy weather. Sometimes called Blind Rollers.

BLINK, a glow on the horizon, being reflected light from fields of ice at sea. Land blink is the same phenomenon appearing above snow-covered land.

BLINKER, is a set of electric lamps at a mast-head or spreaders, connected with a telegraph key. With this device signals are sent in International Morse code with great facility.

BLINKER GUN, a hand-held device for the same purpose, its light visible only in the direction in which it is pointed.

BLISTER, an outer skin constructed on the hull of a vessel to increase the beam and stability or to provide tankage. It is used in naval construction for torpedo protection with compartments within. If in the original design, it may protect the whole underbody, but if added to a vessel it may only go down a short distance below waterline. There are smaller blisters for other purposes such as submarine bells.

BLIZZARD, a gale of wind with a temperature below freezing and accompanied by snow.

BLOCK, a contrivance consisting of a frame or shell which supports a sheave or roller over which ropes are run. There is a great variety of blocks in shape, size and design, such as single, double, treble, secret, gin, leading, clump, sister, check, jeer, dasher, snatch, all of which see elsewhere. Blocks with a rope through them form a *tackle*. (Pronounced Taycle.)

BLOCK AND BLOCK (Two Blocks), the condition when two blocks of a tackle come together; the tackle must then be *overhauled* before another pull.

BLOCK COEFFICIENT. See Coefficient of Fineness.

BLOOD MONEY, a fee given by a master to a shipping master or crimp for the procuring of seamen; a practice which has added many dismal incidents to the history of the waterfronts.

BLOWN UP, a stevedore's term given when a cargo has been so stowed as to raise the center of gravity above that of ordinary stowage.

BLUE NOSE, a facetious name given to a Nova Scotian.

BLUE PETER, the letter P flag of the International Code—blue with a white square center. It is flown at the foremast when a vessel expects to sail within 24 hours.

BLUE PIGEON, the hand lead.

BLUFF, full-bowed vessel, in contradistinction of sharp-bowed, or fine; a steep shore.

BOARD, a leg or tack when close-hauled. There may be *long boards* and *short boards*. To go *on board* a vessel. *By the board* is to be carried overboard.

BOARD NETTINGS, nets formerly hoisted above the rails to hamper the enemy in reaching the decks.

BOARDING PIKE, was a spear-like weapon specially devised to repel boarders. Both boarding pikes and nettings were used by Captain Samuel Reid of the American privateer *General Armstrong* at Fayal, where he defended his ship against a vastly superior British force. He inflicted losses on the enemy greater than in any other naval engagement of the War of 1812.

BOAT, as used by seamen the term does not apply to a vessel, but to small craft, although river and excursion steamers are quite generally called boats, as are smaller submarines. To *boat your oars* is to lay them across the thwarts after rowing. Boat, as distinguished from the general term vessel or ship, is constructed of bent frames and a vessel or ship of sawn frames. (This is the opinion of a shipbuilder.)

BOAT-BOOM, a spar swung out horizontally and at right angles from the side of a vessel supported by topping lift and guys. A small boat rides to it without fouling the ship.

BOAT BOX, a receptacle for axes, lanterns, matches, tools and small equipment of a lifeboat.

BOAT CHOCKS, cradles in which a boat rests on the deck of a vessel.

BOAT COMPASS, a small box compass made convenient for use in small boats.

BOAT DECK, that upon which the lifeboats are secured.

BOAT HOOK, a device for catching hold of a ring bolt or grab line in coming alongside a vessel or pier in a small boat.

BOAT TACKLE, a tackle for hoisting boats.

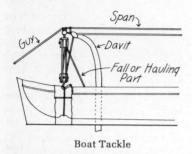

Boat Tackle

BOATSTEERER, a sort of petty officer in a whaler; he is the harpooner. Having thrown the harpoon he exchanges positions with the officer, who leaves the steering oar and goes forward to lance the whale.

BOATSWAIN (Bo's'n), a subordinate but valuable officer; a warrant officer of great importance in naval service, who has direct charge of work under the general supervision of the officer of the deck or the executive officer. Old men of sail used to pronounce the word Bo'z'n.

BOATSWAIN'S CHAIR, a short narrow board suspended by a bridle. It is used to sway a man aloft for scraping masts, tarring, rigging, etc.

BOATSWAIN'S CHEST, is given over to boatswain's stores, such as marlinespikes, rigging screws, marline, ropegear, sail needles, palms, twine, etc.

BOATSWAIN'S MATE, a petty officer proficient in seamanship.

BOATSWAIN'S PIPE, a peculiarly shaped whistle having a shrill call used to give orders or to get attention when orders are to be given on naval vessels and some large yachts.

BOATSWAIN'S STORES. See Boatwain's Chest.

BOBBING, the condition of a vessel lying very close to the wind and sea, as a pilot schooner so often does, making very little way.

BOBSTAYS, chains or heavy wire rigging running from the end of the bowsprit to the vessel's stem to support this spar in position from beneath. Should a bobstay part, a vessel's masts are in great danger of carrying away and falling aft. Hence a vessel in this emergency should be quickly put before the wind to relieve the strain.

BODY PLAN, the end view of the curves and frame lines of a ship; a central vertical line divides the views of the forward and after sections, the latter being on the left-hand.

BOGGIN LINES, a length of chain and a wire pendant shackled to the rudder horn; their purpose is to retain control of the rudder and facilitate steering in case of accident.

BOILER STOOL, a heavy bracket resting on the tank tops or floors and under the boilers.

BOLD, applied to a steep shore.

BOLE, a small boat.

BOLLARDS, two vertical heads of iron or wood to which mooring lines are made fast. Sometimes called *nigger heads*.

BOLSTERS, pieces of soft wood resting on the trestletrees under the eyes of the rigging, which prevent cutting of the rigging. Also the "lip" under the hawse pipe to take the chafe of the chain.

BOLT, a roll of canvas.

BOLTROPE, a rope sewed to the edge of sail to give it strength and prevent the ripping of the fabric. It is named for the side of the sail, as in a square sail, the head rope, the leech rope, etc. It is usually of hemp, but in yachts is sometimes cotton. The term is now applied to a superior quality of rope having long fibers of manila, or hemp. Wire boltropes were used on the last of the square-riggers.

BONAVENTURE, mizzen sail, lateen in character carried on the after-most mast of ancient vessels. See Mizzen.

BONE, the white foam created at the bow by the onward motion of the vessel. She is said to carry a *bone in her mouth* or *teeth*.

BONNET, an additional strip of canvas laced to the foot of a jib or square sail for use in fair weather but which is easily removed when necessary to reef. See Laskets.

BOOBY, a tropical bird so-called by sailors because of its extraordinary stupidity. It is sooty brown in appearance and is about 31 inches in length.

BOOBY HATCH, a small opening in the deck forward or aft of the main hatches. It is used to facilitate communication below or to the deck. A companionway with sliding hatch in small craft.

BOOM, a spar with many uses; the foot of a fore-and-aft sail is laced or tracked to a boom; boat booms swing out horizontally from ship's side for small boats to ride to; cargo booms, which rest at the foot of the masts, are raised and lowered by topping lifts and swung from side to side by guys according to where the pieces of cargo suspended from them are to be placed. There are studding sail (stun-sa'l) booms, extensions of the yards from which studding sails are set. A line of floats or logs secured end to end forming a floating chain for the purpose of obstructing the passage of boats or to restrict a quantity of logs to a certain area, is known as a boom.

BOOM CRADLE, a contrivance so shaped as to receive and hold secure the cargo booms when lowered into a horizontal position for sea.

BOOM HORSE, a circular device of iron made into the boom band for the sheet block to travel on.

BOOM IRONS, bands or withes at the end of a yard arm through which a stun-sa'l boom is rigged out.

BOOM OUT A SAIL, TO, to extend a corner of a sail with a spar.

BOOM TACKLE, leads forward from the end of the boom of a fore-and-aft sail. It serves to steady the spar when running before the wind. It also has been called the *kicking strap,* and more recently the *vang.*

BOOMKIN, a small spar extending over the stern to carry the sheet block aft for an overhanging boom. See Bumpkins.

BOOMS, an elevated rack above the spar deck, usually forward of the mainmast, for the stowage of spars and boats.

BOOT, a newly enlisted man.

BOOT HOOK, a long-handled caulking tool used to drive oakum into out-of-the-way places.

BOOT-TOPPING, a band of paint at the water-line; usually red; the particular kind of paint used is called boat-topping. This is the most vulnerable part of a vessel and should be painted at least every three months.

BORA, a very violent squall characteristic of the northern Adriatic. The weight of the cold air of the high surrounding land accelerates its flow to the sea. This is typically a *Katabatic wind*.

BORE, a sudden rise of tide which rolls up certain rivers and bays in the form of a breaker. In the Seine River it reaches a height of eight feet. See Sand Bores.

BOSOM KNEE. See Knees.

BOSOM PIECE, a butt strap for angle bars.

BOSS, the swelling portion of a ship's hull around the propeller shaft. The rounding hub of a propeller.

BOSS PLATE, a plate curved to fit the swelling part of the hull due to the emerging of the propeller shaft.

BOTTLE PAPERS, blanks furnished to shipmasters by the U.S. Naval Oceanographic Office upon which they state the latitude and longitude, name of vessel and date. They are sealed in bottles and thrown overboard. The date and place of their ultimate recovery furnish valuable information concerning the currents.

BOTTOMRY BOND, a lien on a vessel placed by a master who is obliged to raise money for repairs and who is out of communication with his owners. If the lien is on the cargo it is called a *Respondentia Bond*. The money derived from such liens can only be used for repairs, takes priority over all mortgages, and is primarily for the purpose of getting a vessel to her home port.

BOUNDARY PLANK. See Margin Plank.

BOW, the forward part of a vessel. Sometimes used in the plural as, "in the bows of a ship."

BOW AND BEAM BEARING, a convenient and universal method of locating a ship's position by bearings of a known object. The log is read when the object bears 45° off the bow, the course is not changed until the object bears abeam (90° from bow) when the log is again read, and the distance run between bearings is obtained. This is the distance of the ship from the object when abeam, for we have a right angle triangle, and all three angles combined equal 180°; take away the right angle (90°) there is 90° left; we know one of the remaining is 45° so the other must be also 45°. Equal sides must lie opposite equal

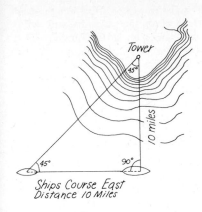

Bow and Beam Bearing

angles, hence the distance run is the distance off. It is also called a *Four Point Bearing*. It is important that allowance be made for current as the distance must be that made *over the ground.*

BOW LINE, a term sometimes applied to that part of a buttock line which is forward of the midship section. The line (hawser) leading forward from the bow chock when a vessel is tied up to a wharf.

BOW PORT. See Cargo Port.

BOW THRUST PROPELLER, in a recess below the waterline of a steamer's bows a propeller is installed. It is operated from the bridge and is of great assistance in maneuvering about the docks.

BOWDITCH, NATHANIEL (1773–1838) the author of the *American Practical Navigator,* the great American epitome of navigation, known popularly among seafarers as *Bowditch.* The latest edition is 1958. It

is published by the U.S. Naval Oceanographic Office.

BOWERS, heavy anchors carried in the forward part of the vessel, and ordinarily used in anchoring. The heavier of the two is the *best bower.* In weight the bowers lie between the sheet and stream anchors. See Anchor.

BOWHEAD. See Whales.

BOWLINE, one of the most useful knots; it is tied in such a way as to make an eye in the end of a rope. A *bowline on a bight* is a similar knot made with the bight of a rope. See *French Bowline.* Also, a bridle on the leech of a square course (sail) by which it is hauled forward, letting the wind into the sail when full and by.

BOWLINE BRIDLE, a short length of rope each end of which is spliced on the leech of a course to facilitate the bowline tackle in hauling the leech to windward when on the wind.

BOWSE, to haul with a tackle, usually downward, as in the case of taking in on the fore tack.

BOWSER BOAT, a craft fitted with tanks carrying gasoline for the bunkering of seaplanes.

BOWSPRIT, a heavy spar projecting forward of the vessel from which the head sails are set. It is guyed by *bowsprit shrouds* at each side, a *bob-stay* from beneath, and the fore topmast stay from above and forward. Bowsprits are rigged to slide inboard on some craft, the Brixham trawlers, for example. They are known as sliding bowsprits in contradistinction to standing bowsprits. A standing or semi-permanent bowsprit that is *rigged in* for repairs or to clear a warehouse is said to be *housed*. See Artemon mast, also Jibboom.

BOWSPRIT BITTS, two heavy timbers vertically placed, between which the heel of the bowsprit rests.

BOWSPRIT CAP, a heavy double band; the lower band goes over the outer end of the bowsprit, and the jibboom is rigged out through the upper band and on the bowsprit.

BOWSPRIT SHROUDS, heavy standing rigging which support the bowsprit at the sides, leading from its end in to the catheads.

BOX BEAM, a built-up beam, hollow and box-like in appearance.

BOX-HAULING, to wear ship within a small space by backing the head yards to pay the bow off quickly under sternway, letting them run square when before the wind, and tending all braces as the vessel comes to the new tack.

BOX OFF, to fall off from the wind with sternway by backing the head yards.

BOXING THE COMPASS, naming the points (and quarter points) of the compass from north through south to north and return backwards. From *Boxar,* old Spanish—to sail around.

BRACES, long whips leading aft from the ends of the yard arms (forward on the last mast if it is square-rigged) by which they are swung at different angles with the keel but still in horizontal positions. Yards are braced *aback* when the wind is on the forward side of the sails; *abox* when the fore yards are aback, and the after yards are filled; they are *braced in* when they are brought more athwartships; they are *braced up* when brought nearer a fore-and-aft line; *sharp up* when they are as far as they will go. When on the wind a square rigger is *braced up*; when the wind is free she is *braced in*.

BRACKET, a small plate used to connect two or more parts such as deck beam to frame, or a frame to margin plate.

BRAIL, a rope of a fore-and-aft sail, leading in from the leech to the mast. It is used to gather the sail in and aid in securing. The lee brails are always used when taking in a sail. The verb is to *brail in*.

BRAKE BEAMS, handles by which the windlass or pumps are worked.

BRAKES, the handles of a deck pump and windlass. See Friction Brakes.

BRANCH, certificate given by pilot commissioners to a competent pilot; in England by Trinity House. A *full branch* is without restrictions.

BRASS BOUNDER, a British sea apprentice.

BRASS HAT, a naval officer with grade of commander or above.

BRAVE WEST WINDS, the westerlies of the north temperate zones. See Roaring Forties. (British Admirality.)

BRAZIL CURRENT, flows southwestward along the coast of South America from Cape St. Roque.

BREACH, is made by seas that break completely across a vessel. This is called a *clean breach.* Whales when they throw themselves well out of water are said to breach.

BREADTH. The moulded breadth is the distance between the outer faces of the frames, while the registered breadth is measured between the outside of the shell plating. See Lloyd's Breadth.

BREAK, a sudden rise or drop in a vessel's deck line. To *break out* any gear is to take it out of stowage. A sea *breaks* when it falls forward in a mass of broken water. *To break bulk* is to commence discharging cargo. An anchor *breaks* ground as it is hove from its bed. To *break off* is to stop work.

BREAK BULK CARGO STEAMER, a steamer in which shipments are discharged at different ports.

BREAK HER SHEER, a phrase applied when a vessel, riding to a port anchor, for instance, is sheered to starboard (perhaps by a little right rudder), but swings with the turn of the tide (or change of wind) so as to pass over, or to port, of the anchor instead of to starboard, the direction in which she was headed. By swinging clear to starboard she would *keep her sheer* and avoid fouling the anchor.

BREAK OF THE POOP (or FORE-CASTLE), the point where these decks stop and ladders lead to the main deck or well.

BREAKER, a broken sea that has been tripped by shoaling water. A water-cask used in a ship's boat.

BREAKS GROUND, when an anchor is broken out of its bed.

BREAKWATER, an artificial embankment, usually of rocks, to break the force of the seas and furnish shelter behind it. A low bulkhead on the forward deck to take the force of a boarding sea and protect the hatches.

BREAMING, the process of cleaning a vessel's bottom with a torch.

BREAST, to meet the sea. To *breast off* a boat from a wharf or vessel is to fend her broad off. A steamer may be breasted off to allow a lighter on the pier side.

BREAST HOOK, a plate structure in a steel ship fitted inside the hull near the bow to give local strength to the shell plating. A horizontal knee in a wooden vessel set in the bows of a boat as well as a vessel.

BREAST LINE, is used to secure a vessel to a wharf. It leads directly to a cleat abreast the vessel without leading forward or aft. Breast-rope or band, a guard for the leadsmen in the chains.

BREECH OF A BLOCK, is the part opposite the swallow—opposite from the end through which the rope passes.

BREECHES BUOY, a ring buoy fitted with canvas breeches for bringing shipwrecked persons ashore. See Lyle Gun.

BREEZE OF WIND, a redundancy often employed in a favorable sense, but also as an understatement in referring to a severe gale.

BRICKFIELDER, a hot northerly

wind in the southern part of Australia.

BRICKLAYER'S CLERK, one who goes to sea but who feels above it.

BRIDGE, an elevated thwartship platform from which the vessel is navigated and all activities on deck are in plain view. See also Flying Bridge.

BRIDGE CRANE, an arched structure having over-reaching cantilever extensions at each end. The cargo pendant is suspended from a carriage which travels under the bridge; the whole moves on rails.

BRIDGE PIECE, that forming the arch over the propeller well; it bridges between the stern frame and the rudder post.

BRIDGE SIGN, a painted sign on a movable stand set on the loading platform of a pier to "spot" a docking vessel so the hatches will line up with pier doors. This is called "spot docking."

BRIDLE, a piece of rope or chain each end of which is fast to a spar or rope. The purchase to be applied is hooked to the bight. A bridle often comprises three or more parts.

BRIDLE PORT, a gun port forward on the gun deck.

BRIG, a two-masted vessel, square-rigged on both masts. There are also *hermaphrodite* and *jackass brigs* (see Brigantine). The ship's prison.

BRIGANTINE. Somewhat before the turn of the century the brigantine in America was square-rigged on the fore and on the main-top mast, but carried a fore-and-aft sail on the main mast.

The square sails aloft on the mainmast of the American brigantine were found to be more trouble than worth and were abandoned, leaving the brigantine on both sides of the Atlantic, a two-masted vessel square-rigged on the fore and fore and aft rig on the main with the familiar gaff-topsail. American sailors, perhaps jeeringly, called this rig an hermaphrodite brig, or in their lingo a "morfidite." The term "morfidite" died naturally though slowly.

The *jackass brig* was similar to the brigantine but its fore-topmast and topgallant mast was in one single spar. The early application of the word "brigantine" or "brigandine" was in the Mediterranean and referred to a small galley propelled by oars.

BRIGHTWORK, all brass that is kept polished, while *bright woodwork* is that kept scraped and varnished in natural wood.

BRING TO, to heave a vessel to (the wind); or with a shot heave another ship to. In desiring to anchor the term is *to bring the ship to an anchor.* To *bring to a sail* is to bend it.

BRING UP, to come to a stop, sometimes with an anchor, sometimes by fouling an obstacle or the bottom. To *bring up all standing* is to stop suddenly as in running ashore. To *bring up with a round turn* is to stop some action, or the movement of a rope, abruptly.

BRISTOL FASHION, is a seaman-like style. The phrase is—Ship-shape and Bristol Fashion.

BRIT, a red or sometimes a yellowish organism which floats in vast quantities on some parts of the sea, and serves as a food for whales; a very small fish an inch or so long.

BRITISH THERMAL UNIT (B.T.U.), the amount of heat necessary to raise the temperature of a pound of water 1°F. when at 39.2°F.

BROACH TO, to swing to the wind when running free, through bad steering or by the force of a heavy sea. This dangerous situation is a frequent cause of foundering, or loss of spars at least.

BROACHING CARGO, the act of breaking into the ship's cargo and appropriating food, drink or other articles for individual use.

BROAD OFF (or **ON**) **THE BOW OR QUARTER,** the term applied to an object that bears about 45° from the bow or stern, respectively.

BROADHORN, a flat-boat used on the western rivers of the United States.

BROADSIDE, the side of a vessel above the water. The simultaneous firing of all guns on one side of a warship.

BROADSIDE ON, sideways, opposite to end on.

BROKEN STOWAGE, where the stowage of cargo is interferred with by parts of the ship that extend into the hold, and odds and ends of freight are used to fill the spaces.

BROKEN STRIPE, a sleeve mark of rank worn by a boatswain or other warrant officers of the Navy. The stripe of alternate gold and blue silk ribbon. *Broken-striper,* a warrant officer.

BROKEN WATER, where the regularity of the waves is broken by shoal water or a breaking sea.

BROKER, a ship agent who acts for her owners or charterers, securing cargos and transacting the ship's business. He also charters, buys and sells ships.

BROTHERS OF THE COAST, an organization of very daring pirates who frequented the Spanish Main; the organization embraced a thousand ships. They operated under a strict code of discipline, the notable penalty of which was marooning; they carried accident benefits for those injured in action.

BROW, a gangway to a vessel.

BROW LANDING, a platform attached to the side of a ship at deck level to support the brow.

BUBBLE SEXTANT, is designed for use when the horizon is not visible. A bubble attachment serves the purpose of an artificial horizon. At sea it is difficult to operate this instrument accurately. It is used principally by airplane navigators.

BUCCA. See Buzzo.

BUCCANEER, a pirate, especially applied to those who formerly infested the West Indies. The term was derived from the word (Fr.) *bucane,* to smoke meat. This was done by bands of lawless men who made their headquarters at Tortuga Island. Their hunting and marauding expeditions changed later to sea piracy on a large scale.

BUCKLING, the dangerous bending of a spar under a heavy stress. The warping under stress of any member of the vessel's structure.

BUFFALO RAIL, a rail rising to a low height above the forecastle deck of a vessel.

BUGEYE, a small vessel characteristic of Chesapeake Bay, with a pointed stern, mutton-leg or jib-headed sails and two extremely raking masts.

BUILDING SLIP, the location where a ship is built; where the foundation and groundways are established.

BULB IRON, a frame bar with an angle at one side and a bulb at the other.

BULB KEEL, a deep keel used in racing yachts consisting of a fin with a mass of lead or iron at the bottom; it served to increase stability.

BULBOUS BOW, has a "swollen" stem below the waterline.

BULGE, a longitudinal swelling or blister constructed along the hull of a vessel below the water-line to serve for greater steadiness.

BULK CARGO, usually a homogeneous cargo stowed in bulk such as wheat or coal.

BULKHEAD, a vertical partition extending athwartship or fore and aft of a vessel. The *main bulkheads* are mostly watertight, and are known as such. They are equipped with *watertight* doors which are so fitted with a rubber gasket and dogs as to make a tight contact through which no water will pass.

If the bulkheads only extend upwards to a certain deck this is called the *bulkhead deck* which is sufficiently high to preserve seaworthiness in a one or two compartment ship if these compartments are flooded. The floor plate in a single bottom ship at a bulkhead is known as the *bulkhead floor.* The connecting angle around the bottom of a bulkhead is the *bulkhead shoe. Fore and aft* or *longitudinal bulkheads* are seen at the sides of the engine-room and fireroom where they form the sides of the *side bunkers.* In order to drain water from one compartment to another, *bulkhead sluices* or openings are found in the bilges and are operated from deck. The bulkheads are reenforced by angle irons called *stiffeners* and often a *web* plate is further provided at the center of the bulkhead. In large tanks *wash bulkheads, or baffle plates* are set vertically to cut down the violent motion of the liquid. The *collision bulkhead* is most important, being as its name implies, near the bow of the ship to restrict sea water from the larger compartments in case of damage forward. A bulkhead is said to be *stepped* when it is carried forward or aft for the accommodation of machinery and is not all in the same vertical plane.

BULKHEAD LINE, the outer limit of solid filled pierheads as laid down by Army Engineers. See Pierhead Line.

BULL LINE, used to run cargo out of the wings to a hatch convenient for hoisting. The line is carried to a winch. When lead blocks are used longshoremen should stand out of the line of the strain.

BULL ROPE, a line leading out through a *bull's eye* in the end of the bowsprit to a mooring buoy in order to prevent its striking against the bow. A line leading from forward through a bull's eye on the boat boom for a boat to ride to. See Geswarp. Bull Rope, by another use passes from the cap of a square-rigged mast through the heel block of the topmast, through a cheek block on the lower mast head (or block hooked to cap) thence to the deck, for use in hoisting or striking a topmast.

BULLNOSE, a sort of hawse pipe set in the top of a vessel's stem for the accommodation of mooring lines or a towline.

BULL'S EYE, a round piece of lignum vitae, doughnut-shaped and scored around the edge to receive the eye of a rope. A heavy piece of glass set in the deck to let light below. A bit of blue sky often seen at the center of a tropical storm.

BULWARK, a vessel's frames extend three or four feet above the weather deck and are planked forming a solid "rail." It serves the crew's safety, helps secure deck cargo and keeps out a certain amount of water in rough weather.

BULWARK PLATING, the strake or strakes above the sheer-strake which form the bulwarks.

BULWARK STAY, an iron brace set at an angle from the deck to a bulwark plate to strengthen it.

BUM BOAT, a small craft used to bring off peddlers who supply the crew with fruit, tobacco, parrots and perhaps illicit wants.

BUMPKINS, short projecting iron bars, port and starboard, on the ship's side well aft on the quarters; the main brace leads to their outer ends. Also on the bows to which the fore tack is bowsed down. A similar strut aft from which the patent log is streamed. The iron stays which secure the bumpkins in position are called bumpkin shrouds.

BUND, a seawall or embarkment.

BUNG UP AND BILGE FREE, a phrase used in the stowage of casks. It obviously means that the bungs should up and that the casks should rest on skids so as to raise the bilge, or middle of the cask, clear of the deck.

BUNGS, the name given to the cooper aboard a whaler.

BUNK, a built in bed aboard ship.

BUNKERING, the charge for putting coal or oil fuel aboard in bunkers or tanks.

BUNKERS, compartments of a vessel for the stowage of coal. There are side bunkers, reserve, wing, cross or athwartship bunkers. The term also applies to fuel oil.

BUNT, is the middle part of a square sail.

BUNT JIGGER, a light tackle which helps to lift a square sail up on the yard in furling.

BUNT WHIP. See Bunt Jigger.

BUNTING, a thin woolen fabric of which flags are made.

BUNTLINES, ropes that are fast to the foot of a square sail. They lead up through blocks that are located above the yard. The buntlines gather up and bring under control the body of the sail when being furled.

BUOY AN ANCHOR, to make a line fast (clove hitch) around the crown of an anchor with a buoy bent on at a depth at highwater. This indicates its position and aids in recovering it. It is called a *buoy rope.*

BUOYS, floating beacons, which by their shape and color convey to the mariner valuable information as to his position. The various types in the United States comprise spar, can, nun (conical or truncated), cask, bell, whistle, and lighted buoys. If painted red they are to be left on the starboard hand in entering port, if black on the port hand; the red buoys carry even numbers and black odd numbers. A black and white vertically striped buoy indicates a fairway, and should be passed close aboard. A buoy painted in red and black horizontal bands indicates a danger and should be avoided. A spar buoy moored close to a bell or lighted buoy is called, and is, a *marker.* A buoy is *watching* when it is on station and floating plainly visible. Green buoys in foreign waters are placed to mark wrecks. White buoys indicate naval anchorages or practice areas and at times race courses. A quarantine anchorage is indicated by a yellow buoy. See Fog buoy.

BURDENED VESSEL, the one obliged to keep clear of those having the right of way.

BUREAU VERITAS, a French society for the classification of ships.

BURGEE, a swallow-tailed flag.

BURGOO, boiled oatmeal; mush.

BURTON, a type of purchase. Where three single blocks are used it is called a single *Spanish burton*; if double blocks, a double Spanish burton. The whip or tackle of a cargo boom reaching over the ship's side and working in conjunction with another boom guyed over a hatch. This is also called the *yard tackle* among seamen. See also Married falls.

BURY OF A MAST, that part below decks.

BUSH, to mark the sides of a secondary channel with young cedar or birch trees which have been stripped of branches except for a tuft at the top.

BUSHING, a replacement lining for a shaft journal or other moving part. The shell of a spark plug.

BUSS, a two-masted schooner rigged vessel having a galley house forward and a cabin house aft. In earlier days the buss carried a square sail on each mast sometimes a main topsail; there was also a riggermast with a square sail. They were very full lined forward and aft. These vessels were early used by the Dutch in the herring fisheries.

BUTT, the end of a plank or plate; the placing of two planks or plates end to end and caulking the seam. A barrel-like container of 126 gallons. If steel plates are butted a small plate is riveted over the joint called a *butt strap*. To *start a butt* is to have the end of a plank loosen.

BUTTERFLY NUT, a nut with two wings to turn by hand. Also called Wing Nut.

BUTTER-RIGGED, applied to English topsail schooners in which the topgallant sail (as Mr. Chatterton says) is set flying by hoisting the yard each time.

BUTTERWORTH SYSTEM, of cleaning oil tanks. It consists of a hose with two nozzles rotating in right angled planes. Steam is cut into the line forcing very hot water at high pressure against every part of the tank. The cleaning begins at the deck and works downward.

BUTTOCK, the rounding part of a vessel's stern.

BUTTOCK LINES, represent what would be longitudinal saw cuts vertically through a vessel's model made at different distances from the line of the keel; sometimes confined to that part of the line which is abaft the midships section.

BUY BALLOT'S LAW, states that by standing with one's face to the wind the atmospheric pressure increases towards the right and decreases to the left in the northern hemisphere. The center will be to the right hand from 8 to 12 points.

These conditions are reversed in the southern hemisphere.

BUZZO, a capacious cargo carrier of the Venetians, propelled by sail rather than oars.

BY THE HEAD, when a vessel is deeper than her normal draft forward.

BY AND LARGE. See Large.

BY THE LEE, the situation when a square-rigged vessel running free on one tack is thrown off by a sea or bad steering sufficiently to bring her sails aback on the other tack. This is a very serious situation. With a fore-and-aft rig, running by the lee is likely to cause a jibe, but is sometimes done purposely when racing as a temporary expedient.

BY THE STERN, when a vessel is deeper than her normal draft at the stern, out of trim by an excess of weight aft.

BY THE WIND, sailing close-hauled.

BY THE WIND SAILOR (Velella spirans), a form of marine life, not greatly unlike the Portuguese man o' war, having swimming bells and long tentacles, and found in warm waters.

C

C, clouds.

C. I. F., cost, insurance, freight.

C AND S, annotations in a liberty book indicating that a returned seaman is clean and sober.

C. T., chronometer time before being corrected for chronometer error (C E).

C-W, the difference between the navigator's watch time and the chronometer time. The watch is set near local or ship time. To get C-W subtract W.T. from C.T., adding 12 hours to C.T. if necessary. Hence to get C.T. add C-W and W.T. C-W is used in both E. and W. longitudes. See W-C.

CAAING WHALES. See Whales.

CABIN, the quarters of the captain on naval vessels and merchant sailing ships. In passenger steamers the word becomes more general and includes the quarters of officers and passengers. The enclosed space of a decked small boat.

CABLE, a heavy rope or chain. It is used attached to anchors, or in towing. It is also a term of measurement, being 200 yards or one-tenth of a nautical mile.

CABLE-LAID ROPE, is composed of three ropes laid up like strands from right to left-handed (holding the end away from you). The ropes which serve as strands are laid up from left to right (right-handed). This is often called *Hawser-laid Rope* in this country. See Right-handed Rope.

CABOOSE, a cookhouse or deck.

CAIQUE, a small sailing vessel of the eastern Mediterranean Sea; a small rowing skiff of the Bosphorus.

CAIRN, a pile of stones formed to serve as a beacon.

CAISSON, the gate at the end of a drydock which excludes the water after pumping out the dock. The pumping engines are often located in the caisson.

CAISSON DISEASE, an affliction

to which divers are subject due to increased atmospheric pressure and artificial conditions. Also called *the bends.*

CALDERETA, a hot sharp squall from the mountain gorges of northern Venezuela.

CALIBER, the diameter of the bore of a gun, measured at the muzzle. The length of a gun is expressed in terms of the caliber.

CALIBRATE, to determine and rectify the error in the graduated scales of instruments. Radio Direction Finders are periodically calibrated in order to furnish accurate bearings.

CALL, the boatswain's whistle.

CALL AWAY (Whaleboat), a preliminary order given when a boat is to leave the ship. "*Away* (Whaleboat)," is the order given by the boatswain.

CALLAO ROPE, a unique mooring line for lighters lying alongside a steamer anchored in a seaway. It consists of two lengths of wire rope (about 15 feet) one fast to each end of a resilient fabrication of woven cordage like a fender about 1 foot in diameter and 15 feet long. Under heavy stress this loosely woven section stretches, relieving the shock of the passing swell.

CALM, a condition of no wind.

CALVING, the process by which icebergs are made, as the foot of a glacier breaks up in the sea. Or, the breaking of fragments from a berg at sea.

CAMBER, the athwartships crown of a vessel's decks. It is usually ¼ inch to the foot. A protected area for small boats.

CAMEL, a floating stage very stoutly constructed and used as a fender to keep a vessel off a wharf or pier. Also a buoyant device chained to the sides of a ship to raise her and reduce the draft so as to allow passage over a bar.

CAMOUFLAGE, deception by means of low visibility or structural changes. Low visibility consists of painting a ship with such colors as will reduce the contrast between ship and sky under favorable conditions. The dazzle camouflage of the First World War was a form of protection consisting of a distortion of the normal lines of the vessel, thereby making it more difficult for the enemy to determine her course and speed.

This system was largely abandoned in World War II in which two fore-and-aft bands of differing shades of slate gray were used with considerable success.

Structural camouflage consists of the elimination of high parts for low visibility, the offsetting of masts, stacks or other parts normally referred to for an indication of the vessel's course.

CAN BUOY, a cylindrical buoy usually painted b'ack, marked with an odd number and indicates the port side of a channel when inward bound.

CAN (CANT) HOOKS, used in hoisting casks by hooking into the chines.

CANCER, the fourth sign of the zodiac.

CANDLEPOWER, a unit of the luminous intensity of light arrived at by international agreement.

CANDY STOWAGE, cargo perishable by heat, such as candy, wax paper products etc.

CANOE, a light craft of canvas, skins, bark, thin wood or aluminum, propelled by paddles on inland or sheltered waters. A hollowed log used by primitive people. A light pulling boat used by pilots.

CANT, to turn a vessel in a river or harbor.

CANT BODY, that part of a vessel near the bow or stern where the frames depart from the perpendicular.

CANT FRAME, one not square to the keel line. Such frames occur at the bow and stern.

CANTILEVER TANKS, are located in the gunwales and are also known as *gunwale tanks*.

CANTLINE, the recess at the center of four casks stowed bilge and bilge. The bilge of a cask of the upper tier rests in the cantline of those below.

CANVAS, a woven cotton (or flax) fabric used for sails, awnings and many other shipboard purposes. It is numbered from 00, the coarsest, to 10, the finest weave. Synonym for *sails*.

CAP, a piece of wood or a metal casting having a square hole, which fits over the lower mast head, and a round hole directly forward through which the mast above passes and is secured. The *bow-*

sprit cap serves a similar purpose with the bowsprit for the jibboom.

CAP JIB, that head sail whose stay is made fast to an eye in the bowsprit cap.

CAP LOG, the heavy timber forming the edge of a wharf.

CAP SHORE, a support for the cap (of a mast) to prevent its slipping down on the forward side.

CAPE ANN OARS, those with a square shaft at the gunwale and used with tholepins. One could not feather with these oars.

CAPE HORN CURRENT, the general easterly drift in the vicinity of Cape Horn and Falkland Islands.

CAPE HORN FEVER, a feigned illness of malingerers.

CAPE PIGEON (*Daption capensis*), a black and white petrel very common in southern seas, especially in the South Atlantic.

CAPPANUS, a worm that bores into the wood of the underbody of a vessel.

CAPSIZE, to turn over.

CAPSTAN, a cylindrical device usually standing on the forecastle and used for heaving in anchors, hoisting yards and other heavy work. It is revolved by steam or electric power or by hand. If, by the latter, *capstan bars* are inserted in *pigeon holes* at the top of the drumhead and manned. Its parts comprise the spindle, barrel, drumhead, pigeon holes, pawls and pawl-rim.

CAPSTAN KNOT, a very useful knot for making a line fast. It jams itself and will not slip.

CAPTAIN, the master of a merchant vessel. In the navy, the commissioned rank next below that of rear-admiral (commodore in certain circumstances); also, by extension, the commander of any naval vessel, irrespective of commissioned rank.

CAPTAIN'S BRIDGE, the bridge off the captain's quarters on a steamer below the navigating bridge.

CAPTAIN'S WALK, a narrow balustraded gangway constructed on the ridgepole of old shipmasters' houses where a vantage point could be gained to view the shipping and at the same time provide for the seaman's traditional exercise of "pacing the deck."

CAR FLOAT, a large decked scow fitted with tracks for carrying railroad cars.

CARAVEL, a vessel of the 15th and 16th century. Many great voyages of discovery were made in caravels, including those of Columbus. They were distinguished over other vessels of their time by having better lines that contributed to speed and seaworthiness. While the rigs varied they usually carried four masts, square rigged at the fore, and lateen rigged on the after masts. The foremast raked forward, the stern was square and there were forward and after castles.

CARRACK, a vessel of about the 15th century and the largest of that general period. The rig varied but may be said to have had three masts, large main, small foremast and lateen mizzen.

CARDINAL POINTS are the N, S, E, and W of a compass. (Northeast, Southeast, Southwest and Northwest are inter-cardinal points.)

CAREEN, to list. A vessel is *hove down* by careening her, when in a light trim, by use of tackles to a dock or trees on a river bank for the purpose of cleaning her bottom. Formerly particularly well adapted locations were called *careening places,* as a *careenage.*

CARGO, merchandise carried for payment of freight. There is *bulk, general, package,* and *homogeneous* cargo.

CARGO BATTENS, planks spiked or bolted across the frames to keep the cargo from contact with the ship's side.

CARGO BOOM or **DERRICK,** a heavy boom resting at the foot of a mast. It is elevated by a topping-lift tackle and controlled by guys. It is arranged to work cargo through deck hatches.

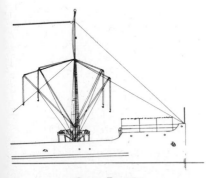

Cargo Booms

CARGO CLUSTERS, groups of electric lights fitted under a reflector to give light for working cargo.

CARGO JACK, a screw jack for moving and stowing cargo, especially where it is to be forced into small spaces; cotton is always jacked into a hold.

CARGO NET, a square net of heavy rope. It is used to sling case goods or small package freight. When old, they are sometimes used to catch and save pieces of cargo that break adrift from the slings by stretching them between the ship and the pier abreast a working hatch. Also called a *save-all.* The save-all is of lighter construction and larger; not necessarily made of old cargo nets.

CARGO PLAN, a plan showing the proposed stowage of cargo. It is usually prepared in the office of the pier superintendent with the endorsement of the master. The cargo is stowed according to this plan, a copy of which goes with the ship for the aid of the stevedore at port of discharge.

CARGO PORT, a large opening in the side of a vessel for removing and loading cargo. Schooners were often seen with an opening just below the hawse pipe for the passage of long timbers. This is called a *lumber port.*

CARGO SLINGS, a piece of rope with ends spliced together making a strop (a circle of rope). Slings are used around a draft of cargo to hoist out or in. Trays or pallets are used when the draft consists of fragile boxes or cartons. They consist of a wooden flat tray with a bridle at each end for hoisting; a spreader prevents the parts of the bridle inclining inward and causing damage to the cases. These trays are also called "airplanes." When the cargo consists of very small articles a tray is used with sides perhaps a foot high called a "scow."

CARGO TON, occupies 100 cubic feet of space.

CARGO WORTHY, a term applied to a vessel adapted to carry the particular cargo being considered.

CARLING BOX, is fitted between the beams and carlings and flush with their lower edges.

CARLING (CARLINE) KNEES, are right-angled supports set horizontally to reinforce the carlings.

CARLINGS, or **CARLINES,** pieces of fore and aft timbers between deck beams.

CARRICK BEND, used principally for bending two pieces of rope together. There are the *single, double* and *open* carrick bends.

CARRICK HEADS, the tops of the old-fashioned windlass bitts.

CARRY AWAY, to give way; break; part, or wash overboard. Used to describe an accident to spars, sails, hull, cargo or any fixtures.

CARTEL, a vessel used to negotiate with an enemy under a flag of truce, usually bearing prisoners of war for exchange. Privateers made a practice of disposing of their prisoners by turning a captured vessel into a *cartel.*

CARVEL-BUILT, smooth-sided. Planking edge to edge on frames and caulked.

CASCO, a natural square-ended flat-bottomed craft of Manila Bay. They are used as lighters.

CASE, see Junk.

CAST, to throw a vessel to port or starboard in getting underway by use of head sails or rudder for sternway or by a spring line to a kedge. It is a seaman's term to throw, as to *cast the lead.*

CAST AWAY, to be forced from a ship by disaster. It may be through foundering when the crew are cast away in the boats; or by stranding when they may be cast away on a barren island. A seaman in this predicament is a *castaway.*

CAST OFF, to let go a line.

CAT, see Catamaran.

CAT THE ANCHⲅR. See Cat Head.

CAT BLOCK, a ʌvy three-sheave block with a he ⱴy hook, used in catting an anchor. See Cat Head.

CAT BOAT, a shallow draft, broad beamed craft with mast stepped far forward. The single sail is usually large with gaff and overhanging boom. The name Cat was early applied to a heavy vessel of Scandinavia. She carried pole masts and the square sails were lowered to the deck for furling.

CAT DAVIT or **CRANE,** is similar to a boat davit from which the cat fall of old-fashioned vessels is rigged.

CAT HEAD, a heavy timber projecting horizontally from the bow of an old-fashioned vessel through which the fall of the cat tackle is rove, the sheaves being set in the cat head. This tackle heaves the ring of the anchor to the cat head.

The process is called *Catting the anchor*.

CAT HOLES, through which a stern line passes in the older ships.

CAT O'NINE TAILS, an implement of punishment in the old navy. It consisted of nine cords each with three knots, all lashed to a short heavy piece of rope. To be so punished was to be *introduced to the gunner's daughter*. Also called *Cat*.

CAT SCHOONER, an early American coastal vessel with fore and aft gaff sails, but no head sails or bowsprit. By some also called a *periguger*.

CAT YAWL, a two-masted boat carrying a main, small mizzen, no bowsprit nor head sails.

CATADIOPTRIC, a lighting system employing the *Catoptric* and *Dioptric* systems.

CATAMARAN, a two-hulled craft joined by a cross structure. Becoming popular in yachts for their qualities for speed. Also called *cats*.

CATCH A CRAB, to get an oar blade caught flatwise under water or as some, probably erroneously, interpret the term—to miss the water in making a stroke with an oar.

CATCH RATLINE, every fifth ratline. If the ratlines cross only a part of the shrouds the catch ratline crosses all of them.

CATENARY, the curve of a rope suspended between two points, as the catenary of a towing hawser.

CATHARPIN (G) S, short legs of rope fast to each shroud a short

distance below the top and leading in to the mast. They serve to take up the slack of the shrouds and allow the yards to be braced up more sharply.

CATHEDRAL HULL, a design in which bottom sections form an arch on each side of the keel. It planes readily with a smooth ride.

CATOPTRIC LIGHT (HOUSE), one in which the reflecting principle of light is employed.

CATS-PAW, the ruffled surface of the water caused by a flaw during light airs. A peculiar twist in the bight of a rope, by which two eyes are formed. The hook of a tackle is passed through them for hoisting purposes.

CATWALK, an elevated fore and aft bridge connecting the midship house with the forward or after part of a vessel. It provides a safe passage in heavy weather and with low freeboard when the well decks are liable to be awash.

CAULK (CALK), to drive oakum or cotton into the seams of a deck or ship's side. The tool used for this purpose is a flat, chisel-like affair called a *caulking iron*. The particular kind of wooden mallet used is a *caulking mallet*. The steel plates at their lap and butt joints are said to be *caulked* when made water-tight by working their edges down to a close contact. *Caulk off*, to sleep. This came from taking a nap on deck and the tar of the seams marked the sleeper's white clothes.

CAULKING MAT, an old sail laid on the deck at night under which seamen, not immediately needed, were allowed to crawl and sleep. In naval parlance, any deck covering from a newspaper up, on which a sailor may sleep.

CAULKING TOOLS, those used in the process of caulking.

CAVIL, a large fore and aft cleat for belaying lines.

CAVITATION, caused by a propeller revolving so fast that the head of water pressure cannot supply solid water for the screw to work in and the blades cut across the suction column of the propeller instead of working in it. This produces heavy vibrations and consumes additional power without effective thrust. (Standard Seamanship.) Cavitation is due to a number of causes; too small a propeller, thickness of trailing edge, poor stream-lining of the blades, propeller too near the surface. The head of water is the pressure which forces the water to follow the blade and amounts to .434 lbs. per square inch for every foot of water over the blade, added to which is 14.7 lbs. for atmospheric pressure. Hence a propeller should be as deep as possible to increase the pressure and aid in preventing cavitation.

CAYUCA, a dugout canoe once used by the Indians of Panama.

CEILING, the inside planking of a ship. A ceiling of planks is laid over the tank tops to serve as a floor and protect the tanks.

CELESTIAL EQUATOR, the projection of the earth's equator to the celestial sphere. For a person standing on the equator the celestial equator is directly overhead. It is everywhere 90° from the celestial poles. It is also called the *Equinoctial.*

CELESTIAL HORIZON, is defined by the extension of a plane at the center of the earth to the celestial sphere which is at right angles to a plumb line at the observer's position. It is the same as the rational horizon. The rational and sensible horizons on the celestial sphere are separated by the amount of the semi-diameter of the earth.

CELESTIAL LATITUDE, the angular distance of a point northward or southward of the ecliptic.

CELESTIAL LONGITUDE, the arc of the ecliptic lying between the First Point of Aries and the circle of latitude passing through the body.

CELESTIAL SPHERE, an imaginary shell, represented to us, in a way by the blue sky of the heavens as its inner surface, situated at an infinite distance away. Upon this sphere all celestial bodies are assumed to move regardless of their actual distance. In order to assist us in locating these bodies the sphere is laid out with a system of poles, equator, parallels and meridians similar to that of the earth. The earth is assumed to be the center of this infinite sphere.

CELLULAR DOUBLE BOTTOMS, the separate compartments between the inner and outer bottoms, formed by fore and aft girders and the athwartship floors of a modern steamer.

CELO-NAVIGATION, the science of finding a ship's position by means of observations of heavenly bodies and the mathematical calculation attending them.

CELSIUS, a measure of temperature formerly known as centigrade (q.v.).

CENTER OF BUOYANCY, the center of displacement. It is the center of upward or buoyant action.

CENTER OF EFFORT, the center of wind pressure on the sail area.

CENTER OF FLOTATION, that point about which a vessel rotates when slightly inclined in any direction from her free position of equilibrium by the action of an external force without change in her displacement. (Shipbuidling Cyclopedia.)

CENTER OF GRAVITY, the center or balancing point of downward pressure. The whole weight of a ship and cargo is assumed to act downward through this point.

CENTER OF LATERAL RESISTANCE, the total lateral resistance centered as a single force in a point where its effect will be the same on the vessel.

CENTERBOARD, a keel-like device that is capable of being hoisted and lowered in a well for the purpose of adding keel area to a sailing craft. When down the leeway is much reduced. The water-tight box inside the vessel that receives the board when hoisted is called the *centerboard trunk.* The centerboard is sometimes called a *drop keel.* The primary object of a centerboard is to improve the sailing

qualities of a shoal draft boat in working to windward.

CENTERING CHAINS, are swung across a dry dock carrying a red and white disc by which a vessel is centered on the keel block in conjunction with range sights.

CENTER-LINE BULKHEAD, one running fore and aft amidships.

CENTIGRADE, a measure of temperature where 0° is freezing and 100° boiling. To change a centigrade reading to Fahrenheit take $\frac{9}{5}$ of centigrade reading $+32°$. This measure of temperature is now called *Celsius.*

CENTIPEDE, a length of rope or strip of oak on each side of the bowsprit and jibboom through which are passed at intervals short stops with which the head sails are secured.

CESSER CLAUSE, a clause appearing in a charter party which reads approximately as follows: "Charterer's liability to cease when the ship is loaded, the master having lien upon the cargo for freight, dead freight and demurrage."

CHADBURN, the name by which the masters and mates of the Great Lakes refer to the engine room telegraph.

CHAFING BATTEN, a strip of wood along the side of a yard to take the chafe of the gear.

CHAFING GEAR, a winding of canvas, rope, or other material, around the rigging, spars and rodes to take the wear. See also, Baggy Wrinkle.

CHAIN, the term usually applied to the anchor cable. A shot of chain is usually 15 fathoms. There are two types of chain—the stud-link and open-link.

CHAIN BITTS, heavy vertical iron castings forward of the windlass to aid in securing the anchor chains. A turn or two of the chain is taken around the bitt and further secured with stoppers.

CHAIN GRAB, the wildcat of the windlass.

CHAIN HOISTS, a combination of gin blocks and chain falls. They possess great power and are an important part of a steamer's equipment.

CHAIN HOOKS, handled hooks for the purpose of hauling the heavy chain cable about the decks or from the lockers.

CHAIN LOCKERS, compartments for the stowage of anchor chains. They are each fitted with a ring bolt to which the end of the chain is secured.

CHAIN PIPE, the casting in the deck through which the chain leads to the locker. Sometimes called also the *Spurling Gate.*

CHAIN PLATES, iron or bronze strips bolted to the side of a ship or yacht to take the stress of the rigging. If these chain plates project out to a narrow platform, abreast the rigging, the whole is called the *chains* or *channels.* This arrangement gives greater spread to the rigging, but is not often seen on modern vessels.

CHAIN RIVETING, two rows of rivets where each is opposite and not alternated with those of the other row. If alternated they are said to be staggered.

CHAIN SLINGS, short pieces of chain provided with hooks for handling rails and similar cargo.

CHAIN SPLICE, a method of securing a rope to a chain.

CHAIN STOPPER, a short length with a slip hook and a turnbuckle for securing the anchor chain. The anchor is often let go by casting off the slip hook from which the anchor is already hanging.

CHAIN SWIVEL, is made into an anchor chain to prevent kinking. One is usually found between the anchor and the 15 fathom shackle, and another at 75 fathoms.

CHAIN TIERER, one who stows the chain in the lockers.

CHAIN WALES, the strakes in old ships to which the chain plates were bolted.

CHAINS. See Chain Plates.

CHANCE, a breeze.

CHANNEL, the deeper courses of a river, harbor or passage between sections of land; they may be dredged or natural.

CHANNEL FEVER, nervousness of a bridge officer in constricted waters.

CHANNEL IRON, a three sided angle iron somewhat resembling a [in cross-section.

CHANNELS. See Chain Plates.

CHANTY (CHANTEY), a song formerly always and now rarely sung aboard ship to lighten and unify labor at the capstan, sheets and halyards. The soloist is known as the *chanty-man* and is usually a man of leadership in the forecastle. He is something of an improviser, for those especially successful make their verses applicable to the existing conditions in the ship, indulging in slight hits at the peculiarities of the different officers. The vociferousness of the chorus indicates the relative delight with which these squibs are received by the men. This was the only privilege allowed to pass in the old days of iron-fisted discipline. They were composed for various kinds of work such as *capstan chanties,* which were timed to be rhythmic with the steady tread around the capstan. They usually dwell upon the joys of being homeward-bound and farewells to the port (and ladies) they are heaving up the anchor to leave. The topsail halyard chanties are the most stirring as they, at their best, are sung in a gale when the reefed topsail is being mast-headed. There are also *short pull* and *long pull chanties.*

The words of some are not for public print and are in the main rather meaningless, but in tune they are very melodious, and are made romantic by the unique and stirring surroundings in which they are sung. Pronounced as if spelled shanty.

CHAPELS, grooves in a built-up mast. The appearance of a vessel was enhanced in the sailing ship days by painting the chapels in contrast with the general color of the mast.

CHAPPELING, the evolution of wearing a vessel taken aback, around before the wind to her original course without bracing the yards. It is not practicable except in light airs. Older authorities refer to chappeling as the act of a careless helmsman. It is said, *he has built a chapel.*

CHARLEY NOBLE, the enlisted man's name for the galley smoke pipe. It is quite the custom to send each landsman to find Charley Noble, a hunt which causes endless amusement for the older men.

CHART SYMBOLS, characters used on charts to represent the aids to navigation, character of land, and the bottom.

CHART WORK, the laying off of courses and distances, plotting of positions, and the study of hydrographical and topographical features.

CHARTER, a contract for the employment of a vessel. There are *time charters* where the crew is furnished and ship kept found, and there are *bare pole* or *bare hull charters* in which the charterer does all the detail of operation. There are also *lump sum, voyage,* and *tonnage* forms of charter.

CHARTER PARTY, a document written for letting to freight the whole or part of a vessel for one or more voyages or a certain length of time.

CHART-HOUSE (or ROOM), a compartment designed for the stowage of charts and books, and usually equipped with a table for chart work.

CHARTS are to the water and coasts what maps are to the land.

They show a fund of information for the use of the navigator, such as all landmarks, contours of the lands, character of the shore, the depths of water, character of the bottom, shoals and reefs, aids to navigation and information concerning tides and currents, etc. They are constructed on different scales, the general, covering large areas, being of small scale; the intermediate or coast charts, and the large scale harbor charts. The larger the scale the greater the detail. They are constructed mainly on the *Mercator* projection, but also on the *polyconic* and *gnomonic* projections.

CHASE, a vessel pursued.

CHASSE MAREE, a small French vessel of the lugger type. It carries a bowsprit and jib and three masts, the fore and mizzen being stepped in the extreme bow and stern, respectively. The mainmast is lug-rigged with a square or lug topsail.

CHEATER, a small staysail used as a save-all under a parachute spinnaker. Also called Spinnaker Staysail.

CHEBACCO BOAT, a seaworthy fishing boat of New England about 30 feet, double ended, masts stepped forward, no bowsprit or head sails; popular about 1800.

CHECK, to slack off slowly, to stop a vessel's way gradually by a line fast to a dock or anchor on the bottom.

CHECK RING, at the base of a pintle to allow the removal of its lignum vitae strips.

CHECKERED PLATES, used for engineroom flooring, having raised sections which tend to provide a foothold. They are used on ladders.

CHEEK BLOCK, one whose sheave is set against the side of a spar with only one cheek to support the pin.

CHEEKS, projecting parts of a mast worked from the "stick" or substantial pieces of timber bolted a short distance below the top of a mast to support the trestletrees. The sides of a block are called cheeks.

CHEESE-CUTTER, a type of centerboard.

CHERUB LOG, a taffrail log which rings a small bell as the miles pass.

CHESS TREES, pieces of wood with a sheave in the end; fayed and bolted to the topsides so as to project at a point convenient for hauling down the main tack.

CHEVRON, the insignia of rank of a petty or non-commissioned officer. There are also service and wound chevrons.

CHIEF, the popular name given to the chief engineer. Also to a chief petty officer of the Navy.

CHILEAN CURRENT, or Humbolt Current flows northward from Antarctic off the west coast of South America.

CHILLED CARGO, that carried at a temperature of 29°F to 42°F.

CHINE, the line of intersection between the sides and bottom of a flat-bottomed boat; the angle in the planking of a V-bottomed boat.

The part of the waterway which is left above the deck that the lower seams of spirketting may more conveniently be caulked. (Falconer) *To Chine Out* is to hollow out. That part of a cask (sometimes called *chime)* at the end of the staves; *chime hooks,* the term usually employed, are used to hoist casks by catching them under the chines. These are also called *can* and *cant hooks.*

CHINE AND CHINE, applies to casks stowed end to end.

CHINOOK, a relatively warm wind caused by flowing down from mountain heights and raised in temperature by compression.

CHINSE, to caulk lightly where the planks will not stand the force of heavy blows.

CHIP, to remove paint or rust with hammers.

CHIP LOG, a device now restricted to a few sailing vessels. It consists of a wooden quadrant about 5 inches in radius with lead placed in the circular edge which causes it to float upright. It is made fast to a log line by a three part bridle. The part fitted to the upper corner is slightly shorter than the other two parts of the bridle and has a socket and a pin which pulls out when a strain is placed upon it. The chip then is easily hauled aboard. The chip is cast over (streamed) with the pin in position. The first 15 or 30 fathoms of line is called the *stray line* which is marked by a piece of red bunting. The line from this point is divided into parts of 47 ft. 3 in. each

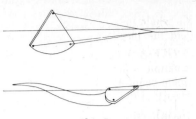

Chip Log

called a *knot.* They are marked by pieces of cord tucked through the strands with knots in their ends corresponding to the number of knots out. Each knot is subdivided into fifths and marked with a white rag. The log line is allowed to run out while a 28-second glass is emptying itself. The result is the rate of speed of the vessel. The length of the knot was derived from the proportion that one hour (3600 sec.) is to 28 seconds as one mile (6080 ft.) is to the length of a knot (47 ft. 3 in.). The clipper ship *Flying Cloud* off Cape Horn once ran out eighteen knots and there was still a little sand in the glass.

CHIPS, a nickname for the ship's carpenter.

CHOCK, an iron casting which serves as a lead for lines to a wharf or other vessel. There are several types—open, closed and roller chocks. A roller chock reduces friction and wear on a line when working a vessel around the docks. A convenient block of wood for shoring up boats, weights, etc. The chocks of a whaleboat were formed in the stem which was grooved down vertically to carry the whale line. A chock pin of oak held the line in the chock.

CHOCK-A-BLOCK (two blocks), the situation when two blocks of a tackle come together. When a hold or cask is full to the top.

CHOKE-THE-LUFF, to put the end of a rope across the sheave of a block to jam the fall and prevent its rendering.

CHOP, a name given to a place where tides meet and cause an irregular sea. The junction of a channel with the sea is sometimes called the *chops of the channel,* as in the English Channel.

CHOW, a sailor's term for food.

CHOW CHOW, rips or overfalls, of the Min River in particular.

CHOW RAG, the meal pennant.

CHRISTMAS TREE RIG, an arrangement of lines in a towing operation. At a point in the main towline is shackled a triangular plate with an eye in each apex: it is known as the *flounder plate.* Into, say the port eye of this plate, is shackled a chain pendant to provide a catenary—a dip to take the shock of stress. This chain pendant is shackled to another flounder plate into whose after eyes is shackled a chain bridle, the legs of which lead to pad eyes or bitts at each bow of the *first* tow. Returning to the forward flounder plate: Into the starboard eye of this plate is shackled a chain pendant of such length as to provide a deep catenary for the necessarily low riding wire rope leading to the *second tow* far astern. This wire is similarly shackled to a third flounder plate with a chain bridle leading to the bows of the second tow.

CHRONOMETER a sea-going clock, fitted with gimbals to neutralize the motion of the vessel. It is made with very superior workmanship and of accurate design, having a variable lever and a compensated balance wheel. This instrument for the purposes of navigation carries Greenwich mean time (G. M. T.).

CHRONOMETER   CORRECTION (C. C.), the amount of instrument is fast or slow on correct G. M. T. It is now ascertained by radio time signals broadcast by all countries. Before this invention came into use time balls, dropped from a conspicuous point in all the principal ports of the world, were depended upon. But before the days of telegraphy navigators took careful observations while in port, or even at sea off a well established point like St. Helena, and the amount (in time) their longitudes differed from the true known longitude was the error of their instrument. This method was subject to many errors. The observations taken in port required the use of an artificial horizon when no sea horizon was available, but as the mean of many observations was taken, very satisfactory accuracy was obtained.

CHRONOMETER DAILY RATE, is the amount the instrument gains or loses each day. It is established by dividing the error accumulated over a certain period by the number of days elapsed.

CHRONOMETER ERROR, the amount the instrument is fast or slow on correct G. M. T. It is another name for chronometer correction.

CHUBASCOS, violent easterly squalls on the western coast of Nicaragua. Short sharp squalls on the Orinoco.

CHUTE, an abbreviation for parachute spinnaker.

CIRCLE OF ILLUMINATION, the twilight line which separates the illuminated from the shaded hemisphere.

CIRCLE OF RIGHT ASCENSION, a great circle that passes through the poles of the equinoctial or celestial equator.

CIRCLES OF DECLINATION, celestial meridians or hour circles.

CIRCLES OF EQUAL ALTITUDE, the circles upon which the altitudes of a body are equal. If an observer walked out a distance from Washington Monument where the altitude of its top was seventy degrees, he would find by experiment that at the same distance in every direction the altitude would still be seventy degrees, a circle of equal altitude. Substitute the sun for the top of the monument and a similar condition will be found to exist. A system of concentric circles each with it own particular altitude lies around the sub-solar point.

CIRCUM-MERIDIAN ALTITUDE, an observation for latitude shortly before or after noon. Also called an Ex-Meridian Altitude.

CIRCUMNAVIGATE, to sail around the world.

CIRCUMPOLAR, a body is said to be circumpolar when during its diurnal revolution in the heavens it does not set for the observer, remaining alway above the horizon.

CIRRO-CUMULUS (Ci-Cu), white flaky clouds or small rounding masses with little or no shadow. Also called *Mackerel sky.*

CIRRO-STRATUS (Ci-S), a thin whitish veil occasionally covering the whole sky. It is this veil that usually brings out halos of moon and sun.

CIRRUS (Ci), clouds that generally take the form of delicate white feathers. They are usually detached but sometimes form belts across the sky; they are the highest clouds and are composed of ice crystals.

CIRRUS VEIL, a thin mist-like cloud covering the sky as a forerunner of a hurricane or typhoon.

CIVIL DAY, is 24 hours long, mean time, divided into antemeridian and post-meridian periods of 12 hours each. The civil day begins at midnight. A method being extensively used is to express midnight as 0000; 6.30 a.m. as 0630; noon as 1200; 8.15 p.m. as 2015, etc. Since 1925 the *American Nautical Almanac* has counted the hours of the day in civil instead of astronomical time. Civil time is measured from midnight.

CLAMP DOWN, to swab a deck when it is not desired to turn on the hose and wash down.

CLAMPS, the heavy planks or timbers forming the ceiling upon which the deck beams rest. The clamp of the forecastle is the strake under the forecastle deck beams. Likewise, the poop or raised quarterdeck clamps.

CLAMSHELL BUCKET, a device for moving coal, ore or mud. It consists of two scoops like a clam's shell hinged at one point so they can be opened as the whip lowers it to the pile of coal or the bottom, but so arranged as to close when the raising tension is applied.

CLAPPER, sometimes called the *tumbler,* or *tongue,* a movable fitting between the jaws of a gaff to prevent jamming.

CLAWING OFF, the maneuver of working a ship off a lee shore.

CLEAN, a term applied to a vessel's lines. If they are very fine at her entrance and at the counter, going through the water without disturbing it unduly, she is said to be *clean-lined.*

CLEAN SHIP, a whaling vessel that returned from a voyage with no oil.

CLEAR, to observe the formalities in connection with ship's papers at the customhouse when a vessel is about to sail. To leave the land. To empty a hold. To work by a shoal. To straighten out a tangle of rigging. To clear away a boat for lowering.

CLEAR AHEAD. A yacht is said to be clear ahead of another, under racing rules, when every part of the leading yacht is ahead, in the direction of the course they are sailing, of an imaginary line drawn at right angles to that course, through the forwardmost part of the other yacht.

CLEAR ASTERN. A yacht is clear astern of another when every part of her is abaft a corresponding line drawn through the aftermost part of the other yacht.

CLEAR or **OPEN HAWSE,** when both anchors are down and the chains are not crossed.

CLEAR FOR RUNNING, when the gear is coiled down *on its ends,* so when cast off the pins it will run out quickly without becoming tangled or fouled.

CLEAR VIEW SCREEN, a device for giving an officer on the bridge a clear vision. A circular disk of plate glass turned at high speed by a motor is kept clear of snow, rain or sleet by the centrifugal action.

CLEARANCE, the permission to sail given by the custom officials to the master of a foreign-going vessel. This is given after the master has called at the customhouse and presented various papers, including his ship's registry, the crew list and articles, receipts for port charges, and bill of health. He swears to the accuracy of the manifest and is granted clearance. A vessel is then said to have *cleared.*

CLEAR-HAWSE PENDANT, a short piece of chain used in clearing hawse, or in using a mooring swivel. One end is fitted with a slip hook and the other with a shackle with a long tail or wire rope spliced into it.

CLEARING FOR GUAM, clearing for no particular port. Originated in gold rush days when there was no homeward cargo and ship sailed to seek one.

CLEARING HAWSE, the process of clearing the turns in the chains which usually occur when a vessel lies in a tideway with both anchors down.

CLEARING PORTS, openings in the bulwarks, to free the decks when a sea has been shipped.

CLEAT, a piece of wood or metal with two horns around which ropes are made fast.

CLEVIS, a shackle.

CLEW CRINGLE (or IRON), a spectacle iron set in the clew or a square sail.

CLEW DOWN, to bring the yard down when the sail is well filled, let go halyards hold sheets and haul down by clew lines. (See Clew Up.)

CLEW GARNET, the clewline of a lower (course) square sail.

CLEW JIGGER, a handy tackle made fast aloft for various uses about the decks.

CLEW LINES, the ropes leading from the clews of a sail to the quarter of the yard and thence to the deck. They haul the corners of the sail up towards the bunt on the after side of the sail preparatory to furling sail.

CLEW ROPE, a single rope to haul down the clew of a course.

CLEW OF A SAIL, in a fore and aft sail the lower corner aft, in a square sail the two lower corners.

CLEW UP, lower away on halyards of a yard, let go sheets, and haul up the clews by clew lines. (See Clew Down.)

CLEWS, the small ropes at the ends of a hammock.

CLICK, the pawl that drops in the rack-wheel of the windlass or capstan as it goes ahead and prevents a reverse movement.

CLINCH, a bend by which a bight or eye is made by seizing the end to its own part. There are two kinds known as the *inside* and *outside clinches.* A *clinch ring* is an oval washer used on spikes and bolts where they are used in wood construction.

CLINKER or CLINCHER BUILT, a method of planking in which the lower edge of a plank overlaps the upper edge of the one below it. This is also called *lapstrake.* This is also done with steel plates by placing a tapering liner underneath and on the frames.

CLINOMETER, an instrument which indicates the pitch or roll of a vessel according as it is placed on a fore and aft or thwartship line.

CLIP, a short angle bar.

CLIP HOOKS, are two hooks similar in shape and so beveled as to lie together and form an eye, also called *Sister hooks.*

CLIPPER BOW, one with a very graceful incurving stem. Strictly speaking it should have concave water-lines forward, but the latter feature is no longer considered.

CLIPPER BUILT, a term applied to vessels wtih very fine lines.

CLIPPERS, swift sailing vessels of narrow beam and very fine lines. Their length was about five times the beam with concave lines at the water-line forward. They necessarily needed high freights in order to pay, owing to their restricted cargo space. The term comprises *extreme, half* and *medium* clippers. The *Lightning* was probably the fastest clipper in the world, having sailed 436 nautical miles in 24 hours, the highest authenticated record. She was designed and built by Donald McKay of East Boston for James Baines & Co. of Liverpool for the Australian trade.

CLOSE ABOARD, in close proximity to.

CLOSE CEILING, the edges of the ceiling planks very closely fitted.

CLOSE-HAULED, the term applied to a vessel with sails trimmed to sail as close to the wind as possible. A fore and aft vessel usually sails within four points of the wind, and a square rigger six.

CLOSE-LINKED CHAIN, that which has short links making a compact chain.

CLOSE WINDED, a vessel capable of sailing very close to the wind.

CLOTH, a width of canvas in a sail. Plural, clothes.

CLOUD SCALE, indicates the amount of the sky overcast. It ranges from 0 when there are no clouds to 10 when there is no blue sky.

CLOUDS. These floating masses of condensed vapor take on many different shapes and colors due to atmospheric conditions. They are described under their different names.

CLOVE HITCH, a most useful and efficient method of making a line fast to spar or to other rope.

CLOVE HOOKS. See Clip Hooks.

CLUB, a spar serving as a boom on a foretopmast staysail or fisherman's jumbo; the spars which spread the club topsail are *clubs.*

CLUB FOOT, a broad fore foot, giving added displacement in the extreme forward section at the lowest part. This section, however, tumbles home rapidly to the load water-line.

CLUB HAULING, an evolution resorted to in heavy weather on a lee shore when a sailing vessel is cast on the opposite tack by use of a line from a kedge anchor leading to the lee quarter. As the vessel comes to, the anchor is let go forward on the lee bow, a strain is put on the kedge by sternway produced quickly by backing the head yards, and she falls off, if successful, on the other tack; the hawser is then cut.

CLUB LINK, the link of special and heavy construction that connects the chain to the anchor.

CLUB TOPSAIL takes the place of a gaff topsail. It is larger, being extended by lacing its foot and luff to two spars, called clubs, which extend beyond the gaff and topmast.

CLUBBING, riding with the current with an anchor just dragging on the bottom. This is also called *kedging* or *dredging* among some seamen.

CLUMP BLOCK, a single sheave, roundish lignum vitae block. These blocks are used in the sheets of the head sails. Their rounding shape facilitates in hauling them across the stays when tacking ship.

COACH WORK, plaited mats and made of hard laid cotton cord.

COAL BUNKER, a storage place for coal used in furnaces.

COAL CHUTE, a small round hatch in the deck with a tube leading to the bunkers.

COAL SACK, a patch of the southern sky near the Southern Cross apparently devoid of stars.

COALING PORT, an opening in the side of a vessel for the handling of bunker coal. Also a port or harbor that offers facilities for coaling.

COALING SHIP, filling a vessel's bunkers.

COAMING, the name applied to the structure raised about a hatchway to prevent water getting below, and to serve as a framework to receive the strongbacks and hatchcovers and for the securing of the tarpaulins. The slightly elevated rail of a yacht. Also *cockpit coaming*.

COAMING BULKHEAD, additional or double plates reenforcing a bulkhead at top and bottom.

COAST PILOT, a man unusually familiar with a certain coast along which he acts as pilot. A book of sailing directions is popularly called a coast pilot.

COAST PILOTING. This highly important part of navigation requires a peculiar skill of the coastal mariner. It does not require a knowledge of Celonavigation, but a great familiarity with the coast and coastal waters. It requires skill in the use of instruments for taking bearings, of the lead and log. The courses are laid from light to light and a vessel in the coastal trade is not usually out of touch with some landmark for more than two or three hundred miles.

COASTER, a vessel engaged in coastwise commerce.

COASTWISE, a term pertaining to the navigation of the coast, in distinction from offshore navigation.

COBBLE, a small English craft with high flaring bows; the greatest draft is forward which diminishes until aft it is almost flat. This is to facilitate beaching which is done stern first. The cobble is usually lug-rigged. Also *coble*.

COCK BOAT, a very small rowing boat used as a tender. It carries a long deep rudder, sails fast and very close to the wind.

COCKBILL, to trim the yards by the lifts in a diagonal manner, as, port yardarm up and starboard down.

COCKBILLED, a term applied to yards when topped to an acute angle with the mast. This is necessary in lying alongside a pier. An anchor is cockbilled when hanging over the bows, by a stopper, ready to let go.

COCKPIT, a small well where the steering wheel or tiller is located in the after part of the upper deck of some sailing vessels. Formerly the quarters of junior officers on the lower gun deck of a man of war; also the place where the wounded were treated, below the water-line.

COCKSCOMBING, the covering of a ring, rail or becket with turns of white cord, fitted snugly and locked with a half-hitch at each turn. There are several designs used.

CODE FLAG, of the International Code is the so-called answering pennant having red vertical stripes alternating with white.

CODLINE, eighteen-thread stuff.

COEFFICIENT OF FINENESS, is that fractional part that the volume of a vessel bears to a box of same length, breadth and depth. That is the amount the ship's lines depart from the box; it may be, say 0.7.

COFFEE GRINDER, a winch located aft or amidships in a racing yacht. It is used particularly to bring in the sheet of a genoa, balloon jib or spinnaker. The drum is operated through gears on a vertical shaft turned by two cranks, 180° apart, worked by hand. The sheet is led through a cheek or snatch block on the rail and made fast to a cleat on top of the winch.

COFFERDAM, a heavy bulkhead on a naval vessel and some types of cargo vessels, particularly tankers. It is doublewalled in construction with a space of 3 to 5 feet between. It can be used for water ballast or oil. A temporary enclosing dam built in the water and pumped dry, to protect workmen.

COG, a double-ended, full-lined, bluff bowed craft of early days in Scandinavia and Holland. It was clinker built and was originated on the Friesian Coast.

COIL, to lay a rope down in circular turns; if the rope is laid up right-handed it is coiled from left to right with the hands of a watch; if left-handed, from right to left; hemp rope is always coiled from left to right. Rope is sold by the coil which contains 200 fathoms standard length and 100 fathoms in so-called half coils.

COIR HAWSER, a rope made of coconut husks and sufficiently light to float; it has about one-fourth the strength of manila rope.

COL, a neck of low pressure between two areas of high pressure. It is an area of light variable winds, frequent thunder storms, and uncertain weather conditions.

CO-LATITUDE, is the complement of the latitude, 90° −Lat. = Co. lat.

COLD FRONT, is the line of separation between a mass of cold heavy air flowing in beneath a mass of warmer lighter air. There is an abrupt drop in temperature in the passing of the cold front. Also a pronounced change in the barometric gradient, hence a wind shift.

COLD WALL, is a counter current of cold Arctic water which flows southwestward close inside the Gulf Stream. It is so close at times that the temperature between that at the bow of a steamer may be 20° in variance with that at the stern when crossing the line between the cold wall and the Gulf Stream.

Such a contrast is most marked in the vicinity of the Grand Banks.

COLLA, a brisk south or southwest wind in the Philippines.

COLLARS, the eyes of standing rigging that go over the mast-head.

COLLIER, a vessel in the coal trade.

COLLIER PATCH, an expedient of placing tar over a thin portion of an old sail.

COLLISION, vessels coming into destructive contact. They are said to have been in collision.

COLLISION BULKHEAD, a partition in the forward part of the ship, built of sufficiently heavy material to stand the great strain should the bow become damaged through collision.

COLLISION CHOCKS, preventer brackets at both ends of a boiler to protect against the dislodging of the boilers in case of collision.

COLLISION COURSE, one which if pursued would lead to a collision, especially applied to the burdened vessel.

COLLISION MAT, a piece of extra heavy canvas roped and fitted with hogging lines spliced into each corner. It is thickly covered with pieces of oakum stitched to the canvas. It is drawn over a damaged section of the hull below the waterline to prevent the inrush of water.

COLORS, a ship's national flag. The naval ceremony which takes place at hoisting of the colors at 8 a.m. and the lowering at sunset.

COLT, a short piece of rope which boatswain's mates used to carry in the boats to use as a "starter" on those slow in obeying orders.

COMB CLEAT, a wooden board with a row of holes to lead the running rigging fair.

COMBER, a high breaking sea in deep water.

COME, a term of several meanings: To come to, is to turn towards the wind; also to anchor. To come up, is to come forward on a rope and slacken it. A kedge anchor comes home when it fails to hold.

COMMANDER, the commissioned naval rank below that of captain, corresponding with lieutenant colonel in the Army. A commander wears three gold stripes ¾ inch wide on his sleeves.

COMMISSION PENNANT, the official pennant flown from a vessel when in command of a commissioned officer of less than flag rank.

COMMITTEE BOAT, with race committee aboard lies near starting and finish lines flying a blue flag with letters R.C.

COMPANIONWAY, a series of steps or "stairs" leading below from the spar deck. With some authorities, companions are skylights, which cover the hatches allowing light and air below; but with others it only applies to the covering leading to a stairway, called a companion-ladder. The latter appears to be the best usage.

COMPARTMENT SHIP, is so called when one or more compartments can be flooded and the vessel remains afloat. Thus a steamer may be a two-compartment ship if she floats when two compartments are flooded but would sink if three were flooded.

COMPARTMENTS, spaces below between bulkheads.

COMPASS, is the most valuable instrument in navigation as it directs the course of the ship. It is known as the mariner's compass. There is also the gyro compass.

COMPASS COURSE, the direction of the ship's head based on the ship's compass. A direction shown by the compass is subject to the errors of both deviation and variation. The compass course can be corrected by applying these errors to the right when easterly and to the left when westerly, provided the directions are taken from an assumed position in the center of the compass.

COMPASS DIAGRAM, the representation of the compass on a chart. Also called a compass rose. From this diagram courses are taken.

COMPASS ERROR, the amount the ship's compass is deflected from the true direction by variation and deviation combined. It is the difference between the true bearing or azimuth of a body and that shown by the compass. It is named East if the true azimuth is to the right of the compass azimuth, if the eye is assumed to be at the center of compass; otherwise it is West.

COMPASS POINT. A compass card is divided into 32 parts or points, each covering an arc of 11¼°.

COMPASS ROSE, a graduated circle engraved on a chart from which courses and bearings can be taken with parallel rulers. Compass roses are graduated by points, or degrees, or both, one within the other. They are true or magnetic, depending upon whether the north and south line lies with the true or the magnetic meridian. The magnetic rose gives by inspection the amount of variation existing at the spot indicated by the location of the rose on the chart.

COMPASSES, a drafting instrument with two legs for transferring distances. Also called *dividers*.

COMPENSATION, the reenforcing of plates, beams and stringers around a hatch by adding strength to offset the weakening of the deck by cutting the hatch. *Compensation of the Compass,* the placing of bar magnets in such a manner beneath a compass as to counteract the semi-circular deviation, and by setting a sphere of soft iron at each side of the compass to rectify the quadrantal deviation.

COMPLEMENT OF AN ANGLE, what it lacks of 90°.

COMPOSITE SAILING. When the great circle course between two points leads into dangerous latitudes or intervening land, recourse is made to Composite sailing. This expedient comprises three sections, a great circle to the parallel of latitude passing comfortably on the safety side of the danger, a course along this parallel until the danger is passed, then another great circle to the port of destination. The two principal routes where composite sailing is practiced are from the

Cape of Good Hope to Australia where a great circle course leads into the far Antarctic; and in the Pacific on the run from Cape Flattery to Yokohama where the Aleutian Islands intervene.

COMPOSITE VESSEL, one whose hull is planked with wood upon a steel frame. Composite sometimes also is used to describe boat hull construction of other dissimilar materials, such as wood and fiberglass-reinforced plastic.

COMPRESSOR, a device which grips the out-going anchor chain by choking it against the side of the spurling gate or deck pipe.

CON (or **CONN**), to direct the helmsman as to the movements of the helm, especially in maneuvers, in narrow channels, or heavy traffic. One is said to be *at the con* when one is directing a vessel's movements in this way. The expression appears in an old Navy log "Stood into the Tagus with the pilot at the conn."

CONCLUDING LINE, a small rope rove through the middle of the steps of a Jacob's ladder. (Soule's Naval Terms.)

CONDUCTION, is the process of carrying heat from one molecule of an element to the next. Air in contact with the warm earth is at first heated by conduction before convection sets in. Conduction is a slow process of transmitting heat.

CONICAL BUOY, is in shape as its name implies. In the United States it is usually red in color, marked with an even number to indicate the starboard side of a channel when entering port.

CONJUNCTION, two heavenly bodies are said to be in conjunction when one passes over the other.

CONNECTING BRIDGE, a fore and aft structure or walkway leading from the bridge deck to either the poop or the forecastle. It is sometimes called the *flying bridge* or in a sailing vessel *monkey bridge*.

CONNING TOWER, the armored control station of a fighting ship.

CONNING A VESSEL, to direct the quartermaster as he steers through narrow or congested waters.

CONSOLAN (CONSOL), is an electronic system that provides bearings from a Consolan station which transmits dots and dashes in alternate arcs of about 15°. The moving boundary between the dots and dashes gives signals that are indeterminate as they overlap. The observation should be made at the moment that this boundary passes. The dots and dashes, of which there are 60, should be counted then. If less than 60, several being lost in the blurred boundary, the lack should be distributed between the dots and the dashes. The bearing is obtained by referring to a table or special chart.

CONSTANT (latitude), a formula used to expedite the reporting of the latitude at noon to the captain. By its use the problem is worked in advance and the observed altitude is merely added to or subtracted from the constant to obtain the latitude.

CONSTELLATIONS, particular groups of stars.

CONSTRUCTIVE TOTAL LOSS, when the damage exceeds the value of a stranded vessel.

CONTAINER SHIP, a vessel so constructed as to receive and closely stow freightcar sized containers in turn stowed full of merchandise. By this method one draft handles a large amount of cargo with greater facility than by older practices.

CONTINENTAL SHELF, is roughly limited by a line which indicates the contour where the declivity of the coastal slope steepens to the ocean depths. This is usually at 100 fathoms.

CONTINUOUS FLOOR, an unbroken steel frame from the keel to the turn of the bilge in a cellular double bottom.

CONTINUOUS VOYAGE, DOCTRINE OF, the principle which justifies the capturing of contraband of war when consigned to a neutral port but really intended for a belligerent.

CONTINUOUS WAVE, a type of radio transmission in which the frequency and amplitude do not vary. It is of very low frequency and is used for radio direction finding. In broadcast practice the continuous wave is changed by modulating its amplitude (the height above or below a median line). The result is the AM of voice radio. When frequency is modulated the result is FM broadcasts.

CONTOUR LINES, if on the land, represent the line of a certain elevation; if in the water, the line of a certain depth. For instance, if a great imaginary saw should cut the hills off everywhere, 100 feet above the sea, the edge would be represented by the 100-foot contour line.

CONTRA PROPELLER, stationary blades attached to the rudder post or forward of the propeller, by which the benefit of a thrust is derived from the currents of the revolving propeller.

CONTRABAND, munitions or other goods prohibited entry into a belligerent state. There is *absolute contraband* which is always recognized, and *conditional* which may be declared contraband.

CONTROLLER, a device by which the anchor chain is jammed and controlled when riding to the anchor or when heaving in.

CONTROLLING DEPTH, the least depth in the approach and channel to a port which governs the draft of vessels that can enter.

CONVECTION, a term much used in meteorology and oceanography. It is the process of transmitting heat by the movement of the heated air or water. The heat of the earth expands the air at the surface, it becomes lighter and rises. The cooler air above then descends to take its place. This is also true of the waters of the oceans; warm water rises and the cooler flows to the lower depths.

CONVOY, one or more merchant vessels proceeding under the protection of naval vessels.

COOLASHI WATCH, all hands

standing by, with no regular watches set.

COOPER, a member of the shore personnel who lays dunnage, shores, braces and toms cargo. Formerly the man who made and maintained the water casks and barrels for whale oil.

COORDINATES, a system of lines, planes or angles, by which, with certain data, a position can be determined. A line or plane is selected from each system as a prime or reference line (as the Greenwich meridian from the system of meridians and the equator from the system of parallels of latitude). The lines or planes cut each other at right angles in the geographical or spherical system used principally in navigation. The given number of degrees is measured from each line or place of reference and the point desired lies at the intersection of the secondary lines.

COPEPODS, primitive crustaceans resembling tiny shrimps. They feed on minute plant forms and in turn constitute food for fish.

COPPERS, large cooking kettles usually connected with the vessel's boiler.

CORBITA, an ancient Roman merchantman. She was high-pooped, one mast with square sail and raffed above, bowsprit and spritsail. The mast was heavily stayed.

CORD, several yarns with an extra twist laid up the opposite way.

CORDAGE, collectively, rope, hawsers and small stuff.

CORINTHIAN, an amateur sailor.

CORIOLIS EFFECT, is the tendency of ocean currents, drift ice, hurricanes, airplanes, etc., to drift to the right in the northern hemisphere (left in southern). It is due to the rotation of the earth.

CORK FENDER, a bag of granulated cork covered with woven tarred stuff.

CORK LIGHT, wholly without cargo.

CORK PAINT, used to prevent sweating on the inside of a steel vessel. Granulated cork is mixed in the paint.

CORNET, a signal for all hands to report aboard a naval vessel at once; a general message from a flagship to a squadron; a signal for every ship to prepare to receive a message.

CORONA, a small ring of 5° radius around the sun or moon, the colors of which range from blue on the inside through the spectrum to red on the outside. They are caused by diffraction of light on the particles of ice and water.

CORPOSANT, a ball of glowing electrical energy appearing about the spars of a vessel. It was considered a good omen among the old sailing ship sailors when a corposant was seen to rise, but bad luck if it descended to a lower position; it was also ill luck to have the light of a corposant shine on one's face.

CORSAIR, a privateer of the Mediterranean, whose activities often verged on piracy.

CORVETTE, an armed vessel with a row of guns along one deck only. It ranked next below a frigate and was called a *sloop of war* in the United States. It was used on light cruiser service. In World War II the corvette was a lightly armed vessel used for convoy protection and patrol. It carried about one-half the crew of a destroyer.

COTIA, a native vessel of the Malabar coast, having two masts lateen rigged.

CO-TIDAL HOUR, the interval between the moon's transit of Greenwich meridian and the time of high water at any port.

CO-TIDAL LINES, those along which the tide is high at the same time.

COTTON CLOUDS, appear beneath the cirrus veil and are forerunners of a tropical cyclone. They are squalls clouds and usually drive low.

COUNTER, the after part of a vessel's hull where the lines converge towards the stern; the under side of the overhang.

COUNTER BRACED YARDS, a situation when those of the fore are braced on the opposite tack from those on the main mast, as in tacking ship; *abox*.

COUNTER-CURRENT. An ocean or tidal current usually is accompanied by a counter-current outside its own limits which flows in the opposite direction. Inside the Gulf Stream, that is, between it and the American Continent, is a cold current flowing southward counter to the Gulf Stream. The counter-current is of less volume and slower than the main current.

COUNTERFLOODING, is the action of admitting sea water to uninjured compartments for the purpose of overcoming a dangerous list (or trim) caused by damage water in flooded compartments.

COUNTRY, the space adjacent and used for access to a compartment or quarters, as, the cabin, wardroom or hatch country and head country.

COURSE, the direction steered by a vessel; the sail set from a lower yard.

COURSE MADE GOOD, that course which a vessel would have steered had she sailed directly for her point of arrival. It disregards different intermediate courses, current set, leeway, etc.

COURSE PROTRACTOR, an instrument consisting of a compass rose and a movable arm by which courses may be laid down on a chart or bearings noted. It serves the purpose of parallel rulers.

COVE, a recess in a coastline. The arch moulding sunk in the lower part of the taffrail, as Hamersly says. A sailor.

COVERING BOARDS, planks that cover the top of the frames; plank sheers.

COVERING STRAKES, narrow steel plates covering the joint of plating laid flush.

COW HITCH, a lanyard hitch.

COWL, the upper part of a ventilator which flares out bell-shaped at right angles to the main tube. This is faced in the direction of the wind.

Cowl

COXCOMB, a small piece of wood sawtoothed on the upper side and bolted to the yardarm to keep the turns of the reef earing from slipping inward.

COX'S TRAVERSE, frequent personal errands for the purpose of evading work.

COXSWAIN (pronounced coxs'n), a petty officer in charge of a small boat.

COXSWAIN BOX, the space behind the backboard of a cutter or whaler.

CRAB, a small capstan or winch.

CRABBER'S EYE KNOT, a running eye that will not jam.

CRADLE, a frame of timber erected under a vessel to support her on the ways until she is waterborne. Supporting skids under a boat; a rest for the lowered ends of a cargo boom at sea; the bracket which holds the lower topsail yard out from the mast.

CRANCE or **CRANZE IRON,** a band at the head of the bowsprit fitted with eyes to receive the bowsprit shrouds and bobstay. A boom iron.

CRANE, an apparatus for hoisting purposes appearing in many forms, adapted for many demands. Some cranes are designed for heavy and others for light weights, even to a single davit used for a minor purpose. A *trolley crane* consists of a car on a projecting track over a hatch from which depends a whip fast to a bucket or cargo hook. A *revolving crane* consists of a small structure, containing machinery and an operator, which is capable of circular movement; a derrick boom equipped with a cargo whip reaches over the hatch of a vessel and swings its load to a pier. See types of derricks and cranes viz: A-frame, stiff-leg derrick, guy derrick, tower crane, hammerhead crane, bridge crane, gantry and straight-line crane.

CRANK (not cranky), a term given to a vessel which is unstable and tender. It is due to build or the stowage of cargo.

CRANK HATCH, the opening in the deck of a side-wheel steamer over the engines.

CRAYER, a food ship which attended a fleet in early days.

CREEPER, an iron contrivance with prongs for dragging the bottom.

CREPUSCULAR RAYS, fan-like rays of red and dark color apparently radiating from the sun at dawn and twilight. The dark beams are shadows of distant clouds.

CRESSET, a light formerly displayed from the stern of vessels. An iron basket-like receptacle to hold burning material in a whaling vessel.

CREST, the highest point of a wave.

CRIBBING, the blocking under the keel blocks.

CRIMP, a despicable person who preys upon seamen, getting their advance and other money from them by various underhand and contemptible practices. The term is also applied to joggled plates.

CRINGLE, the piece of a rope worked into a circular eye on the leeches or clews of sails. Usually it is made around a clew iron or thimble.

CROJIK (CROSS-JACK), the lowest yard on the mizzen-mast.

CROSS BEARINGS, are two or more bearings of as many known objects, taken and plotted on the chart. The ship being somewhere on each bearing will be at their intersection. In taking two objects, an error may creep in without detection, but if three objects are used and they plot at or close to the same intersection, the mariner may feel confidence in this position.

CROSS BITT, a horizontal timber across two bitt-heads.

CROSS BUNKERS, those running athwartships.

CROSS DECK TACKLES. See Thwartship Tackles.

CROSS HEAD, the fixture at the rudder head connecting with the hand steering gear.

CROSS-JACK (CROJIK), the lowest yard on the mizzen-mast of a sailing ship.

CROSS LEECH, a rope sewn in the middle of a strip of tabling which runs from the head cringles of a square mainsail to the middle of the foot where the midship tack is shackled. The reason: sometimes when running it is desirable to clew up the weather half of the mainsail to let wind into the foresail.

CROSS SEA, confused, irregular and often running contrary to the wind. It is caused usually by the shifting wind of a cyclonic storm.

CROSS SPALES, timbers temporarily fastened across the frames to secure them until the deck beams are in place during the construction of a vessel.

CROSS SPRING, a line used in maneuvering about a pier or in mooring with lines to a wharf.

CROSS STAFF, an old-fashioned device for measuring altitudes.

CROSS-TREES, comparatively light timbers placed thwartships across the trestletrees. They support the tops and spread the rigging. The term without qualification refers to those at the topmast head. See King Port.

CROSS WHISTLE, to answer a steamer's signal with another of different meaning as, for instance, when one blast is answered with two blasts. This is unlawful. If the signal received cannot be complied with, four or five short blasts should be given.

CROSS WIRES or **HAIRS,** fine wires or spider web placed at right angles to axis in the focus of object and eye piece glass of a telescope.

CROSS YARDS, to lower them into a horizontal position after they have been sent aloft *on end.*

CROWD, to carry excessive sail. To steam or sail close to a vessel that has the right of way.

CROWFOOT, a bridle of many parts made fast along the ridge rope of an awning which is hoisted and suspended in position by the *Crowfoot halyards.*

CROWN, the part of an anchor where the arms are welded to the shank. So to tuck the strands of a rope's end as to lock them, and to prevent unravelling by backsplicing the strands. A wall knot with a *crown* on top of it forms the beginning of a man rope knot.

CROW'S NEST, a lookout station usually placed on the foremast. It is usually cylindrical in form for convenience and protection. It was carried by whaling and exploring vessels at a very early date.

CRUISER, a naval vessel of light armament and wide cruising radius. A *day cruiser* is a small cabined motor boat suitable for short runs. An *express* cruiser is one capable of making high speed.

CRUISER STERN, one in which overhang does not exist, the projecting part of the stern being under water. The rudder in this type is well protected. Or, a pointed, somewhat projecting, rounded stern.

CRUISING RADIUS, is calculated with two points of view—one, the vessel's capacity in miles without refueling; the other, her capacity to remain at sea expressed in days running at normal speed.

CRUTCH, a stanchion so formed at its upper end as to receive and support a boom or other spar. *Crutches* are breasthooks at the stern. The term is sometimes applied to rowlocks.

CRYSTALLIZATION, a structural change in metals, causing the collapse of shafts, hooks and chains. It is often called "fatigue," a condition that is induced by heavy loading.

CUCKOLD'S NECK, the round turn thrown in the standing part when making a bowline.

CUDDY, a cabin in a small boat; the cookhouse on deck.

CUL DE SAC, an inlet connected with the sea by a small entrance.

CULMINATION, the position of highest altitude of a body, when it passes the meridian. This is the upper culmination. When the body crosses the meridian below the pole it is called the lower culmination, thus a circumpolar body makes two culminations each 24 hours.

CUMULO-NIMBUS (Cu.-N.), clouds rising high above the horizon forming into many majestic shapes which are characteristically shower clouds.

CUMULUS (Cu.), clouds which lie horizontally near the horizon but whose upper edges are rounded with dome-like shapes. The sunlight according to its direction makes remarkable changes in them from dark deep shadows to great brilliance. They are popularly called *wool pack clouds.*

CURRENT, the movement of water in a horizontal direction. There are the periodic currents due to the effect of tides, seasonal currents due to seasonal winds, and the permanent flowing currents of the ocean.

CURRENT, DETERMINATION OF. Current is the difference between the dead reckoning position (corrected for all errors such as, leeway, bad steering, and scend of the sea) and a fix by astronomical observations, electronic readings or land bearings. The direction and velocity of current is thus estimated. The leeway of a steamer should not be ignored.

The log (corrected) registers the amount of water distance that passes by the rotator, and the propellors of the ship turn up a sufficient number of revolutions to drive her this water distance. This number of turns is in no way affected by current, provided it extends down well below the keel. Locally the whole ocean is moving, and the current has no more effect than would be the case were the steamer in a great tank which was being carried along over the bottom at the same rate and direction as the current moved. Hence there can be no effect on the propeller revolutions due to a uniform current.

When a log shows an increase or decrease of speed with engines running the same r.p.m. it is due to wind pressure, wave effect or irregular currents about the ship. When the r.p.m. increase or decrease the alteration is due to mechanical changes, wind, or wave influence and not to a uniformly moving current.

CURRENT SAILING, laying the courses in such a manner as to offset the drift of the current and bring the vessel to the desired destination.

CUSP, a horn of a crescent of the moon or similar projecting point.

CUSTOM HOUSE, the place where imports are entered, clearance papers are obtained, and other official nautical business is transacted.

CUSTOM OF THE PORT. The rules and regulations that form the manner of doing business in the port.

CUT-OF-THE-JIB, the appearance or impression of a person or vessel; something characteristic.

CUT-SPLICE, made with two rope ends so spliced as to make an eye.

CUT YOUR PAINTER, a term meaning to be on your way.

CUTTER, a single masted vessel of particular design, the cutter being narrower of beam and deeper of draft than a sloop. Formerly they were characterized by a straight plumb stem and fidded topmast. Strictly, in the cutter the mast is stepped farther aft than in a sloop to admit a double headsail rig. The mast of a sloop is farther for-

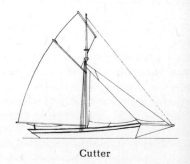

Cutter

ward as it carries a single head rig. The small powerful seaworthy patrol vessels of the Coast Guard are called Cutters, a term probably handed down from the fast sailing craft of the service.

CUT WATER, is the forward side of the stem.

CUTTING A FEATHER, the onward movement of a vessel rolling off a wave of foam at the bow.

CYCLONES, circulation of air around a vortex; violent agitations of the atmosphere where the wind blows in spirally to a vortex.

D

D. D., the enlisted man's laconic abbreviation of Dishonorable Discharge.

D. W. T., dead weight tonnage.

DACRON, a textile made of synthetic fiber which is desirable for use in rope and sail-making. It holds shape and resists mildew.

DAGGER, a steel bar used to release a vessel when launching. It acts as a trigger when the dog shore is knocked out.

DAGGER KNEES, those formerly set at an angle with the beams.

DAILY MEMORANDUM, mimeographed sheets published by the Naval Oceanographic Office in the late afternoon containing important items of navigational information that are received during the day.

DAILY RATE, the amount a chronometer gains or loses each day.

DAMAGE CONTROL, consists of methods of design and action of a ship's personnel in resisting the conditions which cause vessels to sink. In design multiple compartments have vertical access rather than bulkhead doors add resistance to foundering. Serious flooding may cause the capsizing moment to take charge and judicious use of reserve buoyancy by carefully flooding in certain compartments might counteract the list. It is a complex subject with many phases, including fire extinguishing.

DAMAGE WATER, is the sea water which has entered a ship's compartments due to collision, explosion or structural failure.

DAN BUOY, a small float to mark fishing gear and mine sweeping operations. A light staff, often of bamboo, from which flies a signal flag, passes through the center of the float. It is extensively used for vacant yacht moorings.

DANDY, a yawl rig seen in British waters in which the jigger is a mutton leg sail.

DANDY FUNK, a man-of-war pudding of other days, consisting of broken crackers and molasses.

DANGER ANGLE, an angle, between two objects, which if not allowed to get larger (or smaller as the case may be) as the vessel proceeds, will clear an offlying danger. For instance, if the horizontal angle between two lighthouses is 120° on a safe course outside a danger, a navigator would not allow the sextant to show a greater angle than 120°. Vertical angles are also used on objects whose height is known.

DANGER BEARING, a method by which the navigator is warned by a compass bearing when the course is leading into danger. The danger is avoided by laying off a bearing from a lighthouse or other landmark to a point well clear of the rock or shoal. So long as the bearing of the light from the ship does not alter so as to show the ship on the danger side of the charted bearing she is safe.

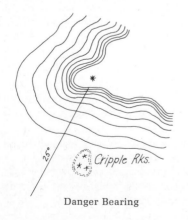

Danger Bearing

DANGER BUOY, a buoy of any shape but painted in red and black horizontal bands. These buoys are moored close by dangerous reefs, rocks, and sunken wrecks in United States waters. In European waters wrecks are usually marked by buoys painted green.

DANGER SECTOR, a red sector of a light indicating the presence of rocks or shoals within it.

DANGEROUS SEMICIRCLE, the right-hand side of a storm track in the northern hemisphere.

DANUBE RUDDER, an extension to after edge of ship's rudder to increase the effect.

DANUBE RULE (for propelling-power deductions). The so-called Danube Rule states that to machinery and boiler spaces should be added 75 per cent of such space for propelling machinery deductions, in the case of screw vessels, and 50 per cent in case of paddle steamers. As an example take a ship in which machinery and boiler space is equal to 14 per cent of the gross tonnage; the deduction for propelling power under the Danube Rule equals 14 per cent × 1¾ equals 24.5 per cent of the gross tonnage. (Mr. J. L. Bates.)

DARBIES, handcuffs.

DASHER BLOCK, the ensign halyard block at the peak of the gaff.

DATUM, a level to which depths and elevations are referred, as, Mean Low Water (MLW), the reference for soundings on Coast Survey charts.

DAVID, a small boat carrying a torpedo and submerged until almost awash. Boats of this type were constructed by the Confederates in the Civil War.

DAVID'S STAFF, an ancient instrument for taking altitudes of the sun.

DAVITS, small cranes that project over the ship's sides for hoisting boats. Many improved styles are now in use by which a boat is readily swung outboard and inboard. The *davit guys* trim them at the side while a span of wire rope, chain or spar maintains the proper space between a pair of davits. The wire or chain is called a *spreader* or *check*, the spar a *strongback*. The *Welin Davit* has a cogged quadrant cast on its lower end and by a geared crank is swung out and in with great facility. *Gravity-davits*, consist of two movable cradles from which the lifeboat is suspended and are mounted on two sloping frames that turn downward at about 45° to the deck at the sheer strake, thence down the ship's side. The cradles and boat, when released by a lever, roll on rollers down the sloping frames and thence to the water.

DAVY JONES' LOCKER, the bottom of the sea where all things thrown overboard find their way.

DAY LOST AND DAY GAINED. Clocks are geared to show an hour's time while the sun travels 15° from east to west. A westbound vessel steaming in the same direction as the sun breaks up this unison of movement between the clock and the sun by causing the latter to exceed the hour in moving an (apparent) 15°. So the hands of

the clock are pushed back to keep pace with the sun. This amount is equivalent to the ship's change of longitude (in time). After doing this each day on a voyage around the world the seamen on the vessel have lived each of these small amounts twice *by the clock,* and they have formed a fictitious day in the aggregate. In order to keep the calendar date correct, a day is dropped when crossing the 180° meridian.

On the contrary, an east-bound vessel meets and passes the sun as it were, causing it apparently to travel its 15° in less than an hour, and it becomes necessary to push the hands of the clock ahead to adjust its reading with the sun's bearing (or hour angle). In this way the seamen are cheated of a part of each day's time, but upon crossing the 180° meridian the day is used twice, that is, there may be two Mondays May 14th in the log book, and the time problem is squared.

DAY'S WORK, consists, at least, of the dead reckoning from noon to noon, morning and afternoon time sights for longitude, and a meridian altitude for latitude.

DEAD ON END, a wind directly ahead; dead ahead.

DEAD FREIGHT, money earned, or claimed, on space reserved by a shipper but not used.

DEAD HEAD, a spar or log floating on end and mostly submerged. A pile projecting above a wharf to which lines are made fast. A wooden buoy.

DEAD HORSE, the debt incurred by a seaman by the advance of a month's wages to the boarding house runner to pay bills and credit for a last wild night. It was the occasion of a unique celebration aboard ship among the crew when their advanced money was worked up. An effigy of a horse was fashioned out of any available material, and the "animal" hoisted clear of the rail and overboard into the sea with ceremony and boisterous hilarity.

DEAD LIGHTS, the round brass plates working on hinges that screw down upon the air ports and serve as preventers to the glass port lights in heavy weather. The term given by some to the glass bull's eyes set in the deck. They are also called battle ports.

DEAD MEN, loose ends of gaskets hanging from a yard; Irish pennants.

DEAD MUZZLER, a strong head wind.

DEAD PEG, to work directly to windward.

DEAD RECKONING (D. R.), the calculation necessary to ascertain the ship's whereabouts by using the courses steered and distances run. The influences of current and wind, as well as the errors of the compass, are taken into account to determine as closely as possible the latitude and longitude without the aid of celestial observation. This is the real test of a navigator's skill. The dead reckoning position is nowadays sometimes referred to as that latitude and longitude worked up without an allowance for current, but the name is erroneously applied.

DEAD ROPE, one for a hauling purpose with no block to assist the work.

DEAD SHEAVE, a half sheave which is stationary but allows a line to pass over it regardless of friction.

DEAD WATER, that water which is drawn along with the vessel at her waterline and especially aft. There is a phenomenon known as *dead water* in which there is a deep overlay of fresh or brackish water. With this condition slow speed vessels of sail or very low power experience a loss of headway due to the generation of subsurface waves between the lighter water above and the heavier salt water below.

DEAD WEIGHT CARGO, merchandise with a stowage factor that is 40 cubic feet or less to the ton.

DEAD WORK, a vessel's sides above the water.

DEADEYE, a round block of lignum vitae somewhat similar to the shell of a block. It has several holes through it and a groove around the edge to receive the lower eye of a shroud or the strap of a chain plate. The deadeye of a shroud and that of a chain plate are connected by a *lanyard* rove through them. A *shroud tackle* hooked in a strop well up on the shroud or stay is clapped on the end of the lanyard which, well greased, renders through the deadeye, setting up the stay or shroud.

DEADRISE, the rise of the floor of a vessel above the horizontal. It is the rise of the sides of a vessel's bottom above the base line at the intersection with the moulded breadth line.

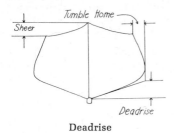

Deadrise

DEADWEIGHT, the carrying power of a vessel beyond her own weight.

DEADWOOD, the solid timbering at the bow but mainly at the stern of a vessel just above the keel.

DECK. What floors are to a building so are decks to a vessel. Their arrangement and character depend on the type of vessel and the trade engaged in. A cargo steamer usually has a main deck with a raised section forward and one aft known as forecastle and poop decks (these two terms also apply to men-of-war); there is also a midship section over the engine and boiler rooms containing quarters, galleys and navigating bridge and chart rooms. Between these different sections the main deck is called the *well deck*. The deck below the main is called the 'tween decks. Where in larger vessels there are several decks, the first above the tank tops or holds is called the *lower*, the second the *main*, the third the *upper deck*. On passenger

steamers appears a fourth or *promenade* deck and the *hurricane* or *sun* deck the highest of all. It is customary for the benefit of simplicity to name the decks below the Promenade A, B, C, D, and E. In naval vessels the upper deck was

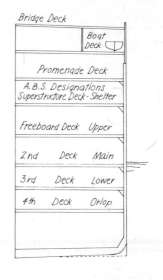

Names of Decks

formerly known as the *spar deck*, the next below as the *gun deck* and the *berth deck* next below. At present, however, the highest full length deck is called the *main deck*; and the latest types carry a deck aft to the mainmast called the *upper deck*; it is becoming the practice to number the decks of these ships from highest down. A deck heavily armored is called the *protective deck*, while one of lighter armor is called the *splinter deck*. A deck not extending to the side of a naval vessel is called a *superstructure deck*. A partial deck below the main deck is known as a *platform deck*. See also quarter, poop, 'tween and orlop decks. An officer of the watch is said *to have the deck*. *On deck* is a hail from a man aloft, from the bridge, from below or from a boat alongside to draw the attention of someone on the deck.

DECK BEAR, a box of stones, scrap iron or other heavy material hauled back and forth on the deck for the purpose of cleaning and whitening.

DECK CHEST, a receptacle for wash deck gear.

DECK GANG (or DECKIES) enlisted men of the seaman branch in the Navy—as opposed to the *black gang,* or engineer branch.

DECK HORSE, a heavy iron rod placed athwartships and parallel with the deck for the traveler ring of a sheet tackle to run on.

DECK HOUSE, a compartment of light construction erected on deck.

DECK LOAD cargo carried on deck.

DECK PIPE, the fairlead for the chains through the deck.

DECK STOPPER, a rope with a hook, or a short piece of chain and a hook, by which the anchor chain is secured when the anchor is down.

DECK STRINGER, a strip of plating that runs along the outer edge of a deck.

DECLINATION, the angular distance, a body is north or south of the celestial equator. The sun's declination ranges between 23° 27′ north to 23° 27′ south; the moon's from about 28° north (maximum) (about 18° minimum) to a like distance south; the planets' declination varies in a complex manner for their orbits differ greatly in size, but they travel within a belt about 8° each side of the ecliptic, and this great circle departs at its vertex about 23° 27′ from the equator.

DECLINATION OF THE COMPASS. The compass needle, if freely suspended by a thread, will lie in the direction of the earth's lines of magnetic force. These lines are not parallel with the earth's surface except in the vicinity of the equator. Northward or southward from this line, the needle begins to dip downward increasingly towards the magnetic poles. This *dip* or declination of the needle is restrained in the mariner's compass, and the horizontal directive force is alone shown. When in the region of excessive magnetic dip, such as Hudson Bay, the horizontal component of magnetic force is so small as to cause a lack of directive power in the compass and it becomes sluggish.

DECLINATION OF THE ZENITH, the angular distance from the equator to the zenith. This distance is equal to the latitude.

DEEP FLOORS, are found at the ends of a vessel where the floor frames are given considerable depth.

DEEP-SEA LEAD, is a heavy lead, about 50 pounds, for sounding in deeper water than is reached by a hand lead.

DEEP SIX, to throw an article overboard is to give it the "Deep Six."

DEEP STOWAGE, to stow cargo in a deep hold where there are no decks to break the depth.

DEEP TANK, a midships ballast tank of considerable capacity by which a vessel's draft can be increased as a whole. It is sometimes used for cargo.

DEEP WATER, means offshore. Often refers to a voyage around either Cape Horn or Cape of Good Hope.

DEEPS. The fathoms of a lead line not marked are called *deeps*. Areas of deeper water than prevail on the surrounding bottom; a depth of over 3000 fathoms constitutes a deep beyond the continental shelf.

DEGAUSSING, is an arrangement of electric coils so installed in a ship that the magnetic field of the vessel is so neutralized as to give a degree of safety in passing over a magnetic mine.

DEMERSAL, are bottom fish such as cod, halibut and flounders, in distinction to pelagic fish as mackerel and herring.

DEMURRAGE, money paid on the undue detention of a vessel. Demurrage commences at the expiration of the lay days. A master should notify the consignees in writing the day before demurrage starts.

DEPARTURE (Dep.), the distance a vessel makes good east or west. It is measured along a parallel of latitude and is always expressed in miles. Departure is converted

into difference of longitude by use of Table 3, Bowditch, 1958. Taking a departure is a procedure at the beginning of a voyage, or on making a landfall. It is necessary to have a definite latitude and longitude at which to commence reckoning, so a lighthouse or prominent landmark is chosen whose position is well known. A bearing is taken and the distance off established. The direction is reversed and entered in the reckoning as the first course of the voyage, just as though the ship herself had started at the lighthouse and sailed this departure course.

DEPERMING, a process allied to Degaussing. Heavy conductors are passed around a ship up one side, athwartship and down the other. A strong current through this coil changes the magnetic field of the ship. The change is temporary owing to the vibration of the propellers.

DEPRESSED HORIZON, is the visible horizon lowered by the height of the observer's eye above the earth. Usually called *Dip*.

DEPRESSED POLE, the opposite of the elevated pole; that one below the horizon.

DEPTH. See Lloyd's depth. The depth from main deck to the ceiling over the floors. The depth by American Bureau of Shipping rules is from the top of the keel to the top of the deck beams at the side of the freeboard deck. Should the bulkhead deck be above the freeboard deck then depth is measured to the bulkhead deck. The depth registered is the *depth of hold* and is the distance from the double bottom, amidship (2.5 inches being allowed for ceiling planks) to the top of the upper deck beams, or main deck in awning or shelter deck vessels.

DERELICT, an abandoned floating vessel. The term also sometimes refers to the foreshore dry at ebb-tide.

DERRICK (Cargo Boom), a boom with its foot set at the foot of a mast, supported by a topping-lift tackle and controlled by guys. It is used for loading and removing cargo. The term *cargo boom* is preferred by seamen. Some other types of derricks and cranes are viz: A-frame, stiff-leg derrick, guy derrick, tower crane, hammer-head crane, bridge crane, gantry crane, and straight-line crane. The modern level buffing crane operates on a track at the pier side (or on a lighter). Its flexible arm rises to a height of 187 feet and is capable of discharging a vessel's cargo into lighters lying on the off side. They have a reach as great as 118 feet.

DERRICK METHOD, cargo handling by. In this procedure a boom is topped over a hatch; when a draft of cargo is raised above the coaming, the boom is swung by guys over the pier and the draft lowered.

DESTROYERS, very fast scout vessels for the protection of capital ships and convoys and for use against submarines.

DEVIASCOPE, an instrument for testing, practicing, and instructing

in the use of magnets for compensating compasses.

DEVIATION, an unnecessary divergence from the accepted course of a vessel. If disaster results, the underwriters are relieved from liability. There are several justifiable deviations allowed—stress of weather, unavoidable accidents and the saving of life. Many hull policies, however, contain a clause which includes the saving of property.

DEVIATION OF THE COMPASS. The ship's compass, if uninfluenced by any local attraction or by any magnetism outside of the earth's lines of force, would point to the north magnetic pole. The construction of ships is so largely of steel and iron that they readily take on magnetism and become in themselves magnets. The different parts of the vessel, as the stack, steel masts, ventilators, davits, etc., are the poles of projecting magnets. The compass needle is affected by these influences and drawn one way or the other by the dominating force. These magnetized projections change their positions relative to the compass needle on the different directions of ship's head and thus make a new deviation for each heading. These are determined by observation and tabulated. For further information see Quadrantal and Semi-Circular Deviation.

DEVIATION TABLE, a tabulation of the ship's heading on each compass point and the deviation which appears when steering on each.

DEVIL SEAM, between the garboard and keel. The old expression "The devil to pay and no pitch hot" comes from the problems of paying this seam.

DEVIL'S CLAW, a heavy hook used in holding the chain when riding to an anchor.

DEVIL'S HOLE, lies between lats. 46° 09′ N. and 46° 55′ N. and longs. 12° 50′ W. and 13° 10′ W. in the distant approaches to the British Isles.

DEW POINT, the temperature at which the saturated air forms vapor in clouds, mist or fog.

DEW VALVE, an automatic draining valve in the cylinders of deck machinery.

DGHAISA, a gondola-like boat peculiar to Valetta, Malta. Pronounced *dicer.*

DHOW, a long flat vessel of the East and Near East. The masts are lateen rigged and usually rake forward. The dhow changes tacks by wearing ship. The lateen yard is brought forward and nearly parallel with the forward-raking mast. It is worked around to the other side of the mast (the side of the new tack) while the sail flows out ahead. As the vessel comes up to the wind the sheet is hauled in and trimmed for a new tack.

DIAGONAL BUILD, a method of planking a boat where the diagonal planks of one layer are covered again by an outer layer lying diagonally with it.

DIAGONAL TIES (or PLATES), deck stiffeners that run diagonally across a vessel.

DIAMOND, an arrangement of shrouds in a lofty-rigged marconi mast that take the diamond shape.

DIAMOND KNOT, a knot sometimes made in the end of a manrope for ornamentation.

DIAMOND PLATES, plates to connect and stiffen the framework where the web frames and stringers intersect.

DIATOM, a minute plant of the sea. It moves by the action of current only, and attaches itself to submerged stones and wreckage giving them a slimy feeling. The diatom is dependent upon sunlight for life; when it sinks below the reach of its influence it dies. It forms the food of copepods, which in turn furnish sustenance to fish. The walls of the diatom cell form a skeleton when the organism dies, which, in quantities, becomes a whitish sediment of silica known as kiselguhr.

DICE-NO-HIGHER, an order not to gamble on letting a close-hauled square-rigged vessel come closer to the wind and risk being taken aback—a hazard; the term may be used as a caution against taking risks.

DIFFERENCE OF LATITUDE (D. L.), the difference in degrees, minutes and seconds between two parallels of latitude. It is the distance (° ′ ″) between the parallel of a vessel's departure and the parallel of destination.

DIFFERENCE OF LONGITUDE (D. Lg.), the difference in degrees, minutes and seconds between two meridians. It is the distance (° ′ ″) that a vessel makes east or west along a parallel of (middle) latitude.

DIFFERENTIAL HOIST, is an endless chain passing over two sheaves and around a lower sheave of smaller size carrying the lifting hook. A part of the chain is the hauling part.

DINGHY (Dingey), a small rowboat. The name is said to come from a Bengal word meaning a small boat belonging to a larger vessel.

DINK, a nickname for a dinghy.

DIOPTRIC LIGHT (HOUSE), one *in* which the refracting principle of light is used.

DIP, a term applied to the descent of the sun after reaching its maximum altitude (at noon) on the meridian. A flag is *at the dip* when about two-thirds way up. As a mark of courtesy, flags are dipped by passing vessels. A tackle is said to have a dip in it when one block becomes accidentally passed through the parts of the fall disorganizing the tackle. Dip is also the error introduced in an observed altitude of a body by the observer being elevated above the sea, as upon the bridge of a steamer. As the height of the eye increases, the horizon extends and falls, making the altitudes measured thereto larger, hence dip is a minus correction, found in the Nautical Almanac. Altitude should theoretically be measured to the sensible horizon, that seen when the eye is at the water's surface.

DIP OF THE NEEDLE, is the inclination assumed by the magnetic needle as the north (or south) mag-

netic pole is approached. Also called Declination of the Needle.

DIP ROPE is of open linked chain or wire used with a mooring swivel or in clearing hawse. The outer end is fitted with a shackle and the inner end with a long piece of manila rope.

DIPPING LUG, a small boat rig. The sail is set from a small yard and the tack is made fast to the stem.

DIPSEY LEAD, a deep sea lead for sounding up to a hundred fathoms.

DISPATCH, a term found in ship's papers meaning that the loading and discharging or the clearance of a vessel shall be expedited.

DISPATCH MONEY (if provided in charter party), is a sum paid upon the completion of loading and (or) discharging to charterer of ship, for time saved on allotted lay days.

DISPERSAL OF THE THRUST COLUMN. A tug with a heavy tow turns her propeller at a rate disproportionate to her onward motion. The distribution of water abaft the propeller results in a disturbance which impairs the efficiency of the thrust. Cavitation is a corresponding disturbance forward of the propeller.

DISPLACEMENT, the weight of the water displaced by a vessel, equal to the weight of the vessel. It is the common measurement of naval vessels. The *displacement curve* shows the displacements at different drafts. See Tonnage. The center of the displacement is the center of buoyance. A cubic foot of sea water weighs 64 lbs., fresh 62.5

lbs. A ton of sea water equals 35 cubic feet and of fresh water 35.9 cu. ft.

DISTANT OBJECT, a term used in swinging ship when a series of bearings is taken of a distant object and the mean of all taken as the correct magnetic bearing. All other bearings taken by compass are referred to this to ascertain the deviation on the different headings of the ship.

DISTRESS SIGNALS are N C of the International Code; the ensign Union down; minute guns, continued blasts of whistle, various pyrotechnics or a burning tar barrel at night; and S O S by radio. Also "May Day" by voice radio.

DITTY BOX or **BAG,** a receptacle for a sailor's sewing kit.

DIURNAL relates to a day; a phenomenon occurring daily.

DIURNAL INEQUALITY OF THE TIDES, the difference between the two daily high waters and is caused by the declination of the moon. On the Pacific coast where one high water is much higher than the other, the diurnal inequality is likewise large. When the moon is in high declination it is near the tropics, and the tides occurring at that time are called *tropic tides.* When the moon is full at the same time it is in high (northern) declination (September) the *September or great tropic tides* occur.

DIVIDERS, an instrument with two legs, each pointed, and hinged at the opposite end. They are used to take distances from a scale and transfer them for use on the chart or vice versa. See also, compasses.

DOCK, the water space between piers. The use of the word through the years indicates the water space, not the pier. But seamen sometimes use the term in referring to wharf or pier, yet it is not considered strictly correct. There are also Dry, Floating, Graving and Wet Docks.

DOCKAGE (usually), the charge made for a mooring, loading or discharging berth.

DOCKING KEELS, additional keels paralleling the main keel which serve to take the weight of the vessel in dry dock as well as to furnish longitudinal strength. Auxiliary docking keels are often set in pairs forward and aft or between the main docking keels.

DOCKING PLAN, a cross-sectional drawing of a vessel giving the important measurements of keel and docking keels.

DOCKYARD, the establishment consisting of a dock, piers, and the buildings which house the facilities for repairing and building vessels.

DOCTOR, the ship's cook. The sea breeze in Jamaica and other tropical countries. A pump for the purpose of testing boilers.

DOCTRINE OF THE LAST FAIR CHANCE, a doctrine which provides that a person shall, when a collision is imminent, do all in his power to avert or lessen the disaster.

DOCUMENTING, the procedure of securing the necessary legal papers that allow a vessel to operate. If in coastwise trade, she must have a certificate of enrollment; if foreign, a certificate of registry.

DODGERS, canvas wind shields for the bridge. Said to be derived from Dodge.

DOG CURTAIN, a canvas flap sewn into the canvas binnacle which when raised allows a view of the compass through the glass face of the binnacle.

DOG SHORE, a timber holding a vessel on the launching ways. As the dog shore is removed, the vessel slides down the ways.

DOG STOPPER, a stopper which secures the anchor chain forward of the bitts and allows slack to bitt the chain. A riding dog serves the same purpose, and is used in modern steamers. The chain passes through a fixture hinged in the top of which is a pawl or dog; thrown one way the dog rides the outgoing chain but when thrown back stops it.

DOG VANE, a tapering tube of bunting at the masthead through which the wind blows and indicates its direction. A wind sock.

DOG WATCHES, those from 4 to 6 and 6 to 8 p.m. The watches are *dogged* when the watch changes at 6 p.m.

DOGBODY, a fishing vessel of Newfoundland in the early part of the 19th century. Those of small size were engaged in the shore fishery, while larger craft fished the Banks. They were square-sterned, carried fore and aft gaff sails, no head sails or bowsprit.

DOGGER, a two masted ketch used by Dutch fishermen.

DOGHOUSE, a shelter forward of a yacht's cockpit, usually opening aft.

DOGS, small bent metal fittings used to close the doors to watertight compartments, hatch covers, manhole covers, etc. The short iron rods with their sharpened ends bent at right angles which are driven into the blocks at the bottom of a dry dock to prevent their floating.

DOG'S EAR (or LUG), the bight of the leach of a sail when reefed. One of the corners of the *shark's mouth* of an awning.

DOGS RUNNING BEFORE THEIR MASTER, heavy swell preceding a hurricane.

DOLDRUMS, a belt of calms and light airs lying between the trade winds of the northern and southern hemispheres.

DOLLOP, a wave that lops over the rail on deck.

DOLLY, a single bollard-like timber head set horizontally in a ship's bulwarks. A bar with concave end, held against the inside end of a rivet.

DOLPHIN, a pile or cluster of piles serving as a beacon; a spar mooring buoy; or as a mooring fast or buffer in the water or on a wharf. A long line of piles between two piers to which a vessel may tie up and load from lighters. A strap around the mast which secures the *puddening* at the slings of the lower yard. Also applied to the guard rail of a vessel.

The derivation of this term "dolphin" for a pile cluster has aroused some speculation. In Europe it was first called a Duca d'Alba, the Duke being the heir apparent of Spain, the name was translated to the languages of other countries. The Spanish Naval Attaché in Washington suggested that the term may have arisen from the tradition that the Duke of Alba, when in command of the Low Countries in the 16th century, had a resemblance of his features carved on the guiding piles along the rivers. In France a cluster is called a Duc d'Albe, but as the dauphin of France had parallel rank with the Duca d'Alba of Spain, used the dolphin (fish) as his symbol of heraldry, it may be a clue to the origin of the American name dolphin for a pile cluster.

The term "dolphin" also applies to two families of sea creatures familiar to seamen. The delphinidae are cetaceans. One group of this family of dolphins has a beak, with pointed teeth. Another group is our common porpoise, known as the bottle-nosed dolphin; has no beak but wedge-shaped teeth; it is about seven feet long, leaps out of the water and plays about a ship's bow, being a fast swimmer. The other family is the coryphaena; they inhabit warm and temperate waters; are edible and change colors as they die on deck. They are about six feet long. While often called dolphins they are perhaps better known as dorados.

DOLPHIN STRIKER, a small spar beneath the bowsprit and forming a truss for the support of the jib-boom with the martingale guys and martingale stays. It is also called the *martingale boom*.

DONKEY ENGINE, a steam engine which furnishes power to hoist anchor and sails, turns cargo winches, supplies heat, and operates fire pumps and radio.

DONKEY'S BREAKFAST, a seaman's mattress, having straw filling.

DORADE VENTILATOR, is an effective water trap that provides fresh air below. It consists of a simple box secured to the deck, into which, say, the after half, an ordinary cowl ventilator is inserted for about one-fourth of the depth of the box. A tube or ferrule passes from the forward half of the box through the deck, letting air below. To exclude water effectively, the upper edge of the ferrule is slightly higher than the lower edge of the cowl. The water that comes down the cowl falls to the bottom, free and clear of the ferrule and flows out through scuppers at the low end of the box. Except in heavy weather the cowl can be headed into the wind without water getting below.

DORY, a flat-bottomed small boat with a sharp, graceful sheer, flaring sides and V transom. It is a typical New England craft and is one of the most seaworthy. It is used on all the Bank fishermen, being readily stowed one in another, making a so-called *nest of dories*.

DOUBLE. See Doubling.

DOUBLE BOTTOM, the space between the watertight plating over the floors and the ship's bottom. This space is utilized for ballast tanks and protects the ship in case of damage to the outside plating.

DOUBLE CARD COMPASS, is one visible from both below and above, so placed as to act as a telltail for the master below.

DOUBLE DANGER ANGLES, two danger angles, one each for two shoals or dangers, one outside the other and the ship's course leading between them. The angle protecting the vessel from the inshore danger must not be allowed to get larger or the angle protecting from the outer danger to get smaller.

DOUBLE-ENDED, having a stern somewhat similar to the bow.

DOUBLE TOPSAILS, two square sails of narrow depth where one large single topsail was carried in the early clippers. The double topsails are more readily handled but are not as efficient in light air. They were invented by an American shipmaster, Capt. Frederick Howes. The idea has also been adapted to t'gallant yards.

DOUBLING (of a mast), the place where the lower part of an upper mast overlaps a lower mast. A vessel is said to *double* a cape when she passes around it.

DOUBLING THE ANGLE ON THE BOW, a method of finding a ship's position. A vessel with an object, say 35° on the bow, can be located by noting the distance run until the object bears 70° on the bow. The

distance run will be the distance off.

DOUBLING PLATE, one fitted outside or inside of another to give reinforcement.

DOVEKIE, a small sea bird found in the Arctic regions. It is about 8½ inches long, with black head, neck and back, wings having a small patch of white, white under parts,

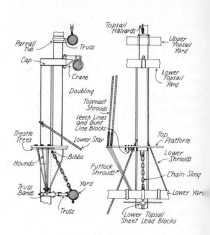

Doubling of a Mast

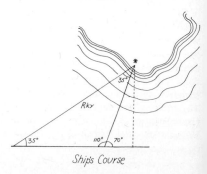

Doubling the Angle on the Bow

red legs, and black bill. The word is applied by many to the black guillemot.

DOWEL, a wooden pin used instead of an iron spike.

DOWN EASTER, a person or vessel from Maine. It is *down* because Maine is down wind from Boston.

DOWN HELM or UP HELM, orders given to helmsmen when a vessel is under sail—down is away from, and up is towards the wind. The helm is put down to tack ship and up to wear.

DOWN THE MASTS. The wind is facetiously said to blow down the mast in a calm.

DOWN THE WIND, to leeward.

DOWNHAUL, a tackle or single rope by which a sail or yard is hauled down.

DOWSE, to spray or duck with water; to lower a sail quickly or to extinguish a light.

DRABLER, a second bonnet added to a jib or square sail in ships of the old days.

DRAFT, a single sling load of cargo.

DRAFT or DRAUGHT, the depth of water necessary to float a vessel. For easy handling most vessels draw a little more water aft than forward; this is called *drag.* The draft aft increases with speed. The draft increases upon entering fresh water from salt (see Sea Water), the rule being:

$$\frac{\text{Displacement in salt water}}{63 \times \text{tons per inch immersion}} = \begin{array}{l}\text{increase} \\ \text{in draft} \\ \text{in inches}\end{array}$$

DRAFT MARKS, figures fastened to the stem and sternpost; the lower edge indicates the draft of the vessel.

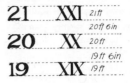

Draft Marks

DRAG, the amount that the after end of the keel is below the forward end when the ship is floating. Vessels are designed and loaded to have a small amount of drag. Weights attached by hawsers to a vessel at launching to kill her way when waterborne.

DRAG or DROGUE, a sea anchor or stop water. It is either in the form of a spar with a weighted sail attached, or a cornucopia bag. The vessel rides to this device and tending to drift faster to leeward than the drag puts a strain on the line which holds her head to windward. See Sea Anchor.

DRAG CHAINS are used in launching a vessel in restricted water area. The chains are fast to weighted drags which bring the vessel up quickly after her slide down the ways. It required 2,300 tons of drag chains to bring the *Queen Mary* to with her stern 250 feet out from the ways.

DRAG RACING, is a contest of acceleration of speed on a short straight-away course. The boats, usually two, start at a slow controlled speed and are clocked electronically at the finish line.

DRAGGER, a rugged fishing trawler that usually operates in the shore fisheries rather than on offshore banks. It has one or two masts that support booms for the handling of its one dory, the trawl and for setting a steady sail. See Otter Trawl.

DRAIN HOLES, holes drilled through floor and frame angles to lead the water from the *bilge gutter.*

DRAW, a term applied when the wind on a sail puts a strain on the sheet. Also a vessel is said to draw so many feet of water according to her draft. The moving section of a bridge which allows the passage of vessels.

DREDGE, a vessel or scow equipped with machinery for removing the material of the bottom of a harbor or channel. This action is called *dredging.* The sea-going dredge is not unlike a steamer in appearance. Suction machinery draws up the material, while underway, filling the hoppers and when the capacity is reached the vessel proceeds to the dumping ground. A device to gather oysters by dragging along the bottom. An anchor dragging up and down along the bottom is said to *dredge.*

DRESSER, the work table in a ship's galley.

DRESSING SHIP, to display flags in honor of a person or event. If a string of flags extends from water to water by way of jibboom, mastheads, and end of spanker boom the vessel is said to be *rainbow dressed.* A sounding lead is used to fly the flags to the water from the overhanging spars.

DRIFT, a vessel's leeway. The part of a rope not in use. The velocity with which a current moves. The amount two rivet holes are out of line, and the action necessary to bring two rivet holes in line. A *drift pin* is used for this purpose. The *drift angle* is that which the line of a vessel's keel takes with her turning circle when the rudder is put over.

DRIFT BOLT, a long punch for driving out rivets. Also a long bolt used in a boat's engine bed and deadwood.

DRIFT CURRENTS, those slow movements of water down the western coast of Europe, which serve to complete the general circulation of water of the North Atlantic Ocean. They are the feeble continuations of the Gulf Stream. Beyond the Grand Banks the Gulf Stream becomes the Gulf Stream Drift.

DRIFT ICE. As an icefield breaks up the drifting pieces are called drift ice and usually are easily navigated by being conned from aloft.

DRIFT LEAD, an ordinary sounding lead and line that is dropped over the side to indicate any dragging of the anchored vessel. This is readily shown if the line begins to lead forward. It can also be used to show the current if on soundings and vessel is stopped.

DRIFT OF A LINE, the angle between the line of the keel and the mooring line out ahead or astern.

DRIFT NET, is buoyed to float in a vertical position and the fish are caught in the meshes by their gills. The fishing vessel lies to the net.

DRIFT SAIL, a sea anchor.

DRIFTER, a fishing vessel that pursues the surface fish (pelagic) such as herring. It is seen more frequently in European waters. It sets nets that, strung together, may extend a mile or two in length. The fish's gills are caught in the meshes —whence the term *gill nets*. A characteristic of the drifter is a riding sail aft which keeps her head up while drifting with her nets out.

DRIFTS, those parts where the sheer is raised according to the heights of the decks, and where the rails are cut off and ended by scrolls. (Hamersly.)

DRIVE, to hard press a vessel with canvas. A vessel *drives* before a gale or *drives* to leeward when out of control or forced excessively.

DRIVER, the name that was sometimes given to the fifth mast of a six-masted schooner. It was the sail set from a yard suspended from the very after part of a vessel in old days. Brady's *Kedge Anchor* says it is a large sail suspended from the mizzen gaff.

DROGHER (DROGER), a bluff modeled vessel engaged in transporting heavy cargoes, as a sand drogher. A type of West Indian trader.

DROGUE, a drag or sea anchor.

DROP KEEL. See Centerboard.

DROP OF A SQUARE SAIL, the distance from the head to the foot. It is used on the courses in contradistinction to the hoist of sails that are set from yards that hoist.

DROP STRAKE. See Stealer.

DRUGG, is a marker-buoy attached to a whale line fast to a whale. A waif is also attached to increase its visibility.

DRUM HOOKS, a group of cant hooks attached by wire strops to a hoisting ring. The hooks proper are in pairs and run loose in the strop. By the use of these drum hooks five oil drums are hoisted at one draft.

DRUMHEAD, that part of a capstan where the bars are shipped.

DRUMHEAD MAN, the winch man; he who operates a winch in the loading and discharge of cargo.

DRY COMPASS, a segmental circle of paper mounted on an aluminum ring, suspended by thirty-two silk threads from the central boss containing a jeweled cup. The needles suspended below the card are single wires and depend from the card ring by a second series of silk threads. This brings the weight of the needles down low and makes the card very steady. The pivot supporting the jeweled cup held in the boss of the card rises from the bottom of the *compass bowl* and the bowl, in turn, is carried on a ring, ring and bowl being supported by *knife edge bearings* placed at right angles with each other. (*Standard Seamanship.*)

DRY DOCK, a watertight basin which after pumping out excludes the water and allows examination and work upon the bottom of a vessel. Vessels are floated in and out through the removal of a bulkhead called a *caisson,* itself capable of floating or flooding. A *floating dock* receives a vessel when it is submerged to a proper depth, after which the watertight compartments of the dock are pumped out and the buoyancy of the dock raises the vessel. A *graving dock,* usually walled with stone, was one in which vessels' bottoms were formerly cleaned by a burning process called *graving* or *greaving,* but the term still applies to the walled up excavated docks seen in Navy Yards. They are more substantial and permanent than floating docks, but are far more costly. There are

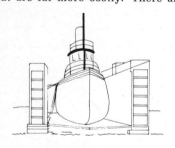

Floating Dry Dock

screw docks comprising a platform which submerges to receive a vessel, the whole being raised by screws or jacks. Other means of working on a vessel's bottom are to haul out on a *railway,* or go on a *gridiron* at high water, or again, to *heave down* at a careenage as they do at Curaçao.

DUBB (DUB), to smooth a timber with an adze. *Dubbing,* the smoothing of the planking of a ship after being riveted or spiked on the frames.

DUC d' ALBE (Fr.), the term used in Europe for a pile (cluster) dolphin, varied according to language.

DUCT KEEL, is box keel, the vertical plates forming the sides are riveted to the ends of the floors, port and starboard. The top plate of the keel is flush with the plating covering the floors. This keel also serves as a conduit for pipes and cables.

DUCTILITY, the quality of a metal which allows it to stretch or be drawn out perhaps into wire.

DUFF, a mixture of flour and water, with raisins added, is Plum (Lum) Duff. It is a sea tradition to serve this dish on Thursdays, perhaps to compensate for the no-meat ration on that day.

DUGOUT, a boat hewn from a log. Boats of ancient people have been unearthed in Europe measuring as much as 48 feet long and 6 feet wide hewn from a log.

DUKW, an amphibious four-wheeled craft of many uses; it was developed for rescue work in World War II.

DUMB-COMPASS, a brass compass diagram oriented to North or if desired to ship's head. A pelorus consists of a dumb compass.

DUMB SHEAVE, a groove in the foot of a spar for a rope to lay in in lieu of a revolving sheave.

DUMP SCOW, a square-built flat-bottomed vessel so fitted as to permit lowering the bottom of her carrying compartment, thus dumping the load of rubbish or dredged material. Watertight compartments keep the scow afloat and a hand windlass gear heaves the bottom back in place. This craft is dependent on tugs for propulsion.

DUMPING PLANKS, a temporary rough floor on the tank tops directly beneath a hatchway to take the wear and tear of falling cargo, such as coal or ore.

DUNGAREES, blue overalls.

DUNNAGE, all kinds of wooden blocking used in the holds of a vessel to raise the cargo above the floors and sides, preserving it from sweat and leakage, and to serve as chocks to prevent it getting adrift. It is a general custom to use approximately 9 inches over the floors, 14 inches at the bilge, from 2 to 6 inches at the sides and 3 inches on the 'tween decks. No hard and fast rules can be laid down beyond a sufficient amount of dunnage to bring the cargo to port in good condition.

DUTCH COURAGE, that which is manifested after a drink of liquor.

DUTCH DOOR, one in two parts allowing the upper and lower sections to swing independently.

DUTCHMAN'S LOG, a crude expedient used in small slow vessels for measuring speed. A distance of 47 feet 3 inches is laid off and marked on deck. A floating object is thrown overboard at the bow, if the vessel takes 28 seconds to pass the object she is making 1 knot; if 14 seconds, 2 knots, etc. A chip log it better.

DYING MAN'S DINNER, a little food served during an emergency.

E

E. D., familiar letters appearing on charts, which mean "existence doubtful."

E. T. A., estimated time of arrival.

EAGER, EAGRE, EAGOR, a sharp rise of tide advancing in shallow estuaries in the form of a wave; a bore; a mascaret, a pororoca.

EARING, a rope used in bending a sail or head cringle to a yard or the clew cringle to a boom. A *reef* *earing* (weather or lee) makes the reef cringle fast to the yard. The weather earing is passed first while the men on the yard, grasping the reef points, attempt to haul the sail to windward. Then they *light out to leeward* and the lee earing is passed up forward and down abaft the yard. Earings are passed.

EARTH, a spherical body about 7,927 statute miles in diameter which rotates on its axis once in

24 hours and revolves around the sun once in a year. It is a planet. The shape of this body is that of an ellipsoid, being compressed along its polar diameter to the extent of $\frac{1}{2935}$ part, or about 27 miles. The equatorial plane is not a true circle but slightly elliptical, there being about one half mile difference in its long and short diameter.

EARTH'S CENTRAL PROGRESS, the difference between a solar and a sidereal day, amounting to 3 m. 56 s. and is due to the earth's movement in its orbit.

EARTH'S SHINE, the reflection of the earth's light thrown on the moon and being faintly visible on the shadowed part when the latter is two or three days old and shows as a crescent.

EASE THE HELM, to reduce the amount of rudder angle.

EASE HER, to luff a sailing vessel when carrying a heavy press of sail; to give a little lee helm to ease a vessel into a heavy sea.

EASTING, the distance a vessel makes eastward.

EASY. A vessel rolls easily when her motion in a seaway is without sudden movements.

EASY SAIL, an amount of canvas under which a vessel rides or sails without laboring or straining.

EBB, the period when the tidal current is flowing from the land. The different phases of the ebb are referred to as the first of the ebb, the strength of the ebb, and the last of the ebb.

EBB TIDE BENDS, a term applied to the outside of the bends in a tidal river. The deeper water is usually there, hence the old piloting rule: "Follow the ebb tide bends."

ECHO BOARD, a structure similar to a bill board but fitted in addition with wings at each end which are set at an angle towards the sea. The purpose is to reflect the sound of a steamer's whistle and enable the pilot to establish his position.

ECLIPSE, the total or partial obscuration of a heavenly body due to its entering the shadow of another body. Closely associated with an eclipse are the *umbra* and *penumbra*.

ECLIPTIC, a great circle of the celestial sphere which lies at an angle of 23° 27′ with the celestial equator. The sun, *apparently*, moves along the ecliptic eastward around the earth due to our onward movement of revolution around it. It is the apparent path of the sun. The plane of the earth's orbit extended to the celestial sphere marks the circle of the ecliptic. The *Poles of the Ecliptic* are the points everywhere 90° from the ecliptic north and south.

EDDY, a circulatory motion of the water.

EIGHTY NINE FORTY EIGHT (89° 48′), a simple method of finding latitude by meridian latitude in which all the corrections for altitude are lumped as 12′ and subtracted from 90° = 89° 48′, the observed altitude is then subtracted for the zenith distance, to which the declination is added (algebraically). It was practised by early navigators and later those of limited knowledge of nautical astronomy.

ELECTRIC ARC WELDING, a process of welding two pieces of steel in which the positive wire of a current is connected to one part and the negative wire to the other, the high temperature occasioned accomplishing the desired results.

ELECTROLYSIS, an electro-chemical action set up by the salinity of the water between the different metals of a ship's underbody. Pieces of zinc are often placed on the run below the waterline in an effort to prevent the pitting that results from electrolysis.

ELEPHANTER, a periodical heavy rain on the west coast of Hindustan.

ELEVATED POLE, the pole that is in the observer's sky. If in north latitude, the north pole is the elevated pole.

ELEVATING, a charge for use of an elevator in loading cargo.

ELLIOTT EYE, a thimble spliced in the end of a hawser.

EMBARK, to go aboard a vessel preparatory to sailing on a voyage.

EMBAYED, a vessel unable to weather the entrance points of a bay, due to wind, current or sea.

END FOR END, to reverse the position.

END ON, head on.

ENGINE ROOM BELLS are signals sent from the bridge or wheelhouse to engine room by means of pulls. There are two, a gong and a jingle. The signals are, or were, as follows:

If stopped, one bell means ahead slow and two bells is astern slow. A jingle added to either of these signals means full speed. When at full speed ahead one bell slows her down, another stops the engines; if full speed or slow astern, one bell stops her.

ENGINE ROOM TELEGRAPH, a mechanical device with a dial and two indicators (one having a handle attached), on the bridge and a similar one in the engine room. The dial shows by subdivisions the various speeds which are sent below according as the indicator is set. The engineer hearing an automatic bell notes by his indicator the desired speed of the engines. As a check against error he similarly returns this signal to the bridge where it is recorded by the second indicator.

ENROLLMENT, a document issued by the customs authorities to vessels in domestic trade. It gives all facts relating to the vessel.

ENSIGN, a flag, the emblem of a vessel's nationality. The lowest commissioned naval rank.

ENTERED, a term used when a vessel has arrived from a foreign port and her master has gone before the customs authorities and taken oath to the contents of the ship's papers. When these have been accepted the ship is said to have *entered.*

ENTERING A PROTEST. A document executed when a shipmaster knows of or suspects damage.

ENTRANCE, that part of a vessel which cleaves the water, displacing it for her passage; the forward part, especially at the water line and below. A river or harbor mouth.

EPACT, the difference between lunar and solar time.

EPHEMERIS, a tabulation of the successive positions of heavenly bodies. A nautical almanac.

EQUATION OF TIME (Eq. t.) the amount of time that the real or apparent sun is ahead or behind the mean sun. It is the difference between mean and apparent time whether expressed in local or Greenwich time. It is tabulated in the nautical almanac for every 12 hours of Greenwich time.

EQUATOR, a great circle whose plane is at right angles with the line of the earth's axis. It is everywhere 90° from the poles.

EQUATORIAL CURRENTS, the great westerly moving streams of water of the equatorial region. One is north of the equator and is probably caused primarily by the rotation of the earth and directly assisted by the Northeast Trades. The other lies southward and is aided by the Southeast Trades. The *Equatorial Counter Current* flows eastward between them.

EQUIANGULAR SPIRAL, a *rhumb line* or *loxodromic curve.* It is a line that cuts the meridians at the same angle, always approaching but never (theoretically) reaching the pole. It is a straight line when drawn on a mercator chart.

EQUINOCTIAL, the celestial equator.

EQUINOCTIAL COLURE, the hour circle passing through the First Point of Aries. This hour circle, with the First Point of Aries upon it, indicates the passage and hour angle of sidereal time. Right ascension is measured eastward from this circle.

EQUINOCTIAL POINTS, the two intersections of the celestial equator and the ecliptic. When the sun is at either of these points it is said to be the equinox, either vernal or autumnal, according as it is spring or fall.

EQUINOCTIAL STORMS, a term applied to those gales which happen to occur at or near the equinoxes.

EQUINOXES. There are two, the vernal and autumnal. The 21st of March (approximately) is called the vernal equinox and the 22nd of September the autumnal. The points in the orbit occupied by the earth on these days. Also the intersections of the ecliptic and the celestial equator in the heavens.

EQUIPPED SHIP, one with bunkers and tanks full, stores and crew on board ready for sea.

ESCAPE HOLES, small manholes for coal trimmers to get out of and for filling the farther corners of the bunkers.

ESCUTCHEON, that part of a vessel's stern ornamented with her name.

ESTABLISHMENT OF THE PORT, the interval between the passage of the moon over the meridian and the next succeeding high water. For practical purposes this interval is constant. The lunitidal interval is also used to obtain the time of high water.

ETESIAN WINDS, periodic winds; especially those which blow from the north over the eastern Mediterranean Sea.

EUPHROE or **EUVROU,** a spreader of brass or wood used with the crowfoot of an awning.

EUROPE, old-time tarred rope.

EVEN KEEL, the trim of a vessel when its keel is parallel with the water surface or, more properly perhaps, when it takes its designed position for normal trim.

EXECUTIVE OFFICER, one who ranks next to the commanding officer, and is his representative at all times; he carries out the routine, has charge of the personnel and the discipline. In the absence of the captain he takes command of the vessel.

EX-MERIDIAN ALTITUDE, an altitude of a body taken near noon or the meridian, and from which the latitude is quite readily computed. The amount the body will rise before it reaches the meridian (or if after noon, the amount it has fallen) is obtained by using tables 29 and 30 (Bowditch). This quantity known as at^2 is added to the true altitude. With this meridian altitude now at hand proceed as with an ordinary noon sight.

EXPANSION BEND, a section of a pipe line bowed sharply with a U, so as to take up the vibration and the working of the vessel, saving the annoyance of leaking joints.

EXPANSION TANK, constructed above a main tank of liquid and so devised as to take up the contraction and expansion.

EXPANSION TRUNK, a contrivance consisting of an oil-tight compartment situated over a tank which keeps the main tank full. A hatch in this trunk is called an *expansion hatch.*

EXPANSION VALVE, in a tanker is designed with a spring valve which under the pressure of expansion opens and relieves the condition of the tank. There is one of these valves in each tank except peak and deep tanks.

EXTENSION OF PROTEST, a document supporting a *Note of Protest* sworn to by a master and signed by an officer, a petty officer· and two seamen before a consul or a notary. It sets forth the circumstances of the voyage, and what action was taken to safeguard the ship and cargo. A protest results in a survey of damage.

EXTRA MASTER, a certificated master in Great Britain who voluntarily takes an examination and successfully shows his superior qualifications.

EXTRA-TROPICAL STORMS, those cyclonic disturbances originating outside the tropics. The *pampero* is an example.

EYE BOLT, one with a looped opening in its head to receive a shackle or a rope.

EYE BROW, a vizor-like projection over an air port to prevent the entrance of water running down the ship's side.

EYE SEIZING, a seizing put on the strop of a block to hold a thimble and to secure the strop firmly in the groove. In general it is a round seizing made on the bight of a rope to form an eye. It is also often called a *throat seizing.*

EYE-SIGHT NAVIGATION. Piloting by estimating distances and color of water.

EYE SPLICE, a loop spliced in the end of a rope, manila or wire.

EYE OF THE STORM. The relatively calm center of a cyclonic disturbance; there exist erratic seas and gusts of wind.

EYES, the very forward part of a ship. The collars of the rigging that go over the mast heads. The holes in bolts, needles, and loops in the ends of rope. A *worked eye* has smoothed edges, while a *shackle eye* is a straight drilled hole. *Eyes in the boat,* an order to men in a pulling boat whose attention has wandered to interesting passing objects.

F

f., foggy.

F. A. S., free alongside.

F. O. B., free on board.

FABRICATED SHIP, one whose parts are made in different mills and assembled in a shipyard.

FACTOR OF SAFETY, the ratio of the ultimate strength of materials to the working stress. A number applied to the materials entering a ship's structure which if multiplied by the allowed working stress will give approximately the real strength of the material.

FAG END, the end of a rope that is untwisted.

FAGGED, to be ragged or untwisted.

FAIR, a line leading straight or running freely. Smoothing out dented plates or restoring dislocated frames in a steel vessel.

FAIR LEADERS, are found in many forms but all serving the purpose of leading lines in the direction desired; they put an angle in the direction of a line so it may be brought to a belaying pin, or to the capstan, etc. A *roller head fair lead* reduces friction and satisfactorily takes the place of a fairlead block.

FAIR WATER CONE, the conical cap covering the after side of the hole of a propeller which takes the end of the tail shaft.

FAIR WIND, a wind abaft the beam. To some few, however, the term indicates a wind with which a vessel can lay a course to her point of destination without tacking.

FAIRWAY, a thoroughfare of shipping—mid-channel.

FAIRWAY BUOYS, buoys of any shape, painted (in the U.S.) with vertical white and black stripes. They are moored at the entrances to channels.

FAKE or **FLAKE,** a complete turn of a rope in a coil. The term *flake* is occasionally heard among old sailors, but is quite often used in referring to long bights of chain cable ranged along the deck or floor of a dry dock.

FAKE DOWN or **FLAKE DOWN,** to prepare a rope for running. It is coiled with the end up, then coiled down on the end so that each fake (flake) overlaps the preceding one in such a way as to run out rapidly without the chance of becoming entangled.

FALL, the rope which with the blocks comprise a tackle. The fall has a *hauling part* and a *standing part,* the latter being the end fast to the tail of the block. With some simply the hauling part is the fall.

FALL or **DROP DOWN A HARBOR** or **RIVER,** to pass down and usually come to anchor.

FALL ASTERN, to be out-distanced.

FALL TUB, a framework resembling a tub into which are coiled the falls of a boat.

FALLING HOME, the same as *tumble home.*

FALLING OFF, paying off from the wind.

FALSE HORIZON, a condition, inimical to the taking of good sights, which is caused by cloud shadows near the horizon.

FALSE KEEL, a timber added to the main keel of a vessel to increase the draft or to protect the keel.

FANCY LINE, a downhaul for a gaff. Also a line for overhauling the lee topping-lifts.

FANG THE PUMPS, to prime the pumps with water.

FANNING. A vessel is fanning along when moving very slowly in light air.

FANTAIL, the aftermost section of a vessel.

FANTOD, a nervous officer.

FAR VANE, of a pelorus, is the outer sight vane.

FARDAGE, dunnage used with bulk cargo.

FARM, the open space in front of a pier used during periods of wharf congestion.

FASHION PIECES, timbers at the after part of a vessel which form the shape of the stern.

FAST, a line securing a vessel to a pier. *Shore fast* being a line to the shore rather than to the pier, and the term "stern fast" is in common usage. To make fast is to secure.

FATA MORGANA, a mirage. Especially that appearing in the Straits of Messina under certain conditions of wind, tide and atmosphere.

FATHOM, six feet. It is the measure of depth in America and many other countries. Its derivation is interesting, based on the ancient and universal custom of measuring a fathom of rope by the spread of the arms. This action is strikingly like a homecoming sailor greeting his sweetheart. The old Anglo-Saxon word "fæðm" meant to embrace; to grasp.

FATHOMETER. A sonic depth finder.

FAVOR, to ease a ship or spar.

FAY, to join a timber so closely to another that they serve the purpose and appearance of a single timber.

FEASE, to untwist the strands and yarns of a rope's end.

FEATHER, to turn the blade of an oar in a horizontal position when out of water. This relieves the wind pressure. There are *feathering paddle-wheels* in which the buckets move on an axis in such a way that their edges enter and leave the water while their whole broadside surface is acting when fully submerged. It is an effort to reduce the resistance at the points where effective propulsion is least. The *feathering screw* is one in which the blades of the propeller of an auxiliary vessel are capable of being set (or which set automatically) with their edges fore and aft to reduce the drag when proceeding under sail. *Feather key,* a tapering wedge of steel or brass for keying a wheel or propeller to a shaft. The wake made by the periscope of a submarine.

FEEL OF THE HELM. A good helmsman with old-fashioned steering gear is conscious of the slightest movement of the ship's head by the feel or pressure on the wheel or tiller.

FEELING THE WAY, to proceed slowly, sounding, and with caution.

FELLOES, the pieces of wood which form the rim of a steering wheel.

FELUCCA, a lateen-rigged vessel of the Mediterranean. It is either two or three masted and has a square stern.

FEND OFF, to exert pressure by various means to prevent a boat or vessel from fouling a pier, gangway, or float, or another vessel.

FENDER, a device to take the shock of contact between ship and wharf or other vessel. There are *cork fenders,* heavy bags of granulated cork for use at the particular point of collision; *fender guards* which are timbers running fore and aft along the side of a vessel; *fender spars* which float alongside of a wharf to keep a vessel off. There are round logs suspended vertically as *fenders. Boat fenders* come in many shapes and materials but all are to prevent chafing. Wharves are protected at their corners by clusters of piles, called *fender piles.* The *riding fender* is the wooden protection at the edge of a concrete pier against which a vessel rides.

FETCH, to make a desired point—particularly applied when there is an adverse condition of wind or tide to be reckoned with. The distance or sweep a wind has from the weather shore to a ship is called the *fetch.*

FETCH LOG, a canvas receptacle for palm and needles, sail hooks, wax and twine.

FIBER GLASS BOATS are those constructed (usually molded) of polyester resin and reinforced with fiber glass. This latter material is glass spun to an extremely fine fiber which possesses remarkable strength and flexibility. Such a boat is not liable to rust, corrode, rot or be attacked by marine borers; it will not swell or shrink. Desired colors are impregnated into the resin, hence surface treatment is not needed for several years. If the first cost is higher, savings may compensate in a few years. Being of recent development the life of fiber glass boats has not been determined, but they have proved durable.

FID, a conical piece of lignum vitae which serves as a marline-spike for certain work. Also a pin of iron or wood which inserted in the hole at the foot of a topmast or topgallant mast, takes the weight as it rests on the trestle trees.

FIDDLE BLOCK, one having two sheaves, one larger than the other and one above the other, tandem fashion.

FIDDLE BOW, a clipper bow.

FIDDLE HEAD, an ornamental timber curved like the head of a violin used in lieu of the more expensive and elaborate figurehead.

FIDDLE RACK, a device to keep dishes on a table in heavy weather.

FIDDLER'S GREEN, a sailor's paradise, where dance-halls and kindred amusements abound. (Hamersly)

FIDDLES. See Racks.

FIDDLEY, a grating hatch over the engine and boiler rooms. In heavy weather, tarpaulins are spread over it and battened down.

FIELD DAY, a carnival of scrubbing and washing aboard ship.

FIFE RAIL, a pin rail in a semicircle around the mast.

FIGHTING SHIP, a steamer, backed by ample capital to withstand losses, which enters a trade for the purpose of crushing competition by offering low rates.

FIGURE OF EIGHT KNOT, one made in the end of a rope to prevent its unreeving through a block. The insignia worn by all enlisted men of the Navy who have passed through the rating of apprentice. A *figure of eight lashing* is made racking fashion around the heads of a pair of sheer legs.

FIGURE HEAD, an ornamented figure that rides beneath the bowsprit. Among the notable figureheads was the beautiful female figure of the famous clipper *Flying Cloud*; the flying fish on the ship of that name; the remarkable dragon, with its alternate green and gold scales, of the ship *Peerless*; the golden eagle of the celebrated clipper *Surprise*; the *Nightingale* carried the figure of Jenny Lind. The bust of the Indian chief Tecumseh carried by the *Delaware*, ship-of-the-line, is preserved at the Naval Academy, where it is known among the midshipmen as the god of 2.5, their passing mark.

FILIBUSTER, an illicit trader, usually applied to a smuggler of firearms, etc.

FILL, is said of sails when a strain is put upon the sheets by a breeze. To fill a yard (or sail), brace so as to bring the wind on the after side of a square sail.

FIN KEEL, a deep keel of small extent usually of lead; it brings the center of gravity very low, and allows the carrying of a large sail area.

FINDS HERSELF (of a ship), a condition of magnetic equilibrium after the magnetic chaos of a newly launched ship has settled to normal.

FINE, knife-like forward, where a vessel enters the water. The more a vessel departs from the shape of a box, the finer her lines.

FIRE BALL, a meteor resembling a ball.

FIRE BILL or **FIRE QUARTERS,** a posted list of the crew and their stations and duties in case of fire.

FIRE CONTROL, the system of communication on a naval vessel by which the ranges are transmitted from the range finders to the plotting rooms, thence to the guns. Also the communication system of the spotters aloft who report to the plotting room the landing of a shell relative to the mark. Also the system of controlling a conflagration by closing compartments and flooding.

FIRE WARP, a fire warp is a long line run out ahead of a steamer lying at a pier as an escape in case of fire on the pier and no steam in the boilers.

FIRING POINT, that temperature, higher than the *flash point,* at which a volatile liquid gives off vapor in sufficient quantity to burn in a continuous flame.

FIRST LIEUTENANT, the commissioned officer having charge of the cleanliness, efficiency and general upkeep of a naval vessel's hull. This is a duty (not a naval rank), as executive officer, navigator, etc.

FIRST POINT OF ARIES or **VERNAL EQUINOX,** the intersection of the ecliptic and the celestial equator which the sun crosses in coming from south into north declination in March. It is the point by which sidereal time is measured westward from the meridian, as the sun measures off the solar time. It is also the origin of right ascension, this element being measured eastward from the hour circle passing through the First Point of Aries to the hour circle passing through the body whose right ascension is desired. This point is slowly moving westward and is now in the constellation of Pisces and close to that of Aquarius, due to a remarkable motion called the *Precession of the Equinoxes.*

FISH, to splice a broken spar by placing "splints" called *fishes* over the break, lashing and wedging them firmly. A spar used for heavy work may be *fished* as a precaution against a strain or fracture.

FISH AN ANCHOR, to bring the flukes to the rail for securing after being hove to the hawse pipe or cathead.

FISH BLOCK, a heavy double or triple sheave block fitted with a hook, sometimes with a short length of chain. It is for use in *fishing* the anchor.

FISHERMAN, a fishing vessel, particularly applied to a schooner or motor driven dragger. See Fishermen's staysail which is often called the *fisherman*.

FISHERMEN'S BEND, a very useful method of making a rope fast to a spar, or particularly, to the ring of a kedge anchor.

FISHERMEN'S GREASE, water for lubrication.

FISHERMEN'S REEF, TO TAKE A, to weather a short, sharp squall by giving to mainsail plenty of sheet.

FISHERMEN'S STABILIZERS, or *flopper stoppers,* consist of booms out, port and starboard, with a whip attached to each. The whips carry devices that plunge freely with the roll, but offer resistance to the recovery, thereby effectively reducing the roll.

FISHERMEN'S STAYSAIL, a light sail whose head hoists to the main-topmast head, its forward upper corner being fast to the fore cap where there is a deep nock. The sheet leads well aft, making a quadrilateral sail of large spread and great pulling power. This sail must be doused when going about on the other tack, owing to the spring stay between the mast-heads.

FIX, the ship's position established on a chart by two or more bearings of known landmarks. The establishment of two or more satisfactory position lines is known as an astronomical fix.

FIXED STARS, those whose distances from the earth are so great that any movements they may have are inappreciable to us for navigational purposes.

FLAG OFFICER, one who flies a flag designating his rank—two white stars on a blue field for a rear admiral, with added stars for higher rank. When the rank is active a commodore flies a one-star flag.

FLAKE, a complete round turn in coiling down a rope. A term used by some sailors as a substitution for *fake.*

FLAM, the concave part of the flare of a vessel's bow section immediately beneath the deck. A puff of wind.

FLANK SPEED, the fastest of which the engines are capable without damaging results.

FLARE, the reverse of tumble home.

FLARE UP, a blazing light shown above the rails by a vessel being overtaken by another, by a pilot vessel or fishermen.

FLARING SIDES, those projecting out from the water-line.

FLASH PACKET, or vessel, showy in appearance; immaculate.

FLASH POINT, that temperature, lower than the *firing point,* at which a volatile liquid gives off vapor in sufficient quantity to ignite.

FLASHING LIGHT, one in which the period of light is less than that of darkness. The word "group" precedes it if the light periods are grouped.

FLAT, a level area of mud or sand which bares at low water.

FLAT ABACK, when square sails have the wind blowing squarely on their forward sides.

FLAT BOAT, a scow-shaped vessel of shallow draft, mostly used in river work.

FLAT KNOT, a square or reef knot.

FLAT SEAM, is used in sewing canvas where the edges overlap. The needle pushed through the lower piece of canvas and up through the upper piece.

FLAT SEIZING. A round seizing has two layers of turns of seizing stuff, but a flat seizing has only one layer.

FLAT SHEETS, those hauled down (square sail), or in (fore and aft sail), as much as possible.

FLATTEN IN, to haul in the sheets of a fore and aft sail.

FLATTIE, a small sailing craft, usually known as *Hampton flattie.* It is a development of the flat-bottomed sharpie, introducing increased beam and a small deadrise. Sometimes the cabin roof is hinged allowing it to be raised to give more headroom. They are from 25 to 35 feet in length and sloop rigged. Also, a one-design class of racing sailboats.

FLAW, a gust of wind heavier than the prevailing breeze.

FLEET, a collection of vessels sailing in company. A locality of shallow tidal water. To move aft or forward; to overhaul a tackle, especially applied when a tackle on the hauling part of another becomes *two blocks* and it is necessary to overhaul it, to take a new haul.

FLEET UP, to promote an officer to the next higher grade.

FLEMISH COIL, according to Patterson, a coil in which each fake rides the fake beneath it so as to insure its running clear. By the same authority a *Flemish fake* or mat is one in which each fake lies coiled flat and concentrically, giving the appearance of a mat. Some other authorities say the mat is a Flemish coil. In American ships common usage is to make a concentric mat for appearance when ordered to *Flemish down* and to lay down for clear running when told to "Fake or Flake down."

FLEMISH EYE, an eye with no strands tucked but all the fibres separated and bound with yarn securely to the main part.

FLEMISH HORSE, a short foot rope at the end of a yard for the use of the men who pass the head or reef earings.

FLINCHING or **FLENSING,** was the process of removing the blubber blanket from a whale while chained alongside the vessel: the whale rotated as a strip of blubber was hoisted. Nowadays flinching is done aboard a mother ship or factory.

FLINDERS BAR, a bar of soft iron placed vertically near the compass to counteract the effect of vertical iron causing semi-circular deviation. This does not apply to semi-circular deviation due to sub-permanent magnetism. It is placed on the opposite side of the compass from the disturbing object.

FLOATING DOCK, a dock which sinks to receive a vessel, is then pumped out raising vessel and all.

FLOATING HARBOR, a collection of timbers, logs or spars moored ahead of an anchored vessel to break the sea.

FLOATING ISLANDS, areas of vegetation whose roots are so interlaced as to give buoyancy when sections of a river bank are washed out and carried to sea. These floating islands have been seen at sea with trees standing as on the shore.

FLOCCULATION, is light muck on the bottom through which a steamer can make way slowly.

FLOE ICE, field ice but in smaller masses.

FLOOD, the period when the tidal current is flowing towards the land. When the tide begins to flow inward this phase is called the "first of the flood"; when at full current it is the "strength of the flood," and towards the end of the flow the "last of the flood." To fill with water.

FLOOD COCK, a valve by which a compartment can be flooded with sea water. It is called a *sea cock.*

FLOOD TIDE, the incoming current.

FLOODABLE LENGTH, that part of a vessel's length that can be flooded and submerge her to within three inches of the top of her bulkheads.

FLOOR, the lower portion of a transverse frame, usually a vertical plate extending from the center line to the bilge and from inner to outer bottom.

FLOTILLA, a fleet, perhaps more frequently applied to small vessels.

FLOTSAM, floating goods or wreckage. There is also *jetsam,* that is jettisoned and *lagan,* that which sinks.

FLOWER OF THE WINDS, an old-fashioned name for a *compass rose.*

FLOWING SHEET, a free sheet, occurring when wind is aft.

FLUID COMPASS, the same as a liquid, wet or spirit compass, in which the card is immersed in a solution of forty-five per cent alcohol.

FLUKES, triangular pieces of iron at the ends of anchor arms. Also called palms. A whale's tail.

FLURRY, the wild, dying struggles of a lanced whale.

FLUSH DECK, an unbroken deck fore and aft, where no wells or erections extend across a vessel.

FLUSH SYSTEM, the plan of laying plates butt to butt with staggered rivets to the continuous butt strap beneath.

FLUTE, a ship rigged vessel of the 17th century. She had a round stern and high narrow poop.

FLUX, the flood tide.

FLY, the outer part, or the length of a flag.

FLY BLOCK, the large upper block of the topsail halyards.

FLY BOAT, a store ship of the 16th century.

FLY-BY-NIGHT, a jib used as a stun'sail.

FLYING, is a term used to describe the manner of setting a sail when controlled only at its "corners." This in contrast from having the head, luff and foot secured by lacing, hanks or rings to spars or stays. Thus a jib with only the halyard, tack and sheet to control it, is said to be "set flying." The stunsails of old sailing vessels were set flying, as are spinnakers in yachts.

FLYING BRIDGE, the highest navigating bridge. The bridge over a well deck to poop or forecastle.

FLYING DUTCHMAN, a mythical Dutch vessel, under Captain Vanderdecken, who is forever striving to double the Cape of Good Hope, homeward bound from Batavia; but whose efforts, owing to his defiance of the Almighty, are in vain. It is (or was) considered to be a bad omen to sight her and superstitious seamen were often reporting her.

FLYING FISH SAILOR, one who avoids cold rough winter seas and seeks the balmy breezes of summer or southern latitudes.

FLYING JIB, the outer head sail whose tack is fast to the jibboom or flying jibboom.

FLYING JIB STAY, one leading from the end of the jibboom or flying jibboom to the fore-topmast head, from which sets the flying jib.

FLYING JIBBOOM, a spar extending beyond the jibboom.

FLYING JIBBOOM GUYS, pieces of wire rope that support this spar at the sides.

FLYING LIGHT, riding high out of water without ballast or cargo.

FLYING MOORING, to moor under sail, using the headway of the vessel to run out double the desired length of chain on the first anchor, then by backing the yards falling back and letting go the second anchor, heaving in half the amount of chain on the first anchor. This same evolution is readily done in a steamer by sheering her with the rudder.

FOAMITE, a fire fighting chemical filled with bubbles of inert gas for use against oil fires.

FODDER, collision mat placed under a vessel.

FOEHN, a warm dry wind in the vicinity of high mountains caused by the drawing of air over the range. The rising air expands, precipitates its moisture and upon descending on the other side compresses with rising temperature sometimes increasing 40° in a very short time. This wind in Northwestern America is called a *chinook.*

FOG, condensed water vapor, which differs from clouds only in that it lies near the earth. A warm air passing over cold water cools, and when, at the dewpoint, its capacity to hold moisture is reached, it condenses into very small spherical particles of water and forms fog. This is a low-lying fog above which the topsails of sailing vessels can often be seen by going aloft. Likewise a cold wind passing over warm water forms visible vapor readily, owing to the lower temperature of the air. This usually becomes a high fog. The warm water of the Gulf Stream penetrating high latitudes is productive of fog, especially in the vicinity of the Grand Banks where the cold water of the Labrador Current makes the contrast in the temperatures of adjacent waters most striking.

FOG BANK, a dense area of condensed water vapor seen at a distance through clear intervening atmosphere.

FOG BOW, a white arch caused by sunlight acting on the fog particles as it does on raindrops in a rainbow. The inner edge is blue tinted and the outer side is reddish.

FOG BUOY, a device towed by a naval vessel at a given distance as a guide for a vessel astern when cruising in formation.

FOG EYE, a spot of sunlight in a fog.

FOG SIGNALS are in two classes: those sounded by vessels, and those by light-stations to aid the mariner. In the first class, there are the fog horn and steam whistle; the latter, outside inland waters, is sounded every two minutes by a steamer during a fog (every one minute in inland waters). Should she be underway but stopped, two blasts are sounded. The fog horn is sounded by a sailing vessel, one blast if on the starboard tack, two blasts if on the port tack, three blasts if running free. The ship's bell is rapidly rung for five seconds by vessels anchored in a fog. In the

second class there are fog signals sounded at the light-stations which comprise bells, submarine bells, steam whistles, sirens, compressed air horns, guns, and radio signals. Each has a characteristic group or interval of sounds to distinguish it from other stations.

FOGY, a period of three years upon which naval officers' longevity is computed. The o has the long sound.

FOIST, a type of barge.

FOLLOWING SEA, one running in the direction of the ship's course.

FOLLOWING WIND, one blowing in the direction of the ship's course.

FOOL-WIND, that blowing out of one sail into another.

FOOT, the lower edge of a sail.

FOOT BAND, a reenforcing strip of canvas along the foot of a square sail on the after side.

FOOT ROPE, a piece of served wire rope hanging in a bight beneath a yard, supported by stirrups, upon which men stand when furling or reefing sail. There are foot ropes beneath the overhang of the main, or spanker, boom of a schooner, beneath the bowsprit and jibboom.

FORCED DRAFT, the use of fans to create an artificial draft in the furnaces.

FORCED MEN, those taken aboard pirate vessels against their will and forcd to serve as members of the crew. Any member of the crew of a captured vessel could, upon reaching home, advertise the fact and perhaps save his shipmates from the gibbet should they be captured.

FORE, referring to the foremast.

FORE AND AFT, in line of the keel.

FORE AND AFT RIG, a method of setting sail from a vertical mast or stay instead of from a horizontal yard as with the square rig. It is superior in windward work but not as efficient with fair winds; it requires fewer men than the square rig type. Through the reasoning of Mr. Chatterton in his delighful book *Sailing Ships and Their Story* the fore and aft rig was a development of the lateen worked out by the Dutch in the 16th century to meet the demands of navigating their inland waters and a more boisterous climate than that of the lateen's native Mediterranean.

FORE AND AFT SAILS. See above.

FORE AND AFTERS, fore and aft pieces which fit in a hatchway from coaming to coaming, and are crossed by cross beams known as *strongbacks*. They all support the hatch covers. Schooners are called fore and afters.

FORE HAND, to take the strain inside a leading block when hauling on a piece of gear so that it can be belayed. Forehanded, is to be prepared for a contingency by foresight; to have money laid up for the future.

FORE HOOK, is a breast hook.

FORE LEECH, the luff of a fore and aft sail.

FORE PEAK, a compartment in the very forward part of a vessel.

FORE REACH, the headway a vessel will make when thrown up into the wind.

FORE RUNNER, the mark of the stray line in a log line.

FORE SAIL, in a schooner, that sail set from the foremast; in a square rigger, that set from the fore yard.

FORE-SHORE, the shore on the margin of the ocean, usually exposed at low water.

FORE SIGHT, the bringing of a body down to the horizon at the point directly beneath it with a sextant.

FORE STAY, one leading from the fore top to the eyes of a ship.

FORE TOPMAST STAYSAIL, a jib-shaped sail that sets from the fore topmast stay.

FORE YARD, the lowest yard on the foremast.

FORECASTLE (pronounced fo'c'sul), the compartment set aside for living quarters of seamen.

FORECASTLE CARD, a statement posted in seamen's galley quarters giving the voyage, estimated duration, pay-off port, legal rations, Master's name stamped by Shipping Commissioner.

FORECASTLE (FO'C'SUL) HEAD, the very foremost part of the spar deck. The raised deck of most merchant steamers in the forward part of the vessel. Its origin was in the raised castellated structure on the bows of ancient vessels used as a vantage point for their fighting men.

FOREFOOT, the point at which the stem joins the keel.

FORELOCK, a wedge or pin driven through a hole in an anchor shackle securing the shackle pin, or to secure the anchor stock in place in the shank serving the same purpose as a cotter pin. The modern method of securing the pin is by driving a lead ring around it when in place in the shackle, a score around the end of the pin locking it. It is removed with a *shearing punch.*

FOREMAST, the first mast abaft the bow except in the ketch and yawl where the first mast is called the main.

FORESTAYSAIL, a jib-shaped sail setting from the forestay. The *forestaysail club* is the boom fitted to the foot of this sail, sometimes called a *jumbo boom.*

FORWARD, towards the bow. Pronounced, "forrard."

FORWARD OF THE BEAM, any direction less than 90° from the bow of a vessel, but usually only in that sector 45° to 90° from the bow; from the bow to 45° being termed, for instance, *Two points on the bow.* An object bearing 45° or 4 points is said to be *broad on (or off) the bow.*

FORWARD PERPENDICULAR, the vertical line at the bow where the load waterline intersects the stem.

FORWARD SQUARE, a clear space around the forward hatch, 'tween decks of a passenger steamer.

FORWARD TRIANGLE, the area between the mast and foremost stay, often called *fore triangle.*

FOTHER, to stitch oakum to the canvas of a collision mat. Some-times applied to the process of heaving the mat under a vessel's hull and over an injury or leak. Also to stop a leak by passing a box filled with sawdust along the seams.

FOUL, the opposite of clear. An anchor is foul if the chain is turned about a fluke or stock; a rope tangled or jammed is foul; the sea bottom is foul if rocky; if a vessel's bottom has a growth of weeds or barnacles it is foul; there is a *foul hawse* if the chains of two anchors become crossed. A vessel fouls another if she touches her, or the bottom, if she slightly takes ground.

FOUL BERTH, an anchorage spot or berth at a pier with a rocky bottom.

FOUND, to be furnished; a vessel is *well found* if well equipped. A sailor is paid wages *and found,* that is, he is furnished food and shelter.

FOUNDATION PLATE, that upon which the keelson rests.

FOUNDER, to fill and sink at sea; to be overwhelmed by the sea in deep water.

FOUR-FOLD PURCHASE or **TACKLE,** one in which the blocks have four sheaves.

FOUR LOWERS, the mainsail, foresail, jumbo and jib of a fishing schooner.

FOUR-MASTED BARK (BARQUE), by the most common usage a vessel square-rigged on the first three masts and fore and aft rigged on the aftermost mast, which is often called the *jigger* or *spanker.* These vessels are also called ships by some authorities. Others claim a four-masted bark is square-rigged on the fore and mainmasts with the mizzen and spanker fore and aft rigged. The bark *Olympic* was thus rigged.

FOUR-POINT BEARING, see Bow and Beam Bearing.

FOUR POSTER, sea slang for a four-masted vessel, usually a four-masted bark.

FOURTH CLASS LIBERTY, scanning the shore, especially with binoculars, when restricted aboard ship.

FOX, the twisted fibers of several rope yarns. They are used for seizings after being twisted against the lay and smoothed out. *To see a fox,* to sight imaginary land—an illusion of overstrained eyes.

FRACTO CUMULUS (Fr. Cu.), clouds of cumulus broken up by strong winds.

FRACTO NIMBUS (Fr. N.), popularly called *scud*. They are broken cloud masses driving below nimbus clouds.

FRACTO STRATUS (Fr. S.), stratus clouds broken into irregular shreds by the wind.

FRAME, the skeleton structure of a vessel; a transverse rib. As a rib it is found in wooden craft built up of pieces called *futtocks*; in a steel or iron vessel it is an angle iron which extends continuously from keel to rail. They are used in three principal forms, a solid frame of the bulb iron type, or a channel iron or Z-bar; a web frame, which consists

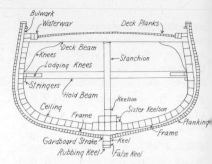

Transverse Frame—Wooden Vessel

of a web plate with angle bars riveted to each edge; and a frame merely made up of two angle bars riveted together. The web frames are widely spaced with lighter frames between. The *knighthead frame* is the first frame in the bow. A *frame mould,* the template for a vessel's frame.

FRAMING, the skeleton structure which supports the planking or plating and decks. It consists of frames, beams, floors, longitudinal framing, keel and keelson, longitudinal stringers, etc.

FRAP, to bind or draw together; to secure with ropes, particularly where two slack lines are hove together, to keep or increase the tension on them, as in the shrouds when they work slack and are hove in across the deck towards each other. To pass ropes about a loose sail to secure it in a wind. In early days ropes were even passed around the hull of a wrecked ship to help hold her together. The noun is *frapping.*

FRAZIL ICE, forms with great adhesiveness on metal and on the underside of solid ice where it may extend down to depths of 15 feet or more and raises the level of the surface ice. Under some conditions it is spongy. It is also called *Ground Ice.*

FREE, to sail with the wind well aft, two points or more abaft the beam.

FREE PORT, a segregated area in which goods may be discharged and stored, graded and packed without the imposition of custom duties. These goods may be reloaded and shipped free to a foreign country. But if they pass from the free area into the domestic market duties are levied as in ordinary importation.

FREE TANKS, those only partially filled. They are said to have a *free surface.* They are also called *slack tanks.*

FREE WATER, is water in a hold not confined but shifting with the motion of the vessel.

FREEBOARD, the distance (in the center of a vessel's length) from the top of the *freeboard deck* to the water; the freeboard deck being the upper seaworthy deck.

FREEBOARD MARKS, painted disks on the side to indicate the load waterlines.

FREEBOARD TABLES, a tabulation of freeboards for standard vessels to which allowances are made according to the time of year, the trade, the deck houses, the strength of hull sheer, etc.

FREEBOOTER, a pirate or buccaneer.

FREEING PORTS, openings in the bulwarks of a vessel to free the decks when a sea is shipped. The doors of these ports are hinged at the top, swing outboard, and are forced open by pressure at the bottom.

FREIGHT, money paid for the transportation of goods; goods transported.

FREIGHTER, a vessel engaged in the transportation of freight.

FRENCH BOWLINE, a form of bowline, having a double bight, which is very useful in emergencies. For a full description and illustration see *Standard Seamanship* (Riesenberg).

FRENCH COIL, sometimes called a Flemish Coil.

FRENCH REEF, a method of reefing square sails. A rope called a *jack-rope* is rove through the grommets of the reef bands. When hove up to the yard the band is held by toggles fast to the jack stay and toggled through the jack rope.

FRESHEN, to shift or renew. An increasing of wind *freshens.*

FRESHEN HAWSE, to veer a little chain in order to bring the chafe of the hawsepipe in another place. This is especially necessary in a hemp hawser. Also called *freshen the nip.*

FRESHWATER STAY, one leading down and aft from the fore topmast truck of a schooner to the cross trees of the next mast aft.

FRET, to chafe.

FRICTION BRAKE, a device which controls a machine by a band about some moving part to which pressure is applied to brake the motion. In case of accident to the steering gear the friction brake controls the tiller or quadrant until the hand gear is thrown in. The friction brake on the windlass controls the veering of chain.

FRIGATE, a vessel of war, full rigged, in size between a corvette and a ship-of-the-line. There were single and double decked frigates carrying 24 to 50 guns. In modern times a lightly armed naval vessel rating under a destroyer escort (D.E.) and used mainly for convoy protection.

FRIGATE BIRD, a great sea bird of the tropics. It has a length of about forty inches; is met several hundred miles from land gliding with a remarkably smooth flight sometimes near the water and sometimes so high as to be nearly out of sight. Its prevailing plumage is black with two long trailing feathers. Also called *man of war bird.*

FRIGATOON, a square-sterned vessel of Venetian days having a main mast, jigger and bowsprit.

FROST SMOKE, a fog produced by a cold wind over warm water; the sea seems to steam. Also called *Arctic smoke.*

FROSTBITERS, dinghy racers who sail during the winter.

FROZEN CARGO, that which is carried at 15°F. and frozen solid.

FUEL FEVER, a shortage of fuel oil.

FUFU, a dish consisting of mush and molasses.

FULL AND BY, when all sails are drawing (full) and the course is as close to the wind as possible.

FULL DUE, to secure, or to set up rigging, with an idea of permanency.

FULL ENDED, said of a vessel whose waterline section is well rounded at bow and stern.

FULL MOON, occurs when the earth, sun and moon are in range with the earth between. The illumined side of the moon is then directly towards the earth and a full round disc of light is seen.

FULL-POWERED VESSEL, one capable of 15 knots or better.

FULL SCANTLING SHIP, one of three decks in which the frames hold the same dimensions to the upper deck.

FULL FOR STAYS, an order to helmsman to bear off a little preparatory to tacking ship.

FULMAR, a large bird of the petrel family seen in great flocks in high latitudes. They have a mantle and tail of bluish gray with dusky wings, white head and underbody, greenish yellow bill, pale, flesh colored feet, and are about nineteen inches long. They attend steamers, whale ships and fishermen with the hope of satisfying a voracious appetite. It is interesting that they still keep the air with the ease of flight of an albatross, even when molting, because the outer wing feathers remain until the inner feathers are grown. They are characteristically a sea bird not usually approaching the land.

FUNNEL, the smoke stack of a steamer. The cylindrical device at the topgallant mast where the jack or spreader is located.

FUNNEL CASING, the outer case of insulating material around a funnel.

FUNNEL STAYS, wire ropes supporting the funnel.

FUNNY, a light narrow skiff seating but one person, and equipped with outriggers for the oarlocks.

FURL, to roll up and secure sails on a yard or boom.

FURNITURE, the masts, sails, rigging and equipment of a vessel.

FUTTOCK, a part of a frame. A frame in wooden-shipbuilding is made up of the first, second, third, etc., futtocks beginning at the keel.

The first futtock is called the *ground* futtock; and if amidships the *navel* futtock.

FUTTOCK BAND, a band below the top which supports the futtock shrouds.

FUTTOCK CHAIN PLATES, chain plates at the sides of the top, up to which the topmast rigging sets.

FUTTOCK PLATE, corresponds with the platform of a top.

FUTTOCK SHROUDS, iron rods which support the top and topmast rigging. They lead from the *futtock plate* to the *futtock band*.

FUTTOCK STAFF, a rod serving as a topmast rigging shear-pole.

G

G. A. T., Greenwich apparent time.

G. C. T., Greenwich civil time.

G. M. T., Greenwich mean time.

GADGET, a convenient name given to objects whose real names are not known, or which have none. Sometimes given to a collection of fittings to avoid enumerating them. If it becomes necessary to distinguish between two gadgets, one of them is usually named a *gilhickey*.

GAFF, a spar that stands or hoists on the after side of the mast and supports the head of the sail. It is hoisted by the throat halyards close to the mast and the peak halyards on the outer part. If it remains standing, the *peak span* leading to the lower-mast head keeps it in position, steadied by vangs on each side. The outer end of a gaff is called the peak; the end at the mast the jaws or tack. A heavy hook fast to the end of handle for landing fish.

GAFF TOPSAIL, a triangular sail set from the topmast and gaff of a fore and aft rigged mast. The sheet is hauled out to the peak of the gaff and the tack to the deck.

Sometimes these names are reversed.

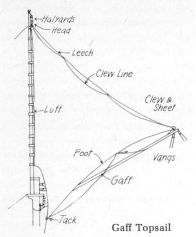

Gaff Topsail

GAGE, a vessel to windward or leeward has the weather or lee gage of another. Also spelled gauge.

GALACTIC POLE, the point at 90° from the galaxy.

GALAXY, a belt of innumerable stars across the sky which is also called the *Milky Way.* This is now thought by some scientists to be the result of an electrical phenomenon.

GALE, a continuous wind blowing in degrees of a moderate, fresh, strong and whole gale and varying in velocity from 34 to 63 knots.

GALLANT, or **T'GALLANT RAIL,** the upper rail above the bulwark rail.

GALLEASS, a large type of galley. It had high poop and forecastle; fore and mainmast square rigged and a lateen mizzen.

GALLEON, a sailing vessel of about the 15th and 16th centuries, although the term appeared in England during the reign of Elizabeth. They often had three or four decks and were used for vessels of war as well as commerce. The galleons were the first line of defense, supported by the lighter but faster galleasses. The English galleon was finer forward than the carrack from which it was developed. During the 16th century the ships of England were painted in brilliant colors of conventional designs, little carving and only the figurehead being gilded. The 17th century brought the elaborate carving and gilding into the ornamentation of ships.

GALLERIES, projections like barbettes at the quarters of ancient vessels, often of fancy design.

GALLEY, the cooking compartment. A single deck vessel of ancient times native to the Mediterranean, propelled by oars or sails, but primarily a rowed vessel. *Galley-built* was an old term for a flush decked vessel.

GALLEY DRESSER, a table for the preparation of food.

GALLEY NEWS, unfounded rumors circulated about a vessel.

GALLIED, a term applied to a whale that has taken off in alarm.

GALLIOT, a small speedy vessel propelled by sail with oars as auxiliary power, formerly used in the Mediterranean. The term is also given to Dutch type, long and narrow, of the yawl rig. The earlier Dutch galliot was full rigged. The distinguishing feature was a short-headed mainsail with long foot.

GALLIVAT, a sailing vessel and large rowboat used by Malay pirates; two masts, triangular sails and armed with a few small swivel guns.

GALLOWS FRAMES, frames rising above the main or spar deck and serving as a place to stow boats, oars and spars. Sometimes called *gallows-bitts*. Aboard a yacht, the gallows, or *gallows frame* supports the main boom when the sail is furled, and may be either permanent or removable. The *gallows* is a distinctive feature of a fishing trawler, where it is an A-frame from which the trawl warps are handled.

GAM. In earlier days when time was not taken seriously, two ships falling in with each other would back their yards and exchange available news by word of mouth. It was the custom for the ship to windward to back her main yards and the one to leeward her fore-yards. In this way they could maneuver with greater facility for their purpose. This was called *gamming*. It was most extensively practiced by whalers who kept the sea for four to six months and more.

GAMMON LASHING, formerly secured the bowsprit at the knight-heads. The *gammon iron* or *gammoning* replaced the lashing in later days.

GANG, a line of hooks made fast by short lines to a heavier trawl line. In handling cargo in American ports a gang consists of two winch-men, one signalman, eight holdmen and nine dockmen.

A *gang of rigging* comprised all the standing and running rigging of a sailing ship.

GANG BOARD, the plank running fore and aft between the oarsmen of a pulling boat.

GANG CASK, a cask of medium size, larger than a breaker.

GANGPLANK, a temporary bridge between ship and shore.

GANGWAY, a passageway aboard or ladder up a ship's side. An order demanding a passageway among the crew. *Gangway boards* are ornamental heavy pieces of mahogany set athwartships in the rail at each side of the gangway of old men-of-war.

GANGWAY DOOR, a hinged section of the bulwark which swings down or to the side and allows a gangway.

GANGWAY LADDER, steps leading down the ship's side to the water.

GANTLINE or **GIRTLINE,** a single whip made fast aloft and especially used for raising or lowering a man in a boatswain's chair, and in hoisting sails aloft for bending.

GANTRY CRANE, a spanning carriage which moves on tracks and from which a hoisting tackle depends for use in moving heavy weights. All wharf gantry cranes have revolving arms and are divided into two classes: the *full arch* which travels on two tracks on the ground, and the *half arch* in which the inner side travels on a rail fast along the face of the warehouse, thus having only one leg on the ground.

GARBOARD STRAKE, the length of plank or plating next to the keel. Sometimes called the *sand strake*.

GARE, to Gare Ship is to tie up to the side of a canal such as Suez, to allow another vessel to pass. Used in Royal Navy. Term taken from Craddock's *Whispers From The Fleet*.

GARLAND, a strop used to hoist spars.

GARNET, a tackle used in hoisting cargo, usually on the mainstay. The clewline of a square course (sail).

GARVEY, a scow-shaped boat of simple construction; native to Barnegat Bay.

GAS FREE, a term applied to a tank after a chemist's test shows no gas.

GASKETS, ropes or bands of canvas by which sails are secured to yards or booms. A rope wound around a sail and yard from the yardarm to the bunt is called a *sea gasket*; canvas or sennitt bands used likewise to secure a sail are *harbor gaskets*. Jibs are secured by *stops*. A packing ring or disc to make a joint water- or gas-tight.

GATEWOOD SYSTEM, a method of heavy longitudinal framing.

GATHER WAY, to begin to make headway.

GAUSSIN ERROR, due to temporarily retained magnetism in soft iron produced by steering a long time on one course or lying at a pier. It is most effectively created when underway on easterly or westerly courses in high latitudes.

GEAR, a general term for a collection of spars, ropes, canvas, etc. The sailor speaks of his personal effects as his gear; his oilskins and boots, his *foul-weather gear* and in his watch below he may change to his *night gear*.

GEMINI. The third sign of the Zodiac.

GENERAL AVERAGE, a term applied to the adjustment of a loss caused by the voluntary sacrifice of part of the ship or cargo by the master for the preservation of the whole. (See Act of Man.) In order to enter a claim for general average, the sacrifice must have been voluntary; it must have been made by the master or upon his order; must not have been caused by any fault of the party asking the contribution; the sacrifice must have been successful and it must have been necessary.

GENERAL QUARTERS, a muster of the entire ship's company at battle stations.

GENOA, a large overlapping jib that sheets well abaft the first mast. Also called *guinny* and *jenny*.

GEOCENTRIC, referring to the motion or position of a body considering the earth's center as a center.

GEOCENTRIC LATITUDE, the position of a body or place as would be seen by a person at the center of the earth, the longitude being measured from the First Point of Aries along the ecliptic.

GEOCENTRIC PARALLAX, the difference in the positions of a body as seen by a person on the earth and as would be seen from the center of the earth.

GEODESY, that branch of surveying which takes into account the curvature of the earth, and comprises surveys to determine its size, shape and dimensions. A little *Geodesy* is of value to the hydrographic surveyor and at least interesting to the mariner. For instance, *mean sea level* is the great datum plane to which is referred the heights of mountains and often the depths or levels of the ocean.

The mean sea level is a difficult plane accurately to establish, for, aside from the uncertain attraction of the sun and moon, great land masses serve to raise the water level through its own attractive qualities for other matter. With the variable height of mean sea level goes a variable error in the plumb line in different parts of the world reaching well over 20″ as a maximum in some mountainous countries.

GEODETIC SURVEYING, operations of such a scale and precision as to form a basis for obtaining data concerning the size and shape of the earth.

GEO-NAVIGATION embraces piloting and dead reckoning in contradistinction to celo-navigation which comprises observation of heavenly bodies.

GESWARP, sometimes met with, could readily be a corruption of the term guest warp (which see), considering that boat booms were once called guest warp booms. When the term *geswarp* is used, it is a line by which a boat rides to a boat boom. This line, or painter leads, through a bull's eye in the boat boom pendant. In this connection a naval officer, who had made a study of terms, gave this interesting derivation: The word *jes*, in falconing days, applied to the leather strap and eye on the bird's leg. The leash led from the falconer's wrist up through an eyelet on the bird's leg, thence to the hand. The French "J" in many words became "g" when assimilated into English, as "jarden" to "garden" and our geswarp may have been so derived owing to its similarity of use.

GHOSTING, a vessel making headway when there is no apparent wind.

GIBBOUS, phases of the moon are those from the First Quarter to Full Moon and thence to the Last Quarter.

GIBSON GIRL, a slang term for the hand-operated transmitter for sending distress signals.

GIG, the captain's boat. It was formerly a light ornamented whaleboat. The crew was carefully selected and the general appearance of this boat and her crew was considered a fair guide to the condition of the ship, hence there was always much pride taken in their appearance. In the naval service this boat carried a gilded arrow on each bow. The crew pulled (single banked) the so-called gig stroke, which involved a pause after each stroke of the oars. The coxswain was the stroke oarsman when the captain was aboard, who in the stern sheets steered with elaborate yoke-ropes. Gigs today are motor-boats.

GILGUY, a term promiscuously applied to objects without well known names, particularly a makeshift for expediting work, but perhaps not efficiently. Also gilhickey.

GIMBALS, a contrivance consisting of two concentric rings bearing at opposite points on knife edges; one circle has its bearings athwart-ships for the pitching motion, the other fore and aft for the rolling motion. Within these rings hang the different instruments that are required to remain level without regard to ship's motion, such as the compass, chronometer, pelorus, and mercurial barometer.

GIMLET, to turn an anchor around after it has been hove to the hawse pipe.

GIN POLE, a spar temporarily set up to serve as a derrick for handling cargo where usual ship's gear is not at hand. The pole is fitted with head tackle, guys, heel blocks and a shoe to prevent slipping.

GINGERBREAD, applies to the light construction of an excursion steamer, fancy work. Gilded work which covered the sterns of 17th century vessels.

GINS, iron sheaves set in iron shells. They are used as single blocks for whips or fairleads in working cargo.

GIRDERS, longitudinal lengths of steel which strengthen the vessel in a fore and aft direction. Also called *stringers*.

Girders

GIRT, a vessel moored without play and unable to swing freely to wind and tide.

GIRTLINE. See Gantline.

GIVE, the stretching of a new rope, or bending of a spar. To give pursuit to an enemy.

GIVE WAY, an order to commence pulling in a cutter or whaleboat.

GLASS, a mariner's name for a barometer; a spy glass.

GLOBIGERINA, small sea organisms which are found in the surface waters of the ocean. They have perforated shells through which minute tentacles or feelers work in and out. The shells of the dead organisms fall to the bottom forming a calcareous layer called Globigerina ooze.

GLORY HOLE, a term formerly given to the firemen's quarters of a coal-burning steamer; sometimes applied to the lazarette.

GLUT, a reenforcement of canvas in the bunt of a square sail to receive the becket of a bunt jigger.

GNOMONIC PROJECTION, one used particularly for finding the course and distance by great circle sailing. The projection is drawn as though the earth's surface were seen by the eye of an observer at the center of the earth, and thrown on a plane tangent to the surface. As every great circle passes through this point, the earth's center, all of them will appear as straight lines on the projection. The plane represented by this chart lies tangent to the earth's surface and a line drawn straight on this chart is a great circle course. Near its center, and point of tangency, there is practically no distortion, but at the margins the land becomes much distorted. The meridians converge towards the poles and the parallels crown away from them.

GO ABOUT, to tack.

GO ADRIFT, to break loose.

GO FOREIGN, to ship on a vessel bound for foreign countries. Spoken also of the vessel itself.

GOB, an enlisted man of the Navy, below the rating of Chief Petty Officer. Is said to have originated on China Station being the Chinese name for a sailor. (Haskins.)

GOB LINE, a martingale guy.

GOB STICK, a wooden spoon; a stick used by fishermen to stun a halibut before attempting to get it aboard a dory.

GO-DOWN, a storehouse on the waterfront of eastern ports, especially in southern China.

GOLDEN NUMBER, the years (about 19 years) of a lunar cycle.

GOLLYWOBBLER, a full cut maintopmast balloon staysail; the term has been cut down to *golly*.

GONDOLA, a light boat always associated with Venice. It is sculled with an oar at the stern, and its stem and stern post are carried upward high above the rail in an ornamental manner.

GOONEY, a name applied to the black-footed albatross by seamen. They have a wing spread of about 7 feet. They are mostly dark in color.

GOOSE-NECK, a metal device that secures a boom to a mast. It allows the boom to swing and to be topped. The fixture at the heel of a cargo boom. The pipe of a ventilator which bends through 180° when above-decks. In modern goose-necks an aluminum ball is fitted in the mouth of the goose-neck ventilator which seats when decks become flooded and prevents water getting below.

Goose-Neck

GOOSE WINGED, the condition of a vessel when lying to, with the bunt of a close reefed topsail up and only a triangular piece of canvas set at the yard arm. This term is used by yachtsmen to describe an unintentional half-jibe resulting in the awkward situation of having the boom and gaff on opposite sides of the mast.

GORES, cloths of canvas cut on

an angle and used at the leeches of a sail to give desired shape.

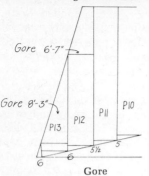

Gore 6'-7"

Gore 8'-3"

P13 P12 P11 P10

5½ 5

6

Gore

GORGE, the groove in the sheave of a block.

GRAB ROPES, those which run fore and aft along a vessel's sides for the assistance of boats coming alongside.

GRABS, flexible claws so hinged at the upper end that upon being lifted by a crane the jaws close. They differ in design to meet various types of cargo such as bulk, ore, pulp wood or scrap iron.

GRADIENTS (Barometric). The upper atmosphere might be said to be made up of "hills and hollows." The areas of high pressure are under the "hills" and those of low pressure under the "hollows." The slope of the atmospheric elevations are called the *gradients.* They may be steep or gentle. If steep, the winds are violent; if easy, the winds are light. Gradients are lines of equal pressure. They are known as isobars.

GRAFT A ROPE, to taper the end and completely cover it ornamentally by a series of half hitches made with small cotton stuff. Sometimes called pointing a rope.

GRAIN FEEDERS, compartments just above the grain holds to keep them full of grain and help to prevent shifting.

GRAIN FITTINGS, a system of stanchions and shifting boards in the hold of a steamer for the safe carriage of grain in bulk. The stanchions are so built up with angle irons as to form a groove into which the ends of the shifting boards are dropped.

GRAINS, a multi-barbed spear used in capturing fish.

GRANNY KNOT, unseamanlike knot made instead of a square knot by a green hand.

GRAPNEL, a small four-pronged anchor, used for dragging for drowned persons, lost articles, or for anchoring dories or skiffs. Formerly it was employed to hold an enemy ship alongside for hand to hand combat.

GRAPPLING IRONS. See Grapnel.

GRATINGS, wooden or iron openwork covers for hatches, bunker holes, etc.

GRAVEYARD WATCH, the middle watch or 12 to 4 a.m., because of the number of disasters that occur at this time.

GRAVING (or GREAVING) A VESSEL, to burn off the barnacles and growth from the bottom.

GRAVING DOCK, a dry dock walled with stone, formerly where graving was done.

GRAVING PIECES, small sections of plank set in a vessel's deck.

GREASING THE GANGWAY, slating a man for discharge.

GREAT CIRCLE CHARTS. See Gnomonic Projection.

GREAT CIRCLE SAILING, the practice of sailing along the great circle passing through the point of departure and that of destination. It is the shortest distance between the two points and, in fact, is the straight line of vision were it possible to see the point of destination. In order to follow this line or circle, it is necessary constantly to change the compass course. The Mercator chart shows a great circle as a curved line but a chart of the Gnomonic projection shows it as a straight line.

GREAT CIRCLES, those whose planes cut through the center of a sphere, dividing it into two equal parts.

GREAVE (or GRAVING), to burn off a vessel's bottom when foul.

GREEN FLASH, is an interesting phenomenon that occurs under certain conditions, viz: at sunrise or sunset, a clear atmosphere and a sharp horizon. When the sun is at the horizon its light is subject to the maximum refraction. The red end of the spectrum (longer wavelength) is bent less than the violet-blue (shorter wavelength) or green, so drops below the horizon first (or last to appear at sunrise). The blue of the spectrum is so scattered by the atmosphere that it is not a factor in sunset (or sunrise) coloring. So the green color under the right circumstances may be seen momentarily at the horizon. This is the green flash.

GREEN SEA, solid water shipped aboard.

GREENWICH APPARENT TIME (G.A.T.), the hour angle of the apparent or real sun referred to the 180° meridian—the midnight meridian of Greenwich.

GREENWICH HOUR ANGLE (G.H.A.), the angle at the celestial pole between the Greenwich meridian and the hour circle passing through the sun (or star).

GREENWICH MEAN TIME (G.M.T.) is measured by the passage of the mean sun beginning at the 180° meridian—the midnight meridian of Greenwich.

GREENWICH TIME OF SIDEREAL NOON, is the G.M.T. when the First Point of Aries is on the local meridian.

GREGALE, a wind with the characteristics of a bora (q.v.) that is met in the vicinity of Malta.

GRETA GARBO, a quadrilateral jib with the triangle at the clew cut off making two clews, upper and lower, with a sheet to each.

GRIDIRON, a framework foundation with a cradle built just above low-water mark. A vessel is floated upon it at high water, and while left exposed at low water work is done upon the bottom.

GRIPE (or GRIP), the abnormal and sudden tendency of a sailing vessel to come to; when a vessel is crank she is often said to gripe. *Gripes* are pieces of plaited small stuff, ropes or short pieces of chain with turnbuckles, used to hold boats into the strong-backs or to secure them in chocks in a seaway.

GROG-RUM, name coming from Old Grog Admiral Vernon who wore a cloak of coarse cloth called grogram.

GROIN (GROYNE), a small masonry breakwater. Also a projecting wall or wooden structure for the purpose of breaking the current and thereby causing the deposit of silt and holding the land.

GROMMET, a ring of rope made from a single strand by laying it up until there are three parts. They are used for various purposes about a vessel, sometimes being served in the center, forming two eyes. Grommets are also metal rings sewed into the edge of a hammock or sail. They are often of brass in two parts punched together from each side of the canvas, forming eyelets through which stops or robands are passed. The removable metal ring in an enlisted man's flat hat.

GROSS TONNAGE, is the cubical capacity of a vessel divided by 100 cubic feet. However, some spaces are excluded by the so-called Moorsom Rules.

GROUND, a vessel grounds if she touches the bottom. There is usually the meaning of touching in a harbor or alongside a pier rather than striking a rock in the open sea. See Stranded. The ground futtock is the lowest section of a wooden frame of a vessel.

GROUND LOG, a sounding lead bent to a log line, instead of a chip log, in order to get the speed over the bottom. It obviously can only be used in shoal water.

GROUND SWELL, long undulations especially noticeable in calms and light airs, due to the waves running into shoal water and "feeling" the bottom.

GROUND TACKLE, anchors, chains, etc.

GROUND TIER, is the lowest tier of casks; those above are called *riders*.

GROUNDWAYS, two timbers laid on the ground to serve as a foundation upon which a vessel under construction may rest. The sliding ways are placed on the ground ways with launching tallow between.

GROWLERS, low-lying masses of ice which are not easily seen by approaching vessels owing to their dark indigo color. The term more particularly applies to isolated fragments of ice.

GROYNE. See Groin.

GUARD RAIL, a timber bolted fore and aft to a ship's side to serve as a fender.

GUDGEONS, devices set in the stern or rudder post having an eye which receives the pintle of the rudder and about which the rudder swings in lateral motion. See Pintle.

GUESS WARP, a term applied to a line used when warping a vessel. It is coiled in a boat and is paid out as the mooring buoy or wharf is approached. It is necessary to estimate the distance in connection with the amount of line coiled in the boat, hence the name. In present day usage this is a *running line*.

GUEST FLAG, a blue rectangular flag with a white diagonal bar across it, flown from the starboard spreader of a yacht to indicate that the owner is absent and that guests are aboard.

GUEST WARP, a line by which a boat rides at a boat boom. It is led from forward through a bull's eye near the end of a boat boom. A figure of eight knot from 6 to 10 feet from the end prevents the line unreeving. By slacking away forward a boat can be dropped aft to the gangway. Also, a line to assist the towline when towing, either to steady the tow or to lengthen the towline or act as a preventer; the grab rope that runs alongside to assist boats coming to the gangway. Boat booms were, according to Smyth, called *Guest warp booms*.

GUFFY, a marine.

GUINEA CURRENT, an eastward moving stream close in to the Guinea Coast of Africa. Its southern edge cuts into the westgoing Equatorial Current.

GULDER, a tidal phenomena at certain points on the south coast of England occasioned by a double low water. After first low water a slight rise of perhaps six inches occurs followed by a corresponding recedence at second low water. At Portland and Weymouth the two low waters are about four hours apart, the tide then rising for about four hours and falling four.

GULF STREAM. The North Equatorial Current flowing in great volume across the Caribbean Sea and through Yucatan Channel, fills the Gulf of Mexico with warm water. This further increases in volume by the expansion due to a higher temperature. The outlet is the Florida Straits where the current flows with considerable velocity and to great depth, and is the beginning of the Gulf Stream. This wonderful ocean current continues off Cape Hatteras and flows eastward of the Grand Banks, the effect of its relatively warm waters being felt even to the coasts of Northern Europe.

GULFWEED, a branching sea weed having small air vessels resembling berries which keep it afloat. It is found in great quantities in the Sargasso Sea and the Gulf Stream. It is also called Sargassum Weed.

GUN TACKLE, a purchase comprising two single blocks and the necessary rope.

Gun Tackle

GUNBOAT, a light, unarmored naval vessel.

GUNDELOW, a shoal draft, beamy bluff-bowed craft used in New England inland waters in former times. These vessels were used for freight and transporting salt hay. They were propelled by tide, oars and by a lateen sail. A vessel of this type was built in 1934 on the Piscataqua River on the lines of the old craft.

GUNK HOLE, a small narrow channel dangerous to navigate owing to current and to numerous rocks and ledges. Also *gurnet*. A small anchorage, usually shallow. Gunkholing adds much interest and pleasure for shoal draft boatmen.

GUNTER'S SCALE, a device in the form of a two foot ruler, upon one side of which are shown the trigonometric functions and on the other side their logarithms.

GUNWALE (GUNNEL), the rail of a boat.

GUNWALE TANKS. See Cantilever Tanks.

GURNET. See Gunk Hole.

GURRY, fish entrails and waste, oil, skin and blood. It is kept in a gurry tub.

GUSSET, an iron plate fitted over the ends of beams or bilge brackets, etc. Also a triangular segment cut from the tack of a spinnaker to relieve turbulence and improve the draft.

GUSSET STAY, an iron plate fitted diagonally at the ends of a boiler to strengthen it.

GUST, a sudden increase in the velocity of wind and of short duration—a *squall* when the gust is very heavy.

GUT, a small channel.

GUTTER, a waterway at the side of the deck along the inside of the bulwark, leading to the scuppers.

GUY, a rope or whip that supports or steadies a spar usually in a horizontal or inclined position, such as a bowsprit or a cargo boom. A stay supports in a vertical position.

GUY DERRICK, consists of a mast and boom: the mast being stayed in several directions.

GUZZLE, a small channel making into flats exposed at low water.

GYBE, a variation in the spelling of jibe; to change tacks by running off before the wind.

GYN, a device consisting of three legs (tripod) for hoisting heavy weights.

GYN TACKLE, a purchase consisting of a double and a three sheave block, the standing part of the fall being fast to the double block.

GYPSY, the drum of a winch, around which a rope or chain is turned for heaving in.

GYRO-COMPASS, one which receives its directive power from a gyroscope which in turn is operated by electrically driven rotors. The compass card at all times indicates true north. It is the realization of a navigator's dream—no variation, no deviation. A rotating gyroscope with a weight hung from it, aligns itself with the axis of the earth—true north, a condition which lends itself for adaptation in a non-magnetic and magnetic free compass. The *master gyro* is usually located below decks near the center of motion, and is connected electrically with *repeaters,* so-called, placed anywhere for convenience—beside the steering wheel, on the wings of the bridge, or as a telltale in the cabin.

GYRO-STABILIZER, the characteristic of a rotating gyroscope that keeps it in the same plane unless overcome by a greater force has been used in the development of the Sperry gyro-stabilizer. The rolling of a ship is mainly the result of synchronism, one wave not ordinarily having a sufficient force to cause a heavy roll. So by detecting a wave at the inception of the roll with a sensitive *pilot-gyro,* the opposing force of the *main gyro* is turned against the force of the wave, reducing greatly the tendency to roll and preventing the accumulating rolls of synchronism.

H

H. A., hour angle.

H. O., Hydrographic Office, U.S. Navy. Now U.S. Oceanographic Office.

HACK WATCH, used for noting the time when taking astronomical observations and afterwards comparing with the chronometer to convert into G. M. T.

HAGDON, a common name for the seabird called the Shearwater.

HAGUE RULES, those drawn up in 1922 to define the risks to be assumed by ocean carriers under a bill of lading, and to unify various laws and practices. They are a long step toward uniform bills of lading.

HAIL, HAILS, the attention call of one vessel to another. A man or vessel *hails* from his or her home port. Frozen pellets of snow covered with layers of ice.

HALF BEAMS, brackets at the head of alternate frames, between the beams.

HALF BRIG, an old term for a brigantine.

HALF DAVIT, a single davit.

HALF DECK, in some small vessels, a deck extending aft over only a part of the boat. The after part of the gun deck of a naval vessel. In the high pooped ancient vessels the deck which ran aft from about the center of the vessel.

HALF A GALE, a wind of about force 7, Beaufort Scale.

HALF HITCH, a turn made around a rope or spar with the end coming through the bight.

HALF-MAST, a mark of respect for the dead. The flag is always full-masted before lowering to half-mast and is always full-masted before lowering to the deck.

HALF SEAS OVER, well on toward being a drunk.

HALF TIDE, is midway between high and low water. This level is the same whether considered at Springs or Neaps.

HALO, an illuminated ring of about 22° radius around the sun or moon. It is caused by refraction of light in the ice crystals of the upper air. When colored, the red of the spectrum is on the inside and the shades of blue on the outside, but are seldom visible.

HALYARD RACK, an open "tub" consisting of balusters topped by a circular rail. The topsail halyards were coiled in it. Similar racks were also used for boat falls.

HALYARDS or **HALLIARDS,** ropes or tackles for hoisting sails and yards.

HAMBROLINE (HAMBER), three-stranded (laid right-handed) seizing stuff.

HAMMER HEAD CRANE, a crane constructed on the cantilever principle, in which the weight on the hoisting arm is counter-balanced by weights and the hoisting machinery. The name comes from its appearance. It is of a heavy-duty type, and is capable of swinging its load in revolution as well as backward and forward on tracks.

HAMMOCK, a rectangular piece of heavy canvas fitted at each end with a number of small ropes called *nettles* spreading from a ring. The nettles collectively are called *clews*. The hammock was used at sea for the berthing of seamen, especially on naval vessels.

HAMMOCK CLOTHS, canvas covers that are laced down over and protect the hammock nettings.

HAMMOCK NETTINGS, the space in the rail of a naval vessel for the stowage of hammocks.

HAMPTON BOAT, a type of small center-board fishing boat used on certain sections of the New England coast, having two small masts easily unstepped, and carrying spritsails. They have now been motorized.

HAND, a member of the crew. To furl a sail. To *bear a hand* is to hurry up.

HAND GEAR, a contrivance where man power is used instead of machinery, especially applying to the hand wheel and its steering gear.

HAND LEAD, a 7- or 14-pound lead for sounding in up to about 15 fathoms.

HAND MAST, a term used in Europe for a pole mast.

HAND OVER HAND, to climb a rope or stay without the use of the legs, but with one hand alternately above the other.

HAND RAIL, a rail used for support, running beside a ladder or up a ship's side.

HAND SPIKE, a level for lifting heavy weights; a capstan bar. When used for this purpose, one end is squared. Also used for working on heavy lashings and setting up the rigging.

HANDICAP, an advantage given to a boat by agreement either in time or distance, usually due to size and sail area.

HANDSOMELY, to ease off on a line gradually and moderately; sometimes, as in the case of a cable, little by little.

HANDY, a term applied to a vessel quick in stays.

HANDY BILLY, a watch tackle; also a hand pump.

HANGING IN THE GEAR, the condition of square sails after they have been clewed up (with buntlines hauled up) and loosely gathered to the yard.

HANGING KNEES, fit under a beam at the ship's side, in a vertical position.

HANGING PENDANT, one used in carrying out an anchor with a small boat. It holds the weight of the anchor to the belly-strap.

HANKS, peculiarly shaped rings for bending the luff of head sails and stay sails to the stays. Snap hanks of several designs are used.

HARBOR DUES, expenses incident to the visit of a ship to a foreign port. They include tonnage taxes, light dues, and fees for the execution of papers and to various port authorities.

HARBOR GASKET. See Gasket.

HARBOR LINES, the bulkhead and pierhead lines laid down by the Army Engineers. Improvements under the River and Harbor Act do not extend inside the harbor lines.

HARBOR MASTER, an official charged with the enforcement of the regulations of the port and the proper berthing and anchorage of vessels.

HARD, a landing place for hauling boats and small vessels out on a sea beach. It is at right angles with the shore line and is constructed of concrete, stone or gravel.

HARD CHANCE, a tight situation; a strong wind for making a passage.

HARD DOWN, a hard-a-lee helm.

HARD-A-LEE, to put the helm hard over away from the wind. The command given on a sailing vessel preparatory to coming about.

HARD OVER, to put the helm as far as possible in one direction.

HARD UP, a hard-a-weather helm.

HARD-A-WEATHER, to put the helm over towards the wind.

HARDENED SHEETS, those hauled in close on the wind. To harden the sheets, take in a little more.

HARDTACK (or bread) is really a hard, dark flour product that survives climatic changes, but softer products now carry the name.

HARMONIC ANALYSIS, conceived by Lord Kelvin, resolves a series of periodic values, such as the diurnal range of temperature, the ebb and flow of tide, etc., into components the resultant of which forms a smooth curve. The tides, being produced by the attraction of the sun and moon, form a composite wave made up of a simple wave produced by each body. As these bodies are constantly changing their relative positions between themselves and the earth, the resultant of their combined influence is the composite wave. The mathematical process of separating the moon tide wave and the sun tide wave from the composite wave is called a harmonic analysis. And by using the relative positions of the sun and moon again to combine them the tides may be predicted for any future date.

HARMATTAN, a very dry wind on the west coast of Africa in the dry season (winter). It being cooler than the humid atmosphere of the Guinea coast it flows in and replaces it. It gives relief to the coastal plain and is known as the "doctor." The harmattan is usually accompanied by dust which often forms a heavy haze.

HARNESS CASK, one kept on deck from which are served the daily rations of salt meat.

HARPINS, the forward part of the wales at the bow. Also temporary pieces of wood to support frames near the ends of the ship when erecting them.

HARPOON, a barbed spear used in the whale fishery. It was thrown by the bow oarsman known as the harpooner or harpooneer, for the purpose of getting attached to the whale which was accomplished with a long line fast to the harpoon and coiled in a tub. After the mammal exhausted itself he was again approached and lanced. The harpoon was invented by the Basque sailors of the Bay of Biscay, who were the original harpooners and are supposed to have first used the word.

HARPOON LOG, a rotating device with blades or wings which is drawn through the water by a vessel. The distance run is recorded on dials set in the body of the log. It is necessary to haul it in to obtain the reading and for this reason is inconvenient. There is also a Taffrail Log.

HARPOON OAR, the foremost in a whaleboat.

HARRIET LANE, canned beef.

HARTER ACT, a law which protects a ship owner against claims for damage incurred through the acts of the ship's officers or crew, provided she left port in a seaworthy condition, properly equipped and manned.

HARVEST MOON, is a phenomenon of the higher latitudes in which for several nights of full moon nearest the autumnal equinox, that body rises only a little later each night instead of the average 51 minutes. Even in middle latitudes the rising is markedly earlier at the harvest moon than in April for example. The moon ordinarily rises later each night by the average of 51 minutes, but at this time she is coming northward very rapidly in declination and an earlier rising results which overcomes much of the usual retardation owing to her eastward movement of revolution.

HASH MARK, a red diagonal stripe across the sleeve of a man-of-warsman, signifying that a previous enlistment has been served.

HAT MONEY (HATCH MONEY), a bonus given to ship masters for the successful delivery of cargo.

HATCH. This term in common usage among seamen is indiscriminately applied to the opening on a ship's deck and to the covers that close it. However, it would seem that the best usage applies *hatch* to the opening, *hatch covers* to the heavy sections that close it, *hatchway* to the clear vertical space through the hatches of several decks to the hold, and tarpaulins to the three (in a seagoing vessel) canvas covers that protect against the entrance of sea water. In connection with a hatch there are Strong Backs, Fore-and-afters, Hatch Beams and Head Ledge.

HATCH BAR, a bar secured across the hatch covers to keep them in place.

HATCH BATTENS, strips of steel or wood wedged to the side of the hatch coamings to make fast the tarpaulins.

HATCH BEAMS, serve as supports for hatch covers. They are denoted king beams and blind beams. The former has a vertical member extending longitudinally with the beam, and serves to restrict movement of the hatch covers when in position.

HATCH BOOM, a cargo boom guyed over a hatch and used with a yard boom. The whip used with a hatch boom is called a hatch whip or tackle.

HATCH CLEATS, secure the battens to the hatch coaming.

HATCH COVERS, sections of planking (usually four) that fill the hatch opening in the deck.

HATCH MONEY. See Hat Money.

HATCH ROLLER, a heavy portable pipe roller which is clamped to the top of a hatch coaming, on the inside, to take the chafe of the cargo whips.

HATCH TACKLES or **WHIPS,** tackles suspended over the hatches to facilitate the handling of cargo and stores. See Burton.

HATCH TENDER, the man stationed at a working hatch who under the gang boss gives signals to the winchman and sees that the cargo moves properly.

HATCH TENT, a canvas protection from rain over a hatch and over the men working the hatch. An opening on the shore side allows the movement of cargo.

HAUL, to pull; the particular nature of the pull usually brings out other terms such as, *bowse down, sway away, sweat,* or *swig.* Sometimes the term *heave away* is used where it is a case of a "long pull, a strong pull, and a pull all together," but *heave away* more particularly refers to capstan work, heaving the lead, and heaving a vessel down. To haul is an extended task when done by hand while we heave with power yet, confusingly, we heave the lead and a line by hand. To *run away* or *walk away* is to make a steady haul instead of a succession of short pulls while standing in the same place. Seamen speak of hauling a vessel to another pier; of hauling her across the river even though she goes under her own power and no particular hauling is done. The wind hauls when it changes direction with the hands of a watch, but the more popular term for this is *veering*. (See Back.) On a sailing vessel when the wind changes it is said to *haul forward*.

HAUL AWAY, an order to pull on a line.

HAUL OUT, to pull a boat or vessel out of water for purposes of repairs, hull maintenance, or storage.

HAULING PART, that part of a rope making up a tackle which is hauled upon. The part made fast is the *standing part*.

HAULS HER WIND, a term applied to a vessel coming on the wind after running free.

HAUNCH, a sudden decrease in the size of a piece of timber. (Ansted.)

HAVEN, a sheltered anchorage.

HAWSE, the space forward from a vessel to a point directly over her anchor. A vessel crossing this space *crosses the hawse*. With two anchors down and the chains leading without turns, there is a *clear* or *open hawse;* if there is a cross or a turn in these, there is a *foul hawse*. See Athwart Hawse and Freshen Hawse. The term hawse originally referred to the bows of a ship.

HAWSE BAG, a cornucopia filled with granulated cork or oakum used in the hawse pipe to prevent the entrance of sea water. This is also called a *jackass*. A *hawse block* is a wooden plug and the *hawse buckler* is an iron plate for the same purpose.

HAWSE BOLSTERS, blocks which are placed beneath the hawse pipes to take up the chafing.

HAWSE HOLES and **PIPES,** the iron castings in the bow through which the anchor chains run are called the *hawse pipes*, the openings the *hawse holes*.

HAWSER, a heavy line, five inches or over, used in kedging, warping, or towing. *Hawser laid* rope is that whose strands, which are right-handed ropes, are laid up left-handed. It is also called Cablelaid.

HAWSER BOARD, a piece of wood at the stern of a tug designed to reduce the chafe of a towing hawser.

HAWSING. A vessel lying uneasily to an anchor, probably due to a weather tide, is said to be hawsing.

HAZE, a thin obscurity in the atmosphere due to smoke or dust. Applies when a mate selects a seaman for unjust discrimination.

HEAD, the compartment with toilet facilities. The *head* of a *sail* is the upper side or, if a jib or staysail, the upper corner. The *captain of the head* is the enlisted man whose cleaning station is at the head.

HEAD BLOCK, the single block at the head of a cargo boom.

HEAD CRINGLE, the iron ring worked into the upper corners of a square sail and the upper and after corner (peak) of a fore and aft sail.

HEAD EARING, a rope making the head of a square sail fast to a yard.

HEAD HOLES, the grommets in the head of a sail for securing to the yard of a square sail or to the gaff in a fore and aft sail.

HEAD LEDGES, the thwartship pieces of a hatch.

HEAD REACHING, making slow headway under short canvas but not hove-to.

HEAD ROPE, the bolt rope at the head of a sail.

HEAD SAILS, the sails forward of the foremast. They are of fore and aft type, coming often under the term jibs.

HEAD SEA, waves coming from ahead.

HEAD SHEETS, those of the head sails.

HEAD STICK, a batten in the head of a jib. The halyard is bent to its center to prevent the head's twisting.

HEAD YARDS, the yards on the foremast.

HEADROOM, the clearance between decks. In yachts *full headroom* is usually reckoned as slightly more than six feet.

HEADS UP, naval slang used by mess cooks hurrying with a load of chow calling for a passageway.

HEALTH OFFICER, a government sanitary officer who examines the sanitary conditions of a vessel on arrival as well as the health of the passengers and crew. The health officer of a port issues the bill of health to departing vessels when it is not done by a consul. See Bill of Health.

HEART, a small rope or core running through the center of a heavy rope. A kind of dead eye, heartshaped, with a single hole in it.

HEART YARNS, those in the center of a strand.

HEAVE, to throw; to throw one's weight on a capstan bar or in a steady pull on a line. To heave is otherwise associated with power, as to heave ahead to the next berth at a pier using the capstan. In general to heave means to accomplish a task by mechanical power, as in heaving up the anchor or heaving the vessel ahead by a line to the capstan, while hauling is done by hand. Sailors also speak of hauling a vessel farther up the dock. The terms *heave* and *haul* become confused. Although in heaving we use power, still it means to throw by hand as in heaving a line and, of course, we heave the lead. See Haul. To haul snug the tucked strands of a splice using the marline-spike as a lever. The rise and fall of a vessel at sea.

HEAVE AHEAD, to move forward by taking in on a line, warp or chain cable.

HEAVE AROUND, an order to work the capstan. *Heave away* is used as an order to pull when the work is heavy, but the term *heave around* applies to capstan work.

HEAVE AWAY, to commence heaving on a capstan or windlass, or to haul on a line.

HEAVE AND AWEIGH, an order to man the windlass and break out the anchor.

HEAVE DOWN, to heel a vessel on her side in order to examine or repair her bottom. This expedient was formerly much resorted to in ports where repairs were necessary and drydocks were not available. It was done by use of heavy tackles at the lower mastheads attached to trees on the shore or anything stationary on a wharf. The vessel was first put in *cork light* trim. See Careen.

HEAVE THE LEAD, to take a sounding.

HEAVE THE LOG, to cast the log and ascertain the speed. It is more proper to say "stream the log."

HEAVE AND PAWL, an order to heave on the windlass and not ease up until a pawl drops.

HEAVE OF THE SEA, the scend of the waves; the amount a vessel is thrown over to leeward by the force of the seas.

HEAVE SHORT, heave in on the chain until nearly over the anchor with but little more chain out than depth of water.

HEAVE TAUT, to put a strain on a line or chain.

HEAVE TO, to lay the vessel on the wind with helm to leeward, sails shortened down and so trimmed that she will come to and fall off, but always head up out of the trough. A steamer heaving to heads up to the seas, just turning her engines enough to hold her there by using the steerage way. Some steamers are allowed to drift slowly with seas on the quarter using oil and sometimes long steamers even heave to in the trough. Hence, to heave to means to lay a vessel where she takes the seas most comfortably, the thought being to ride out the gale rather than to make progress on

the voyage. The less onward motion a vessel has the safer she rides. See also Lay (verb).

HEAVER, a lever bar; a steel spike with wooden handle, used to heave strands in splicing.

HEAVING LINE, a light line having a manrope knot or small weighted bag at its end to aid in throwing. It is thrown to a pier or another vessel as a messenger for a heavy line. See Monkey's Fist.

HEAVISIDE LAYER, is that ring of the ionosphere, far above the earth, that deflects radio waves back to the ground. The ionosphere is composed of widely spaced atoms that are electrically charged. A radio wave encountering these atoms undergoes a change in polarity: its front travels faster where these atoms are more highly charged, causing a change of course toward an area of less ionization which is the earth's atmosphere.

HEAVY LIFTS, pieces of cargo, such as locomotives, so heavy as to require special gear.

HEAVY WEATHER DAMAGE, as its name implies is damage caused by heavy seas. It may be due to improper loading which sets up abnormal stresses causing sheered rivets, cracked plates, etc.

HEEL, the after part of the keel at the stern post; the foot of a mast; a list or inclination.

HEEL BLOCK, the single block at the foot of a cargo boom which acts as a fairlead to the winch.

HEEL CHAIN, a short chain designed to aid in supporting a topmast. It leads from the lower mast head to the keel of the topmast.

HEEL LASHING, the line securing the foot of a sheer-leg or derrick boom.

HEEL AND TOE WATCH, is four hours on and four off.

HEELING ERROR, the change in the deviation of the compass due to the relative change of vertical and horizontal iron in the heeling of a vessel. It is corrected by the introduction of a permanently magnetized bar, vertically beneath the compass in the binnacle.

HEIGHT OF EYE, the distance in feet that the observer's eye is above the water when taking the altitude of a body. See Dip.

HELENA. See Corporsant.

HELIOCENTRIC, referring to the motion or position of a body considering the sun as a center. *Heliocentric longitude* is the distance from the First Point of Aries to a point along the ecliptic with the sun as the center.

HELM, the tiller. In modern times a quadrant is fitted to the rudderhead. In giving orders to the quartermaster the helm was referred to in the merchant service, but the rudder in all services now. That is, formerly the order *Port your Helm* meant that the helm was to be put to port by turning the wheel to starboard, the ship's head then going to starboard. The terms *helm up* or *helm down* refer to orders given in a vessel under sail, as do *helm's alee* and *helm's aweather.* The order *Right Rudder* now means that the wheel is to be turned to

the right. The rudder will go to the right and the ship's head will go to the right or starboard.

HELM PORT, the hole through which the rudder stock passes into the hull of a vessel.

HELMSMAN, the man who steers —the quartermaster.

HEMP ROPE, rope made from the fiber of the hemp plant. There are Italian, Russian and American hemp; then there is Phormium hemp from New Zealand and Sunn hemp from the East Indies. The rope made of this fiber is usually tarred but if not is called *white rope.*

HEN FRIGATE, a vessel in which the captain's wife accompanies him to sea.

HERMAPHRODITE BRIG, a two-masted vessel, square-rigged on the fore and fore and aft on the main mast. This term was applied to a brigantine by some sailors in the last days of sail, owing to the fact that it is rigged half as a brig and half as a schooner. Long ago it was used when minor changes in sails and spars made a brig a snow and a snow a brig. See Brigantine.

HERRINGBONE GEAR, one in which the teeth have an angle in order to reduce lost motion.

HERRINGBONE STITCH, a round seam crossed forward by the returning part. It is very serviceable for repairing rips in canvas and covering standing rigging with leather or canvas.

HIGH DAWN, a condition when the day breaks above a cloud lying on the horizon.

HIGH AND DRY, the condition of a vessel or anything else left wholly out of water.

HIGH LATITUDES, those parallels remote from the equator.

HIGH LINER, the schooner (or other vessel) with the largest catch.

HIGH PRESSURE, an abnormal weight of atmosphere. The greater pressure on the mercury of the barometer forces it higher up the column, making a so-called high barometer.

HIGH PRESSURE HAT, an officer's cap.

HIGH SEAS, the ocean beyond the three-mile limit where no nation has special privileges or jurisdiction. However, the high seas limit is often in dispute.

HIGH WATER (H. W.), a periodic high level of water after a periodic low level of water.

HIGH WATER FULL AND CHANGE (H. W. F. and C.), the interval of time between the time of the moon's transit and of high water on the days of full and change of the moon. This is used as a constant. Added to the time of moon's passage on any subsequent day it will give a sufficiently accurate time of high water. Or, if the time of moon's passage is not available then add 51 minutes for each day past new or full moon to the time of high water full and change.

HIGH WATER MARK, the line on the shore made by the average of the high waters.

HIKING, to get live weight out beyond the weather rail in an effort to keep a racing boat on her feet. Sometimes a plank is extended to windward to give a man's weight greater leverage. Hiking is commonly practiced in sailing dinghies.

HIT THE DECK, a phrase used in breaking a naval crew out of the hammocks; the same as *Rise and Shine.*

HITCH, a combination of turns for making a rope fast to a spar or stay, etc. A term of enlistment in the Navy.

HOBBLER, a coastwise pilot in England who, without a license, assists vessels in various ways. His small boat was called a hobble.

HOG FRAMES, trusses running fore and aft on river steamers to support the hogging stress.

HOG PIECE, the keelson of a small wooden boat.

HOGGED, a term applied to a vessel whose bow and stern have drooped. It is opposite of *sagged* where the amidship section has fallen. A *hogged shear* is one in which the conventional shearline is flattened or reversed.

HOGGING, scraping barnacles at sea.

HOGGING LINES, lines attached to the corners of a collision mat, which pass under the keel and serve to work the mat over the injured part.

HOGGING STRESS, the force tending to produce a hogged condition.

HOGSHEAD, a barrel-like container of 63 gallons capacity.

HOIST, to elevate a sail, spar or piece of cargo. As a noun, the length of a sail measured between the boom and the jaws of the gaff, or the head if a jib-headed sail. Also the amidship depth of a square sail that is set by hoisting the yard. The height of a flag along the staff.

HOLD, a large lower compartment of a vessel for the stowage of cargo.

HOLD BEAMS, the same as deck beams in the hold but without the deck planking.

HOLD ON TO THE LAND, TO, to keep in touch with a coast by soundings and an occasional bearing, but not necessarily to be always in sight of it.

HOLD WATER, to dip the oars and retard a boat's progress.

HOLDING DOWN BOLTS, those securing an engine or boiler to its bed.

HOLDING GROUND, the character of the bottom in relation to the degree of bite it gives an anchor, that is, its power of holding; it varies according to whether the holding ground is good or bad. Clay, marl and mud are good, while soft mud and sand are poor holding ground. Rocky bottom is liable to cause the loss of or damage of an anchor.

HOLIDAY, an unpainted, unvarnished or unscraped spot on the spars or about the vessel.

HOLLOW ENDED, a vessel whose water line section at the bow and stern are concave with the water; a fine lined vessel. The famous clippers were so constructed.

HOLLOW SEA, a condition usually occurring where there is shoaling water or a current setting against the waves. The line from crest to trough makes a sharp angle and the sea is consequently dangerous.

HOLLOW SEAM, is the condition when the inner side of a seam between two adjacent planks is the same or wider than the width on the outside. In order to hold caulking the inside of the seam must be narrower.

HOLYSTONE, a brick of sandstone used for cleaning decks by hauling it back and forth; small ones used around corners are called *prayer books.* Pieces of stone from a church were used to scrub decks in Royal Navy, hence the term.

HOME, a sheet is home when hauled well out at a yard arm. An anchor comes home when it drags when used in kedging. To bring into place. A spike is driven home.

HOME PORT. If sailing in foreign trade any American port is called a home port. But *the* home port is that in which a vessel's documents are issued.

HOMEWARD BOUND PENNANT, one hoisted on a naval vessel when returning from at least a year's cruise on a foreign station. It is of great length, usually requiring an inflated hog's bladder to keep the end afloat. It formerly was equal in length to a foot for every man aboard, and was cut up on this basis for souvenirs, the captain taking the first star at the hoist, the executive the second, and so on.

HOMEWARD BOUND STITCHES, unusually long stitches in sewing, to hurry the completion of a job.

HOMOGENEOUS CARGO, one composed of merchandise of the same nature, as all grain or all cotton.

HONG, a warehouse on the waterfront of Chinese ports.

HONG KONG MOORING BUOY, consists of arranged cylindrical floats horizontally, and has a "hawse pipe" through the bilge of the buoy. The chain from the mooring buoy leads up through the hawse-pipe to a ring, which cannot pass back. The stress is carried by the chain and not the buoy. The buoy merely floats at the end of the chain.

HOOD, a canvas cover for a hatch; the slide over a hatch; or sometimes the trunk or raised part of a deck which gives headroom and ventilation below. The foremost or aftermost planks of strake.

HOOD ENDS (HOODINGS), the ends of planks set in the rabbet of the stem and stern post. Also called *hooding ends.*

HOOK, a general term, but referring usually to a *cargo hook* on the block of a cargo tackle, over which the cargo slings are hooked; or a plain hook at the end of a cargo whip. Such a hook is measured for working load at the back of the hook. Hook is slang for anchor; the *fish hook* of the anchor stowing gear; the hook of any tackle. There are also Slip or Pelican Hook; Breast Hook.

HOOK ROPE, a rope used in clearing hawse; merely a rope with a hook.

HOOKER, a colloquial expression given to an old vessel.

HOOPS, are rings breast high above the crosstrees of a whaling vessel, one to port another to starboard to steady the lookout. Sometimes called spectacles. Also see Mast Hoops.

HORIZON. There are several different horizons; the first and most evident is the line between sky and water. This is called the *visible horizon.* The *sensible horizon* is the circle on the heavens indicated by a plane at right angles to a plumb line passing through the position of the observer. This is identical with the visible horizon of a person whose eye is at the sea level. A similar plane passing through the center of the earth indicates the *rational horizon* on the celestial sphere. There are other terms associated with the Sea horizon: Dip, Refraction, and Parallax; Artificial Horizon and False Horizon.

HORIZON GLASS, usually a piece of glass one half of which is mirrored, and the other half plain. It is erected perpendicular to the plane of the sextant and parallel to the index glass when the zero of the vernier coincides with the zero of the arc. If these glasses are not parallel in this position there is an index error. To test the glass for its perpendicular position, bring the reflected sea horizon in coincidence with the real horizon and swing the instrument to a horizontal position each way. If the horizon does not break, the glass is perpendicular; otherwise it must be adjusted by screws at the back. A more accurate but less practical test is made by bringing a star in coincidence with its reflection. This is called the Index Correction.

HORIZONTAL PARALLAX, the angle at a body between a line drawn from an observer on the earth's surface and one from the earth's center when the body is in the horizon. If the body is above the horizon, this angle is known as *Parallax in Altitude.* Parallax must be added to an observed altitude of a body.

HORN, a projecting spar or helm attached to the after side of the rudder. To this chains are attached and brought to the quarters of the vessel for use in case the rudder heads should carry away. *Horns* are also the ends of the crosstrees.

HORN TIMBER, in small vessels, extends from the keel at an angle to the head of the sternpost; the dead wood being filled in below. Another version is the timber mortised into the head of the stern-post, extending aft in line of the keel and forming the angle of the overhang.

HORSE, the low iron rod parallel with the deck along which the traveler of a fore and aft sheet shifts from side to side in tacking. See Deck Horse. The Boom Horse is a rod welded to a collar around the boom, carrying a traveler from which the upper block of the sheet hangs. The foot rope of a yard. To *horse up* is to harden up the caulking in a vessel's seams with a horsing iron.

HORSE BLOCK, an elevated grating on the quarter-deck from which the officer of the watch formerly gave orders and maneuvered a naval vessel under sail.

HORSE LATITUDES, the region of high pressure on the outer edge of the trades where light and variable winds prevail. The conditions are unlike the doldrums in that the air is fresh and clear and calms are not of long duration. The name is supposed to have originated in the days when sailing vessels in the West India trade lost many horses of their cargoes while becalmed in this area. Some sources think the term was derived from the act of heaving the "dead horse" overboard when the "advance" was paid. This for ships out of England would be near the latitude of the horse latitudes.

HORSE MARKET, an eddy caused by confused tidal currents, to be avoided by small boats in heavy winds as dangerous cross seas are characteristic.

HORSEPOWER, the equivalent of a lift of 550 pounds one foot in one second. The *indicated horsepower* that an engine develops is measured by the pressure on the cylinders during the stroke, no allowance for friction being made. *Shaft* or *brake horsepower* is the actual twisting power given to a shaft and measured by a brake. *Effective horsepower* is that expended to propel a vessel, all losses being deducted.

HORSE'S LEG, a sextant or old quadrant.

HORSING, a sailing ship term used when being carried to windward by current. Often applied when a vessel rides uneasily to her anchor, constantly sheering with the wind on one bow, then the other. See *Hawsing.*

HORSING IRON, a tool similar to a caulking iron but equipped with a handle for one man to hold while another swings the hammer or mallet and *horses* in the oakum.

HOT BUNKS, those occupied by successive watches below. This situation occurs when the crew outnumbers the bunks available.

HOUNDING, that part of a mast between the hounds and the deck.

HOUNDS, shoulders of wood bolted to or a part of the mast. Near the upper end the hounds are sometimes fashioned out beyond the normal taper of the spar to form shoulders upon which rest the fore and aft trestle-trees. The upper parts of the hounds are called the *cheeks.*

HOUR ANGLE (H. A.), the angle at the pole between the meridian and the hour circle passing through the body being considered. It is measured westward. The hour angle of the sun is solar time, while the hour angle of the First Point of Aries is sidereal time.

HOUR CIRCLE, a great circle of the celestial sphere which passes from pole to pole as do the meridians on the earth. The circles are celestial meridians.

HOURLY DIFFERENCE (H. D.), the change in the elements of the Nautical Almanac that occur in an hour of time.

HOUSE, a structure on deck.

HOUSE AN ANCHOR, to heave a stockless anchor into the hawse pipe and secure it.

HOUSE AN AWNING, to cast off stops from the jackstay and make an awning fast to the rail or to ring bolts in the deck upon the approach of a squall.

HOUSE A BOWSPRIT, to rig it on the forecastle.

HOUSE FLAG, a distinguishing flag of a company which is flown from the mainmast of their steamers.

HOUSE-LINE, small stuff of three strands laid left-handed. Sometimes called *housing.*

HOUSE A MAST, to partially lower and lash to the lower mast. Topgallant and topmasts were housed to pass under the New York bridges.

HOUSEBOAT, a pleasure craft of great beam and low power, with commodious living quarters for use on inland waters.

HOUSING OF A MAST, that part below decks.

HOVELLER, a wrecker; one who recovers lost anchors. A coastal vessel.

HOVE-TO. See Heave-to.

HOWKER, a Dutch vessel of the 17th and 18th centuries with a round bow and stern. The foremast predominated the rig, being set well aft as with a bomb ketch; both the fore and main were square-rigged, spanker on the main and large jibs. A spritsail was sometimes carried. Later the term was applied to smaller single-masted vessels.

HUG, to keep close.

HULK, an old unseaworthy vessel unable to propel herself by sail or steam. She is usually devoid of spars, except, perhaps, masts, and serves as a lighter or storeship; the term frequently refers to a *wrecked hull.* Around A.D. 1500, a type of large-sized merchantman was called a *hulk.* They had round bows and stern, high poop; the fore and mainmasts carried square topsails and a lateen sail at the mizzen.

HULL, the main structure of a vessel.

HULLING, an old term for heaving-to on the wind with helm to leeward.

HUMBOLDT CURRENT, a branch of the general drift setting northward out of the Antarctic. It flows up the coasts of Chile and Peru.

HUMIDITY, atmospheric moisture is termed humidity. Absolute humidity is the actual vapor content expressed in grains per cubic foot or per pound of air. The ratio of the vapor content to the vapor content of saturated air at the same temperature, expressed in per cent, is called the relative humidity. For example, given a sample of air at 70° having an absolute humidity of 4 grains per cubic foot. Since saturated air at 70° contains 8 grains per cubic foot, the relative humidity is 50 per cent.

HUNTER'S MOON, the full moon that follows the harvest moon which is the one nearest the autumnal equinox.

HURDY GURDY or **GURDY,** a roller at the gunwale of a trawler's dory to assist in hauling or under-running a trawl.

HURRICANE, a cyclonic storm which blows with a velocity from 64 to 118 knots or over. The name generally applies to those violent agitations that pass over the West Indies, while the name *typhoon* applies to similar disturbances occurring in the East Indies. These storms bring all ships under bare poles and are indicated in the log book by force 12–17 of the Beaufort Scale.

HURRICANE DECK. See Deck.

HUTCH, a shelter over the helmsmen.

HYDRO-AIRPLANE, a sea plane or flying boat.

HYDROFOIL is a boat with underwater wings. These wings or hydrofoils, due to their shape and angle, create an upward pressure on the under sides as the boat's speed increases, while there is a lessening of pressure on the upper sides. This condition creates a lifting power which raises the boat from the water, greatly reducing water resistance and allowing high speed. However, a dragging force accompanies the lifting power and the foil must be designed to create a favorable high ratio between lift and drag. The more drag the more propulsive power needed. The lifting power of a foil increases as the square of the speed. It is necessary to control the lift and as only the submerged part of the foil is effective, the usual practice is to provide a number of foils one above the other. They are so set that as the boat is lifted to the desired height above the water the upper members of the foil become ineffective. The foils take a sweptback angle with the fore and aft line of the boat. The trailing edges of the foils are equipped with controls which when raised decrease the lift and when lowered increase it.

HYDROGRAPHY, the physical features of the bottom and depths of water; the currents and tidal data shown on a chart. The same name applies to the process of surveying by which these data are collected.

HYDROLANT, an urgent warning of a danger to navigation in the Atlantic.

HYDROMETER, an instrument for obtaining the specific gravity of liquids; or measuring salinity of sea water.

HYDROPAC, an urgent warning of a danger to navigation in the Pacific.

HYDROPLANE, a small, light, step-bottom boat designed to plane at speed along the surface of the water. Such boats, equipped with high-powered gasoline engines, have attained great speeds.

HYGROMETER, an instrument for measuring humidity; sometimes hair is used to actuate an index hand. See Psychrometer.

HYPOTENUSE, the side of a right-angled triangle opposite the right angle.

I

I-BEAM, a rolled beam of mild steel used for bulkhead stiffeners whose cross-section resembles an I.

I. C., index correction.

I. H. P., indicated horsepower.

ICE. Fresh water solidifies at 32°F., and forms ice. With a falling temperature the surface of a body of water cools and its greater density causes it to sink, being replaced by warmer water from the bottom. This continues until the water reaches a temperature of about 39°F. (which, curiously enough, is its heaviest point) when it no longer rises, and the surface cools to 32° and freezes. Salt water freezes at slightly lower temperatures than fresh water. See Ice Designations.

ICE ANCHOR, an iron device of a shape particularly designed to drive into ice for the purpose of mooring a vessel.

ICE BREAKER, a powerful vessel of heavy construction used to clear harbors and channels. Specially constructed steamers are used having a "cut under" bow allowing them to ride up on the ice and crush it. An experimental ice breaker has been developed to break the ice by raising it with an underwater extension of the bow. A skeleton iron saddle placed upstream from an exposed lighthouse to break up drifting ice fields.

ICE DESIGNATIONS. The polar precipitation on the mountains of northern Greenland builds an immense ice cap on these elevations of land. The ice mass of the valleys moves slowly down to the sea where great fragments break off or *calve,* forming *icebergs.* About 90 per cent of the bergs of the North Atlantic come from Disko Bay. They float out with the wind and current and are gradually carried into the flow of the Labrador Current making to the southward. The second summer of their drift usually finds the surviving bergs off the Grand Banks. The smaller pieces of ice, fragments of bergs which still constitute a menace to navigation, are called *growlers* and *bergy bits.*

Pack ice is a rough mass of broken floes frozen into a heavy obstruction preventing navigation. The barrier sometimes breaks or opens, forming a clear channel called a *lead,* but a lead may prove to be a *blind* lead if it terminates and prevents a vessel from proceeding. Should the ice close on a ship it would constitute a *nip,* and nips have crushed many a vessel. The *pack* is the ice barrier in the far north which halts navigation.

The great frozen areas of the southern Arctic and bays and rivers of Canada break away in the warming weather and drift southward as *field ice.* It is mostly not navigable. Often by opposing currents or changing directions of wind two fields collide or impinge on each other. The ice at the edges buckles with the impact and large cakes are thrown up on the adjacent field. This is known as *rafting.* The force of the sea often accomplishes the same result on the weather side of a field. When the ice becomes piled high in this manner it is known as *hummock ice.*

As a field becomes dispersed the drifting pieces of ice are called *drift ice.* It is usually easily navigated.

Floe ice consists of drift ice frozen into small fields, a floe carrying the meaning of small field.

The term *sludge* or *brash* is applied when field or drift ice becomes broken up and slushy through action of the sea and warmer water; very slushy ice is also known as *lolly.* *Slob ice* is found along the weather side of a floe or field and along the coast, but the term seems to apply more to the white, broken-up new snow ice; it is more or less slushy and is usually easily navigated.

Sheet ice, as its name implies, is a sheet; smooth and level and is new ice. It is found off the bays of Newfoundland where it has formed the previous winter and broken away with the coming of spring.

Ice rind, thin ice (less than two inches) found in bays and harbors where the discharge of fresh water overlays the colder sea water; it is tough, cutting and is noisy when a vessel works through it.

A pan is a small sheet of flat ice. Pancake ice is new ice which becomes detached in small cakes or sheets around whose edges the ice has built up higher than the inner parts.

Anchor ice, that which forms on the bottom.

ICE DOUBLING (Ice Lining), additional plates riveted on the bow plates at the water line to protect against the impact of drifting ice.

ICEBERGS, portions of a glacier which break off and float to sea. They vary widely in size and shape. About one-eighth of the volume is above the water, but the height is not necessarily one-seventh of the depth under water. The shape of the mass determines its draft and height. In the North Atlantic they drift southward from Greenland with the Labrador Current and those that do not become lodged on the coast of Labrador usually become dissipated in the warm waters of the Gulf Stream, where, on the ocean lanes, they become a great menace to shipping. This is due particularly to the difficulties and uncertainties of detecting their presence in fogs which prevail so extensively in this locality. The use of radar reduces this danger.

In the Southern Ocean great quantities of ice break away from the Antarctic ice barrier and work northward into the navigable waters of this ocean. The ice masses are enormous, being often many miles in extent. The bergs are very frequently plateau-shaped (flat-topped). Antarctic ice occasionally reaches latitudes north of 40°S.

ICEBOAT, a framework mounted on three metal-shod runners, one at each end of a crossbeam and the third, which is turned by a tiller and acts as a rudder, at either the forward or after end of the fore-and-aft backbone of the frame. A mast and rig—usually a sloop but sometimes a single sail, is mounted on the framework, as is a cockpit to hold the crew of one or more persons. Iceboats, under favorable conditions, attain speeds over reasonably smooth ice considerably higher than that of the wind that is driving them.

IDLERS, members of a ship's company who have an all night in.

IN, a seaman sails in a vessel, not on her.

IN BOWS, an order to bow oarsmen to boat their oars and prepare for coming alongside.

IN AND OUT SYSTEM, the arrangement of plating where of three strakes the two outer ones are riveted to the frames while the middle strake overlaps the other two and is riveted to them. The outer plate requires a liner on the frame.

IN SAIL, an order to lower fore and aft sails and clew up square sails.

IN STAYS, said of a vessel when in the wind while going about to tack ship.

INBOARD, towards midships.

INCHMAREE CLAUSE, a clause of an insurance policy covering loss or damage to the hull or machinery through the negligence of masters, charterers, mariners, engineers, or pilots, or through any latent defect in the machinery or hull.

INCIDENCE, ANGLE OF. Rays of light striking the surface of a mirror are reflected at the same angle as the direction of the direct ray; from a perpendicular to the mirror the angle with the direct rays is called the angle of incidence and with the reflecting rays the angle of reflection.

INCLINATION OF THE EARTH, the angle of 23° 27′, which the earth's axis takes with the plane of its orbit.

INDEX BAR, an arm pivoted at the top of a sextant. It carries the venier and tangent screw at its lower end which swings across the graduated arc, and the index mirror at its upper end.

INDEX CORRECTION (I. C.), a correction necessitated by an error in a sextant which exists after the index and the horizon glasses have been made perpendicular with the frame, but are not parallel with each other, when the zero of the arc and the zero of the vernier are in line. The amount the zeros are off when the reflected and real sea horizons are in one is the Index Correction. If the zero of the vernier is to the right of the zero of the arc, the Index Correction is that much plus; if to the left the Index Correction is minus. This is easily remembered by the rule: *If it's on it's off; if its off it's on.*

INDEX ERROR. See Index Correction.

INDEX GLASS, a mirror erected perpendicular to the plane of a sextant at the top or pivot of the instrument. To test the correctness of this glass, place the index arm in the center of the arc, and holding the instrument flat with the arc away, look closely at the inner edge of the index glass and note if the direct and reflected image of the arc form a straight line. If so, the glass is perpendicular, if not, adjust by screws at the back.

INDIAN HEAD (bow), was a type of stem first appearing in New England fishing schooners in 1897. The stem dropped in a slow convex curve, sharpening as the waterline was approached. The term came from a fleet of Duxbury schooners having Indian names.

INDIAN SPRINGS LOW WATER, approximately low water tropic springs.

INITIAL STABILITY, that which exists when a vessel is upright or listed at small angles.

INNER BOTTOM, the plating forming the upper side of the double bottom.

INNER JIB, the head sail usually next outside the fore-topmast staysail.

INSHORE, toward the land.

INSOLATION, is the radiant heat the earth receives from the sun; it then heats the air close to the surface by conduction and distributes it by convection.

INSURANCE HAWSER, is kept reeled, one forward and one aft. Is required by underwriters and only used for towage purposes.

INTERCEPT. See Altitude Difference.

INTERCOSTALS, *parts in the* structure of a vessel placed fore and aft between frames and floors and not continuous girders.

INTERMITTENT LIGHT, an occulting light.

INTERNATIONAL CODE, a set of signal flags, including one for each letter of the alphabet, adopted by the leading maritime countries for communicating between ships and shore-stations. There are also ten numeral pennants, three repeaters and a code and answering pennant. See Publication 102 of the U.S. Naval Oceanographic Office.

INTERPOLATION, the process of selecting proportionally an intermediate quantity lying between two tabulated quantities.

INVOICE, an account of goods consigned; a description of marks and numbers, costs, name of ship and master and the merchants interested.

IRISH HURRICANE, a calm.

IRISH PENNANT, a loose end hanging about the sails or rigging.

IRONS, handcuffs and leg-irons. A ship is *in irons* when caught in stays and unable to cast on either tack. A steamer is said to be in irons when she is loaded so by the head that the propeller is raised and she is unable to maneuver.

IRRADIATION, the apparent enlargement of a heavenly body due to its brilliancy against a dark background. This error is very small and does not affect the results in navigational observations.

ISHERWOOD SYSTEM, that method of ship construction in which the main framing is longitudinal (fore and aft) instead of transverse as in the usual method. The stringers are closely spaced and the transverse beams widely spaced. It is a very satisfactory and successful method of modern construction, especially in long vessels.

ISO, equal—from the Greek.

ISCBARIC CHART, one showing by isobars the normal barometric pressure of different parts of the world.

ISOBARS, lines along which the normal barometric pressure is the same.

ISOGONIC LINES, those upon which the magnetic variation is the same.

ISOSALINES, lines of equal salinity of sea water.

ISOTHERMS, lines along which the temperature is equal.

J

JACK, a device for moving heavy pieces of cargo and for forcibly stowing in a small space. Also called a *jack screw*. The name given to the flag consisting usually of the union of the ensign. This flag is displayed from a jack staff forward on a naval vessel at anchor. It is displayed at a yardarm when a general court martial or board of inquiry is in session on a man-of-war. A vessel shows a jack at the foremast when in need of a pilot. A horizontal iron bar used at the head of the topgallant mast where the topgallant and royal masts are in one spar. It spreads the rigging at that point. (Also called *jack cross-tree*.) An iron rod along the top of a yard to which sails are bent or reefed. They are called *bending* or *reefing jackstays* according to their particular use. The wire rope running through the heads of the awning stanchions to which the awning is stretched is called the *jackstay*. A vertical stay immediately abaft the topmast of a schooner. The lazy jacks are bridles from the topping lift to the boom of a fore and aft sail to restrain the sail on the boom when lowered.

JACK ROPE, the lacing rope that bends the foot of a sail to the boom. The rope that is rove through the grommets of a reef band for reefing with the use of a toggle on the *jackstay*. This is called a *French reef*.

JACK STAFF, a short pole erected near the bowsprit cap or stem from which the jack is flown.

JACK TOPSAIL, an English term for a club topsail (which see). Its club is called the *jack yard*.

JACKASS, a cornucopia canvas bag filled with oakum and hove into the hawse-hole to prevent the entrance of sea water.

JACKASS BRIG. See Brigantine.

JACOB'S LADDER, one consisting of served wire rope sides which support rungs usually of iron. Such ladders are found hanging from the stern of a ship, from the boat booms, abaft the masts where trysails and spanker are brailed in, and above the topmast rigging. The English call the condition of the "sun's drawing water," Jacob's ladder.

JACOB'S STAFF. See Cross Staff.

JAEGT, a Norwegian vessel of small tonnage rigged with one mast from which is set a square sail and topsail.

JALOUSIE FRAMING, a system of tongue and grooved sheathing by which light and air can enter a cabin.

JAMAICA DISCIPLINE, the articles governing (or supposed to govern) the routine of a pirate ship in the 18th century. By its terms the captain took two shares of booty, the officers one and a half and one and a quarter according to rank, while men shared alike. Quite unlooked for is an article forbidding gambling and also the bringing of women aboard ship. It was stipulated that the use of strong drink must be indulged in only on deck after 8 p.m. These rules were formulated to prevent quarrels aboard ship.

JAMIE GREEN, a sail set beneath the bowsprit and jib-boom of a tea clipper. The halyard hauled the sail to the end of the jib-boom and the tack to the lower end of the martingale boom.

JANGADA, a raft-like boat used in South America.

JAPAN CURRENT. The Kuroshio, the current of the Pacific corresponding to the Gulf Stream of the Atlantic.

JASON CLAUSE, a clause in the bill of lading which provides that the shippers, consignees or owners of the cargo shall contribute with the ship owner in General Average in the event of danger, damage or disaster resulting from any cause whatever (whether due to negligence or not) for which the shipowner is not responsible.

JAVA, Coffee.

JAW, the distance between two points on the same strand measured along a rope. If hard laid, bringing the strands close together, the rope is said to have a *short jaw;* if soft laid with the strands rather loosely twisted it has a *long jaw.*

JAW ROPE, the parral leading around the mast between the jaws of a gaff.

JAWS (of a Gaff or Boom), the horns that partly encircle the mast.

JAY HAWKING, using a tender to tow a sailboat in a calm.

JEERS (JEARS), a heavy tackle of double or treble blocks, called *jeer blocks,* used for hoisting heavy yards. A deck capstan used to heave in the fall (*jeer fall*) of this tackle is called the *jeer capstan.* A jeer was originally a hawser or heavy rope supporting the types of heavy yards.

JETSAM, goods thrown overboard to lighten a vessel. See Flotsam and Lagan.

JETTISON, to heave cargo overboard to lighten a vessel in peril.

JETTY, a breakwater built to protect a river mouth or harbor entrance or to divert or control the current.

JEWEL BLOCK, the stun'sail halyard block at a yardarm.

JEWS HARP, the shackle connecting the cable to the anchor, also called the *anchor ring.*

JIB, a triangular sail set forward of the foremast. It came into general use about the middle of the 18th century, displacing the square spritsail. The hoisting arm of a crane.

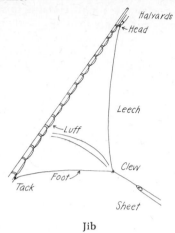

Halyards
Head
Leech
Luff
Clew
Foot
Tack
Sheet

Jib

JIB HANKS. See Hanks.

JIB O' JIB, a sail set as a jib topsail on the fore royal or fore-topgallant stay. It was primarily to overcome some of the weather helm due to the raking masts of a clipper ship.

JIB MARTINGALE, a length of wire rope that leads from the jib-boom to the dolphin striker to support the boom from beneath.

JIB NETTING, network rigged under the jib-boom and supported by the whisker booms. It serves to keep the jib from falling to the water and also as a guard to seamen when losing their footing.

JIBBER THE KIBBER, to lead ships ashore by false lights.

JIB-BOOM, a spar extending beyond the bowsprit. *Jib-boom guys* steady this spar at the sides.

JIBE or **GYBE,** to swing off before the wind, to the other tack, the boom shifting itself, sometimes violently.

JIB-HEADED RIG. A rig wherein all sails are triangular. Also known as marconi rig.

JIB-HEADED SAIL, a triangular sail, without a gaff; also called a marconi or Bermudian sail.

JIBSTAY, a stay leading forward from the foretopmast, in a square-rigged vessel, and from near the head of the foremost mast of a fore-and-aft rig; from it the jib is set.

JIB-TOPSAIL, a light jib set aloft in a similar manner to other head sails. It is hoisted on the outer of the head stays with its tack well up above the jib-boom instead of being fast to it.

JIGGER, a light luff tackle for various work about decks. A boom jigger is used to rig stun'sail booms in and out. In fore and aft rigged vessels, a jigger is sometimes used on the standing part of the throat and peak halyards. After the sail has been hoisted by these halyards, they are *swigged* or *sweated* up by the jiggers. Also, the sail set on the jiggermast.

JIGGERMAST, the small after mast of a yawl or ketch. This mast is called the mizzen. The fourth mast of a five- or six-masted schooner. Sometimes applied to the last mast in a so-called four-masted bark—the fore and aft rigged mast. Also called *jigger*.

JIMMY LEGS, the master at arms.

JIMMY THE ONE, a slang expression used in the Royal Navy to indicate the officer charged with the everyday running of the ship. Generally the First Lieutenant or Executive Officer.

JIMMY SQUAREFOOT, a mythical being at the sea bottom; *Davy Jones.*

JINGLE (BELL), an auxiliary bell used with a gong to signal the engineer from the pilot-house. It indicates the desire for full speed whether ahead or astern. See Engineroom bells.

JOE DECOSTE, a piece of sail spread in the weather fore rigging of a fishing schooner to serve as a lee for the lookout.

JOGGLING, the offsetting of the edges of plates of outer strakes to avoid the use of liners. *Joggled frames* are those whose outside faces are so cut as to receive the planks in such a way as to give the appearance of a clinker built boat.

JOHN or **JON BOAT,** a small pulling boat, adaptable for outboard; square at bow and stern. Used as a tender or for hunting and fishing.

JOLLY BOAT, a work boat carried by a merchantman, usually at the stern of a schooner. Also called a *yawl.*

JOLLY ROGER, the black flag of piracy. The word *roger* in the sixteenth century appears to have carried the meaning of a vagrant or thief, being possibly derived from rogue. The adjective *jolly* was applied by pirates for effect.

JUMBO, the fore staysail of a fore-and-after.

JUMBO BOOM, a heavy lift cargo boom, usually equipped with a 4-sheave tackle and capable of lifting some 30 tons.

JUMP SHIP, to leave without permission; to desert.

JUMPER STAY, a truss stay on the forward side of a mast. Sometimes applied to the spring stay of a schooner, and to the stay running from the funnel to foremast, or to a preventer stay set up with a tackle.

JUMPERS, chain stays leading from the outer end of jib-boom of a schooner to the lower end of the dolphin striker or martingale boom; short lengths of wire rope which lead down from the whisker booms to the lower end of the dolphin striker supporting the booms from beneath.

JUNK, discarded rope, blocks, and other gear. A Chinese or Japanese vessel; it is usually of lateen rig, with bat-wing sails of woven matting. The models of hulls are the result of experience running back for centuries of long voyages. They are very seaworthy craft. Salt meat that has become hard is called *salt junk.* The lower part of a sperm whale's forehead; the upper part being the *case* from which comes the valuable spermaceti.

JUPITER, the fifth planet from the sun.

JURY, a makeshift rig used to work a vessel to port. Probably from the French *jour*—for a day.

JURY ANCHOR, any heavy weight

to serve as an anchor in an emergency.

JURY MAST, a makeshift spar from which to set a sail after being dismasted.

JURY RIG, the expedient in the way of spars and sails resorted to by a master to bring a dismasted vessel to port.

JURY RUDDER, an improvised contrivance by which a disabled vessel is steered to port.

JUS ANGARIA, a belligerent's use of a neutral's ships, etc., by consent or force, through the necessity of war. The ship must be taken in the belligerent's harbors, not on high seas.

K

KAMCHATKA CURRENT, a branch of the Kuroshio which flows more northerly in the direction of the Aleutian islands.

KAPOK, a very buoyant vegetable substance resembling down. It is much lighter than cork and serves very satisfactorily as the filling for mattresses and pillows, life jackets and vests. It is raised mostly in Java.

KATABATIC WIND, cold air flowing down to a lower level by gravity due to greater weight. The wind down a glacier and that down a mountain valley are katabatic winds. The bora of the Adriatic is an excellent example of this type.

KAYAK, an Eskimo canoe constructed with a covering of seal skin.

KECKLING, chafing gear on a cable, consisting of old rope.

KEDGE, a light anchor for kedging or warping.

KEDGING, moving a vessel by heaving in on a *kedge* rope or warp fast to a *kedge anchor* that has been carried out to a desired position by a small boat. The term is sometimes used when a vessel desires to drift with the current but keeps her anchor just touching the bottom. This is also called *clubbing,* and *dredging.*

KEEL, the backbone of a vessel, from which rise the frames or ribs,

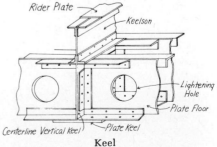

Keel

stem and sternpost. The *flat keel plate* is a plate serving as a keel. A flat-bottomed barge for the conveyance of coal in the British Isles. A barge load of coal is called a keel.

KEEL BLOCKS, those forming the foundation upon which the keel is laid in building. Also the blocks upon which a vessel rests in dry dock.

KEELEK, a small kedge.

KEEL-HAUL, a punishment in which a man was hauled down one side of a vessel under the keel and up the other side. This was accomplished by weighting the man's body and using whips from port and starboard yardarms.

KEELSON, a timber or steel stringer bolted on the keel in the hold for reenforcement. An *intercostal keelson* fits between the floors and is not a continuous stringer.

KEELSON KEY, TO FIND THE, a fool's errand upon which a green hand is dispatched to furnish amusement for the rest of the crew.

KEEP AWAY, to give weather helm and fall off from the wind.

KEEP HER FULL, to keep sails drawing.

KEEP THE LAND, to remain in sight of shore.

KEEP OFF. See Keep Away.

KEEP YOUR LUFF, an order to the man at the wheel to keep close to the wind when full and by.

KELDS, smooth patches in the midst of ruffled water.

KELP, marine growth that accumulates on rocks. It is valuable for fertilizer and the manufacture of iodine. It is also a warning of rocks beneath.

KELPIE, a sea spirit haunting the northern British Islands.

KENTLEDGE, ballast along the keelson in the form of pigs.

KENTLEDGE GOODS, heavy pieces of cargo that, stowed low, will contribute to stability.

KEPLER'S LAWS. The eminent astronomer, Kepler, born in Württemberg in the year 1571, determined the true laws governing the motions of the planets around the sun. The *three laws* which he discovered are:

First. The orbit of each planet is an ellipse having the sun in one focus.

Second. As the planet moves around the sun its radius-vector, or line joining it to the sun, passes over equal areas in equal times.

Third. The square of the time of revolution of each planet is proportional to the cube of its mean distance from the sun. (Patterson.)

KETCH, a two-masted vessel similar to a yawl but with the jiggermast or mizzen stepped forward of the rudderpost instead of abaft it. The original ketch was known as a *bomb ketch;* its rig comprised a large, lofty, square-rigged mast stepped well aft, leaving a wide clear forward deck: it carried a comparatively small jigger. The term *ketch* has had many applications, since the bomb ketch. The Dutch originated a type with three masts—gaff at the mizzen, sprit mainsail, square-rigged at the fore with head sails. The sprit gave way in time to a loose-footed mainsail fitted with brails, and the square-rigged foremast at length disappeared. Ketches with the after mast raking forward were common on the coast of England, especially the North Sea side, and called *Billy Boys*.

KETTLE BOTTOM, a flat-floored vessel.

KEVEL, another name for cavil. The *Kevel-heads* are timber heads used as a cleat.

KEYING RING, a lead ring that is driven around a forelock pin in an anchor shackle to key it in place.

KHAMSIN, a hot wind of Egypt usually from a tropical cyclonic disturbance.

KI YI (phonetic vernacular), a scrubbing brush made of stiff coir bristles used on board ship. A sailor's corruption of coir.

KICK, the throw of a vessel's stern to leeward (or toward the side the helm is thrown), when the helm is put hard over.

KID, a tub or pan in which the forecastle rations are carried.

KIESELGUHR, the sediment, usually white, on the sea bottom composed of the skeletons of diatoms.

KILLICK, a small grapnel. A stone adapted to serve as an anchor.

KILLICK HITCH, a timber hitch with a half hitch added.

KING BRIDGE, the truss extending athwartships between the heads of a pair of king posts forming a solid unit of support for cargo booms.

KING POST, a facility of cargo handling. It is a derrick-mast to support cargo booms. They stand athwartship, in pairs, port and starboard. When heavier drafts of cargo are expected in a steamer's trade the heads of the king posts are connected across the deck by a span which may be of plain steel or latticework. The span is known by various names: crosstrees, trestletrees, truss, king post spanner, king bridge and goal posts. Masts are often stepped in these spans.

KINGSTON VALVE, an outboard valve seated in a casting which is fastened to the inside of the bottom of a ship.

KINK, a twist which disturbs the lay of a rope.

KITE DRAG, a sea anchor made of crossed spars carrying a piece of canvas across them to act as a drag.

KITES, all light sails, such as jib topsails, stun'sails, skysails, spinnakers and light staysails.

KITTIWAKE, a sea bird differing but little from offshore gulls. It is about fifteen inches long, has a mantle of dark pearl gray with head, neck, tail and under parts white; it is black tipped on the wings. This bird inhabits the higher latitudes.

KNEES, right angled strengthening and supporting pieces of natural growth, if of wood, with arms. They fit at the intersection of timbers and strengthen the joint. They take different names according to their particular position, as *Lodging knee,* one that lies horizontal at the forward side of a beam and at the side of a ship. A *bosom knee* does the same duty at the after side of the beam. A *hanging knee* fits under a beam in a vertical position; if not vertical it becomes a *dagger knee.* A *carling knee* fills the right angle between a carling or ledge and a beam, while a *stern knee* is set at the intersection of the keel and stern post.

KNIGHT HEADS, two timbers rising inside and from each side of the stem; the bowsprit heels between them. The knighthead *frames* are the foremost frames in a vessel carrying a bowsprit.

KNITTLES, a kind of reef points. Yarns twisted together for pointing a rope or for seizings. They are also called *Nettles.* See Hammock.

KNOCK OFF, to stop work.

KNOCKABOUT, a sloop or schooner without a bowsprit and whose jib sets from a stay on the stem.

KNOCKED DOWN, to be thrown on the beam-ends by a sudden squall.

KNOT, strictly, a tucking of strands in such a way as to form an ornamental or useful enlargement of a rope. A man-rope knot is a good example. Combinations of turns and tucks in the manipulation of rope are roughly divided into three classes—knots, bends and hitches, and splices. This classification is not strictly adhered to even by seamen.

KNOT, a measure of speed, not one of distance. The term *knots* means velocity in nautical miles per hour whether of a vessel or a current. It is the measurement of a section of a log line being 47 feet and 3 inches. See Chip Log. (A nautical mile = 6,076.1 feet.) However, in navigation 6000 feet and 2000 yards are usually used.

KNUCKLE LINE, the line where the stern plating takes a sharp angle upward near the taffrail.

KNUCKLE MAST, is so hinged near the deck as to allow laying down with truck aft to allow passing under bridges.

KOFF, a two-masted vessel with sails of the sprit type, seen in the Baltic and North seas; it is of shallow draft and is especially adapted for use on the inland waterways.

KONA WINDS, storms or southerly winds over the Hawaiian Islands.

KUROSHIO, the Gulf Stream of the Pacific. It flows northeastward along the eastern coast of Japan, and its warm waters affect beneficially the climate of Southern Alaska, Canada and the American Pacific coast. It is also known as the *Japan* or *Black Stream.*

L

L's OF NAVIGATION, lead, log and lookout.

LABOR, the heavy working of a vessel in a seaway; the motion being irregular and severe, occasioned by a confused sea or by unstable stowage conditions.

LABRADOR CURRENT. See Arctic Current.

LACING, the small rope used in lashing a sail to a gaff or boom.

LADDER, a general term applied to all accommodations by which one proceeds below or on deck. They take obvious names, such as *mast ladder, bridge ladder, poop ladder,* etc., and there are also the Jacob's Ladder, Sea Ladder and Accommodation Ladder.

LAG, delay: lost motion.

LAG SCREW, a heavy wood screw, driven by a square head.

LAGAN, any heavy article thrown overboard and buoyed. (Also spelled ligan and logan.) See Flotsam, Jetsam.

LAGGING. See Priming and Lagging.

LAID UP, to be out of use at a pier.

LAKE TYPE STEAMER, one with engines located aft. Called stemwinders by sailors.

LAND BREEZE, an evening wind coming off the land as it cools to a point below the temperature of the sea. It is this wind that carries the odor of the land far off-shore towards morning.

LAND EFFECT, the deviation of a radio bearing due to passing over tangent to intervening land.

LAND ICE, that attached to the shore.

LANDFALL, a sighting of or coming to land; the position of the land first sighted in coming in from the sea. Sailing ships from Good Hope used to steer to sight St. Helena to check position, that is, make a landfall.

LANDING STRAKE, that just below the sheer strake, the second below the gunwale.

LANDMARK, a conspicuous object or characteristic formation of land whose position is known and which aids the mariner in establishing his position.

LANDSMAN, a man on shipboard with no experience in sea-going.

LANG-LAY-ROPE, a type of wire rope with which the individual wires are twisted the same way as the strands which comprise the rope. The individual wires of regular lay are twisted opposite to the turn of the strands.

LANYARD HITCH, is used in many ways and got its name through its universal use in making fast the hauling part of the lanyard running through the deadeyes of a shroud. The two parts pass through the bight in the same direction, while they pass in opposite direction in a clove hitch.

LANYARDS, the ropes that reeve through the deadeyes and set up the rigging—four-stranded tarred hemp. A rope used for making anything fast. An ornamental braid or plait around the neck of a sailor to secure his knife. A *lanyard knot* is made in the end of a lanyard to prevent its unreeving through a deadeye.

Lanyard

LAP, the overlap of two plates.

LAPSTRAKE or **LAPSTREAK,** a way of planking a boat where the lower edge of one plank overlaps the top of the next below it. See Clinker.

LARBOARD, formerly the port side, and *larbowlines* were the men comprising the larboard watch.

LARGE, a vessel with sheets well eased off is said to be *sailing large*. *By and large* the wide range from *by the wind* to *sailing free* or *large*.

LARK'S HEAD, a hitch used for making fast a line to a spar or ring

bolt. A piece of wood locks it and prevents jamming. It is merely a lanyard hitch through a ring or spar.

LASCAR, an East Indian sailor extensively employed on British vessels.

LASH, to secure by binding closely with rope or small stuff.

LASH AND CARRY, an order to lash the hammocks and stow them in the nettings.

"LASH" SYSTEM, a modern method of expediting the loading, transportation and discharging of cargoes. The ship is of novel design, receiving loaded lighters which are taken aboard through her unconventional stern and stowed compactly in the hull. At the port of discharge the process is reversed. The loaded lighters float out and are taken by tugs to their discharging berths. It is not necessary for the ship to dock, the operation being carried out at anchor. There is a variation of this system called a *SEABEE*.

LASH-UP. A derisive term for a job badly done.

LASHING, the rope used in lashing an eye to a spar, a spar to another, and so on.

LASHING EYES, the loops in the ends of two ropes through which is passed the lashing securing them together. An example is seen in the eyes in the ends of the double fore stays that are lashed abaft the foremast head.

LASKETS, small loops of cord used in lacing the bonnet to the jib. Also called the *latchings*.

LASKING, to sail large, or with wind about a point abaft the beam.

LATCHING KEY, the loop which runs through the laskets and keys them, preventing their unreeving.

LATCHINGS, the beckets in the bonnet of a jib to facilitate lacing it to the foot of the sail.

LATEEN, a triangular sail set from a yard that lies obliquely with the mast. It is a picturesque and ancient rig native to, and characteristic of, the Mediterranean Sea.

LATITUDE, the distance in degrees, minutes and seconds of a ship's position or location of a port north or south of the equator. A minute of latitude is equal to a nautical mile.

LATITUDE BY ACCOUNT, the latitude by dead reckoning.

LATITUDE FACTOR, the change in latitude from a given point in a position line that would be brought about by a change of 1′ in longitude.

LATTICE BOOM, a cargo boom built of structural steel, for lifting heavy weights.

LAUNCH, a small boat with power, sail or oars. To set anything desired afloat. To slide a vessel down the *launching ways*; an operation in which a vessel rests on the *sliding ways* and slides over the *ground ways*. A vessel may be launched end to the water, sideways, diagonally or by filling the dry dock in which she was built.

LAWS OF STORMS. In northern latitudes, the cyclonic storms move bodily along a track which follows a right-hand curve. In the case of a West India hurricane, it forms usually in or eastward of the West Indian Islands and proceeds to the northwestward, turning to the right as it approaches the American continent, which shoulders it off to the northeastward, passing off Cape Hatteras and the Grand Banks. Oftentimes, however, it moves westward over the Gulf of Mexico and sweeps the Gulf Coast. The observer facing along the track as the storm goes has the right semi-circle on the right hand and the left semi-circle on the left hand. The mariner can determine which semi-circle his ship is in by observing the changing direction of the wind, which, if in the right semi-circle, changes to the right, if in the left semi-circle, to the left. No change in the wind indicates a position on the storm track. The right hand semi-circle is considered the dangerous one in the northern hemisphere. The rotary motion of the moving air is counterclockwise in this hemisphere. The center of agitation is situated eight to ten points on the right hand when one faces the wind. If in the right semi-circle, heave to on the starboard track, or if there is considered sufficient time to pass ahead of the storm, put wind on the starboard quarter and run to the left semi-circle.

The right semi-circle is dangerous because the center is curving towards the ship. If in the left semi-circle, heave to on the port tack, or run with wind on starboard quarter. The barometer indicates by its fall or rise the approach or departure of the storm center. The conditions found in cyclonic storms of the northern hemisphere are reversed in the southern hemisphere.

LAY (verb). To *lay to*, or better (lie-to), is to heave to. There is a shade of difference recognized by some seamen, that *heave to* implies heavy stress of weather or the action following a shot across the bows while *lay to* is slightly less imperative, as lying to for a pilot, lying to, to receive a salute or awaiting a clear berth. *Lay aft* or *forward* is an order to proceed in the indicated direction. *Lay out* is to go out on a yard arm or bowsprit. *Lay on your oars* is to stop pulling. To *lay down* a boat or vessel is to draw the curves of her lines on a floor. To *lay up a vessel* is to tie her up and allow her to remain idle. A sailing vessel *lays her course* if when close hauled she is able to make her objective point. A vessel lies at anchor. Old gunners who hit the marks knew how to *lay* their guns.

LAY (noun), the twisting of a rope's strands. The rope may be soft, medium or hard laid, right-handed, left-handed or hawser laid which is a combination of both right- and left-handed lay. A share of a fishing or whaling voyage. For instance, a green hand on a whaler gets (or got) $\frac{1}{175}$ lay or one barrel of oil in one hundred and seventy-five.

LAY BY, usually a row of piles or dolphins to which a vessel ties up as steamers in Suez do to allow other ships in opposite direction to pass.

LAY DAYS, allotted days for the discharging or loading of a vessel; after which demurrage is to be paid. In agreeing on lay days, *running days* are every day; otherwise Sundays and holidays are not lay days. In some ports there will be found a remarkable number of holidays.

LAZARETTE (Lazaretto), a compartment for storage purposes in the stern of the ship; an isolation hospital for patients with contagious diseases from vessels in quarantine.

LAZY GUY, a piece of gear to steady a boom when rolling heavily and to prevent gybing.

LAZY JACKS, small ropes leading down vertically from the topping-lifts to the boom to hold a fore and aft sail when taking it in. In large schooners they are simply called *jacks*. The lee topping-lift is slacked as the sail is lowered, throwing it into the slackened jacks to leeward, then by carrying the topping-lift fall to a winch, the whole sail is rolled neatly on the boom.

LEACH. See Leech.

LEAD LINE. See Leads.

LEADER, a fairlead.

LEADING BLOCK, one used as a fairlead and having an arrangement which opens the block and allows the bight of a line to be inserted. This is also called a *snatch block*.

LEADING PART, the hauling part of a tackle after leading through a snatch block.

LEADING WIND, a free wind; one that blows from aft.

LEADS. There are two types of lead—the hand lead and the deep-sea (pronounced dipsey) lead. The former is used in shallow water and weighs either 7 or 14 lbs., the latter 50 to 100 lbs. The line attached is marked (when wet) as follows:

2 fathoms from the lead, with 2 strips of leather.

3 fathoms from the lead, with 3 strips of leather.

5 fathoms from the lead, with a white rag.

7 fathoms from the lead, with a red rag.

10 fathoms from the lead, with leather having a hole in it.

13 fathoms from the lead, same as 3 fathoms (Sometimes blue cloth.)

15 fathoms from the lead, same as 5 fathoms.

17 fathoms from the lead, same as 7 fathoms.

20 fathoms from the lead, with 2 knots.

25 fathoms from the lead, with 1 knot.

30 fathoms from the lead, with 3 knots.

35 fathoms from the lead, with 1 knot.

40 fathoms from the lead, with 4 knots.

And so on.

LEAGUE, a measurement of distance which varies in different countries from 2.4 to 4.6 statute miles. The English and American marine league is equal to three nautical miles.

LEAK, a hole or crack which allows water to enter a vessel.

LEAK STOPPER, a cellulose stopper designed to be inserted in a hole from inboard, which then expands and prevents the entrance of water.

LEAPFROGGING, landing an amphibious force in the enemy's rear. It was practiced in the Pacific in World War II by taking islands in the Japanese rear.

LEDGE, one or a number of rocks upon which the depth is less than the surrounding soundings and dangerous to navigation. A piece of timber placed thwartships between the beams.

LEE BOARD, a device similar in principle to a centerboard but used on the lee side of a vessel. Also a board placed on the lee side of a weather bunk to keep the occupant from falling out.

LEE BOWING A TIDE, the advantageous situation of having the current setting against the lee bow.

LEE HELM, when the position of the helm necessary to keep a vessel on her course is towards the lee side. This is not as desirable as weather helm.

LEE HO, a command given by English yachtsmen preparatory to bringing a boat about; same as *hard-a-lee.*

LEE SHORE, a coast that lies under a vessel's lee.

LEE SIDE, away from the direction of the wind.

LEE TIDE, one running with the wind.

LEE WHEELMAN, one who stands on lee side of wheel and assists the weather wheelman. The latter is the senior and is responsible for the course steered.

LEECH or **LEACH,** the after side of a fore and aft sail and the outer sides of a square sail. A *leech rope* is the roping of a leech and a *leech line* leads from a square sail's leech up to the yard through a block, thence to deck. Its purpose is to get the leech up to the yard.

LEEWARD, towards the lee. Pronounced, *looward* or *lu'ard.*

LEEWARD SQUALL, one met with on the lee side of the islands of the South Pacific which changes direction and often takes vessels aback.

LEEWAY, the amount a vessel is carried to leeward by force of the wind.

LEFT HAND SCREW, a propeller which turns in the upper half of its revolution from starboard to port when viewed from aft.

LEFT RUDDER, formerly starboard helm. The rudder takes an angle to the left of the keel causing the vessel to change course to the left.

LEG, a tack. In working to windward a vessel may, if her port is not directly to windward, sail a *long leg and a short leg.* One part of a bridle is called a leg. A voyage from New York to Rio Janeiro, thence to London and home, has three legs. A vessel is said to be long-legged when built with a long deep keel.

LEG OF MUTTON, a small boat rig. The sail is triangular, one corner hoisting.

LEMURIA, the lost continent of the Pacific Ocean.

LENGTH, AMERICAN BUREAU OF SHIPPING RULES, the distance from the forward side of stem to the after side of the rudder post along the summer load line. If there is no rudder post measurement is taken from the center of the rudder stock.

LENGTH BETWEEN PERPENDICU-LARS, the distance measured from the fore part of the stem to the after part of the sternpost.

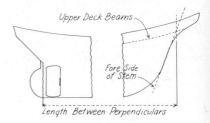

Upper Deck Beams

Fore Side of Stem

Length Between Perpendiculars

LENGTH FLOODABLE. See Floodable Length.

LENGTH OVER ALL, the distance from the foremost part of the stem to the aftermost part of the stern.

LENGTH REGISTERED, the distance from the fore part of stem to the after side of head of the sternpost.

LENGTH TONNAGE, the distance measured along the tonnage deck from inside the inner plate at the bow to the inside inner plate at the stern, making an allowance for rake of the bow and stern.

LEO, the fifth sign of the zodiac.

LESTE, a hot dry wind of Madeira.

LET FALL, an order to a man on a yard standing ready to loose sail. When oars have been tossed preparatory to getting underway, the order *let fall* is given.

LET GO AND HAUL, an order in tacking ship. It is given when past the wind and the after sails have filled. The order is to let go the then weather fore braces and haul the lee braces, filling the forward sails which were aback.

LET GO BY THE RUN, to cast gear off the pins and allow it to run out without control.

LETTER OF MARQUE, a commission given by a government granting a vessel authority to fight off or attack an enemy's commerce or privateers, primarily to get her cargo through. While a letter of marque is (or was) a privateer there is a distinction in that she carried cargo while the privateer's main object was to prey on enemy commerce. The vessel herself was referred to as a letter of marque.

LEVANTER, a strong northeasterly wind of the Mediterranean also called the Meltem and the Euroclydon.

LEVECHE, a hot dusty wind in Spain.

LEVEE, an embankment built along a river to withhold its waters from the adjacent land.

LEVEL, an instrument consisting of a telescope fitted with cross hairs and set on a tripod with leveling glasses to preserve a horizontal position. By the use of a graduated leveling rod, the difference in elevation of surrounding points can readily be determined. This instrument is used in marine surveying.

LIBERTY, leave for a ship's personnel to go ashore for a designated period. A restricted seaman inspecting the port with a spy glass was said to be enjoying fourth-class liberty.

LIBRA, the seventh sign of the zodiac.

LICENSE, a certificate of competency issued by the United States Coast Guard which allows a ship's officer to act in a capacity according to his ability and experience. Yachts usually sail under a document called a license issued by custom authorities.

LIE-TO. See Heave-To.

LIFE CAR, a tank-like vessel designed to haul shipwrecked people through the surf from a stranded vessel.

LIFE LINES, lines stretched fore and aft along the decks to give the crew safety against being washed overboard. Also lines carried along a yard or boom for safety.

LIFE PRESERVER, a buoyant device which comes in many forms; life belts, vests, coats, mattresses and pillows. They are all filled with buoyant material, commonly cork or kapok. The legal life preserver must support a weight of twenty pounds for twenty-four hours.

LIFE RAFT, a contrivance depending for buoyancy upon cylindrical air chambers or balsa wood, which support a thwartship structure. A modern type is elliptical with netting within it. It is carried on deck in such a way as to float when the vessel sinks or at least be easily cut adrift.

LIFE SAVING STATION, a building on the coast which houses a life saving crew, lifeboat, line carrying guns, etc. Such stations are indicated on charts. These stations are now called Coast-Guard Stations. Some are being replaced by modern systems, such as radio and air patrols.

LIFEBOAT, one especially designed for heavy weather, such as is used by the Coast Guard. Lifeboats of various designs are carried by law on the decks of all steamers, sufficient in capacity to accommodate all persons on board. A lifeboat has a watertight compartment or tank in the bow and stern and must be equipped with the following articles: rowlocks, life preservers, mast and sail, oar, boat hook, hatchets, bucket, breadbox, bailer, compass, container, lantern, ditty bag, one gallon oil, distress signals, sea anchor, matches, flashlight and container, drinking cups, pistol and cartridge, water breaker, flare, Gibson Girl, shark repellent and dye marker.

LIFEBOAT CERTIFICATE, a paper certifying to a man's ability to pull an oar, lower, and properly equip a lifeboat.

LIFEBUOY, usually a canvas-covered ring, filled with air, gas, cork or kapok. A gold star on a lifebuoy signifies it has saved a life. Horseshoe-shaped lifebuoys are now preferred by yachtsman.

LIFT. The weather or a fog is said to *lift* when it clears.

LIFT BOLT, the bolt at a yardarm to which the lift is made fast, and the bolt in a boom to which the topping-lift is attached.

LIFTS, pieces of wire rope leading from a position near the cap of a mast, or other convenient position, down to the ends of the yardarms. They support the weight of a yard.

LIGAN. See Lagan.

LIGHT, to lift anything along, as a sail to windward when reefing topsails on a square-rigger. To be without cargo and floating high out of water. A lighthouse or other illuminated aid to navigation.

LIGHT BUOY, one equipped with a lighting apparatus for the guidance of mariners.

LIGHT DUES, charges for the use of lights in navigating a coast which is used to defray the cost of maintenance.

LIGHT LOAD LINE, the waterline of a vessel with no cargo aboard.

LIGHT SAILS, skysails, royals, light staysails, studding-sails, flying jibs, spinnakers, balloon jibs, balloon staysails, mizzen staysails, etc.

LIGHTEN, to ease off as in *lightening* the head sheets. Or to jettison cargo to lighten a vessel.

LIGHTENING HOLES, holes cut mostly in the floors to reduce weight.

LIGHTER, a small vessel used for discharging or loading vessels anchored in the stream or open roadstead.

LIGHTERAGE, a charge for the use of lighters.

LIGHTHOUSE, a tower displaying a brilliant light, erected at a danger point to guide mariners.

LIGHTSHIP, a vessel moored off a harbor, danger or point of navigational advantage, equipped with lights, fog signals and usually radio and submarine signal apparatus. They are gradually being replaced by modern aids, established on "Texas" towers, improved nearby lights ashore and large powerful lighted buoys. In a few years in United States continental waters only Nantucket Lightship and a few others on the Pacific coast will remain.

LILLY IRON, a small harpoon used principally in the capture of swordfish. Its length is increased by setting it on a metal and wood pole which is withdrawn when fast in the fish. There are two lines attached when thrown, one to the pole and one to the iron.

LIMB, SUN'S UPPER or **LOWER,** the sun's upper or lower edge relative to the horizon directly beneath it. The lower edge of the sun is usually brought down to the horizon with the sextant in order to ascertain the altitude, but if cloud, or even an eclipse, should obscure it the upper edge is used. As the altitude desired is of the center of the sun, the semi-diameter must be added if the lower limb is used. The nautical almanac carries the correction required.

LIMBER BOARDS, removable boards over the limbers. The *limber strake* is the plank of the flooring next to the keelson. The *limbers* are holes in the lower part of the frames which allow bilge water to run aft to the bilge pump. A small chain called a *limber chain* passes through these holes, which when pulled occasionally clears any accumulated refuse.

LIME JUICER, a nickname for a British sailor and a British vessel. The British law requires a ration of lime juice, hence the name, but other countries now have similar requirements, the object being to prevent the development of survy.

LIMEY, same as lime juicer.

LINCH PIN, a forelock pin; any pin which passes through a shaft to secure a pulley in position.

LINE, a term applied by sailors to the Equator. A general term for a piece of rope in use, such as clewline, buntline, the lines which make a ship fast, etc. In general, use of the word *rope* is avoided aboard ship, and nearly all ropes are lines.

LINE OF BATTLE SHIP. Also and more commonly called a Ship of the Line. They mounted 74 guns or more.

LINE CARRYING GUN, a small cannon carried by all American steamers for the purpose of shooting a line to another vessel or to the beach if stranded. There should be three projectiles aboard with powder, primers, shot line, etc. It should be fired once a month and the fact entered in the log book.

LINE HONOURS, an Australian term for being the first yacht to finish an ocean race.

LINE OF NO VARIATION (agonic), a line on a chart along which there is no magnetic variation of the compass. It is usually indicated by a plain line paralleled very closely by a line of dots.

LINE OF NODES, the line drawn between the moon's nodes, which correspond to the equinoxes of the earth's orbit.

LINE OF POSITION, a Sumner line. It is a line established by one of several methods, and upon which the ship is somewhere located. Practically all navigation is worked by use of position lines derived from tables. This term also applies to a bearing taken of some known landmark which if drawn on a chart indicates a line upon which the ship is somewhere located.

LINE SQUALL, one caused by a wedge of low pressure passing over an area with a wake of high pressure rolling up in its rear, accompanied by a squall whose strength depends upon the steepness of its gradients. There is a veering wind and a drop in temperature. A dark cloud in a long line or arched in form characterizes the line squall.

LINE STORM, one occurring when the sun is near the equator in September or March; an equinoctial storm.

LINER, a flat or tapered strip placed under a plate or other part to bring it in line or flush with another part that it overlaps. A liner is placed over a vessel's frames under the overlapping plates. A steamer employed on a regular route, usually applied to fast express and passenger vessels.

LINES, ropes used for various purposes such as clewlines, buntlines, leechlines, spilling lines, etc. The fasts which hold vessels to a wharf are particularly called the *lines*.

LINES OF A VESSEL, drawings comprising three separate plans, depending one upon the other, which must correspond in all particulars and be used in conjunction. These three plans are known as the sheer plan, body plan, and half-breadth plan. The first shows the outline of the longitudinal vertical section; the second the vertical cross-sections, and the third the longitudinal transverse section of the vessel at the deckline, the waterline, and at other stations on the same plane as the waterline. In steel ships the lines show the outer surface of frames, while in wooden vessels they represent the outer side of the planking.

LINESMEN, men on a pier to take lines.

LINING CLOTH, strips of canvas sewed to a sail to take the chafe.

LIPPER, a small sea coming over the rail.

LIQUID COMPASS, one in which the card floats in a solution of 45 per cent alcohol and 55 per cent distilled water.

LIST, the learning of a vessel due to a greater weight upon one side.

LITTLE BROTHER, a secondary hurricane following a main disturbance.

LITTORAL, the coastline of a country.

LIVE LOAD, a moving load, as the

swinging of cargo from ship to dock, or the traffic on a bridge.

LIVERPOOL, SEE YOU IN, used to be a sailor's goodby to a shipmate. It is supposed to have been derived from the belief that all seamen would sooner or later meet again in Liverpool.

LIVERPOOL BRIDLE, a salvage device sometimes used when a vessel is stranded broadside. It consists of two heavy wires from a tug, one to the bow, the other to the stern of the vessel. The tug by putting a stress on the hawsers alternately can be very effective in working a vessel afloat.

LIVERPOOL HEAD, a device on the top of the galley smoke pipe comprising two drums one inside the other with staggered openings so as to prevent the entrance of water.

LIVERPOOL PENNANTS, ropeyarns used instead of buttons. Quoted from "The Bird of Dawning."

LIZARD, a piece of rope with a thimble or a bull's eye spliced into one end. It is a fairlead.

LLOYD'S, an English association of underwriters. It is a great and ancient organization for the collection and distribution of maritime intelligence. It is the leading authority on classifying vessels according to their strength and efficiency for carrying cargoes, and its specifications are quite generally followed the world over.

LLOYD'S BREADTH, the greatest moulded width, that is, to the outside of frames but not the outside plating.

LLOYD'S DEPTH, the moulded depth plus the camber of the deck.

LLOYD'S INDEX, a list of merchant vessels giving particulars of each.

LLOYD'S LENGTH, the distance measured from the after side of stem to the fore side of sternpost.

LLOYD'S LIST, a daily publication of shipping news issued with the authority of the corporation.

LLOYD'S REGISTER OF CAPTAINS, a record of the licensed masters of the British merchant marine, giving details of service, ability and character.

LLOYD'S REGISTER OF YACHTS. There are two volumes, one for American and Canadian yachts and the other for British and those of other countries.

LOAD WATER PLANE, the water plane at which a vessel floats with full cargo aboard.

LOAD WATERLINE, established by law and shown by the Plimsoll Mark.

LOBSCOUSE, a hash made of seabiscuit, onions, potatoes, sometimes with meat added. Usually called Scouse.

LOBSTER CAR, a float in which live lobsters are kept until shipment. A *lobster pound* is a pen in which lobsters are turned loose to live, shed and grow until ready to sell.

LOCAL APPARENT TIME (L. A. T.), an hour angle of the apparent sun measured westward from the ship's meridian.

LOCAL ATTRACTION, magnetic influence outside the ship which causes a deflection of the compass needle. It is caused by beds of magnetic ore lying beneath the water or in high land near the water, or by steel-framed buildings. It is seldom of serious consequence except when very close to the land as the vessel quickly passes out of its influence. A sunken vessel may have an influence on passing vessels.

LOCAL MEAN TIME (L. M. T.), the hour angle of the mean sum measured westward from the local meridian.

LOCAL TRANSIT, the term applied to the passage of a body across the observer's meridian.

LOCH, a lake or inlet in the northern British Isles.

LOCK, a compartment resembling a dock fitted with gates at each end. A vessel enters the down end, the gate is closed and the lock is flooded to a higher level by the natural downward flow. The upper gate is opened and the vessel proceeds along the new level, some feet higher than before. In going down, the operation is reversed.

LOCKER, a small stowage space either in the form of a chest or a closet. There is aboard every ship a *paint locker, boatswain's locker* and two *chain lockers.*

LOCKING BARS, are used to secure a cargo hatch for sea. They consist of strips of flat iron and are placed across the tarpaulins of a hatch. The ends are curved to hook under the top of the coaming.

They are in pairs and bolt together in the center of the hatch. When a hatch is bonded the custom seal is placed on the bolt of the locking bars.

LODGING KNEES. See Knees.

LOG. To log a seaman is to deduct pay from wages as a punishment. The fact with circumstances must be entered in the log book in the presence of seamen and witnesses. There are patent logs, harpoon and chip logs, for determining distance run.

LOG BOOK, a record of all the activities aboard a ship, her movements and a record of all meteorological conditions. There are *rough, smooth, official,* and *abstract* log books. The official log book is a record of the crew, punishments, sicknesses, deaths, desertions, etc., and the circumstances of each. At the end of a voyage this book is forwarded to the government. The abstract log book is a synopsis of the voyage. The mate prepares the smooth from the rough log and submits it to the master for his signature. Also called *log.*

LOG GLASS, an "hour" glass with an interval of 14 or 28 seconds.

LOG LINE, the line of hard-laid woven or braided rope which tows the patent log. See Chip Log.

LOG RAFT, principally constructed on the Pacific coast for the transportation of lumber logs. They are about 1,000 feet long with logs 4 to 6 feet in diameter and 40 to 50 feet long.

LOG SHIP, another name, not now used, for the chip log.

LOGARITHMS (Logs), auxiliary numbers used to facilitate mathematical calculations. By adding them, the process of multiplication is accomplished, and by subtracting, a long division is avoided. The logarithm of any number is the exponent of a power to which 10 must be raised to give the number: For instance, 2 is the logarithm of 100 because $10^2 = 100$; 3 is the logarithm of 1,000 because $10^3 = 1,000$.

LOGGED, a term meaning that a record has been put in the log book. When a seaman's wages are docked, he is said to be *logged*. A vessel is said to have *logged* twelve knots.

LOGGER-HEAD, the bitt in the stern of a whale boat with which the harpoon line is controlled with several turns. The harpooner forward heaves his harpoon and the line leads aft between the oarsmen to the officer in the stern who handles the turns around the loggerhead. A sea turtle common along the Florida Keys.

LOLLEY NEEDLE, a short spur or roping needle.

LOLLY, ice broken into small pieces with slush between, easily navigated.

LONG BOARD, a long tack or leg.

LONG BOAT, a large boat carried by sailing vessels. It is the lifeboat and is usually kept fully equipped for use if the ship is abandoned.

LONG LEG AND A SHORT ONE. If the point of destination is not directly to windward of a sailing vessel she will sail a long and a short tack in attaining it.

LONG-LEGGED. A vessel with a long deep keel.

LONG SCOPE, ordinarily with ninety or more fathoms of chain out on an anchor. If in shoal water and anchored with a disproportionate amount of chain to the depth. About three fathoms of chain to a fathom of depth with good holding ground and moderate weather is customary, but a long scope is veered in heavy weather in an exposed anchorage.

LONG SEA, where the crests are far apart.

LONG SHIP, a designation given to those ancient vessels of relatively narrow beam for their length; they were propelled by sails and oars. The galley was a long ship whose length was perhaps six or seven times the beam. The phrase, "This is a long ship," means that it is time for a drink.

LONG SPLICE, joining the ends of two ropes in such a manner that the splice does not enlarge the rope and it will pass freely through a block.

LONGER, a fore and aft row of casks end to end.

LONGITUDE, the distance in degrees, minutes and seconds of a ship's position or a port east or west from the meridian of Greenwich (0°) through 180°.

LONGITUDE BY ACCOUNT, longitude by dead reckoning.

LONGITUDE FACTOR, the change in longitude from a given point in a position line that would be brought about by a change of 1′ in latitude.

LONGITUDINAL, a part of the structure of a ship running fore and aft through the double bottom. As a rule, they are intercostal in merchant ships.

LONGITUDINAL BULKHEAD, one running fore and aft.

LONGITUDINAL FRAMING, the structural parts of a vessel that run in a fore and aft direction.

'LONGSHOREMAN, a laborer who works loading and discharging cargo.

LOOF, that part of a vessel where the beam begins to come in towards the stern.

LOOKOUT, a seaman assigned to the forecastle, on the bridge or aloft, to search the sea ahead and report any vessel or obstruction sighted.

LOOM, the part of an oar that is in the boat when rowing, by some called the part from blade to handle. It is also a form of mirage in which the land is raised by refraction. The loom of a light is the reflection on the clouds when the light itself is below the horizon.

LOOM-GALE, a moderate gale.

LOOSE, to let go; to cast the gaskets or stops from a furled sail.

LOOSE-FOOTED, a fore and aft sail not laced to (or without) a boom.

LORAN, an electronic system of finding a ship's position. The operation of Loran involves measuring, to a microsecond (millionth of a second), the time interval between the reception of short pulses transmitted from pairs of radio stations on shore. One transmitter of a Loran pair emits a number of uniformly spaced pulses each second; this station is known as the "master station." Several hundred miles away a second transmitter, at the "slave station," emits a corresponding series of pulses which are kept *accurately synchronized* (by an electronic timing device) with those from the master station. The time difference between the reception of a master pulse and the corresponding slave pulse establishes the Loran line of position.

LORCHA, a single masted Chinese boat of western model but junk rigged.

LOST ATLANTIS. See Atlantis.

LOUVRE, a ventilating device, like blinds of a window, in the side of a deck house; as screening fixture on the lower end of a ventilating pipe.

'LOW AND ALOFT, an expression applied when all sails including stun'sails are set.

LOW PRESSURE. This term signifies that the atmosphere is not as deep as normal, hence weighs less and there is less pressure exerted on the column of mercury with a resulting low pressure barometer. Winds blow inward spirally, or incurving, towards the center of an area of low pressure, counter clockwise in the northern hemisphere.

LOW WATER (L. W.), the periodic low level of water after a periodic high level of water, due to the tidal action produced by the attraction of the moon and sun.

LOWER or **LOWER AWAY,** to slack away on halyards or boat falls and lower the sail or boat.

LOWER DECK, a term applied to the enlisted force in a British naval vessel, as, "Liberty is granted to the lower deck."

LOWER LATITUDES, those parallels in the vicinity of the equator.

LOXODROMIC CURVE, a thumbline on a Mercator chart; it cuts the meridians of the chart at the same angle but forms a curve on the earth's sphere.

LUBBER, a green or clumsy hand.

LUBBER'S HOLE, the opening in the top at the eyes of the rigging. It is so named because a real sailor is supposed to go over the futtock shrouds to the topmast rigging rather than through the less hazardous lubber's hole.

LUBBER'S LINE (or **POINT**), a black line on the forward inner side of the compass bowl, placed there to represent the bow of the ship, and used to steer a course.

LUCKY BAG, a locker into which pass stray articles found about a naval vessel. It is (or was) in charge of the master at arms. These articles were subsequently sold at auction.

LUFF, to allow a vessel to come up toward the wind and relieve the pressure on the sails. It is the forward side of a fore and aft sail. The *luff of the bow* is the place at which a vessel's rails begin to converge toward the bow. A lieuten-

ant is called the luff. To *take a luff* out of a man is to humble him either by force or speech.

LUFF CRINGLE, the iron ring in the corner of a fore and aft sail at the jaws of the gaff.

LUFF UPON LUFF, one luff tackle placed on the fall of another.

LUFF TACKLE, comprises the rope, a double and a single block.

Luff Tackle

LUG FORESAIL, a gaff sail without a boom, the sheet leading abaft the main mast.

LUG PAD, a small plate with an eye, screwed or bolted in the deck or ship's side, to receive a hook or shackle.

LUG SAIL, a small boat rig. There are Standing, Dipping and Balance Lugs. Also see Lugger. The lug rig was used in larger vessels a hundred years ago and more; for instance, the Spanish *barkalonga.*

LUGGER, a vessel with one or several masts setting *lug sails.* These sails are quadrilateral in shape, bent to a yard which is swung obliquely in a fore and aft position. The lugger goes back into the 18th and even the 17th century, when they sometimes carried three masts, lug-rigged with a lug main-topsail and jib.

LULL, a temporary lowering of wind velocity during a gale.

LUMBER PORT, an opening in the bow of a schooner to facilitate the loading of lumber of unusually long lengths.

LUMINOUS RANGE, the distance a light is visible in a straight line. It is used in distinction to geographic range, in which the curvature of the earth and height of the observer's eye are taken into consideration. It may have an actual visibility of twenty miles, yet have sufficient power to project its luminous range thirty miles. With a high luminous range a light will cut through to its tabulated visibility despite considerable obscurity in the atmosphere.

LUMP SUM CHARTER, an agreement to hire a vessel for a certain sum of money, the conditions being stipulated.

LUMPER, a man who loads or unloads vessels.

LUNAR, pertaining to the moon. A method, now obsolete, of obtaining longitude by measuring the angular distance between the moon and the sun or a star and observing their altitudes. It was in use before chronometers were perfected.

LUNAR CYCLE, a period of approximately nineteen years. All the phases of the moon then come the same in relation to the calendar as in the preceding cycle. The tides likewise act in cycles under the moon's influence.

LUNAR DAY, the interval between two successive transits of the moon over the meridian.

LUNAR INEQUALITY refers to the irregularity of the moon's motion of revolution due to the earth's position in its orbit and its obliquity.

LUNATION, a lunar month or the interval between two new moons, which averages 29 days, 12 hours and 44 minutes.

LUNDIN LIFEBOAT, a self-bailing, seaworthy and convenient small boat for steamers. They are so designed as to nest for compactness of stowage.

LUNITIDAL INTERVAL (Lun. Int.), the interval that elapses from the passage of the moon across the meridian until the next high water. The mean of a number of these intervals is a characteristic for every port and once determined, remains correct for all practical purposes. Thus by taking the moon's passage from the Nautical Almanac, for the day, correcting for longitude, and applying the mean lunitidal interval, the time of high water is at hand. To establish the mean lunitidal interval, observations must be made at least through one month.

LYLE GUN, a life-saving gun designed to shoot a projectile with a line attached. This line is shot from the beach and establishes a connection with a stranded ship by which an endless line and tail block is hauled off and afterwards a hawser. With the hawser fast to a mast and the tail-block, through which the endless fall is rove, fast about two feet below it, the apparatus is ready to take the crew off in the *breeches buoy* sent off by the life savers ashore.

M

---

m. p. h., velocity or speed in miles per hour.

MACHUAS, two-masted, lateen-rigged sailing vessels of the Malabar Coast, which in their hull lines are reminiscent of the caravels of old Portugal. They are among the last of the world's commercial sail.

MACKEREL SKY, patchy clouds (cirro-cumulus), resembling the scales of a fish.

MADE or **BUILT MAST,** one constructed of several pieces of wood banded together into a round spar.

MAE WEST, a slang term for a big parachute spinnaker. Some inflatable life jackets are also called Mae Wests.

MAGAZINE, a compartment for the storage of ammunition. It is fitted with facilities for flooding in case of fire.

MAGELLAN CLOUDS, luminous patches near the southern pole, which are composed of innumerable small stars like the Milky Way.

MAGNETIC AMPLITUDE, the bearing of a body at rising or setting uncorrected for variation. See Amplitude.

MAGNETIC AZIMUTH, the bearing of a body uncorrected for variation. See Azimuth.

MAGNETIC BEARING, the direction of an object uncorrected for variation but with no deviation.

MAGNETIC COURSE, the direction of the ship's head based on the magneitc compass, whose north and south line lies in the direction of the magnetic pole. By applying the variation to the right from the center of the compass if easterly, and to the left if westerly, the true course will be obtained.

MAGNETIC DECLINATION. See Declination of the Compass.

MAGNETIC EQUATOR, a somewhat irregular line, which lies at right angles to the magnetic meridians, but not coincident with the geographical equator. The freely suspended compass needle has no dip on the magnetic equator.

MAGNETIC MERIDIAN, a sweeping line which connects the north and south magnetic poles. The general direction is towards the magnetic poles.

MAGNETIC POLES, the northern and southern centers of the magnetic influence of the earth. The northern one is in approximately Lat. 70° N.; Long. 97° 30′ W.; the southern in Lat. 72° 53′ S.; Long. 156° 42′ E.

MAGNETIC STORM, a fluctuation in the earth's magnetic forces which may cause the compass needle to be deflected. It may last but a short time or continue for several days. Sometimes the magnetic lines of force are affected over the whole earth and sometimes the phenomenon is restricted to a certain area. This phenomenon restricts the availability of radio frequencies and under certain unusual conditions causes a radio blackout.

MAGNETISM, SUB-PERMANENT. The materials of which a steel ship is built take up magnetism during the course of construction and through the percussion of the excessive hammering the whole structure becomes a magnet. Upon launching, a great change takes place with the new headings of the vessel and much of the magnetism is lost. That remaining is called sub-permanent magnetism.

MAGNETISM, TRANSIENT, that which comes and goes in soft iron as it comes into favorable or unfavorable positions with the earth's lines of force.

MAGNITUDE, a measurement of the brilliancy of stars. There are twenty first magnitude stars; those of 1.50 or brighter; those from 1.51 to 2.50 are second magnitude. Sirius is the brightest star = mag – 1.6.

MAGNUS HITCH, a turn around a spar, and jammed by a half hitch.

MAIN DECK, the principal deck of the main hull, being the highest of, and giving strength to, the main hull. It runs the full distance fore and aft and is usually next below a complete upper deck.

MAIN HOLD, a large compartment under the main hatch, usually located in the central part of the vessel.

MAIN TOPSAIL SCHOONER, an obsolete type in which there were square topsails on both fore and main masts; by some known as *two topsail schooners.*

MAIN YARDMEN, the men whose station is on the main yard; those on the binnacle list according to nautical slang.

MAINMAST, the second mast from the bow. The first mast in ketches and yawls.

MAIN-MIZZEN, the third mast of a four-masted ancient vessel.

MAINSAIL, the square sail set from the main yard; the large fore and aft sail set from the mainmast. In ketches and yawls the mainsail is set on the first mast.

MAINSAIL HAUL, an order given in tacking ship when the wind is nearly ahead, and in obedience to which the main yards are swung to the new tack.

MAINYARD, the lowest yard on the second mast from the bow.

MAKE, to attain an objective position, as a harbor; to *make the land* is to see it in the distance as a landfall. To *make fast* is to secure. To *make eight bells* is to strike four double strokes. To make sail.

MAKE SAIL, to set sail.

MAKE WATER, to leak.

MALLET. See Caulk.

MAMMATO-CUMULUS clouds often follow or precede a thunder squall, the mass of bulges are downward due to churning of the atmosphere.

MAN, to put the requisite number of men in a vessel, or on a halyard or brace to properly perform the work required.

MAN-OF-WAR, an official armed vessel.

MAN THE YARDS, to place men standing on each yard from the lift in to the mast. They are supported by life lines between the lift and the mast. This is done to honor a high official.

MANGER, a space made by a low coaming running athwartships abaft the hawse pipes. It prevents any water running aft.

MANHOLE, an opening in a boiler, tank or bulkhead to allow a man to crawl through.

MANIFEST, a document necessary when entering or clearing a ship at the customhouse. It contains ship's name, port of registry, registered tonnage, master's name, information concerning marks and numbers on cargo packages—in fact, full particulars of ship, voyage, crew, passengers, and cargo.

MANIFOLD, a distributing fixture for steam, vapor and water pipes.

MANILA ROPE, made from the fiber of the wild banana stalk and principally found in the Philippines.

MANROPE KNOT, a round knot in the end of a man rope. These ropes serve as safety lines in going up and down the ladders.

MANTISSA, the decimal part of a logarithm.

MARCONI RIG, a lofty mast from which is set a jib-headed sail. It replaces the gaff-headed sail and top-sail. It is also known as the Bermuda or Bermudian rig.

MARES' TAILS, plumes of white clouds with feathery edges somewhat resembling a horse's tail. They portend wind.

MARGIN ANGLE, an angle iron set on the top plank of a composite vessel where the planking breaks off above the waterline and steel plating begins.

MARGIN PLANK, usually a piece of teak surrounding a deckhouse or hatch against which the deck planks are laid or butted. Also called *Boundary Plank.*

MARGIN PLATE, the outer boundary of the inner bottom connecting it to the shell plating at the bilge.

MARIMETER, a sonic depth finder.

MARINE GLUE, a composition for paying the seams of a deck.

MARINE INSURANCE CERTIFICATE, a negotiable insurance document issued by a merchant and duly countersigned to give evidence that a certain individual shipment is covered under an open cargo policy. This evidence is needed in many ways to facilitate business under the open policy system. The more important features of the original policy are embodied in the certificate.

MARINE RAILWAY, an inclined railway extending beneath the water to a depth to receive vessels and haul them out on a cradle with power.

MARINER, a seafaring man of experience.

MARINER'S COMPASS, an instrument invaluable to the navigator, consisting of a card graduated to points and degrees. This card rests on a sapphire-pointed spindle, in a bowl containing a liquid composed of distilled water and about 45 per cent of alcohol or an oil similar to varsol. The weight is all but taken up by a round air float attached to the center of the card. The glass top is set on a rubber gasket, and in the bottom is an expansion device which takes care of the change in volume of the liquid due to temperature. The card derives directive value from the earth's magnetic force passing through bundles of wires attached to it in a north and south direction. A black mark on the bowl, called a *lubber's line,* indicates the bow of the ship and the mark to steer by. In order to preserve a level position the bowl is supported by gimbals—rings with knife-edge bearings set at right angles which take up the motion of the vessel. A mariner's compass may take on a descriptive name appropriate to its location or use, as follows: *azimuth compass,* if fitted with sight vanes for observing the sun; *compensated compass,* if fitted with compensating magnets for neutralizing the deviation; *elevated, pole* or *masthead compass,* if raised above the bridge in an attempt to get it out of the influence of the ship's magnetism; *liquid* or *spirit compass,* if the card is immersed in alcohol or oil; *dry compass,* if the card is placed so as to swing without submersion in a liquid. The *Kelvin compass* is of this type. There are also Standard, Dry, Gyroscopic, Boat, and Steering Compasses.

MARINER'S SPLICE, a splice in a cable-laid rope similar to a long splice; but the strands being ordinary ropes are themselves spliced instead of being tucked.

MARITIME, of, or to do with, the marine.

MARITIME LAW, the jurisprudence prevailing in the courts which has to do with maritime causes and concerns.

MARITIME POSITIONS, the latitudes and longitudes of various seaports and prominent landmarks. Appendix E—Bowditch 1958.

MARKET BOAT, a small vessel carrying fish or produce to market. A dinghy used by the steward to bring off provisions.

MARL, to secure parceling with a series of marling hitches, which are made against the lay of the rope. "Worm and parcel with the lay; Serve and marl the other way." *Marl,* a bottom largely composed of clay.

MARLINE, two-stranded tarred stuff laid up left-handed. There is *common marline* (222 feet to the pound), *medium* (360 feet) and *yacht marline* (520 feet).

MARLINE-SPIKE (Marlingspike), a

pointed steel tool for making splices, etc.

MARLINE-SPIKE HITCH, a simple hitch by which the spike can be used as a lever to heave in the seizing stuff.

MARLINE-SPIKE SAILOR, an expert in splicing, knotting and manipulation of rope.

MARLING HITCH, a round turn around a hammock, rope or spar with the end passed out, in through the bight. It will not slip like an ordinary half hitch.

MARK, the call given by a helmsman or other, when, in comparing compasses, taking azimuths, noting chronometer time, etc., the ship is on her course, or a distant object is accurately sighted.

MARKS, the fathoms of a lead line indicated by leather, cord or cloth. Those not marked are called deeps. Short pieces of cord are often wound around the lifts and braces to indicate the point where the yards are square by the lifts and braces and are called *marks*.

MAROON, to leave a person ashore with no facilities for leaving the place.

MARRIED FALLS, gear used in handling cargo where two falls are brought together at a single hook. A draft of cargo can be swung from one fall to the other, one boom being topped over the hatch and the other (the *burton boom*) over the pier. In discharging, the draft of cargo is hoisted while the burton fall is slack; when clear of the hatch the burton takes the load.

MARRY, to bring two ropes together, holding or temporarily seizing them. When a cargo sling transfers two casks at a draft the term *married* is applied.

MARTINGALE BOOM. See Dolphin Striker.

MARTINGALE GUYS or **BACK ROPES,** pieces of rigging leading from the lower end of the martingale boom aft to each side of the bow. The purpose is to guy or give it support from aft.

MARTINGALE STAYS, those leading from the jib-boom to the martingale boom, staying the former from beneath. Also called *jumpers*.

MARTNETS, an early name for leechlines.

MARU, a term which accompanies the name of all Japanese vessels and carries the hope or assumption of perfection or completeness, being derived from its original meaning of a circle or sphere.

MARY ANN, a utility craft of broad beam, equipped with a derrick to use in salvaging seaplanes.

MASCARET. See Eager.

MAST, the daily ceremony of bringing delinquents in discipline before the commanding officer. See also Masts.

MAST COAT, a piece of canvas around the mast, where it passes through the deck, to prevent water getting below.

MAST-HEAD, the top of a mast.

MAST-HEAD KNOT, one used to support a jury mast or hold a spar in a vertical position. The loops are pulled out to become stays.

MAST-HEAD LIGHT, a light carried by a steamer on her foremast to show over twenty points of the horizon from a head to two points abaft the beam. It must be visible five miles in clear weather.

MAST HOOPS, are rings of oak or metal encircling masts of small craft. The luff of the sail is seized to these rings and they run up and down the mast as the sail is hoisted or lowered.

MAST HOUSES, deck structures built around a mast for the stowage of gear and to serve as a foundation for winches.

MAST LINE, a term used in yacht racing rules. It is an imaginary line extending from the mainmast at right angles to the fore and aft line.

MAST LINING, a reenforcing cloth to protect a sail from the chafe against the mast.

MAST PARTNERS, are pieces of hard wood set about a mast where it passes through the deck. They support the mast at this point.

MAST PEDESTAL, a skeleton structure to support a mast which does not extend below decks. Sometimes called a *mast tabernacle.*

MAST ROPE, one used to send a mast up or down.

MAST STEP. At the foot of a mast is a tenon; this fits into a corresponding squared hole in the keel or heavy block of oak, as a tenon fits to a mortise joint.

MAST TABERNACLE. See Mast Pedestal.

MAST TABLE, a horizontal plate surrounding a mast supported beneath by struts and used as a supporting platform for the cargo booms.

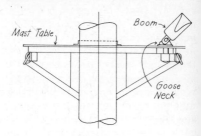

Mast Table

MAST WEDGES, pieces of wood driven around a mast where it enters the deck. They wedge the mast between the partners.

MASTER, the commander of a merchant vessel.

MASTER AT ARMS, was in early days the leading seaman, but was later assigned to "police" duty. He used to be known aboard ship as Jimmy Legs. This rating has been abandoned and the duties assigned to, usually, a bos'n's mate.

MASTER COMPASS, the main compass of a gyroscope equipment. All other compasses distributed at convenient positions about the ship are called *repeaters.*

MASTER MARINER, one who holds a master's license and acts as master of a merchant vessel.

MASTER STATION. See Loran.

MASTS, vertical spars set in ships primarily for setting sail, but also used for supports of cargo booms the suspension of radio aerials and as a means for setting signals. They are divided into two classes, *fore and aft* and *square-rigged* masts. The *fore and aft* comprises usually a tall *lower mast* and *topmast*. The sails set from booms and gaffs. The masts are usually named *fore, main, mizzen, jigger* and *spanker* in a schooner of five masts. To attempt to name the masts of a six or seven masted schooner would be to open one of the most divergent and perennial controversies of American seamen. The most generally favored sequence is jigger and spanker in a schooner of five masts, but good authorities often reverse the names of the last two masts. In modern sailing yachts the tall marconi mast is the most popular: it is supported by shrouds and spreaders so arranged as to act as trusses: the sail hoists on a track on the after side of the mast. The first mast of a ketch or yawl is called the main and the after mast the mizzen. In a *square-rigged mast* the *lower mast* is short compared with that of a schooner; the *topmast* is next above and then the *topgallant mast*. In tall ships a *royal mast* surmounts all. These masts are supported from forward by fore, main or mizzen *stays* as the case may be, which are named for the mast they support, as fore topgallant stay; at the sides they are supported by rigging or *shrouds*, as fore shrouds, main topmast rigging; from aft they are supported by *backstays* named also for the mast they support, as mizzen topmast backstay. These masts support yards from which the sails are set. The yards are horizontal spars which can be swung horizontally by ropes leading aft from the yardarms (forward on mizzen) called *braces*; they can be topped one side or the other by *lifts,* if desired. The yards, excepting the lower, and lower topsail, are hoisted up the masts by halyards in order to set the sails, and take their names according to the mast they hoist on, as fore topgallant yard. *Topsails to the mast* indicates these sails are aback, the wind laying them against the mast. The masts of steamers are merely *pole masts* sometimes offering opportunity to set a staysail, but mostly to support cargo booms, signal yards and radio aerials. The lower masts of large sailing ships called for such large trees that builders resorted to the "built-up mast," the segments of which were bound at intervals with mast bands. To reduce weight aloft yachts are provided with hollow masts—elongated boxes. There are also wooden cored masts made up of four longitudinal sections glued together so as to form a rounded spar with a hollow core. In some small racing yachts the masts have a core of light wood which lends itself to a desired flexibility. Aluminum is also used for yachts' spars.

MATCH HOOKS are similar to clip hooks (which see) and sister hooks.

MATCH ROPE, an inflammable rope used in early days for the firing of guns.

MATES, officers under the master who assist him in operating a merchant vessel.

MATE'S LOG, the smooth log. It is the mate's duty to prepare the smooth log from the rough log for the master's signature.

MATLO, an enlisted man in the Royal Navy. Compare *gob*.

MATTHEW WALKER KNOT, used in the end of a rope.

MATTRESS, a coarsely woven fabric of any suitable material, sunk on the banks or bottom of a stream to protect against excessive erosion by the current.

MAUL, a heavy hammer.

MAXIMA, an area where the barometer is normally higher than the surrounding region.

MAYDAY, the distress call of voice-radio, being from the French "m'aider" ("help me").

McINTYRE TANK, a tank between the double bottoms.

MEAL FLAG, a white rectangular flag shown from the starboard spreader of a yacht at anchor to indicate that the owner is at mess.

MEAL PENNANT, a red triangular flag hoisted from the port arm (or spreader) of a naval vessel (or yacht) at anchor when the crew is at mess. Popularly called *chow rag*.

MEAN LOW WATER, the average of all low waters.

MEAN NOON, the moment of the mean sun's crossing the meridian of the observer. Greenwich mean noon occurs when the mean sun crosses the Greenwich meridian.

MEAN REFRACTION, the average refraction used in the Nautical Almanac for correction of a celestial body's altitude under average condition, when the temperature is 50°F. and the atmospheric pressure stands at 29.83 inches.

MEAN SEA LEVEL, the average height of the sea without abnormal attractions or disturbances. See Geodesy.

MEAN SOLAR TIME, the hour angle of the mean sun. Hour angle is the measure of progress of a body past a meridian.

MEAN SUN, a fictitious body assumed to revolve around the earth at a uniform rate of speed once in twenty-four hours, and in the plane of the equator.

MEAN TIME (M. T.), that indicated by the passage and hour angle of the mean sun. The time carried by ordinary clocks and watches is the mean time of a standard meridian. The 75th meridian west longitude is used in the eastern United States.

MEASUREMENT, calculating the tonnage of a part or whole of a vessel according to measurement taken from carefully laid down rules.

MEASUREMENT FREIGHT. See Stowage Factor.

MEASUREMENT TON, the value of the ton used for measurement—100 cubic feet.

MEET HER, an order to the helmsman when the vessel is swinging say under a port helm; he starboards a little to steady her and prevent swinging by the desired course.

MELTEM. See Levanter.

MEND, to rebend a sail on a spar. A closely furled sail is often spoken of as a *mended sail*.

MERCATOR CHART, one projected according to the method originated by Gerardus Mercator (1512–1594). If the surface of the earth is considered as being developed into the form of a cylinder, tangent to the equator and unrolled, it would be similar to a Mercator chart. The converging meridians of the sphere have been spread to parallel lines on the chart; the parallels of latitude are still parallel, but instead of being equidistant, the distance between them increases poleward keeping proportional with the spreading of the meridians. Thus, islands near the equator are shown close to their normal size, but poleward they are proportionally enlarged with the increase in latitude. However, up to 60°N. this chart is in practical use universally. A straight line upon it represents a *rhumb line* and if steered will lead to the point of destination but not in the shortest distance.

MERCATOR SAILING, navigating by a Mercator chart and by the Mercator principle. See Mercator Chart.

MERCHANTMAN, a commercial vessel.

MERCURIAL BAROMETER, an instrument for measuring the pressure of the atmosphere. It consists of a metallic tube about 43 inches long within which is a glass tube containing a column of mercury. The top of the tube is sealed and the lower end is in a cup of mercury. It moves in a vacuum, like a thermometer, under the varying pressures of the atmosphere averaging a height of 30 inches. Different localities have a different normal barometer and while 29.90 inches may be normal in one place, 30.10 inches may be normal in another. A section of the metallic case is removed to expose the top of the mercury tube and a graduated scale with vernier is attached. It is hung in gimbals for use on shipboard. See Aneroid Barometer.

MERCURY, the planet nearest the sun. See Planets.

MERIDIAN ALTITUDE, a method of finding the latitude by observing the altitude of a body on the meridian. This is corrected by the usual corrections and the true altitude thus obtained is taken from 90° to secure the zenith distance (z). The declination (d) is taken from the Nautical Almanac for the Greenwich mean time of sight; then z plus $d =$ latitude, having regard to signs. If the body bears south, z is $+$, if north the sign is $-$. If the declination is south, d is $-$, if north it is $+$. Latitude north is $+$, south is $-$.

MERIDIAN DAY, the day gained at the meridian of 180° when sailing eastward.

MERIDIAN OBSERVATION, a meridian altitude.

MERIDIAN SAILING, when the course of a vessel is true north or south. In such circumstances there is no departure, and the ship is sailing a great circle course.

MERIDIAN ZENITH DISTANCE, 90° less a meridian altitude; or the distance of a body from the zenith when on the meridian.

MERIDIANS, great circles passing around the earth from pole to pole and at right angles with the equator. These are called terrestrial meridians in distinction from celestial meridians which pass from pole to pole of the celestial sphere.

MERIDIONAL DIFFERENCE OF LATITUDE, the amount representing the same proportion to the difference of latitude that the difference of longitude represents to the departure.

MERIDIONAL PARTS. On a Mercator chart, arcs of the parallels of latitude are increased by spreading the meridians from their natural converging direction to their parallel direction of this projection. It becomes necessary in order to preserve the proper proportion between a degree of latitude and a degree of longitude to also expand the arcs of the meridians, or in other words, the distance between the parallels. The amount that these arcs are expanded is called the Meridional parts. They are tabulated for each latitude in Tables 4 and 5, Bowditch, 1958.

MERRY DANCERS, the luminous wavy streamers of the aurora borealis.

MERRY MEN OF MAY, the tide rips in the Pentland Firth.

MESS, to eat. A group of persons eating together as, wardroom mess,

C.P.O.'s mess. The different persons are *messmates*. They eat from mess *tables* and are waited upon by messmen or mess *cooks*.

MESS GEAR, knives, forks, spoons, etc.

MESSENGER, a light line made fast to a hawser for the purpose of heaving the latter in. Formerly hawsers were too large to take conveniently to the capstan, and the messenger was resorted to. Any line sent ahead by which a larger line is run to a dock, buoy or similar use. A light line (3″ Manila) given by a steamer to a boatman to run to a mooring. The enlisted man, corresponding to an army orderly, who attends the *officer of the deck* of a naval vessel.

MESSENGER CHAIN, one connecting an engine with the windlass or capstan. Also simply called a messenger.

METACENTER, the point of intersection between a vertical line, passing through the center of gravity of a vessel upright and a vertical line passing through the center of gravity of the displaced water of a vessel, listed or heeled. If the metacenter is above the center of gravity, the vessel has stability; if separated by an insufficient distance, she is *crank,* and if below, she is *unstable.* The met acentric height, the abbreviation being G.M., is the distance from the center of gravity to the meta center.

METAL MIKE, a popular name given to an automatic steering device.

METAZOA, many-celled marine organisms.

METEOR (Aerolite), a mass of matter from the celestial spaces which, entering our atmosphere, becomes white hot and visible from the friction of the air. Fallen meteors (meteorites), upon being analyzed, have been found to possess no elements not already familiar to our geologists but in different combinations of elements.

METEOROLOGY, the science which treats of the atmosphere, variations of heat and moisture, winds, storms, etc.

METONIC CYCLE, lunar cycle.

MIDDLE GROUND BUOY, a buoy (in American waters painted in red and black horizontal bands and if lighted shows interrupted quick flashing) to mark a shoal of some extent lying with channels on either side.

MIDDLE LATITUDE (Mid. Lat.), the mean latitude between that of the point of departure and that of the destination. That is, if a vessel were in a position on the parallel of 30° N. and proceeded N. 35° E. until on the parallel of 38° N., the middle latitude of this run would be parallel of 34° N.

MIDDLE LATITUDE SAILING, that method used when a course is steered that lies obliquely with the meridians and parallels and the distance is not great. The whole amount of the departure is approximately the same as though a course were laid that distance along the parallel of the middle latitude.

MIDDLE MAST, a name sometimes given to the third mast of a five-masted vessel; when this term is used the sails and rigging of this mast take on the name of *middle,* as *middle topsail yard.*

MIDDLE PASSAGE, the passage from Africa to a port in the Southern States, with slaves. Middle because it was the second of a usual voyage of three legs: viz., out from New York or New England with rum and other cargo; slaves to New Orleans; cotton and other merchandise north.

MIDNIGHT SUN, a phenomenon of high latitudes which occurs when the observer's co-latitude is less than the sun's declination. With these conditions the sun will not set.

MIDSHIP TACK, a rope shackled in the center of the foot of a main course to aid in trimming the sail, especially with a quartering wind when the weather clew is raised.

MIDSHIPMAN, a student at the Naval Academy. In early days of the American Navy midshipmen served on shipboard learning the profession of a naval officer through direct association with the officers and the work. Farragut at 12 years of age served with Commodore Porter in the *Essex.* Sometimes applied to certain apprentices on merchant vessels.

MIDSHIPMEN'S BUTTER, the pulp of alligator pears.

MIDSHIPMEN'S HITCH, a running eye in a rope which will slip; a noose is made by a half hitch around the standing part, with another turn to jam it.

MIDSHIPS, the center fore and aft line of a vessel. Sometimes applied to the waist or middle of the fore and aft length. Also *amidships.*

MILDEW, a mould of black and gray spots on canvas due to dampness and heat.

MILE, a term given to two different units of measure. The first is the statute mile of 5,280 feet; the second the nautical or sea mile, a somewhat varying quantity. It is the length of a minute of latitude, and as the minutes are not of the same length through all latitudes, the value of a nautical mile varies with the latitude. The plane of a meridian is a slight oval due to the compression at the poles of the earth, and equal angles at the earth's center do not subtend equal arcs at the surface. The length of the nautical mile varies from 6,046 feet at the equator to 6,109 feet at the poles. The value of each degree of latitude is found in Table 6, Bowditch, 1958. In practical navigation, 6,080 feet is probably taken as standard mile by a majority of persons, and in dealing with short distances 6,000 feet or 2,000 yards is used. Nearly all maritime nations have adopted the international nautical mile of 1852 meters and 6,076.10333 U.S. feet. It was adopted by the U.S. Departments of Defense and Commerce on 1 July 1954.

MILK SEA, a remarkable whitish appearance of the water due to pelagic plant life belonging to the species *trichodesmiums.*

MILKY WAY, a belt of innumerable stars across the heavens which gives the appearance of a band of mist. It is also called the *Galaxy.* It is a theory with some scientists that this phenomenon is due to electrical energy.

MILLIBAR (mb.), a measure of atmospheric pressure—one millibar equals about .03 of a mercury inch, or 1000 dynes per square centimeter. Thirty inches of mercury equals, more accurately, 1016 millibars.

MINIMA, an area of normal low pressure in the midst of surrounding normal high pressure.

MINUTE, a measurement of arc (1′) which is one-sixtieth part of a degree; a measurement of time (1^m) which is one-sixtieth part of an hour.

MINUTE DIFFERENCE (M. D.), the change in the elements of the Nautical Almanac that takes place in 1 minute of time. Only very rapidly changing elements use minute differences; others use hourly differences.

MIRAGE, a delusive appearance caused by abnormal refraction. It appears in many forms, raising the horizon and distant land abnormally, distorting it and often causing images to appear above the horizon, even on occasions showing them upside down. The abnormal refraction is due to layers of air of different densities and temperatures. The rays of light from a distant ship or shore become curved by these irregularities in the atmosphere.

MISS STAYS, to fail in the attempt to tack ship.

MIST and fog are clouds which cover the surface of the earth. The term *fog* is applied by seamen when there is obscurity of vision, while mist is thin and allows navigation to proceed unimpeded. The wet and dry bulbs of a psychrometer differ but little during the prevalence of mist. See Fog.

MISTRAL, a cold northwest wind of the Mediterranean Sea, usually blowing down the Rhone Valley of France. It sometimes bears the name *maestrale* when blowing over the Aegean Sea.

MITCHBOARD, a support for a boom, serving as a crutch.

MITTEN MONEY, an additional fee charged for winter pilotage.

MIZZEN, the third mast of a vessel or after mast of a yawl or ketch. The rigging, stays, and shrouds of this mast take their name from it, such as *mizzen rigging, etc.* It was originally a large fore and aft (lateen) sail carried by the ancient caravels; also known as the *bonaventure mizzen.* The word mizzen came from the Italian *mezzana* and the French *misaine,* both carrying the meaning of a forward mast. But through a confusion it became applied to the English *aftermast.* In four-masted ancient ships the names were fore, main, main-mizzen and bonaventure.

MOCK SUNS, bright spots near the sun, being associated with a halo.

MODEL, a miniature counterpart of a vessel.

MODERATE, applied to wind or sea signifies a lesser degree. A gale *moderates* when it lessens its intensity and abates.

MOHN EFFECT, the erratic transmission of sound due to differing densities of air. Fog Signals are sometimes blanked out in certain areas while audible nearby.

MOLD (Mould), a pattern of a certain part of a vessel; a template.

MOLD LOFT, a loft where the lines of a vessel are laid down.

MOLDING (moulding) of a frame is its measurement athwartships; of a stem, fore and aft; of a keel, its depth vertically.

MOLE, a loading and discharging place of vessels. It is usually a substantial masonry structure, and often serves as a breakwater on its outer side while offering facilities for ships on its inner side.

MOLLYMAWK, a name applied by sailors to several small species of albatross common in southern seas. *Mollyhawk* is a modern corruption and *mollie* is the sailor's name. They are large and dusky in appearance, remarkable fishers, very gluttonous, and oily to taste.

MONKEY, the kid from which grog was formerly served in the Navy.

MONKEY BLOCK, a small single block with a swivel.

MONKEY BRIDGE, usually above the pilot or chart house where the standard compass is commonly set. Sometimes the fore and aft bridge on a sailing ship.

MONKEY FORECASTLE, a very short forecastle deck for the stowing of the anchor.

MONKEY GAFF, a light gaff carried on the aftermost mast of a sailing vessel high above the spanker gaff.

MONKEY RAIL, a light rail above the quarter rail.

MONKEY'S FIST, a complicated knot with weight enclosed, used at the end of a heaving line.

MONK'S SEAM, stitching between the seams uniting two cloths of a sail. This is also called middle stitching.

MONSOONS, seasonal winds. The sun in summer warms the land of southern China to a higher degree than the temperature of the ocean. The warm air rises and the southwest monsoons flow in. When the sun is in the southern declination it warms the southern ocean, the air rises and the cool air from the north flows southward to replace it in the form of the northeast monsoons. The same principle applies in other parts of the Indian Ocean and on the west coast of Africa.

MONTYCAT, a 15-foot cat-rigged racing boat.

MOON, a satellite of the earth, making a revolution in 27 ds. 7 hrs. 43 ms. She is a non-luminous body shining by reflected sunlight. The moon's distance from the earth is about 238,840 miles. Her diameter is about 2,163 miles. The attraction of the moon is the chief cause of the tides—about 2¼ times that of the sun.

MOON PHASES, the different positions of the moon relative to the earth and sun, such as full moon, new moon and first and last quarters.

MOON RAKER, a light sail high aloft.

MOONBOW, a rainbow caused by moonlight instead of sunlight; it is usually quite devoid of color.

MOON'S AGE, the time elapsed since the last new moon.

MOONSAIL, a light sail carried above the skysail.

MOORED, to lie with both anchors down. One anchor is let go and double the amount of chain is veered, the second anchor is let go and half the chain hove in on the first. A mooring swivel is sometimes used to prevent a foul hawse as the vessel swings with the tide and wind. A vessel is moored to a pier when well fast with mooring lines. (See Flying Mooring.)

MOORING BUOYS, are attached to heavy anchors.

MOORING PIPES, apertures in the bulwarks to accommodate the mooring lines.

MOORING STAPLE, a device which serves the purpose of an eyebolt but whose opening is rectangular and very much larger. Such staple are attached to the side of a ship and her lines are made fast to them when tying up alongside a pier.

MOORINGS, heavy anchors and chains permanently in position. The chains, in big-ship moorings are attached to large flat-topped mooring buoys which have a large ring in the top to which the anchor chain of a vessel is shackled.

MOORSOM'S RULE. A commission appointed by the British Admiralty in 1849 at the request of the Board of Trade reported certain recommendations for a change in the rules of measurements for vessels. A Mr. Moorsom was honorary chairman, and did not approve the findings. He worked out a mathematical formula for determining cubical contents of vessels which, with modifications, is now in force. In order to make as little change as possible in the registered tonnage Mr. Moorsom suggested that 100 cubic feet be used. The United States adopted this in 1864 for use in calculating the gross tonnage of a vessel.

MORSE, to signal with a Morse lamp. See Blinker.

MORSE CODE, a system of dots and dashes that represent letters and numerals.

MORSE LAMP, a device used on the bridge to signal by flash light.

MORTICE BLOCK, one with the shell made in one piece.

MOTHER CAREY'S CHICKENS, stormy petrels. They follow vessels continuously and used to be held in superstitious regard by sailors. They are about 6 inches long, are dark in color except for a white spot on the rump. They have a bat-like flight and tickle their toes on the waves.

MOTORBOAT, a boat driven by one or more internal combustion engines.

MOTORSAILER, a motorboat with a capability of moderate sailing pleasure while possessing power to proceed with more speed than an auxiliary sailing craft.

MOTORSHIP, a vessel mechanically propelled by a screw propeller actuated by an internal combustion engine. The installation of this machinery costs considerably more than that of the reciprocating or turbine types. A motorship, however, has from 10 to 15 per cent more cargo space, and it is estimated that such a vessel costs less to operate at sea than the older types. Among other advantages of the motorship is her cruising radius; she is obliged to bunker only once to about three times for the old coal burner.

MOULD (Mold), a light pattern of a part of a ship.

MOULDED BREADTH, the measurement over the frames but not the outside plating at the greatest breadth of the vessel.

MOULDED DEPTH, in one, two and three deck vessels the measurement at the middle of the length from the top of the keel to the top of the upper deck beams at the side of the vessel. This measurement is made to the top of the main deck beams at the side of an awning- or spar-decked vessel.

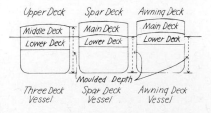

Moulded Depth

MOUSING, a piece of small stuff seized across the hook of a block for the purposes of safety.

MOVING BLOCK, the one that travels, in distinction from the block of the tackle that remains fast.

MUD BOX, a receptacle inserted in the line between the valve chest and the pump line to catch any sand that may pass.

MUD PILOT, a river or harbor pilot who relieves a bar pilot and takes a vessel to her pier; one who operates by eyesight, gauging the depth by seeing the bottom and by changes in the color of the water.

'MUDIAN RIG. Also called Bermuda Rig.

MUFFLED OARS, those with chafing gear around them to kill the sound in the rowlocks.

MUG UP, to have a drink of coffee or tea which is always on the galley stove of a fishing schooner.

MULE, a triangular sail set from a back stay of a yawl or ketch which leads from aloft to the foot of the mizzen. The mule is sheeted to the mizzen head.

MUMBLE BEE, an English cutter, typical of the south coast, whose mast is stepped well aft.

MUNTZ METAL, an alloy of three parts copper and two of zinc. It is used in lieu of copper in the sheathing of vessels' bottoms.

MUSHROOM ANCHOR, a bowl-shaped piece of iron with the shank coming from the center of the concave side. These anchors are used for mooring boats, yachts, vessels, buoys and lightships.

MUSHROOM VENTILATOR, is one with a head shaped like a mushroom and so devised as to prevent water from getting below.

MUSTANG, a term applied to a naval officer who by ability and merit while serving as an enlisted man, earned a commission.

MUTTON-LEG SAIL, triangular in shape, tapering aloft with a boom at the foot.

MUZZLE, to bring bellying canvas under control when furling sail.

N

N. A., Nautical Almanac.

NADIR, the point on the celestial sphere opposite and 180° from the zenith.

NAKED, the term applied to a vessel with her copper sheathing re-moved from her bottom.

NANTUCKET SLEIGH-RIDE, the tow given a whaleboat by a whale after being harpooned.

NAPIER DIAGRAM, a valuable device from which the magnetic course can be obtained from the compass course and vice versa. It embraces a central line graduated to represent the rim of the compass card. The points or the rhumbs are intersected by two sets of parallel lines at angles of 60°. One set is of dotted lines and the other set is plain. A curve representing the deviations is plotted on the diagram by measuring out (from central graduation) the number of degrees of deviation from each compass heading on, or parallel to, the dotted lines. The points thus established are joined by a free curve. In order to find the compass course from a given magnetic course, the plain lines should be followed, or paralleled, until the deviation curve is intersected from which the return is made, parallel to the dotted lines, to an intersection with the vertical scale where the course is read off. If the magnetic course is desired and the compass course is at hand, the above procedure is reversed.

NARWHAL, a whale of high northern latitudes.

NATURAL, a term found in navigation referring to natural trigonometrical functions and numbers whose values in usual practice are calculated from radii valued at 1.

NAUTICAL, pertaining to ships and navigation.

NAUTICAL ALMANAC, a tabulation of the positions of all heavenly bodies relative to the Greenwich meridian and the equator, for the use of navigators. It is published annually by the Nautical Almanac Office of the U. S. Naval Observatory.

NAUTICAL ASTRONOMY, that part of astronomy used in the navigation of ships at sea. It comprises the coordinates of the heavens with which bodies and points are located, the movements of heavenly bodies, the astronomical triangle, time and the movements of the earth.

NATIONAL OCEANOGRAPHIC SURVEY (formerly U.S. Coast and Geodetic Survey), an office under the National Oceanographic and Atmospheric Agency (NORR). The survey gathers data and publishes charts and books for the information of the mariner. Its activities are largely confined to the land and waters of the United States and its possessions.

NAUTOPHONE, a fog signal either through air or water produced by an electrically operated oscillator.

NAVAL, pertaining to the establishment of sea offense and defense.

NAVAL ARCHITECT, a designer of vessels. He is responsible for the vessel's stability, strength, trim, etc.

NAVAL CONSTRUCTOR, a constructor and repairer of vessels.

NAVAL OFFICER. A commissioned officer of a navy; a customhouse officer whose duties are to cooperate with the Collector of the Port in estimating the duties to be levied on manifests and entries.

NAVAL STORES, such stores as pitch, resin, turpentine, oils, etc.

NAVEAM, an urgent notice to mariners in eastern North Atlantic and Mediterranean Sea.

NAVEL FUTTOCK, the lowest section of a wooden frame in the amidships part of a vessel.

NAVICERT, a certificate issued by a belligerent to the vessels of a neutral to expedite passage through the blockaded zone of that belligerent.

NAVIGABLE, capable of being navigated. *Navigable Semicircle,* the left-hand side of a storm track.

NAVIGATION, the art of conducting a vessel from one port to another both by means of landmarks and by observation of celestial bodies, or by electronic beacons. It also includes the method of keeping track of the vessel's position by the courses steered and distances covered, known as *dead reckoning.*

NAVIGATOR, the officer responsible for the position of the vessel and the condition of her navigating equipment. This officer is third in command. In a merchant vessel the master is ultimately responsible for the navigation; in naval service it is shared by the captain and the navigator.

NEAP TIDES, those tides that occur near the moon's quadrature. They have a less range at this time, the high water being lower and the low water higher than the average. This condition is due to the fact that the attractive influences of the moon and sun are opposing each other. It is the opposite condition from spring tides.

NEAPED, a vessel is said to be neaped when her draft is greater than the depth at high water neaps and she cannot leave port until the greater rise of spring tides. Same as beneaped.

NEKTON, those organisms of the sea which possess the ability to move about actively.

NEPTUNE, "A mythical god of the sea. When crossing the equator for the first time a foremast hand, in former days, was conducted blindfolded to a seat consisting of a piece of board laid across a tub filled with water. He was informed by his messmates that Father Neptune would be along shortly to interview him and give him a pass to cross the line. Shortly after this, a tremendous bellowing would be heard from over the bows; the blindfold would then be removed, and the poor greeny treated to a view of the most astonishing looking object coming over the bows. A tremendous rope-yarn beard, deck-swab hair that had been dipped in green paint and dried for the occasion, a spare royal, or some other light sail for a robe, a trident in one hand and a speaking trumpet in the other, completed the *tout ensemble* of this mythological deity, who roared his questions into the victim's ears through the trumpet. Neptune would then decide that the applicant required shaving, so the face of the sufferer would be covered with Stockholm (tar) and then scraped off with an iron barrel hoop. Next the victim would be congratulated for passing the ordeal, and again blindfolded; Neptune would disappear, the board be pulled away from across the tub, and the final scene would be the newly initiated floundering about in the water to the intense amusement of all hands." (Capt. Howard Patterson.) This ceremony with some minor modifications is still observed when a ship crosses the equator.

NESS, a cape or promontory.

NEST OF DORIES. Line-trawling fishing schooners carry a large number of dories on deck by lowering one inside another after thwarts are removed. As many as ten dories are often carried in one of these nests.

NET TONNAGE, is the freight earning space—the gross tonnage with deduction of certain non-earning spaces, such as machinery, crew and ship's stores compartments. Tonnage space is reckoned at 100 cubic feet to the ton.

NETTLES, a kind of reef points. Rope yarns twisted together for grafting or pointing purposes. Small line for hammock clews.

NICHOLSON LOG, a device that registers speed by the pressure of water in a tube exerted through the ship's onward motion. The lower end of the tube is outboard and open to the bow.

NIGGER HEADS, a name for bollards, and sometimes applied to winch heads.

NIGHT EFFECT, the erratic changing and broadening of the minimum in a radio bearing. The effect is most pronounced at twilight and dawn. Bearings taken at these times should be repeated for a mean.

NIGHT PENNANT, a blue pennant shown at night from the main truck of a yacht at anchor.

NIMBUS (N.), thick dark rain clouds without ragged edges.

NINEPIN BLOCK, one resembling a ninepin in shape. It is a swivel block.

NIP, a twist in a rope. The term is used when a ship is caught between two closing ice fields.

NIPPERING, racking.

NIPS, the part of a rope around a thimble—the nip of an eye splice.

NO HIGHER, an order to keep a vessel from heading nearer the wind.

NO MAN'S LAND, the space between hatches and between a hatch and a bulkhead. Sometimes called the Winch Country when winches occupy the space.

NOCK, the short luff of certain staysails that extends down a mast. Sometimes refers to the corner of a sail at the jaws of the gaff commonly known as the throat.

NODAL POINTS, those places where there is little or no rise and fall of tide, but where there are tidal currents. They lie between a place where the water is high and one where it is low.

NODDIES, very familiar sea birds in almost all tropic seas. They frequent the open sea, feeding upon fish that come to the surface. Their plumage is deep sooty brown, paling on the neck and shading to white on the forehead. They are about fifteen inches long.

NODES, the two points at which the moon's orbit cuts the ecliptic. The inclination of these two great circles is about 5° 08′. What equinoctial points are to the earth's orbit, the nodes are to the moon's orbit.

NON-TOPPLING BLOCK, one so weighted as to remain upright. The moving block of a cargo whip is usually of this type.

NOON. The instant when the apparent sun is on the meridian is *local apparent noon,* when the mean sun, *local mean noon* and when the First Point of Aries, *local sidereal noon.*

NORMAN, a preventer pin through the rudder head to guard against its loss. Iron pins or staple-shaped bolts, to prevent the chain from fouling at the windlass. A device like a belaying pin set horizontally in the head of a bitt.

NORTH RIVER JIBE, is applied when a boom shifts sides violently without hauling in the sheet to ease the shock.

NORTHERN LIGHTS, Aurora Borealis. A wavering illumination of northern skies believed to be caused by solar particles which upon entering the ionosphere near the magnetic pole become illuminated. Aurora Australis is a similar phenomenon in the Antarctic zone.

NORTHERS, strong, cold and often violent winds, particularly in the Gulf of Mexico and western Caribbean Sea in winter.

NOSE, the cutwater.

NOTHING OFF, to hold a vessel on a course and not allow her to head farther from the wind.

NOTICES TO MARINERS, weekly publications of the United States Naval Oceanographic Office. They contain information of changes which require correction to existing charts and books of sailing directions and light lists. They cover all changes such as new lights, buoys, recently discovered shoals and rocks, dredged channels, changes in the aids to navigation, decreased depths, etc. Each maritime country issues a notice to mariners.

NUGGER, a small Egyptian boat which had one mast and carried a square sail set obliquely—a cross between a lateen, and a true square sail.

NULL, that desired point of no sound, or minimum, when rotating the loop of a radio direction finder.

NUMBER, the combination of four letters assigned to each ship for recognition purposes. A vessel shows her number by hoisting the alphabet flags denoting these letters.

NUN BUOY, a truncated cone or conical buoy. These buoys are according to the American buoyage system found on the starboard side of a channel in entering port. They are marked with even numbers. Conical buoys are now quite generally being substituted for truncated cones. Most are painted red, but some are red-and-black vertical striped.

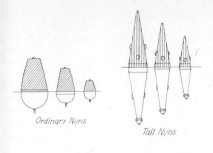

Ordinary Nuns

Tall Nuns

Nun Buoys

NURSE, an experienced officer assigned to a ship or bridge watch to assist in performing the duties of an incompetent or incapable officer.

NUT, the ball on the end of an anchor stock. This nut or ball aids in bringing the stock flat on the bottom by not allowing the end of the stock to bury itself before the anchor cants.

NUTATION. The earth's axis, due to the influence that produces the Precession of the Equinoxes, describes a circle around the Poles of the Ecliptic. This circle is a wavy line due to the attraction caused by the periodic revolution of the moon. This effect is known as Nutation, being derived from the Latin *nuto,* to nod. The sun's influence is similarly noticeable, requiring the distinction sometimes of *solar* and *lunar* nutation.

NYLON, a synthetic fiber extensively used in rope-making. Such rope has greater strength than the comparable size of manila, deteriorates less, and has great flexibility making it excellent for anchor and mooring lines. Nylon is also used for making sails, especially light sails such as spinnakers where its light weight and high strength are important.

O

O. O. D., officer of the deck.

OAKUM, a caulking material made of tarred rope fibers. It was formerly made aboard ship from rope junk but is now a commercial article.

OAR, an implement used for pulling a boat. Its parts are the *blade,* the flat part, the *loom,* the round part between the blade and handle, and the *handle.* Some authorities consider the loom that part in the boat from oarlock to handle. A *steering oar* is used as a rudder where the seas are liable to keep the rudder much out of water and where a boat must be turned quickly, as in whaling.

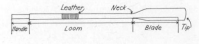

Oar

OARLOCK, a device with jaws to hold the oar when pulling and a shank which sets in the rail. It is also called *rowlock*. The distinction sometimes given is: Oarlock for steering oar; rowlock for rowing oar. Sometimes a square piece is cut in the gunwale for this purpose, and, again, two pins fitting in sockets serve to hold the oars in rowing. They are also called thole pins.

OARS, an order given to a boat's crew to hold all oars horizontal with blades flat.

OBJECT GLASS, the lens at the outer end of a telescope.

OBLIQUE SPHERE, that seen by an observer at any point between the pole and the equator. The apparent diurnal path of the stars intersects the horizon at an oblique angle, and will be above the horizon for varying times according to the latitude of the observer and the declination of the body.

OBLIQUITY OF THE ECLIPTIC, the angle the equator takes with the ecliptic. This is also expressed as the inclination of the earth. The angle amounts to 23° 27′, but is decreasing at the rate of 0″ .5 annually.

OCCLUDED FRONT. When a faster moving cold front overtakes a warm front they merge in what is called an occluded front.

OCCULTATION, the concealment of one heavenly body by another.

OCCULTING LIGHT, one in which the period of light is equal to or more than the period of darkness. If the periods of darkness are grouped, it becomes a group occulting light. A light with a period of one minute, being lighted 40 seconds and eclipsed 20 seconds, is an occulting light.

OCEAN CURRENT, consistent movement of water in the open ocean which is not produced or affected by tidal influence. Very slow moving currents are called *drifts;* thus, to the eastward of the Grand Banks where the velocity of the Gulf Stream becomes much reduced, it is known as the *Gulf Stream Drift.* Probably atmospheric pressure plays the major part in the creation of ocean currents, but wind, temperature, rotation of the earth and salinity are factors.

OCEANOGRAPHIC OFFICE, an office of the United States Navy, formerly called the Hydrographic Office, which serves the merchant service as well as naval vessels. It collects oceanographic as well as hydrographic data and publishes charts, books and current publications through which it dispenses all available information for the use of mariners. Its activities are largely confined to foreign waters.

OCEANOGRAPHY, that branch of science which deals with tides, ocean currents, temperatures, salinity, waves and other phenomena of the ocean.

OCTANT, an instrument differing from the sextant only in that its arc is one-eighth of a circle and measures angles to 90°.

OFF AND ON, to lie first on one tack, then on the other, endeavoring to maintain the same approximate position. Or, to lie hove to under very easy sail and allow the vessel to come to and fall off as she desires; but particularly applying to a vessel waiting for some purpose and not caring to anchor. The term would be used thus: The ship arrived off the port at night and was lying *off and on* until dawn before attempting to enter the harbor.

OFF SOUNDINGS, beyond the 100-fathom curve.

OFF THE WIND, to sail with the sheets well eased, that is, slacked off, with a fair wind.

OFFICER OF THE DECK, an officer taking his turn in charge of a naval vessel. He acts as the captain's representative. He is, during this duty, senior to all other officers but the captain and the executive.

OFFICIAL LOG BOOK, a record of all important events of the voyage, the list of crew, deaths, births, marriages, accidents, fines, punishments, sickness, etc. The log book is furnished by the government and is used by the Shipping Commissioner in paying off the crew.

OFFICIAL NUMBER, that given by the authorities when a vessel is documented and it is burned into a conspicuous place on a hatch header or beam.

OFFING, in sight of land but well to seaward.

OFFSHORE WIND, one blowing off the land. Formerly, in some localities, it referred to a wind coming from the "offshore."

OIL, used to prevent the seas from breaking is called *wave* or *sea-*

calming oil, sometimes *sea-quelling* oil. It was used as early as the 5th century, at least, for this purpose.

OIL BAG, a contrivance from which oil is allowed to drip slowly and spread on the water, in order to form a slick and reduce the seas.

OIL BURNER, a steamer using fuel oil for making steam.

OIL KING, naval slang for the chief petty officer who has charge of all the fuel oil.

OIL TIGHT, capable of holding oil. This requires more careful riveting and caulking than water-tightness.

OIL WASH, a light gas oil used in a tank for cleaning after it has been thoroughly steamed.

OILING, a steamer taking on oil fuel is *oiling*. She flies International Flag B in the daytime and a red light at night during the operation.

OILSKINS, cotton garments waterproofed by repeated coats of linseed oil.

OLD BUILDERS' TONNAGE: Early vesesls were measured for tonnage as follows: The length was along the rabbet of the keel from the after side of the sternpost to a perpendicular from the forward side of the stem under the bowsprit. The breadth was from and to the outside planking (not double planking). By subtracting 3/5 of the breadth from the length they got the "length of keel for tonnage." Multiplying this "length of keel for tonnage" by the breadth, by half the breadth and dividing by 95 the tonnage was obtained. The half-breadth was substituted for depth. This shows why in early records the tonnage carried fractions of 95ths.

OLD HORSE, the same as Dead Horse.

OLD MAN, a name universally given to the captain of a ship.

OLD MAN'S HAT, a bilge well where bilge water collects and where the suction pipes of the bilge are located. A sump.

OLERON, LAWS OF, a code of sea laws adapted at the time of Richard Coeur de Lion from the Rhodian laws. From these, all modern maritime law has developed. They were in some ways rather stringent, but the days of Richard called for drastic action; for instance, a pilot who cast away a vessel through ignorance was in great danger of death, for a master could cut his head off without accountability; false and treacherous pilots were condemned to suffer a most rigorous and unmerciful death. A lord found implicated in a case of barratry to his profit was to be apprehended, his goods confiscated and sold, and he himself burned in the midst of his own mansion which was to be fired at all four corners.

ON THE BEAM, the direction at right angles to a ship's heading or line of her keel.

ON BOARD, aboard; anywhere on a vessel; *on deck* means on the weather deck. See Deck.

ON THE BOW, a direction of four points or less from the bow.

ON THE QUARTER, a direction of four points or less from the stern.

ON SOUNDINGS, to be within the 100-fathom curve.

ON THE WIND, close-hauled, or sailing as close to the wind as possible.

ONE POINT BEARING, a rough estimate of a vessel's distance from a lighthouse obtained by observing the distance run by log from the time it bears one point forward of the beam until it bears abeam and multiplying this distance by five.

ONLY MATE, an old grade in the British merchant service on vessels where no other mates are carried.

OPEN. A distant object seen clear outside another point of land is said to be *open*. It is used in contradistinction to the term *shut in* as would be the case when a point of land is hidden behind a nearer point. An unprotected anchorage is said to be *open*.

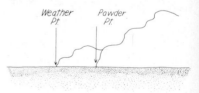

Open

OPEN BOAT, an undecked boat.

OPEN HAWSE, two anchors down and the chains leading clear.

OPEN LINKED CHAIN, that which has long links with no studs.

OPPOSITION, the relative position of two heavenly bodies which are 180° apart, with the earth between. At full moon the sun and moon are in opposition.

ORBIT, the path of a heavenly body through space. Also the path of man-made satellites and capsules.

ORDINARY, the technical condition of a naval vessel tied up at a navy yard having only a skeleton crew aboard but still in commission and ready for quick service. A merchant steamer with this status is known as a *spot ship*. A short term used for ordinary seaman.

ORDINARY SEAMAN, one who is subordinate to an A.B. (able-bodied seaman) but has learned a part of the trade, usually in a sailing vessel, knowing how to reef, furl a sail, and to steer. In recent times, an ordinary seaman is not at first required to know much real seaman's work.

ORIENT, to square an instrument with the true directions of the compass; to fix a position with reference to the east. The engraved compass diagram of an alidade or pelorus is *oriented* to agree with the ship's head.

ORLOP DECK, the lowest deck. The beams may be in place with no deck laid or it may be only roughly laid. It does not necessarily run the whole length of the ship.

OSCILLATION, PERIOD OF, the time of a roll or oscillation from port to starboard. A double roll is the return roll back to port. The number of seconds required for a complete roll remains the same regardless of the angle of the roll provided there is no change in trim. The swinging of a compass needle before coming to rest indicates its period of oscillation.

OTTER GEAR, a torpedo-shaped device used for cutting mines adrift. Also called *paravane*. In World War II the O-type or Oropesa gear was used in sweeping moored mines. A wider path was swept than with paravanes. The serrated wire and explosive cutter were more effective than cutting jaws. The name "otter" came to the Otter Gear and Otter Trawl from a board called an otter used in catching salmon. It was so rigged with a line and bridle as to sheer away from the shore as a man walked and towed it. Lines and hooks were attached to the line. It was called an otter because that animal was the salmon's greatest enemy.

OTTER TRAWL. This term is synonymous with beam trawl and a dragger is a small scale otter trawl. It consists of a funnel-shaped net, kept open by otter or dragger "boards," which act as paravanes (kites) used by the Navy in minesweeping. These boards are towed by bridles so angled as to make them tend outward from the headway of the vessel. The net has a wire footrope which scrapes along the bottom and a headrope held up by metal floats. The towing wire is led through a sheave in a boom, which keeps the gear from the vessel's side, thence to a winch amidships.

OUT OARS, to place them in the position of "oars"—horizontal with blades flat.

OUT POINT, to sail closer to the wind than another vessel.

OUT OF TRIM, to carry a list or to be by the head or stern.

OUTBOARD, out from the vessel; away from the center fore and aft line.

OUTBOARD MOTOR, a portable motor which can be attached to the stern of a boat for propulsion. It is capable of being tipped upward when not in use, when in shoal water or becomes tripped by striking an obstruction.

OUTDRIVE an arrangement of the power plant of a motor yacht in which a conventional engine is set far aft. The shaft passing through the transom operates a propeller similar to that of an outboard motor's, through an assembly of two 90° gears. The propeller is capable of being tripped upward.

OUTER JIB, that just beyond the inner jib, or jib.

OUTFOOT, to outsail another vessel.

OUTHAUL, a line used to haul the corners of a sail out to the end of a boom or gaff.

OUTLYING, offshore, usually referring to rocks and reefs, or islets.

OUTREACH, the reach of a cargo boom beyond its base.

OUTRIGGER, an extension bolted to each side of the crosstrees to spread the topmast backstays in a schooner or top-gallant and royal backstays in a square-rigger; an extended frame on a narrow racing pulling boat which allows the oarlock to be in a more outboard position; a framework run out on the weather side of a native canoe of the South Pacific and elsewhere, to allow a man or several men to shift their weight to windward as the breeze demands. The breeze is named according to this necessity, as a *three-man breeze.* The upper mast tables which support the cargo boom topping-lifts are called outriggers.

OUTSAIL, to lead another vessel by superior speed due to lines of the hull, trim of sails, or management.

OVER ALL, the length on deck from end to end.

OVER THE HILL, absent without leave with no voluntary intention of returning to the ship, in other words, *jumped ship.*

OVER RAKE, the fore and aft wash of the seas when a vessel is anchored in heavy weather and taking water over the bow.

OVER RIGGED, the carrying of unnecessarily heavy rigging.

OVERBOARD, over the side of a ship.

OVERFALLS, breaking waves caused by a weather current (that is, one moving against the wind), by a current moving over a shoal, or by a conflict of two currents. Any of these causes may lead a wave to become sharper and break. It is very frequently the case that rips and overfalls occur at the same time and through the same cause.

OVERHAND KNOT, a simple turn and the end through the bight. It is useful as a beginning of other knots.

OVERHANG, the amount a vessel's bow or stern projects beyond the waterline at the stem or sternpost.

OVERHATTED, oversparred, having too much sail.

OVERHAUL, to haul the parts of a tackle so as to separate the blocks. To overtake a vessel.

OVERHAULING WEIGHT, usually a globular iron weight sufficient to separate the blocks of a cargo tackle. Sometimes a whip is used and is known as an *overhauling whip.*

OVERLAP, in yacht racing, can exist only when two vesesls are more or less on the same course. There is an overlap when one yacht is not *clear ahead* (q.v.), that is, her stern line not completely ahead of the other yacht. No overlap is considered if the boats are over two overall lengths apart.

OVERSPARRED, masts too lofty and yards too long for a vessel's stability.

OVER-STOWED, a term used when cargo for the next port is stowed under that for a subsequent port of call.

OX EYE, a forerunner of a storm or squall on the African coast. The peculiar shape of this cloud suggested its name.

OXTER PLATE, the shell plate which connects to the sternpost, usually of very sharp curvature or twisted and therefore incapable of being developed. (Steel Shipbuilder's Handbook, Cook.)

OXYHYDROGEN TORCH, a device arranged to burn oxyhydrogen gas in an intense flame that burns away metal. It is used for cutting and welding.

P

P. A., position approximate, referring to a shoal or rock on a chart.

P. D., position doubtful. These familiar letters appearing on charts mark reported shoals or reefs whose position as given does not satisfy the hydrographers at Washington as to accuracy.

P. D. L. See Pass Down the Line.

p. l. r. (log-book abbreviation), patent log reading.

p. s. c., per standard compass.

PACIFIC IRONS, the goose-neck at the heel of a cargo boom; the casting capping the end of a yardarm to which the Flemish horse was made fast and supported the stunsail boom irons. The withes on a yardarm through which the stunsail booms were run out by some, though erroneously, called Pacific irons.

PACKET, a vessel making regular voyages between the same ports with mails, passengers, and express freight; a liner of the sailing ship days.

PAD BOLT or **EYE,** one fitted with a square plate which rivets to a ship's side or elsewhere.

PADDLE, an implement of the nature of an oar but of large blade area.

PADDLE BOX, the guard which covers a paddle wheel.

PADDLE WHEEL, one having projecting boards or buckets for propelling a steamer. Such revolving wheels are located about midships; one to each side of the vessel. There are also a few *stern wheelers* left, with one paddle wheel at the extreme stern.

PADDY'S or **IRISH HURRICANE,** a dead calm. The wind is then said to be blowing *up and down.*

PAINTED PORTS, alternate black and white rectangles painted in a band along a ship's side in imitation of gun ports. It was a practice quite generally followed in British sailing ships.

PAINTER, the rope in the bow of a boat for towing or making fast. A condition occurring in Callao, Peru, when the water becomes discolored and nauseating in odor. The paint on a ship's sides is stained a very dark rusty red by it. It is due to a seasonal change of the ocean currents when the equatorial warm current displaces the cool Peruvian Current.

PAIR MASTS, a cargo working unit of two masts abreast with their usual booms. Their heads are connected by a heavy spanner stay. Pair masts are double king posts.

PALLET, a square wooden platform upon which a draft of cargo is loaded. It is hoisted with a four-part bridle, each leg being fast to a corner of the pallet. A stretcher near the top of the bridle prevents the converging parts from damaging the bags or cases. Sometimes there are eyes at the corners and the bridle legs are equipped with hooks. Some pallets have a pipe framework in lieu of the bridle.

PALM, a sailor's thimble. It is of leather and fits over the hand. A piece of iron is secured by rawhide on the inside and with this a needle is pushed through the fabric. There are two types, *seaming* and *roping* palms, the latter being heavier. The flat part of the fluke of an anchor.

PAMPERO, a storm which forms in the pampas of Argentina, and comes off the land with great suddenness. Pamperos are often very violent and their period of duration is variable, lasting sometimes less than an hour and at other times for several days.

PANGA, a flat-bottomed rowboat of Central America.

PANS, cakes or blocks of ice.

PANTING, the in and out vibrations of a vessel's structure.

PANTING STRAINS, those produced by head resistance in forcing a vessel through the water. Also applied to the pressing in or out of a ship's plates due to the pressure of waves. The *panting stringers* reinforce the plates against these stresses, along the sides, and *panting beams* and *frames* at the bow.

PAPAGAYO, a northeast gale blowing off the coast of Central America.

PAPER JACK, a master in name only. One who secures a command through influence and depends professionally on his mate.

PAR LINE, the normal height of a barometer at a given place.

PARACHUTE SPINNAKER, a large, light sail, triangular in shape, hoisting to, or almost to, the foremast head, forward of the head stays: the tack at the end of spinnaker boom and the sail sheeted at the side opposite the boom. This sail has a much greater width than a regular spinnaker.

PARALLAX, the error applied to an observed altitude due to taking it from a position on the surface of the earth and not at its center. It is the angle at the body between a line drawn ot the center of the earth and one to the eye of the observer.

PARALLEL RULERS, an instrument used in chart work for transferring courses and bearings to and from the compass roses. It consists of two rulers attached by two metallic straps which allow the rulers to separate but always to remain parallel with each other. They can be stepped across a chart, preserving the same direction.

PARALLEL SAILING, that method used when the course of a vessel is east or west, running along a parallel of latitude. The distance made is *all* departure. There is no difference of latitude. The parallel becomes the middle latitude and is used as a course in Table 3, Bowditch (1958), from which the difference of longitude is readily taken.

PARALLEL SPHERE, that seen by an observer at the poles where the diurnal circles of the bodies are parallel with the horizon. The sun's daily change of declination causes its diurnal circles to become very fine spirals and not strictly parallel with the horizon. There are also Right and Oblique Spheres.

PARALLELS OF LATITUDE, circles that pass around the earth everywhere parallel with the equator. They grow smaller as the latitudes of the parallels increase.

PARAVANES. See Otter Gear.

PARBUCKLE, a purchase consisting of two ropes which pass down a ship's side, down inside and up outside a spar or cask which is hove to the rail by the last part of the rope.

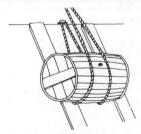

Parbuckle

PARCEL, to wind strips of canvas tightly around with the lay of a piece of wire or other rope. The *service* is placed upon the parceling.

PARHELIA, bright spots or mock suns that are sometimes seen on each side of the sun; sun dogs. See Halo.

PARRAL (Parrel), a ring or *tub,* so called, which goes around a mast and holds a yard close to it. It allows the yard to be hoisted and lowered. Also the band with revolving balls of lignum vitae that connects the jaws of a gaff forward of the mast.

PART, to break, as of a rope. A section of the rope of a tackle is a *part.* There is the hauling part and the standing part.

PARTICULAR AVERAGE, a term applied to the mode of adjustment for damage or partial loss unavoidably happening to one of the individual interests through some peril insured against. See Act of Providence.

PARTNERS, planks, usually rising a little above the decks, fitted around a mast, hatch or capstan, for the purpose of closing the opening.

PASS A LASHING, an earing, etc., to make the necessary turns to secure the sail, spar or other object.

PASS A LINE, to carry a line to or around something or reeve through, and make fast.

PASS DOWN THE LINE, to repeat a message from a flagship to another naval vessel when three or more are in extended formation. This relay method of signaling is employed when the flagship is not in visible communication with her entire squadron and so cannot send a *cornet.* Popularly abbreviated P. D. L. With modern communication this relay system has lost much of its usefulness.

PASS THE WORD, to repeat an order for the information of the crew.

PASSAGE WINDS, those prevailing from same direction over a great oceanic area.

PASSAREE, a rope used to guy out the clews of a fore course when before the wind in order to keep the foresail flat. In the clippers and others with large foresails which extended well outboard, booms were necessary to accomplish this. *Passarees* were boomed outboard some 30 feet at the fore, and when before the wind the foresail was set as flat as possible with its clews hauled well out on the passaree booms. (Mr. Basil Lubbock describing the sails of a tea clipper.) Sometimes spelled pazaree.

PASSPORT, a document issued by the government certifying to a person's, or vessel's nationality. It contains an identification of the person, and it is expected that safe conduct will be accorded its bearer.

PATACHE, a Mediterranean two-masted vessel rigged much like a brigantine of later days.

PATENT BLOCK, one in which the sheave turns on rollers like ball bearings.

PATENT EYE, a metallic device fitted on the end of a wire rope as a substitute for a spliced eye. After the eye is in place, hot zinc is poured in among the separated strands of the wire rope, holding the eye in place.

PATENT LINKS, used in connecting pieces of chain. The link is made in two parts cut obliquely with a small angle making the parts wedge-shaped. The surfaces are notched so when meshed and riveted a complete link is formed.

PATENT LOG (Taffrail Log), a mechanical device used for the purpose of measuring the distance a vessel has sailed. It has a registering contrivance at the taffrail which shows by hands the number of miles and tenths covered. There is a rotator drawn through the water astern, consisting of a brass cone fitted with wings which cause it to rotate according to the speed. The line connecting the rotator with the registering device is a hard laid cotton type, which does not twist. It is usually about 400 feet long, depending, however, on the size and speed of the vessel. There are also patent logs operated by an electric current, and by compression due to passage through the water.

PATENT SLIP, a marine railway.

PATENT STERN, an overhanging deck at the stern of certain Chesapeake Bay bugeyes, the purpose being to widen deck space. This deck is supported by beams extending beyond the sides of the vessel.

PAUNCH MAT, heavy tarred stuff plaited into a strip for use as chafing gear in the rigging. Also called a *wrought mat.*

PAVISSES, protection erected around a ship's rail against the boarding of an enemy or against water. The shields (pavisses) of the Vikings used to line the rails of the ancient Norse ships.

PAWL, a short piece of iron hinged by a pin at one end of the barrel of a capstan. As the capstan is revolved, it is dragged along the pawl rim and falls into the pockets and prevents any backward motion.

PAWL (PAUL) RIM, a rim or groove on a capstan fitted with indentations into which the pawls fall ratchet-like, and hold the capstan from turning backward.

PAY, to fill the caulked seams of a deck with pitch. To cover with paint, tar or pitch.

PAY OFF, to swing off from the wind.

PAY OUT, to let out chain or ease off on a rope.

PAY WITH THE TOPSAIL SHEET, to run away without paying a bill.

PAYING OFF WITH THE MAIN BOOM is the legend of a convenient way to rid the ship of a homeward-bound sailor with a large credit of wages. When he was standing in an exposed position, the main boom was *"accidentally"* jibed and the sailor disappeared without trace. It is said that Bloody Point, Chesapeake Bay, used to be the chosen spot for this "accident."

PAZAREE. See Passaree.

PEA (Pee), the point of the palm of an anchor.

PEA COAT, the blue broadcloth reefer worn by U. S. N. enlisted men below the grade of chief petty officer.

PEAK, the end of the gaff. It is the upper and after corner of a sail. An anchor chain is said to *stay peak* when leading a little forward; to *short stay peak* when the anchor is underfoot. A compartment at the extremity of a ship designated *fore* or *after peak* as the case may be.

PEAK HALYARDS, those which hoist the peak of a gaff.

PEAK SPAN, a piece of wire or rope leading from the lower masthead to the peak of a standing gaff to support it in position.

PEAK TANK, a tank situated in the fore or after peak.

PEAPOD, a small rowing or sailing boat of the Maine coast whose name comes from its shape, being pointed at both ends and round-bottomed.

PELAGIC ORGANISMS, those found off-shore in the surface waters of the ocean.

PELICAN HOOK, a hinged hook which is held in place by a link. When the link is knocked off the hook collapses. It is also called a *slip hook*. It is used to make shrouds fast to chain plates and for boat gripes.

PELORUS, an instrument for the purpose of taking bearings and celestial azimuths. It consists of two sight vanes, revolvable about a dumb compass. The latter is set to the ship's heading by standard compass and the bearing is read off as from the ordinary compass. It is hung in gimbals, and usually the compass plate is of ground glass with an electric light bulb beneath for night work.

PEMMICAN, a condensed food used on Arctic voyages, made of lean meat dried and smoked, which is then more or less pulverized and mixed with an equal part of fat.

PENDANT, a piece of wire or rope with a block spliced in one end. A whip (or tackle) is used at the block end and the other is made fast to a yard or gaff, and serves as a brave or vang, etc. A short piece of wire rope fitted with an eye at each end placed athwart the trestletrees for use in hooking tackles. A pendant's usual function is to shorten the distance necessary to use a tackle or whip.

PENDANT TACKLES, those two-fold purchases which are usually hooked to the lower mast pendants, and are used for moving weights on the deck, or setting up the lower rigging.

PENNANT, a streamer of bunting. There are *answering, commission, meal, homeward bound* pennants, etc.

PENUMBRA. The area of partial light during an eclipse.

PERCH, a pole driven into the bottom to serve as a beacon to mark a channel, or a danger. It usually has a topmark or bush surmounting it.

PERIAGUA. See Piragua and cat schooner.

PERIGA, a small lateen-rigged vessel of the Mediterranean.

PERIGEAN TIDES, occur one to three days after the moon passes perigree. These tides are higher than the mean range.

PERIGEE, the point in the moon's orbit nearest the earth. The opposite point is called *apogee.* These two points are joined by the long diameter of the orbital ellipse. The tides tend to increase in range as the distance of the moon from the earth decreases.

PERIHELION, the point where the earth's orbit is intersected by the long diameter of the orbital ellipse; that is, nearest the sun. The opposite point is called the *aphelion.*

PERIOD OF OSCILLATION, the time occupied by a vessel rolling from port to starboard. See Oscillation, Period of.

PERISCOPE, an arrangement of prisms in a small projecting tube by which an observer below can see objects above.

PERMISSIBLE FACTOR, a margin of safety that must be allowed in spacing bulkheads. It varies with the length of a vessel. If a vessel has a factor of 0.5 and floodable length of 100 feet, she would be obliged to have a bulkhead at 0.5 of 100 feet or 50 feet.

PERPENDICULARS. See Length Between Perpendiculars.

PERSONAL EQUATION, a certain lag or anticipation characteristic of an observer in noting the instant of taking an observation. Also a personal characteristic of observing angles too large or too small. This is also termed *personal error.*

PERTURBATION, an irregularity in the movement of a heavenly body.

PERUVIAN CURRENT. See Humboldt Current.

PHOSPHORESCENT SEA, a phenomenon of glowing light frequently seen at sea at some point of agitation such as the breaking crest of a wave, the bow wave and wake of a vessel, or the dipping of an oar. It is supposed to be caused by the oxidation of a secretion emitted by jellyfish and other animalculae when agitated by some disturbance. The jellyfish causing this condition have been found in a wide variety of forms. The pale light of phosphorescence sometimes attains considerable brilliancy, one shipmaster reporting that a bucket of the water from overside at such a time was sufficient to cause a glow of illumination in the cabin. Another reported great difficulty in making out the lights of vessels until close aboard owing to the brilliance of the sea.

PICAROON, a pirate or pirate vessel.

PICK AND STRIKE METHOD of discharging cargo: In this operation a draft of cargo is swung from the hatch, over the coaming, to the deck where the hatch tackle is unhooked; the burton is then hooked and the draft swung over the side to the pier. The first movement is the *pick* and the latter the *strike.* Sometimes two hatch tackles are rigged, the second being suspended from the middle part of the hatch boom. By this arrangement the drafts come up alternately on the hatch tackles.

PICKET BOAT, an outpost scouting or guard boat.

PICKLE, to creosote timbers or piles for preservation. To give steel plates an acid bath to remove mill scale.

PIE-PLATE, is a cargo net with a circular wooden bottom for fragile cargo.

PIER, a construction work extending into a harbor with a sufficient depth of water alongside to accommodate vessels. It carries a suggestion of greater length than a wharf.

PIERHEAD LEAP, to desert a ship as she reaches a wharf. Sometimes also to join a ship at the last moment before she sails. Also called pierhead jump.

PIERHEAD LINE, is established by the U. S. Army Engineers and limits the length of open piers through which the water can flow. See Bulkhead Line.

PIG BOAT, a submarine.

PIG STEAMER, a sailor's name for a whaleback steamer.

PIG YOKE, a name for an old-fashioned wooden octant.

PIGEON HOLES, those in the drumhead of a capstan to receive the capstan bars. A hole in the top platform for the running rigging to pass through.

PILE DRIVING, the action of a vessel in a head sea when, not being of sufficient length to bridge two seas, she pitches heavily into the second sea and rises violently.

PILLAR, a hold stanchion.

PILLAR LADDER, one consisting of rungs fitted between two supporting pillars or stanchions.

PILLOW, a timber upon which the inner end of the bowsprit rests.

PILOT, a person with expert local knowledge in the piloting of vessels. While he usually takes charge of the navigation, his presence does not relieve the master of his responsibility. Also a book of sailing directions.

PILOT BOAT, a seaworthy vessel, either steam or sail, that lies to or cruises off a port with pilots for incoming vessels.

PILOT CHARTS, invaluable aids to the navigator, containing an immense amount of information, including data on meteorology, ice, fog, currents, floating obstructions, sailing and steaming tracks, distances, and scientific articles. These charts were originated by Lieut. M. F. Maury, U. S. N., and have been published by the Hydrographic and Oceanographic offices.

PILOT SIGNALS. An inbound vessel desiring a pilot shows P.T. of the International code, the jack at the fore, a blue light every 15 minutes at night, or a white light shown at intervals above the rail. Nowadays contact with the pilot boat is made by radio.

PILOT or **WHEELHOUSE,** a room under or on the bridge where the steering wheel is located. The officer of the watch often stands his watch in the wheelhouse.

PILOTING, the navigation of a vessel alongshore, or into a harbor, by means of bearings of landmarks, soundings, and the guidance of buoys and beacons.

PILOT'S LUFF, to make a desired distance to windward by shooting the vessel into the wind until she runs her way off. Sometimes called a *fisherman's luff.*

PIN RACK, a substitute for a pin rail, being a stout piece of wood, bored to receive belaying pins and seized horizontally across the shrouds well above the rail. They were used when deck loads prevented access to the regular pin rails.

PIN RAIL, a thick narrow plank secured inboard to the ship's rail abreast the shrouds. It is pierced with holes to receive belaying pins to which the running rigging is made fast.

PINCH HER, to hold a vessel so close to the wind as to shiver her sails slightly.

PINK STERN, a sharp stern usually with a false overhang having considerable sheer.

PINKY, a small sharp-sterned vessel employed primarily for fishing. Developed in late colonial days the type persisted "way down East" until fairly recent times. In general the pinky had a full bow and a finer stern; a prominent feature was the sheer of the bulwarks that swept up gracefully to a peak abaft the sternpost. The pinky was usually steered with a tiller. Some of the type carried a two-masted fore-and-aft rig without bowsprit or jib. Except for a few yacht versions the type is extinct. The long-disappeared Mediterranean pink or pinque was a vessel of 200 or 300 tons; three masted, lateen rigged with the foremast raking heavily forward; the forward end of the fore lateen yard was controlled by a line to the end of a bowsprit or beakhead.

PINNACE, a double-banked pulling boat; a heavy tender to old naval and merchant vessels. Sometimes propelled by sail. Also in olden times a sea-going decked vessel of comparatively small tonnage.

PINNACLE, a tall spindling rock rising from the sea bottom.

PINTLE, the hook or pin that fits into the gudgeon and upon which the rudder hangs and turns.

PINWHEELING, turning a twin screw steamer within a small space by going ahead on one propeller and backing on the other.

PIPE, a boatswain's whistle.

PIPE DOWN, the silence signal at night on a naval vessel; a call from the boatswain's pipe to go below. A term used to stop talking.

PIPE THE SIDE, to blow the boatswain's pipe in honor of an officer or official coming aboard for an official visit.

PIRAGUA (Pirogue), a large Indian dugout, or canoe, constructed out of the trunk of a tree. It resembles the Malay proa, and in the South Sea Islands is constructed double.

PIRATE, a sea thief. A vessel cruising without legal status in search of booty, and perhaps ready to fight for it. See Buccaneer, and Jamaica Discipline.

PIROGUE. See Piragua.

PISCES, the twelfth sign of the Zodiac.

PITCH, the fore and aft motion of a vessel. The distance between rivets on the same line. The distance a propeller of a vessel moves forward in one revolution, as in cold grease, due to the angle at which the blades are set. The amount, or percentage, of this distance that is lost through the mobility of water is known as *slip*. A by-product of tar which in a melted condition is poured into the deck seams.

PITCH POLE, a disaster to a boat or small vessel in which a breaking sea astern casts her stern over bow in a sort of half somersault.

PITTING, areas of metal eaten away by corrosion or electrolysis.

PIVOTING POINT, that point within a vessel around which she turns on her helm.

PLAIN SAILS, regular working sails, exclusive of light sails such as flying jib, skysails, light staysails, spinnakers, gollywobblers, drifters, etc.

PLANE, a surface with no curvature. The plane of the equator is the course of an imaginary saw should the earth be cut in half along the line of this great circle. As Captain Lecky carefully explains, "a plane is represented by the paper covering the hoop of the circus rider; it is the plane of the hoop."

PLANE CHART, a representation of the earth's surface as though it were flat. The curvature of the earth not being considered, an error will creep in which renders this chart useless in anything but small areas.

PLANE SAILING, a method dealing with the courses and distances sailed and the determination of the point arrived at. The meridian, parallel of latitude, and distance sailed form a right triangle of which the distance is the hypotenuse; with the course angle and one side, the other sides can be computed or picked out of Table 3, Bowditch, 1958. The curvature of the earth is not considered, hence departure and not difference of longitude represents the distance made east or west.

PLANE TABLE, an instrument designed to run in coast lines and locate prominent topographic features on a rough sheet. It consists principally of a small table, supported by a tripod, upon which the sheet is secured. A movable steel straight-edge surmounted by a telescope set in the same line as the straight edge is leveled and oriented by known landmarks after which lines of position of unknown points desired may be ruled in. These lines are crossed by similar lines when another position is taken up. Distances are accurately estimated by the use of horizontal hair lines in the telescope and a graduated rod called a *stadia*.

PLANETARY HOIST, a chain hoist which has a combination of reduction gears in the upper block. There are some with 40 tons capacity.

PLANETS, nine heavenly bodies which form part of the *solar system*. They revolve about the sun in orbits varying greatly in size. The earth is a planet. Mercury and Venus have orbits smaller than the earth's, and are called inferior planets, while Jupiter, Saturn and Mars, the principal navigational planets, have orbits outside that of the earth and are called superior planets. These bodies are very valuable for determining position at sea, if the horizon is clearly seen. The best time for observations is at twilight or dawn. The other planets, besides those mentioned, are Uranus, Neptune and Pluto.

PLANISPHERE, a device for locating stars. They are shown on a circular map which can be revolved between two pieces of cardboard forming a frame. Those stars above the horizon appear within a circular opening, when it is set at the proper time of day.

PLANK SHEERS or **COVERING BOARDS,** those planks placed over the top of the frames and sheer strake.

PLANKS, lengths of wood spiked to the outside of a vessel's frames forming the outside skin, and upon the beams to form the decks.

PLANKTON, those oragnisms of the sea which float or swim feebly, among which are jellyfish and diatoms.

PLAT (or Plait), to braid small stuff into mats and chafing gear.

PLATES, sheets of steel forming the strakes or outside skin of a vessel and the decks.

PLATFORM DECK, one constructed below the lowest regular deck.

PLATFORM SLING, a small platform capable of suspension from a tackle by bridles reaching the four corners. It is used for cargo which does not safely lend itself to ordinary slinging. Also called a pallet.

PLAY, lost motion.

PLEDGE, a length of oakum rolled for caulking.

PLIMSOLL MARK, a figure marked on the sides of cargo carriers. The different horizontal lines indicate the depth to which the vessel can be loaded in different trades. The law governing drafts was a hard-fought victory won by Samuel Plimsoll, M.P., for the protection of seamen. In 1929 an international convention adopted general laws regarding load lines. The world was divided with zones relative to the risks of prevailing weather and load lines assigned thereto. The United States ratified this convention. The abbreviations signify drafts as follows: FW, fresh water; IS, Indian Ocean summer; S, summer; W, winter; and WNA, winter in North Atlantic.

PLOT, to lay down on a chart a vessel's course, her position, or the position of landmarks.

PLOTTING CHART, one showing only the meridians and parallels, laid down on the Mercator projection. It is for the purpose of plotting position lines.

PLOW, an anchor whose holding section has the shape of a farmer's plow. Stress on the shank digs the point effectively into the bottom.

PLUG, a short wooden pin with its grain running from side to side.

not lengthwise, used for plugging holes in a wooden deck above the spike or screw which secures the deck to the beams. A tapering pin used in the drain hole of a boat.

PLUM DUFF. See Duff.

PLUMMER BLOCKS, structural supports or blocks of wood for holding the alignment of the shaft.

PLY, to beat to windward. Steamers *ply* between their regular ports loading and discharging.

PNEUMATIC RIVETER, a compressed air hammer for the heading of rivets.

POD, a group of several whales.

POINT, a division of a compass, being an arc of 11¼°, or ¹⁄₃₂ of the circle of the card. To *point a rope* is to taper off the strands and cover with an elaborate protection of innumerable half hitches made of small stuff. A vessel *points well* if she sails close to the wind.

POINTERS, a name given to two stars forming the outer edge of the Big Dipper. They indicate the position of the pole star by their direction.

POLACRE. A rig and model of the Mediterranean. It usually had three pole masts with no tops or crosstrees. They were square-rigged on fore and mainmast with a lateen mizzen and a square topsail above. The bow was sharp with pole bowsprit.

POLAR ANGLE. See Hour Angle.

POLAR CIRCLES, the Arctic and Antarctic Circles.

POLAR DISTANCE, the angular distance from the pole to a celestial body. It is found by subtracting the declination from 90°, if the latitude and declination are of the same name, that is, both north. But if one is north and the other is south, the declination must be added to 90°.

POLARIS FOR LATITUDE. The altitude of the pole is the latitude of the position of the observer. In order to obtain this the altitude of the star Polaris is taken and corrected for dip and refraction, and further corrected by reducing the altitude of the star to the altitude of the pole. For the last correction, the location of Polaris in its small orbit must be determined by calculating the local sidereal time and entering the proper table of the Nautical Almanac.

POLE, to push a boat by means of a pole reaching the bottom. See Poles.

POLE COMPASS. See Mariner's Compass.

POLE MAST, one all in one spar as seen in most steamers, and in marconi-rigged yachts.

POLES, the points at the surface of a rotating body, as the earth, penetrated by the line of the axis. The poles of a great circle are the points above and below that are everywhere 90° from the circle; thus the poles of the ecliptic are everywhere 90° from that great circle.

POLYCONIC CHART, a projection based on a series of cones. This means that every parallel of latitude represents the base of a cone which is tangent to the earth's surface and whose apex lies somewhere in the axis of the earth according to the latitude. It is as though a dunce cap were placed over the earth, its edge coinciding with the parallel of latitude and its apex directly over the pole. In this projection, the central meridian is straight, but the others converge towards the (pole) top of the chart. The parallels are slightly curved. A great circle is represented, for practical purposes, by a straight line. The polyconic chart represents the earth's surface with less distortion than other navigational projections, but, the Mercator projection being sufficiently accurate for small scale charts, the polyconic is used principally for surveying purposes, and occasionally for large scale harbor charts.

PONTOON, a vessel used in wrecking for lifting power; a scow used for bridge platforms of a so-called *pontoon bridge;* air floats of considerable size are called pontoons. A *pontoon lifeboat* is divided into compartments for seaworthiness.

POOP, the deck abaft the mizzen in a flush decked three-masted vessel; the raised deck and after structure at the stern of a vessel. This raised structure is comprised of *poop framing, poop stringers, bulkhead, beams, sheerstrake* and *poop deck.*

POOPED, a term applied when a wave breaks over the stern.

POP UP CABIN, a device to increase the headroom over a portion of the cabin in a small boat, as over the galley. This section is raised by rods at each corner; it is usually provided with curtains.

POPPETS, blocks set under the fore and aft part of the bilgeways to support a vessel in launching. The name also is given to pieces of wood, forming rowlocks secured to the rail of a boat.

PORCUPINE, a term applied to a wire rope when its threads of wire begin to part and the ends protrude.

PORPOISE. Porpoise, to breach, as a torpedo or a paravane. A mammal of the dolphin family.

PORT, the left side of a vessel, formerly called the larboard side. Originally derived from the fact that the ships of the 17th century had their only loading port on the left side. This became the loading side or ladeboard, later larboard, but the term *port* as applied to the left side of a vessel was used in the 17th century according to R. C. Anderson, Esq., the eminent authority on such matters. It is obvious that port was adopted owing to its contrast of sound from starboard. A harbor for embarkation and discharge of cargo, etc. An opening in the side of a vessel, which takes its name from its location or from the purpose it serves, such as a *gun port, light* or *air port, lumber* or *cargo port, coal, bulwark, bow, ballast gangway, hawser port,* etc.

PORT OF CALL, a subsidiary place at which a vessel calls regularly along her route.

PORT CAPTAIN, an officer of a line who attends to the berthing, repairs and general oversight of vessels while in port. A naval officer in charge of harbor activities.

PORT CHARGES. See Harbor Dues.

PORT OF ENTRY, one having custom authorities.

PORT HELM, the helm (tiller) swung to port carrying the rudder to the right and turning the vessel's course to starboard. The order "port helm" has been abandoned for "Right Rudder."

PORT HOLES, openings in the ship's side for light, air and guns.

PORT LIGHT. The usual round openings closed with glass for light and air are called ports. The glass is set in a hinged brass frame called the *port light* which is screwed against a rubber gasket with lugs. In heavy weather, a metal shutter is screwed against the inner side by lugs as a preventer. This is called a *dead light.*

PORT TACK, sailing with the wind coming over the left or port side.

PORT WARDEN, an officer of a port whose duties include the safeguarding of a vessel's seaworthiness, as by proper stowage; the holding of surveys on vessels or on cargo ashore, and the measurement of vessels.

PORTAGE BILL, the account of the crew's wages.

PORTOISE, an old term for gunwale; a term applied to yards resting on a ship's rails.

PORTUGUESE MAN OF WAR (Physalia), a kind of jellyfish often seen floating or sailing on the warm waters of the ocean. The lower portion under water is provided with long, hanging tentacles, which are poisonous to the touch. The gas-filled body above water is surmounted by a fluted ridge which catches the wind.

POSITION LINE. A line drawn on a chart derived by a celestial observation or bearing of a known object ashore, somewhere upon which is the ship's position. A crossing of two or more position lines definitely locates the vessel.

POUNDING, heavy pitching that causes a shock through vessel's structure.

POWDER RAG, slang phrase for the alphabet flag "B" that is flown when a vessel handles ammunition or highly inflammable fuel.

POWER TONNAGE, a measurement used in classifying vessels, derived by adding the indicated horsepower to the gross tonnage of a vessel.

PRAM (Praam or prahm), a Dutch lighter; a small tender.

PRATIQUE. The temporary quarantine of a vessel arriving from foreign ports is raised by the giving to the master a *pratique certificate.* This is done by the health officer upon becoming satisfied as to the state of health aboard and the *bill of health* issued her at the last port. If *granted pratique* or *admitted to pratique,* she becomes unrestricted, otherwise she is quarantined. An incoming vessel flies the yellow quarantine flag until granted pratique.

PRAYER BOOKS, small holystones.

PRECESSION OF THE EQUI-NOXES, the slow westward movement of the First Point of Aries (vernal equinox) due to a circular motion of the earth's axis around the pole of the ecliptic. The movement is about 50″ each year. As all right ascensions are measured eastward from the First Point of Aries, it is evident they are all increased by 50″ each year due to the precession movement of their point of origin westward. This action of the axis is caused by the unequal distribution of matter in the earth's shape. The equatorial bulge is acted upon by the sun's attraction which tends to draw the earth from its inclination of 23° 27½′ to an upright position. This attraction is at its maximum at the time of the summer and winter solstices when the equatorial bulge is well above or below the plane of the ecliptic; the result is the circular movement of the earth's axis around the pole of the ecliptic. This revolution occupies 25,800 years.

PREDICTED LOG CONTEST, is one in which a motorboat skipper carefully estimates the hours, minutes and seconds that his boat will take to cover a prescribed course set by the judges. He must accurately know his speed at certain revolutions and must evaluate the favorable or adverse effect of current and wind expected to be encountered. The winner is the best predictor.

PRESS-GANG, a naval party ashore who with authority formerly shanghaied British merchant seamen, and others, for service in the navy.

PREVENTER, an additional rope or wire placed alongside an overburdened brace or backstay to relieve pressure and prevent accident. Sometimes loosely used to mean a spare part of any sort.

PRICKER, a small marline spike.

PRIMAGE, a percentage of the freight money given to a master as a bonus. The former custom in sailing ships averaged 5 per cent primage. A percentage of freight money held out by a steamship company which is returned to a shipper as a rebate provided the company has received all the business of the shipper.

PRIME MERIDIAN, the meridian arbitrarily chosen as the origin of longitudes. From this meridian, the measurement of longitude commences. The different countries formerly used the meridian of their principal observatory, as France—Paris; Portugal—Lisbon; Russia—Pulkowa; but virtually all maritime countries have now adopted the meridian of Greenwich as their prime meridian for all navigational purposes. The British Admiralty has been the most active hydrographic surveying organization of the world and its set of charts and sailing directions are the most original and complete, which in a way has influenced the general adoption of Greenwich as the prime meridian.

PRIME VERTICAL, a great circle passing through the zenith and nadir and east and west points of the horizon. It is square with the meridian and is a vertical circle.

PRIMING and **LAGGING.** High water occurs on an average of about fifty minutes later each day; when by reason of the sun's and moon's relative positions the high water occurs earlier than the fifty minutes, the term *priming* is applied to the tide. When the positions of the bodies are such as to cause it to be later, the term *lagging* is applied.

PRISMATIC COMPASS, one fitted with a prism, by which the rays of sunlight are thrown down upon the compass card indicating upon it the bearing or azimuth of the sun.

PRIVATEER. See Letter of Marque.

PRIVILEGED VESSEL, the one with the right of way and privileged to hold her course and speed.

PROA, a vessel native with the Malays of the East, averaging in size about 30 feet long by 4 feet wide.

PROPELLER, the rotating wheel in a screw steamer which furnishes propulsion. The wings are called *blades* and the hub the *boss*. See Pitch. The propeller is often called the *wheel* or the *screw*. Generally *single propellers* are right-handed. *Twin-screws* turn outward. (River steamers turn inward to reduce water disturbance.) *Triple screws;* wing propellers turn outward, and center screw is right-handed. *Quadruple screws;* starboard screws are right-handed, and port screws are left-handed. (Nautical Magazine) Authorities differ as to what the direction of screws, shape of hull, location of struts, rudder post and rudder contribute to the problem.

A suitable design it is thought will accommodate itself to either rotation. In a twin screw vessel when turning it is good practice to slow but not to stop the inside screw; this keeps screw current on the rudder. In quadruple screws the center pair have the greatest effect on the rudder due to screw current. Propellers are right- and left-handed according to the motion, clockwise or anticlockwise when going ahead and viewed from a point outside the vessel facing the propeller, as in a dry dock.

PROPELLER INSPECTOR, a dangerous, waterlogged, derelict log floating upright in the path of shipping. Also called a Tide Walker.

PROPELLER POST, the upright frame erected on the midship line just forward of the space in which the propeller turns. This frame is also called the *stern frame*. The space between the propeller post and the stern post is called the *propeller well*.

PROTECTION and **INDEMNITY CLUBS,** associations of shipowners formed for the purpose of mutual insurance. This particularly applies to insurance against liability for loss of life and injury, and to that portion of collision liability not covered by the ordinary insurance policy.

PROTEST, a document sworn to before a notary or consul declaring that the weather conditions encountered on the voyage were such that if the ship or cargo reveals damage, it was caused by "wind and weather." This is called *enter-*

ing a protest. It is a protest against the ship's owners being held accountable through any fault of the ship, master, officers or crew. No hatches should be removed until a board of surveyors has made its survey.

PROTRACTOR, an instrument graduated into degrees for the purpose of determining direction on a chart. This instrument is found as whole circles and semi-circles and in many forms.

PROW, the bow structure of ancient ships. Not now used by seamen.

PSYCHROMETER, a lattice box containing two thermometers, one of which has its bulb wrapped with muslin and kept wet. The difference in the readings indicates the saturation of the atmosphere. A type of hygrometer.

PUDDENING, a soft pillow of yarns, strands and oakum (junk) for fending and chafing purposes. The anchor rings were protected in old days with old rope to take the chafe from the hemp hawser.

PUFF BALLS, a strip of canvas laced to the foot of a square sail like the bonnet of a jib.

PULL, to pull is a short task, as a pull on a sheet to bring in the boom a little. To haul is a more extended task. We pull a boat with oars. Also, a faster boat *pulls ahead* of another.

PULLING BOAT, a term used to distinguish a boat propelled by oars.

PULPIT, the harpooning platform on the bowsprit of a swordfishing vessel. A yacht may have an inboard pulpit to facilitate handling sails.

PUMP, a machine operated by hand, steam or electricity. It is used for transferring water, fuel oil, and gases. An air pump may be used to create a vacuum or to compress air. Perhaps the most important pump is that one which clears the bilges of water. A barometer is said to pump when it oscillates in an unusual manner. It is mostly caused by the motion of the seaway, and by the changing pressure due to wind. The mercury at such times should be read when at the lowest point of its movement.

PUMP BRAKE, the handle by which a pump is operated.

PUMPKIN SEED, a dinghy of large beam.

PUNCHEON, a barrel-like container of 70 to 84 gallons.

PUNGY, a flat-bottomed Chesapeake Bay sailboat.

PUNT, a small flat-bottomed boat. A punt is usually carried on a vessel for use in painting and cleaning the boot-topping.

PURCHASE, a tackle.

PURSER, a clerical officer on a ship.

PURSE SEINE, a large net which is floated vertically by floats, and towed around a school of fish by boats. When the school is surrounded the bottom is drawn together—pursed, and the vessel comes alongside, the seine hoisted and fish spilled on the deck.

PUT, to go; as *put* to sea.

Q

QUADRANT, a name commonly given to an instrument differing only from a sextant in that its arc is one eighth of a circle and measures an angle of 90°. This is, however, an octant. The term also applies to a quadrant of steel used as a tiller in powered ships and boats. A segment of a circle with a 90° angle, as, for example, the *Northeast quadrant.*

QUADRANTAL DEVIATION, that produced by induced magnetism in the horizontal iron such as deck beams, longitudinal stringers, etc. The error increases and diminishes in each quadrant, being the greatest when the ship is heading on the intercardinal points.

QUADRANTAL SPHERES, hollow balls of soft iron placed to port and starboard of a compass to compensate *quadrantal deviation.*

QUADRATURE. The moon is said to be in quadrature when she shows one half of her disc illuminated and the position is 90° from the sun. The moon is said to be at the *First Quarter* when between new and full and *Last Quarter* when between full and new moon.

QUARANTINE, a restriction placed on vesesls having disease aboard or coming from unhealthful points. During this period the flag Q, called the quarantine flag, or yellow jack, is exhibited. See Pratique.

QUARANTINE BUOY, one yellow in color to make a quarantine anchorage.

QUARTER, the part of a vessel forward of the stern and abaft the after rigging; *off the quarter* is in a direction 45° from astern. The part of a yard immediately outside the mast; about one-fourth the distance out of the yardarm. If the wind persists, say, from the northeast, seamen refer to it as being still in the same quarter.

QUARTER BILL, a list of all men and officers and their stations.

QUARTER BLOCKS, those serving as leads for clewlines and located under the quarters of the yards, but often shackled to the sling yoke. Quarter blocks are fast to ring bolts and serve to secure additional purchase on the boom. The sheaves which act as fairleads for the wheel ropes (or chains) to the steering tiller or quadrant.

QUARTER BOATS, those swung at davits at the quarters of a vessel.

QUARTER DECK, usually the space abaft the gangway to the mizzenmast. However, the quarter deck on a naval vessel is clearly defined by the commanding officer, it may even be forward. In ancient vessels with high poops the deck which began at a point one quarter of her length from the stern was known as the quarter deck.

QUARTERING SEA, one running toward either quarter of a vessel, as also a *quartering wind*. A sea running toward either bow is often, but *entirely erroneously*, referred to as a quartering sea.

QUARTERMASTER, the helmsman and signalman, who also has charge of much of the navigating equipment such as log line, lead line, sounding machine, etc. He also serves as an assistant navigator in naval vessels.

QUARTERS, living compartments.

QUAY (pronounced key), a loading and discharging place for vessels. It is usually filled in behind solid masonry. This type of pier is very common in Europe.

QUEEN SAIL, a staysail set on a main topmast stay.

QUICK CLOSING GEAR, the apparatus for closing all bulkhead doors from the bridge.

QUICK WATER, is that agitated by and around the rudder when put over and operating to port or starboard.

QUICK FLASHING LIGHTS make 60 or more flashes per minute.

QUICKEN, to sharpen a curve in the lines of a ship.

QUICKSANDS, areas with a high saturation of water resulting in a loose bottom in which heavy material sinks rapidly. Notable areas are the waters of lower Hoogly River and the Marquesas Quicksands west of Key West.

QUICKWORK, the planking of the bulwarks of a wooden ship between ports and on the inside. Also that part of a ship's plating and planking under water when loaded.

QUILTING, a covering of woven ropes or sennit on the outside of a container used for water.

QUOIN, a piece of wood formerly used for elevating guns, differing from a wedge in that only one face is tapered; it has a right angle.

R

r. p. m., revolutions per minute.

RABBET, a channel or longitudinal recess cut in the face of a timber to receive another timber or plank, as the rabbet in the keel to receive the garboard strake, or in the stem and stern frames to receive the hood ends of the planks, or the ends of the strakes of plating. The *back rabbet* is the face of the rab-

bet to which the garboard strake is nailed. The *rabbet line* is the lower edge of the rabbet or the line of the outside of the garboard as it is in contact with the keel; the *bearding line* is the line of the upper edge of the rabbet where the inside of the garboard lies against the keel.

RACE, the rapid revolving of a

propeller when the pitch of a vessel raises the stern and brings part of the propeller out of water. A very rapid current, usually marked by rips especially if two currents are conflicting. The term is not applied to offshore currents.

RACK, sometimes called *Fiddles,* a device to prevent dishes from leaving the tables in seaway. Racks appear in many forms, but usually only as a combing around the edge of a table. A more elaborate type consists of several compartments of appropriate size for a plate, cup, glass, and wine glasses. A cruder variety is merely a tablecloth of canvas with heavy rope sewn to it in such a way as to form individual squares before each person. See Halyard Rack.

RACK BLOCK, a series of fairlead sheaves set in a piece of wood.

RACKING SEIZING, small stuff passed around two ropes or spars in an over and under figure-of-eight fashion.

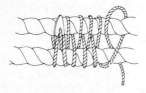

Racking Seizing

RACKING STRESS, exists in a rolling vessel tending to fracture the union of the frames and the beams. A primary purpose of the knees is to resist this stress.

RADAR, is a system of radio ranging and detection. A radio signal is transmitted in a desired direction, it meets an object and returns as an echo. The time these radio pulses require to go out to the object and return gives an accurate determination of distance. It takes about 6.18 millionths of a second to travel a nautical mile. The echo is brought to the A-scope, for the scrutiny of the navigator, by means of a cathode ray tube, on the order of a picture tube in a TV set.

RADDLE, small stuff woven over and under into a mat, gasket or gripe.

RADIATION, transfers heat in waves. The heat from a stove comes largely from heat waves radiating from the hot iron. The heat of the earth's surface comes from radiation from the sun.

RADIO, wireless telegraphy or telephony.

RADIO BEACON, a radio station on shore which sends at regular intervals an assigned characteristic of dots and dashes. The mariner aboard ship taking a bearing of this signal obtains a line of position. See Radio Direction Finder.

RADIO DIRECTION FINDER may be established aboard ship or ashore. It is equipped with an aerial that can be oscillated on a vertical shaft leading down to the operator. It is a characteristic of such an aerial that the radio impulses become more or less distinct depending on the angle at which they are picked up. By means of a large compass diagram the operator by turning the aerial can establish the bearing of a vessel or station by the intensity of the radio waves. At the point where the intensity is least—the null—is the bearing of the radio beacon ashore, or of the ship from a shore station. By obtaining another such bearing from a second beacon the master will have two lines, whose intersection when plotted on the chart establishes the position of the ship. The directions given are great circle bearings and should be corrected, if plotted on a Mercator chart, should the distances be large.

Radio direction finders are also installed aboard ship to enable navigators to ascertain the bearing of shore stations or other vessels.

Such radio direction finders must be carefully calibrated as they are subject to deviation. All these instruments, either ashore or afloat, are also subject to an indeterminate, so-called, *night effect*—also a *land effect*.

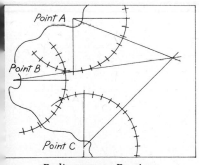

Radiocompass Bearings

RADIO SEXTANT, an electronic instrument by which altitudes of the sun and moon can be observed through an overcast.

RADIO SHACK, the radio operator's headquarters.

RADIO TICK, a time singal sent broadcast for the rating of chronometers at sea.

RADIUS VECTOR, the line drawn from the sun to the earth.

RAFFEE, the same as a *moonraker* or *skyscraper*—a triangular sail set from the truck and the yardarms of the highest yard.

RAFT, a structure of floating logs or lumber which serves various purposes through its simplicity of construction.

RAFTED ICE, that in which cakes have ridden one on another.

RAGHIEHS, easterly gales, shifting to westerly, experienced in the Levant off the coast of Syria.

RAIL, the top of the bulwarks or the plank sheer covering the frames when they extend above the decks; the uppermost of the lines of pipe railing.

RAILWAY or **RAILWAY GAFF,** one fitted with an iron so shaped as to carry the hanks seized to the head of the sail. Now called a *sail track. Railway* is an inclined structure at the water's edge which extends below the water. It carries a cradle which moves on rollers or wheels. The cradle run below the water receives the vessel, usually at high water, which is then hauled out by steam or electric power. Also *marine railway.*

RAINBOWS are caused by refraction and dispersion of light. The sunlight passing through raindrops creates a bow in the sky opposite the sun. The center of the bow, the eye of the observer and the sun are in a straight line. The red of the spectrum is on the outside of the rainbow. In a secondary rainbow, often visible outside the primary rainbow, the order of the colors is reversed.

RAISE, to *raise a light* is to come within the range of its visibility. It is a familiar expression to say "We stood on and raised the land at Cape Horn." *To raise the wind* is to raise money.

RAISED DECK YACHT, is one in which the top of the cabin is carried out to the full beam of boat and usually forward to the stern.

RAISED QUARTER DECK, that deck of a steamer where the raised poop is carried forward, doing away with the after well deck. This deck is of heavy construction.

RAKE, the angle a vessel's masts or stacks, or the angle the overhang of the stem or stern, takes with the perpendicular. To fire shells lengthwise of a vessel's decks.

RAKISH, to have a look of speed through raking masts. A suggestion of illicit employment.

RAM, a protruding portion of the lower stem of a naval vessel, so constructed as to receive the impact of an attacking collision.

RAM LINE, one used for centering a spar in shaping it, and also in determining on deck the fore and aft line of the keel.

RAM PLATE, heavy pieces of structural steel in the bow of a battleship to support the ram at the bow.

RAM SCHOONER, one carrying no topmasts, but tall pole masts. Also called a bald-headed schooner.

RAMP, an incline which takes the place of a few steps. Many ramps are now built from dry ground down the shore to well underwater, to facilitate the launching and hauling out of boats carried on trailers.

RAMPINU, a land wind in the Mediterranean.

RANDAN, an English arrangement of oarsmen in a small boat where the bow and stroke are single oars on opposite sides while a man amidships works a pair of oars (sculls).

RANGE, the distance in yards from the ship to the enemy, or the target. Two or more objects in line to indicate a course to steer, a danger to avoid, or a line of position.

RANGE ALONGSIDE, to lay a vessel close beside another.

RANGE THE CABLE, to run out all the chain in the locker when at anchor over a clean sandy bottom for cleaning or in a dry dock where it is laid down in long fakes (flakes) for inspection as well as cleaning. This allows an opportunity to clean and paint the chain locker. To haul the chain from the locker to allow the anchor to go down with greater ease.

RANGE FINDER, an instrument for finding the distance of an object.

RANGE LIGHTS, two lighthouses or beacons which, when in line, indicate a channel or a danger. The white lights shown on a steamer's fore and main masts to indicate the direction of her course. The forward light is 15 feet lower than the after light.

RANGE OF TIDE, the actual rise

and fall of water at springs or neaps, hence we have spring range, mean range and neap range.

RAP FULL, a little off the wind, all sails drawing well.

RASE KNIFE, a tool for clearing seams of oakum.

RAT GUARD, a metallic conical hood convex towards the shore, or plain disc that fits over a hawser or line leading ashore to prevent rats from boarding a vessel.

RATCH, a tack or reach or as a verb, to reach. To ratch off, to work offshore or to ratch to the westward around the Horn, implies an able vessel and good seamanship.

RATE, the class a naval vessel belongs in. In the grading of enlisted men, those having special qualifications are given *ratings,* such as boatswain's mates, quartermasters, yeomen, machinists, etc. *To rate* in Navy slang is to deserve or to be entitled to.

RATIO OF RANGES (tide), shows the ratio between the height of H.W. and L.W. at a reference port and that of a subsidiary port. By multiplying the height at the former port by the ratio of range at the latter port its height of H.W. or L.W. may be obtained. It is especially valuable when the ratio is less than .6.

RATIONAL HORIZON, a great circle of the celestial sphere everywhere 90° from the zenith and indicated by a plane at right angles to a plumb line at the center of the earth.

RATLINE STUFF, twelve- or fifteen-thread but usually eighteen-thread righthanded, tarred rope, used for ratlines, heavy lashings and heavy lines.

RATLINES, the rope rungs, clovehitched and seized to the shrouds, for seamen to use in going aloft.

RATTLING DOWN, the work of fitting new ratlines to a vessel's shrouds. Ratlines are seized to the forward and after shroud with small stuff—marline or houseline —through an eyesplice in the ends of the ratlines. They are clove hitched around each shroud.

RAZEE, to cut down the spar deck of a vessel, thereby reducing her freeboard. The word is also applied as a noun to such a vessel.

REACH, a point of sailing on which sheets are eased. It is a *close reach* if the wind is forward of the beam; a *beam reach* if it is abeam; a *broad reach* if it is on the quarter. Formerly the term had a narrower meaning, viz: it was a reasonably

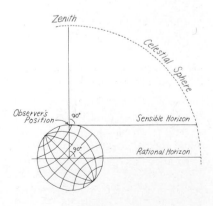

Rational Horizon

long tack to windward, with the wind never abaft the beam. A *reach* is also a straight stretch of navigable water between two bends in a river.

READING A CHART, to glean from it all the information it gives by its symbols.

READY ABOUT, an order to prepare to tack ship.

REBATE, the recessing of a keel to receive a floor frame or futtock.

RECIPROCAL BEARINGS, a method of swinging ship to obtain a set of deviations. A compass is taken ashore and set up in full view of the ship. If at anchor, the ship is swung by a kedge or launch to the various headings of the compass. By prearranged signals, simultaneous bearings are taken by an observer at the standard compass aboard and an observer at the compass ashore. The readings of the shore compass are reversed, and as this compass is free from magnetic influence, it has no deviation. Hence the difference in each set of readings is the deviation of the standard compass for the heading of the ship.

RECKONING, the process of keeping the ship's position at hand.

RED ENSIGN, the British merchant flag.

REDUCTION, the changing of arc into time; the changing of various quantities given in the Nautical Almanac for G.M.T., to their value in L.M.T. the changing of the altitude of the sun near noon to what it would be at noon; the changing of a solar interval of time to a sidereal interval.

REDUCTION GEAR, a mechanical contrivance by which high engine speed is stepped down to low propeller speed. The tendency in modern motor boats is to employ a light, small, high-speed motor in conjunction with a reduction gear which turns the propeller at one-half to one-third crankshaft speed. Among the advantages of this installation are economy of space and fuel consumption and minimized vibration.

REDUCTION TO THE MERIDIAN. See Ex-Meridian Altitude.

REEF, a ridge of rock or coral (usually in an exposed locality) lying at or near the surface of the water.

REEF, to reduce sail area. A fore and aft sail is partly lowered and the surplus canvas is secured along the boom by a band of *reef points,* placed parallel with the foot of the sail. A square sail is raised by reef tackles and secured to the yards by reef points. To *close reef* is to shorten to the last band of reef points. There are also *single* and *double reefs.* A lacing is sometimes used instead of reef points. The sail being free of the points there is less wind resistance. Also in cruising a reef lacing saves wear on the cloth.

REEF BAND, a strip of canvas sewed to a sail in which at regular intervals are short pieces of small rope for reefing purposes called *reef points.*

REEF CRINGLE, a sort of rope grommet worked around a thimble in the leech of a sail at the end of a reef band.

REEF EARING, a short length of rope spliced into a reef cringle to lash the cringle to the yard or boom. In reefing topsails the first man on the yard goes to windward and passes the *weather earing,* the next to leeward; an earing is passed up forward and down abaft the yard.

REEF HOOK. See Rase Knife.

REEF KNOT, a square knot.

REEF POINTS, short pieces of small rope set in the reef bands of a sail for reefing purposes.

REEF TACKLE PATCH, a reenforcing strip of canvas to protect a sail against the chafe of the ref tackle.

REEF TACKLES, purchases which hook into the reef cringles and heave the reef band to the yard to take the weight of the sail and aid the seamen in tying the reef points.

REEFER, a short, double-breasted overcoat.

REEFER SHIPS, are refrigerator vessels and cargo reefer space consists of the refrigerator compartments.

REEVE, to pass a rope through a block or a hole.

REEVING LINE BEND, a method of connecting two lines in such a way that they will reeve through an opening, offering as little obstruction as possible.

REFLUX, the ebb tide.

REFRACTION, the downward deflection of rays of light from a heavenly body upon entering the atmosphere of the earth. The increasing density causes the light rays to take a curved path from the outer atmosphere to the eye. A striking case of refraction is seen when looking at an oar half submerged in the water; a remarkable break is seen at the water's edge. Refraction causes the body to appear higher than it actually is, and it becomes necessary to apply this correction. It is made with the altitude correction given inside the cover of the Nautical Almanac. The higher the altitude the less the refraction, for the reason that the rays take a more direct course through the atmosphere. The rays from a body near the horizon pass at a sharp slant, and hence a greater deflection results.

REGATTA, a race of sail, power or rowing craft. A water carnival.

REGISTER, a document issued by custom authorities allowing a vessel to engage in foreign trade. It is a document of identification as it contains a description of the vessel's characteristics and measurements. It must bear the name of the master.

REGRESSION OF THE MOON'S NODES, slow westward movement of the nodes along the ecliptic, similar to the precession of the equinoxes. This movement in the case of the moon is much faster, for her axis revolves about the pole of the orbit in 19 years while the earth's axis takes about 25,800 years to revolve around the pole of the ecliptic. See Precession of the Equinoxes.

RELIEF, a man standing by, or assigned, to take over the wheel or other duty with the change of watch. One whose duty is to relieve another assigned to a certain post or station; it can be a man, a crew or a ship, as a relief light ship.

RELIEVING TACKLES, purchases placed on both sides of a tiller or quadrant to ease up on the shock of heavy seas that strain the steering gear, an endless fall being used.

RENDER, easing off; the free passage of a rope through a bull's eye, block or deadeye.

REPEATER COMPASS, one operating from the main or master gyroscope compass of a vessel. The repeaters are placed at different convenient positions.

RESERVE BUOYANCY, that of all enclosed watertight space above the waterline.

RESIDUAL ERRORS, the deviation remaining on the different compass headings after compensation.

RESPONDENTIA BOND. See Bottomry Bond.

RETAINED MAGNETISM. A vessel steering on the same course for some time will pick up magnetism by induction over and above her normal subpermanent magnetism. After a change of course, this will be retained for some time, causing an error in the normal deviation on the new course.

RETARD or **AGE OF THE TIDE,** the time that elapses between the passage of the moon and the tide which is produced by it.

RETURN TRADES, upper currents of air flowing from the equatorial regions poleward. They are also called the Anti-Trades.

REVERSE FRAME, an angle iron riveted in a reverse manner to an ordinary frame bar.

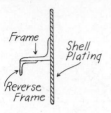

Reverse Frame

REVERSE TRANSOM, one which rakes forward, lessening the overall length of a yacht.

REVOLUTION, the movement in a circular path of one body around another. Turn of a propeller. Engine speeds are generally figured in *revolutions per minute (r.p.m.).*

REVOLVER, the indeterminate position of an observer who, using the three-point problem, finds himself and all three objects in the circumference of the same circle.

RHUMB LINE. A straightaway compass course steered by a vessel is a rhumb line, not a straight line of vision. Such a rhumb line is a straight line on a Mercator chart, and cuts each meridian at the same angle. A rhumb line followed would be a curve on a sphere and would eventually pass about the earth spirally, always approaching but never reaching the pole.

RHUMBS. The rim of a compass is divided into sectors of 15° each, called rhumbs. This is usually done where the compass is graduated from 0° to 360°.

RIBBAND, a fore and aft wooden strip or heavy batten used in ship construction temporarily to support and mark the position of the transverse frames.

RIBBON, a narrow band of contrasting color painted along a sheerline or above the waterline.

RIBS, the frames of a boat.

RICKERS, light short spars.

RICOCHET, the bound of a shell or stone from earth or water when its course is deflected by striking at a small angle with the surface.

RIDE, to lie at anchor. The way a vessel takes the seas is the way she *rides* them; a vessel may ride heavily or easily. A rope *rides* when a turn lies on an adjacent turn rather than close alongside of it. The bunt of a sail may require a seaman to *ride it down,* to force it on the yard. A vessel proceeding with the current may be said to *ride a fair current. Let her ride,* a general expression signifying no change will be made.

RIDER PLATE, rests on the angle irons forming the top of the keelson.

RIDERS, the upper tier of casks or barrels stowed in a hold.

RIDGE ROPE, the "back bone" of an awning into which the crow's foot is tucked.

RIDING BITTS, those to which the anchor chains are secured.

RIDING CHOCKS, devices through which the anchor chains pass inboard. They are fitted with compressors to hold the chain and often a pawl which prevents the

chain from slipping back while being hove in.

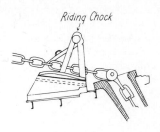

Riding Chock

RIDING DOWN THE RIGGING, in tarring down, a seaman works his way down the stays in a boatswain's chair.

RIDING LIGHT, anchor light.

RIFFLE, small rips causd by current or underlying rocks.

RIG, a vessel's particular character as to sail and mast arrangement. To rig a vessel is to send her spars aloft, and set up the necessary rigging to support them, as well as the sails and their attendant running rigging.

RIGGER, an artisan skilled in the rigging of ships, the hoisting of heavy weights, and the care and use of cordage, wire and hemp.

RIGGING, the ropes of a ship. The wire rope supporting the spars is called *standing rigging* and the manila, dacron, nylon or hemp ropes used in setting and furling sail are known as *running rigging.*

RIGGING SCREW, a clamp for forcing the parts of a wire rope together for splicing purposes. Also British yachtsman's term for turnbuckle.

RIGHT, to return to normal, as a vessel with heavy list or a hard over helm.

RIGHT OF APPROACH, that right accorded to any naval vessel to approach a merchantman in order ot verify her flag and character.

RIGHT ASCENSION OF THE MEAN SUN (R. A. M. S.), the distance in sidereal hours that the mean sun is *eastward* of the First Point of Aries (Vernal Equinox).

RIGHT BANK OF A RIVER, that on the right-hand side facing downstream.

RIGHT-HANDED ROPE, that which is laid up from right to left, and should be coiled down with the hands of a watch. In a right-handed rope held up vertically before you, the direction of the strands is *diagonally upward* to the *right*.

RIGHT-HANDED SCREW, a propeller whose upper blades turn from port to starboard when viewed from aft.

RIGHT RUDDER, old port helm. The ship turns to right under a port helm. Orders are now given in terms of the rudder.

RIGHT SAILING, when the course of a vessel lies either along a parallel or a meridian.

RIGHT OF SEARCH, the right of a belligerent naval vessel to board neutrals and search for contraband goods.

RIGHT SPHERE, the celestial sphere shown to an observer on the equator where the planes of the diurnal circle of the stars or sun lie at right angles with the horizon. The heavenly bodies are above the horizon twelve hours, and below twelve hours.

RIGHTING LEVER, the distance between the two vertical lines passing through the center of gravity and center of buoyancy of a listed ship. When the vertical line of the center of buoyancy meets the central line of the ship above the center of gravity the lever is a *righting* one, but if below, it is an upsetting lever.

RIGHTING MOMENT, the force tending to right a listed ship.

RING BOLT, a bolt with an eye.

RING ROPE, a rope used to bend the chain to the anchor ring.

RING STOPPER, a short length of chain used to secure an old type anchor at the ring while the flukes, resting on the billboard, are secured by a *shank painter.*

RING TAIL, a jib-like addition to the after side of a spanker. In early days it was rectangular in shape. It was used extensively in the tea clippers.

RIP RAP, blocks of stone to protect a bank or breakwater from the wash of sea or current.

RIPPING IRON, an implement used to remove sheathing and to clear the seams of a deck of old oakum.

RIPS, agitation caused by the meeting of currents or by the impinging of one current upon another moving in a different direction. Rips are mostly a vertical oscillation rather than a progressive wave. Rips are further designated as current rips if caused by ocean currents, and tide rips if caused by tidal streams. See Overfalls.

RISE AND SHINE, a rising call used on a man-of-war.

RISE TACKS AND SHEETS, an order to haul up the lower corners of the courses preparatory to swinging the yards.

RISE OF TIDE, the rise of water above the datum of a chart. See Range of Tide.

RISING (or RISER), a fore and aft piece of wood made fast to the inner side of a small boat's frames to serve as a support for the thwarts.

RIVETS, bolts to secure plates, angle irons, and other steel members together. One end has a head and the other end is flattened with hammers while hot.

ROACH, the curve in any of the sides of a sail. The foot of square sail is roached, and called the foot roach. If roached at the sides it is called the leech roach.

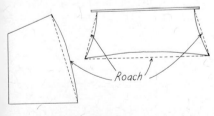

Roach

ROAD (or ROADSTEAD), usually a more or less open anchorage—a bight in the coast.

ROARING FORTIES, the boisterous westerly winds prevailing between 40° and 50° South. Originally applied to that region between Good Hope and Australia.

ROBANDS, pieces of small stuff used to secure a square sail to the jackstays.

ROCKER KEEL, a sharply rounding keel much used in clipper fishing schooners.

ROCKS AND SHOALS, those parts of the U. S. Navy regulations which concern punishment for offenses. They formerly were read periodically by the executive officer of a naval vessel to the assembled company.

RODE, the line attached to the anchor of a small boat.

ROGER, a pirate's flag.

ROGUE'S YARN, a colored yarn worked in rope for identification; formerly as a guard against theft but now as an advertisement.

ROKE, fog or other obscuring element.

ROLL, undulation of the sea; oscillation of a vessel from side to side.

ROLL ON, ROLL OFF SYSTEM. The steamers using this method of cargo handling are designed with a ramp at the stern. Over this ramp, connected with a pier, loaded vans pass aboard, stowing themselves under their own power. They are secured by turnbuckles to pad eyes in the decks.

ROLLER FURLING AND REEFING, the jib, with a wire luff rope, is set flying. At the tack is a drum operated by a *furling line* that (with the sheet) leads aft to the cockpit. Up at the head (jib) is a swivel.

The drum and swivel are capable of rotating in both directions. By hauling the furling line the sail rolls around the luff rope; by hauling the sheet the sail is set. There are other applications of the roller principle.

ROLLER REEFING, a method of reducing sail by which the boom is rotated and the sail rolled around that spar. It is an advance over tying reef points.

ROLLERS (Swell), a wave phenomenon occurring at St. Helena and Ascension Islands where with great frequency heavy swells roll in from the northwestward and break with violence on the coast. They persist against the prevailing winds and periods of calm weather.

ROLLING, the sidewise motion of a vessel.

ROLLING CHOCKS, blocks under the engines and boilers to take up the strain of the motion of the vessel. A great many seamen call bilge keels *rolling checks.* Pieces of wood fastened to a yard to take the thrust when rolling heavily.

ROLLING DOWN TO ST. HELENA, a romantic phrase used on the old sailing route from the Far East. It applied to that part of the voyage within the southeast trades on the run from the Cape of Good Hope to St. Helena. The weather is exceptionally fine with a long even swell, and the steady winds allowed the use of stun'sails alow and aloft.

ROLLING HITCH, a hitch used on a spar that will not slip. It is used to take the strain off a large line

with a smaller one (or stopper) made fast to it with a rolling hitch, such as on boat falls when the boats are hoisted to take the strain while the fall is being made fast to the davit.

ROLLING ROPE AND TACKLES, used to steady yards in heavy weather. They are set up between the yardarm and the mast to relieve the strain on the crane, slings or parral. *Rolling jaws* are pieces fitted to a yard to take some of the stress when rolling, also called *rolling chocks.*

ROMBOLINE, cordage junk.

ROOSTER'S TAIL, the arching plume of spray in the wake of a high speed motorboat.

ROOT, the shore end of a wharf or mole.

ROPE, cordage of greater than one-inch circumference, made up of strands which in turn are made up of yarns. To form the strands the yarns are twisted together in the opposite direction to that of the rope. The twist to make the strands and the twist to make the rope are opposite, and each twist continually tries to escape with the result that the rope remains compact. In the parlance of rope-makers the twist in the strands is called the *foreturn,* while the twist in the rope is called the *afterturn.* In other words, the ordinary rope is composed of yarns in which the fibers are twisted right-handed, of strands in which the yarns are twisted left-handed and the rope in which strands are twisted right-handed. If three ropes are laid up left-handed into a hawser, it is called cable-laid. *To rope* is to sew bolt rope, usually tarred hemp, to the edge of a sail or awning when it becomes known as the *roping*. The term *rope* has, in a nautical sense, been abused in this work— a piece of rope put to work on shipboard becomes in nearly all cases a line. There are but few ropes on a vessel, among them being the man ropes, top ropes, foot ropes, bolt ropes, bell ropes, back rope, yard rope and bucket rope.

Working Rules for Ropes and Tackles

1. To find safe working load of Manila rope: Square the circumference in inches and divide by 7 for the load in tons.

2. To find the size of Manila rope for a given working load: Multiply the load in tons by 7, and take the square root of the product for the circumference in inches.

3. To find the size of rope when rove as a tackle to lift a given weight: Add to the weight $\frac{1}{10}$ of its value for every sheave to be used in hoisting, this gives the total resistance including friction; divide this by the number of parts in the movable blocks for the maximum tension on the fall, reeve the fall of a size to stand this tension as a safe load.

Example: We propose to lift 10 tons with a 3-fold purchase, which means 6 sheaves and 1 for a fair-lead. To the 10 tons add $\frac{1}{10}$, or 1 ton for each sheave. There are 7, which makes 17 tons. Divide this 17 tons by the number of parts at the mov-

ing sheaves, which are 6, and we have $17 \div 6 = 2.8$ tons. Using Rule 2 above, we find the size (the circumference) of rope needed is approximately 4½ inches.

4. To find the weight which a given purchase will lift with safety: Find the safe working load for the rope to be used (Rule 1). Multiply this by the parts at the movable block, this gives the total including friction. Multiply the total resistance by 10, and divide by 10 + the number of sheaves used; the result is the weight that may be lifted in tons. Modern nylon ropes sustain much greater stresses than manila.

ROPE YARN, the untwisted strands of a rope. These are knotted together for various uses aboard ship. The trick of knotting a rope yarn was the first instruction given an embryo marline-spike sailor.

ROPE-YARN SUNDAY, the naval half-holiday of Wednesday afternoon, for the purpose of washing, repairing and making clothes, etc.

ROPE'S ENDING, a punishment applied with a rope's end.

ROPES OF MAUI, a poetic South Sea term given to the radiating sunbeams from the sun behind the clouds, a condition better known as the "sun drawing water" or the term "sun's backstays" of seamen.

ROPING, the sewing of the edges of a sail to a rope called the bolt-rope. Roping has at least one advantage over a taped sail in that it uses a double waxed thread that lies between the strands of the bolt-rope, all contributing to durability. The rope is sewed on the port side of a fore and aft sail and on the after side of square sails.

ROSE BOX, the strainer at the foot of the suction pipe of a bilge pump.

ROSE LASHING or **SEIZING,** a fancy cross lashing woven through the different parts of an eye to secure it to a spar.

ROTE (Rut), the sound of breakers or surf.

ROUGH LOG, the record, kept on the bridge or in the chart house, of the movements of the vessel, activities carried on on board or any items concerning ship or personnel. The smooth log, sometimes called the mate's log, is copied from the rough log.

ROUND OF ANGLES, an operation often resorted to in order to test a sextant or a theodolite. It consists of a series of angles taken from one object to another in a horizontal plane until the first object is reached. By adding all these angles, a result close to 360° should be obtained if the instrument is accurate.

ROUND DOWN, to overhaul a hanging tackle.

ROUND THE FLEET, an old punishment in which a man was secured across a boat and towed alongside each ship of a fleet to receive lashes.

ROUND IN, to haul in quickly on a weather brace or other line.

ROUND SEAM, is used in sewing the edges of two pieces of canvas together by passing the needle through both pieces. In other words over and over.

ROUND SEIZING, a method of securing two ropes together or two parts of the same rope to make an eye.

ROUND SHIP, an ancient designation for those vessels of relatively wide beam for their length, that is about a third of the length. They were propelled by sails but with oars available.

ROUND TO, to come to the wind.

ROUND TURN, to pass a line completely around a bitt, spar, or another rope. A round turn and two half hitches is a most useful and popular way of making a line fast.

ROUND UP, to heave away on a tackle, taking up the slack preparatory to completing the hoist.

ROUNDHOUSE, a cabin aft on the poop or quarterdeck, sometimes used as a privy for the after guard. On some later sailing ships a compartment on main deck aft for petty officers and apprentices.

ROUNDING, the serving of a rope for chafing purposes.

ROUNDLINE, three-stranded seizing stuff laid up right-handed.

ROUSE, to heave heavily on a line; to *rouse out the watch* is to get on deck the watch below, a touch of alacrity being implied.

ROW, to propel by use of oars.

ROWLOCKS. See Oarlocks.

ROWSER CHOCK, a closed chock.

ROYAL, the sail next above the topgallant sail.

ROYAL MAST, that next above the topgallant mast, although the topgallant and royal masts are usually in one spar.

ROYAL POLES, the upper extremities of the mast above the eyes of the royal rigging over the royal yard provided there is no skysail yard.

ROYAL POOP, a small platform deck, the highest and aftermost in the old high poop of ancient ships.

ROYAL YARD, next above the topgallant yard.

RUBBER, a sailmaker's tool to smooth or flatten the seam of canvas in sewing.

RUBBING STRAKE or **WALE,** a piece of half-round, running fore and aft just beneath the rail to protect the planking.

RUCKING, lowering away on the peak and throat halyards, bringing down the gaff-topsail.

RUDDER, a contrivance consisting of pieces of plank or steel plates bolted together or to a frame forming a flat structure. It is hung vertically on the after side of the sternpost with *pintles* and *gudgeons.* These do not carry the weight, but serve only as hinges for lateral motion. There is a bearing within the *rudder port* upon which the weight is carried. The *rudder stock* enters the hull through the rudder port. A *helm* or *quadrant* is secured to the top of the rudder stock called the *rudder head* by which the rudder is swung. By taking an angle with the keel the resistance offered turns the vessel in that direction. A *balanced rudder* is one pivoted on its central axis, and is more practical where the weight is great. A *bow rudder* is used by ferry boats and by hydroplanes. The orders to the quartermaster are now given in terms of the rudder and not the helm, by international agreement.

RUDDER ARMS, steel arms which fasten the rudder stock to the main rudder.

RUDDER BRACE, a gudgeon, the eye set in the stern post to receive the pintle.

RUDDER CASE, the watertight compartment, or well, in which the rudder head works.

RUDDER CHAINS, those secured to the horn of the rudder and leading to each quarter where, in case of accident to the rudderhead, they are available to keep control of the rudder, and to aid in steering the vessel.

RUDDER CHOCK, a wedge used to prevent the working of the rudder when at anchor or when otherwise desired.

RUDDER EYE, the eye bolt in the top of the rudder stock; also the eye on the after edge used for hooking relieving tackles in an emergency.

RUDDER HATCH, a small opening in the deck immediately above the rudder stock; this latter part is raised through the hatch when unshipping the rudder.

RUDDER HORN, a projection on the after side of the rudder for use as a reserve helm in case of accident to the rudderhead. Chains lead from the horn to the vessel's quarter by which she can be steered.

RUDDER IRONS, pintles and gudgeons.

RUDDER LOCK, a device at the bottom of a pintle which prevents its rising and unshipping the rudder.

RUDDER ORDERS, are those given to the steersman when changing the course of a vessel. *Right Rudder* directs that the rudder be turned to the right. The wheel is turned to the right (starboard) and the ship's head goes to the right. The angle is sometimes specified as 10° left rudder; which means that the rudder is to take a position 10° left of the keel line. *Full left Rudder* means the greatest angle possible to the left. *Hard over* was the old term and is still used.

RUDDER PORT, the entrance to the rudder well through the plating or planking of the ship.

RUDDER POST, the vertical post abaft the propeller which supports the rudder.

RUDDER STOCK, the forward part of a rudder to which the main part is attached; the part which passes through the rudder port into the ship where the helm or quadrant is attached.

RUDDER TABS, small plates, "rudders," attached to the trailing edge of the main rudder to increase the maneuverability of a racing yacht. They are operated by an auxiliary wheel.

RUDDER TACKLES, those used on the rudder chains to steer by in case of accident.

RUDDER TELLTALE, an indicator, sometimes lighted, which always shows the bridge officer the position of the rudder.

RUDDER WEDGES, tapered plates riveted to the sides of the rudder to produce a streamline effect. The forward edge is thick and is placed closest to the rudder post.

RUDDER WELL, the watertight compartment in which the rudder head works.

RUFFLES, the rolls of a drum given in salute to officers of high rank.

RULES OF THE ROAD, the navigation laws which bear on the avoidance of collision. They include steering rules, lights, fog signals and whistle signals.

RUN, the part of a vessel where her lines converge towards the sternpost. To scud before a squall or gale is to run. To run *down a coast* or to *parallel* is to steam or sail along it. To *run a warp* is to carry a line to a buoy or wharf to heave the ship ahead with. The distance a vessel travels, as a *days' run* of 240 miles. The travel of the waves is spoken of as *running*—a heavy sea was running.

RUN AWAY. See Haul.

RUNNER AND TACKLE, a single block in the end of a piece of wire rope that is to be hauled on. This is a pendant. A line made fast at one end, perhaps to an eye bolt in the deck, leads through this block making a *whip* and a tackle is clapped on the hauling part.

RUNNERS, preventer backstays used on a yacht; the leeward runner is cast off and the weather one is set up when going about.

RUNNING BOAT, one which serves as a regular ferry between a ship anchored in the stream and the shore.

RUNNING BOWLINE, a bowline made around the main part with the end of a rope and serving as a slip knot.

RUNNING BOWSPRIT, one that can be rigged in and out. When it is in it is said to be *housed.*

RUNNING DAYS, lay days, every day, counting Sundays and holidays.

RUNNING THE EASTING DOWN, a term particularly applied to the long eastward run from the Cape of Good Hope to Australia. It is considered one of the most taxing experiences of regular seafaring, when the passage is made in a sailing vessel.

RUNNING LARGE, sailing with eased sheets off the wind.

RUNNING LIGHTS, the usual lights carried when under way.

RUNNING LINE, one run by a boat to a wharf or buoy that is at some distance. See Guess Warp.

RUNNING RIGGING, all those lines that are used to control the sails, such as halyards, clewlines, buntlines, sheets, etc. Lines that move when in use in distinction from standing rigging such as shrouds, backstays, etc., which work in a permanent position.

RUT. See Rote.

S

SACK, SACK OUT. Sack time, all refer to turning out or in a bunk in the watch below.

SADDLEBACK, plates so set in a coal hatch as to divert coal to different parts of the bunker.

SADDLES or SADDLE CRUTCHES, brackets of wood fastened to the lower part of the mast for the boom to rest on. A block of wood so shaped as to receive the heel of a jib-boom.

SAFE WORKING LOAD (of a tackle), the circumference of the (Manila) rope squared and multiplied by 285. The result of the calculation is taken off in pounds.

Nylon and Dacron ropes of the same circumference have higher strength.

SAFETY ANGLE, the point in the roll of a vessel beyond which the righting power is dangerously reduced.

SAG, to make excessive leeway.

SAGGED, when a vessel has settled structurally amidships.

SAGITTARIUS, the ninth sign of the zodiac.

SAIC, a sailing vessel of the eastern Mediterranean Sea. It is usually two-masted, carrying a square sail forward.

SAIL, a sailing vessel, particularly in the distance. If a fleet there may be twenty *sail.*

SAIL HOOK, a small device used to hold canvas while sewing a seam.

SAIL NEEDLE, one of a special shape, being three-sided except near the eye. There are two types —sewing and roping, being known as short and long spur needles respectively. Sewing needles come sizes 6 to 14—then sizes and half-sizes to 17½—size No. 15 is 2½ inches long and is the most used. Roping needles are known as flat-seam, tabling, old work, store, large, small and middle bolt-rope, small and large marline.

SAIL TACKLE, one used for sending sails aloft, usually a top-burton.

SAIL TRACKS, a railway fitted to the after side of a mast; slides attached to a sail instead of mast loops, travel up the track by halyards.

SAILING BOARD, a blackboard placed at the gangway giving the date and time of sailing and destination.

SAILING ON HER OWN BOTTOM, said of a vessel that has paid for herself. Before 1956 a challenger for the America's Cup had to be seaworthy enough to cross the Atlantic on her own bottom.

SAILING LAUNCH, a heavy work boat, not unlike a cutter, carried by naval vessels. They formerly were used as water boats, being fitted with a large plug hole by which they were flooded at a desirable point on fresh water streams, re-

plugged, and, deeply laden, were towed back to the ship.

SAILING THWART, a fore and aft board running amidships on the thwarts of a boat to support the masts when sailing.

SAILING TRIM, to be loaded to the proper draft fore and aft.

SAILINGS, the problems that arise when working with course and distances, differences of latitude and longitude and departure.

SAILMAKER, a proficient seaman who makes and repairs sails and awnings. The sailmaker is called *sails.*

SAILMAKER'S SPLICE, the joining of two ropes of different sizes. A *sailmaker's eye splice* differs from the ordinary eye in that the tucking is made round and round with the lay of the rope instead of over and under.

SAILOR'S BLESSING, a curse.

SAILS, a nickname given the sailmaker.

SAILS, pieces of canvas of any size and shape set from masts, yards, booms, stays and gaffs for the purpose of propelling a vessel by wind power. They are divided into two general classes, *square* and *fore and aft sails.* The square sails are set from yards with their corners hauled out to the ends of the yard below, and give a forward impulse when the wind blows on their after sides. The yards swing in a horizontal plane, within certain limits, allowing wind pressure on the after side of these sails on courses steered six points from the wind on one tack to six points on the other. The sides of the sail are called the *head, foot* and *leeches,* and in its construction besides the regular vertical cloths, are found *lining cloths, tabling, bellybands, reefbands, top lining, mast lining,* etc. The sail is controlled and set by *sheets, clewlines, leech-lines, bunt-lines, buntwhips, spilling lines,* and secured by *gaskets.* The sails are named for the yard and mast from which they are set as, for instance, the *fore-topgallant sail.* Fore and aft sails are set from masts, gaffs, stays and booms. These sails allow a vessel to sail within four points of the wind but are at a disadvantage with a squarerigger when running free. These sails comprise *jibs, trysails, spencers, gaff topsails* and the ordinary schooner's *fore and main sails.* In yachts there are more sails of various shapes and names. The deck erection of a submarine is called the sail. Also the term is being applied to that area of a vessel particularly exposed to wind pressure. For example, a vessel down deep by the stern, with bow high, would, by this new application, be having a lot of *sail* forward.

SAINT ELMO FIRE, a luminous brush-like appearance on the ends of yardarms, stays, or mast-heads, etc. It appears most commonly when the air is surcharged with electricity. The discharge which takes place in the form of St. Elmo Fire is the relieving of the difference in potential between the electricity in the atmosphere and that in the earth. See Corposant.

SAINT HILAIRE METHOD, the process of establishing a position line by computing the altitude of a body. It has been largely superseded by the use of tables which facilitate the operation of obtaining the altitude of a body.

SALINITY, the salt content of sea water. This varies between 33 and 37 parts salt in 1,000 parts of water. The water on the Grand Banks is not as rich in salt as in the tropical regions owing to the lower percentage in evaporation and to the dilution by the fresh water from ice and snow. A *salinometer* is a form of hydrometer graduated in 32nds for the measuring of the salinity of boiler water, and is based on temperatures 180°F, 185°F and 190°F. A hydrometer, graduated to show specific gravities at 59°F is, the more serviceable to the navigator.

There are many elements found in sea water. Those with the largest content per million parts are: Calcium 408; Chlorine 19,353; Magnesium 1,297; Potassium 387; Sodium 10,769; and Sulphur 901.

SALLY SHIP, a rhythmic movement of a body of men on a vessel that has lightly taken the bottom. The movement is athwartship and for the purpose of inducing a roll to aid engines in freeing the vessel. In the case of mud it helps to break the suction.

SALMON TAIL, an extension added to the rudder on its after edge to give the vessel increased turning power. A movable section attached to the outer edge of a canal boat's rudder by which steering power is preserved when the vessel is light.

SALT HORSE, salt beef as used in old sailing ship days.

SALTWATER SOAP, a composition, strong in alkali, which makes a good lather in salt water.

SALVAGE, an allowance given to volunteers and professionals who assist in saving a ship or cargo or a portion of it. The salvage is based on the extent of the prevailing hazard, and the labor and peril of saving the property. From one-tenth to one-half the value of the goods is paid. The crew of a ship can claim no salvage for saving their own vessel or her cargo.

SALVAGE HAWSER. See Insurance Hawser.

SALVO, the simultaneous discharge of a number of guns.

SAMPAN, a flat-bottomed Oriental boat used as a lighter on rivers and harbors of the Far East. It is propelled by oars and sails, and, when provided with a roof, houses many persons. It is used in harbors to deliver goods and ferry people from and to ships.

SAMSON POST, a small derrick mast to support the auxiliary cargo booms; a king post. A single bitt forward in a small boat.

SAND BORES, ridges of sand either shoal or dry.

SAND GLASS, an hour glass.

SAND STRAKE, the garboard strake.

SAND SUCKER, a full-lined steamer equipped with powerful pumps connected with a tube through which water from the bottom is pumped carrying about 15 per cent sand, mud or gravel. It is often moved along with rotary knives or worms to the vessel's hold or even through a long line of pipe to some distant point.

SAND WAVES, ridges of sand which in some points of the North Sea reach a height of 5 fathoms and lengths of a couple of hundred yards. Their crests are so sharp that often a lead will not reveal the least depth of water. Sand waves are formed of grains the size of which bear a relation to the velocity of currents and depth of water.

SANTA ANA, a dust-laden wind driving down to and beyond the Pacific Coast.

SARGASSO SEA, the eddy in the circulation of the waters of the North Atlantic where great quantities of gulf weed float upon the water. It lies eastward of the Bahama Islands, between Lat. 25° and 30°N. and Long. 38° and 60°W., and was discovered by Columbus. Within its area is that storied region where wreckage has a tendency to accumulate through the eddying influence of the ocean currents. The fanciful tradition of ships unable to extricate themselves from this locality was a firm belief with many people in early times. And, in fact, disabled ships and derelicts have spent long periods in this area before they were freed—if ever. There is a somewhat similar eddy in the other oceans, though of little importance.

SATELLITE, a secondary body that

revolves around a planet. The moon revolves around the earth, hence is our satellite.

SATURDAY NIGHT BOTTLES, the bottles of rum formerly sent forward to each watch of an English whaler on Saturday nights.

SATURN, the sixth planet from the sun. See Planets.

SAVE-ALL, a heavy net swung between the ship and the pier to catch any cargo that might fall from the slings. A sail set to catch wind passing under other sails; sometimes called a watersail. See Cargo net.

SAXBOARD, the uppermost plank in an open boat.

SCANDALIZE, to reduce sail in an unusual manner, that is to lower away the peak halyards while leaving the throat fast. New England fishermen scandalize the fisherman's staysail in numerous ways by the manner in which they hoist its corners aloft. To leave a sail partially set.

SCANT, when a vessel is obliged to head as closely to the wind as possible to make her port.

SCANTLINGS, the dimensions of frames, girders, stringers, plating, etc., that form a ship's structure. The American Bureau of Shipping and Lloyd's publish rules for these sizes based on extensive study and practical experience.

SCAR, rocks exposed at low water; steep cliff.

SCARPH, the joining of two timbers by beveling each in such a way as to form one timber in appearance.

SCEND, the quick upward motion of a pitching vessel; *scending* is pitching. An older meaning now not often used is the listing due to the centrifugal force when a vessel suddenly is broached to, or changes course quickly by force of a sea.

SCEND OF THE SEA, the lifting to leeward of a vessel by passing waves.

SCHAT DAVIT, a quick operating davit, being inclined at an angle and held by a brake. Upon releasing the friction the davit swings out automatically.

SCHOOL, a large number of fish moving about as a unit.

SCHOOLSHIPS, vessels supported for the purpose of educating young men in seamanship, navigation and other nautical subjects. The states maintaining schoolships in connection with their maritime academies or colleges are: Maine, Massachusetts, New York, Texas and California. They cooperate with the Federal Maritime Administration in supplying officers for the merchant marine. A passing midshipman receives a third mate's license, or that of a third assistant engineer, a commission as an ensign in the Naval Reserve and a bachelor of science degree.

The Coast Guard maintains the splendid bark *Eagle* for training the midshipmen of its academy at New London. Germany, Italy, Japan, Portugal and the Scandinavian and other nations support such training vessels.

SCHOONER, a fore and aft rigged vessel of any practical number of masts above one, seven being the largest number ever used. A *topmast schooner* carries a square fore topsail and topgallant sail. A *bald-headed* schooner carries no topmasts. A *schooner guy* or *span* is the whip controlling the distance between the heads of two cargo booms when topped in working cargo.

SCHUYT, a small Dutch sloop with full bow and stern lines and equipped with leeboards.

SCIATIC STAY, a wire rope connecting two mastheads. It sometimes serves as a support for a hatch tackle. Also called the *triatic stay.*

SCOFF, in naval slang, to eat.

SCOOTER, an amphibious craft, shallow and beamy, equipped with runners beneath and rigged with a jib and mainsail. It can be used as an iceboat, particularly on Great South Bay, Long Island. It is capable of crossing patches of open water and makes good speed on ice.

SCOPE, the ratio of length of mooring cable to maximum depth of water. For ordinary conditions at least three times the depth is used, but in a moderate gale five times the depth should be let out—veered. In severe gales the more cable the better. In 1650 Sir Walter Raleigh said, "The length of cable is the life of a ship in all extremities."

SCORE, the groove in the shell of a block for the strop.

SCORPIUS, the eighth sign of the zodiac.

SCOTCHMAN, a piece of chafing gear in leather or wood placed on the backstays or swifter shrouds.

SCOUSE, ship's biscuit, salt pork and molasses, baked. Lobscouse.

SCOW, a rectangular vessel of light draft used in the local transportation of goods, coal, etc. A small fast shoal-draft sloop-rigged yacht having bilgeboards instead of leeboards; most popular on the lakes of the mid-west.

SCRAMBLE NETS, similar to boarding nets of old, but reaching over the side to the water. One dramatic use was when a rescuing vessel, in dangerous submarine waters, would pick up a boat's crew of a torpedoed ship. It was highly desirable to scramble up quickly by way of this facility.

SCRAPER, a sharp edged tool used to remove old paint and varnish.

SCRATCH BOAT. Every racing, sailing yacht is assigned a rating, based on her sail area, length and other factors. In an attempt to bring equality among entries in a race, the yacht with the greatest advantage, the scratch boat, gives a "time allowance" to each contestant. This is applied to the "elapsed time" of each boat to arrive at her "corrected time" and her place in the race.

SCREW, the propeller.

SCREW CURRENT, the motion of water due to the revolution of the propeller.

SCREW HOIST, a chain hoist in whose upper block is an endless screw turning on a worm which gives the power.

SCREW MOORING, consists of a worm, flange, shank and shackle which is screwed into the bottom. A chain connects the shackle with a mooring buoy. Usually two or more of these moorings are put down and vessels ride to a bridle.

SCREW STEAMER, one driven by a revolving propeller in distinction from one driven by paddle wheels.

SCREW STOPPER, a short piece of chain with a turnbuckle cut in and a hook in one end and a shackle at the other. The stopper is shackled to a ring bolt in the deck and the other end hooked to the anchor chain. The turnbuckle takes up all slack.

SCRIMSHAW, carved work done by sailors out of the jawbone or teeth of a whale or shark. Etching done on bone, ivory or shells. The incision of the design was filled with India ink or tar and then polished with sailmakers' wax and canvas.

SCRIVE BOARDS, a large section of flooring in a mold loft in which the lines of the body plan are cut with a *scrive knife.* Used for making molds of the frames, beams, floor plates, etc. (Cook's Shipbuilder's Handbook.)

SCROLL, an ornamentally carved piece of timber bolted to the hull in the place of or in addition to a billethead or a figurehead.

SCUD, to run before a gale or squall. Driving mist; or masses of ragged broken clouds driving beneath nimbus clouds.

SCULL, to work an oar over the stern at such an angle as to drive a boat ahead. Light oars used in rowing shells, or other boats, are called *sculls.*

SCULLERY, the ship's pantry.

SCUPPER LIP, a lower projecting lip to keep the water from the scuppers off the side of the ship.

SCUPPER SHUTTERS, doors to scuppers which swing out by pressure of water on deck but exclude the entrance of sea water. They are hinged at the top.

SCUPPERS, drains from the waterways of the spar or weather deck.

SCURVY, a disease formerly common on shipboard due to the salt beef ration and lack of fresh vegetables. It manifests itself in spongy flesh, excessive languor and debility which leads to fatal consequences, but is readily responsive to a diet of citrus fruit, onions and potatoes.

SCUTTLE, to bore holes in a vessel to sink her. To open her sea cocks for the same purpose. Small round hatches for the loading of bunker coal or the passing of ammunition are called *scuttles.* This term is in some localities applied to all small hatches.

SCUTTLE BUTT, a water cask containing drinking water for daily use. A modern vessel's drinking fountain.

SCUTTLE BUTT STORY, a rumor without authority. Sometimes called *galley wireless.*

SEA, the watery part of the earth. A large body of water, the word being applied to the largest arms of the oceans. An undulation of water; a wave. There are several kinds whose names are descriptive of their nature, such as *cross sea, heavy sea,* etc. The waves prevailing at any time are spoken of collectively as the sea, but they must be due to the wind then blowing. See Swell.

SEA ANCHOR, a *drag.* With a hawser fast to a sea anchor the vessel exposed to the wind tends to move to leeward faster than the anchor, hence the resistance brings her head to wind (if the hawser is forward) and she rides in greater safety. There are sea anchors of various types, even a great length of plain hawser often sufficing. The sea anchor was used to advantage back in the 17th century and called a *drift-sail.*

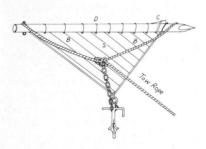

Sea Anchor

SEA BAG, a cylindrical canvas bag in which sailors stow their clothes. A rope (bag lanyard) leading through grommets in the top closes the bag.

SEA BREEZE, a breeze common to the coasts of the tropics, which makes during the forenoon as a result of the heated air rising over the land and causing a gentle indraft of sea air. The term is quite generally applied to any breeze from the ocean.

SEA CHEST, a chest which formerly served a seaman as a trunk. It was usually ornamented by the owner with a painting of his ship, and with fancy pointed rope grommets for handles. Also the portion of an intake between the ship's side and the sea valve.

SEA COCK, a valve which connects with the outside sea water in the lower part of the vessel.

SEA DOG, an old sailor.

SEA FRET, a morning mist.

SEA GASKET. See Gasket.

SEA HORSE (hippocampus), a curious little creature of the sea, about 3 inches long, with a head suggestive of a horse. A mythological creation, whose upper part was horse and lower part fish, for the use of the sea gods.

SEA KINDLY, the condition of a ship when she is in good trim and rides comfortably.

SEA LADDER, a flexible ladder of peculiar construction for use over the ship's side at sea, as in taking a pilot.

SEA LAWYER, a seaman who questions authority by argument.

SEA LETTER, a document issued by the custom authorities to neutral vessels certifying to their ownership and nationality. It is the vessel's authority to proceed on her voyage. In reality a passport.

SEA MEW, a sea gull.

SEA MULE, a small powerful tug, which while only about 40 feet long and 15 feet beam has over 500 horsepower. Two propellers, some 60 inches in diameter with a pitch of 48 inches, are used. This vessel can turn in her own length and has great maneuverability.

SEA PAINTER, a long rope not less than 2¾ inch for use in a steamer's lifeboats. It is led forward before lowering the boat.

SEA PIE, a dish of meat or fish and vegetables, each in layers with a crust between. Each layer is a deck, thus three layers is a *three decker.*

SEA QUELLING OIL, used to modify a rough sea.

SEA RING, an ancient instrument for obtaining the altitude of the sun.

SEA ROOM, offshore with a good safe distance from shoals or a lee shore.

SEA SCALE, indicates the state of the sea in numbers from 0 to 9 as follows:

Scale of State of Sea. (Douglas)

		Height in feet
0	Calm	0
1	Smooth	1
2	Slight	1-3
3	Moderate	3-5
4	Rough	5-8
5	Very rough	8-12
6	High	12-20
7	Very high	20-40
8	Mountainous	40+
9	Confused	

Scale for Swell. (Douglas)

0 No swell
1 Low swell, short or average length
2 Low swell, long
3 Moderate swell, short
4 Moderate swell, average length
5 Moderate swell, long
6 Heavy swell, short
7 Heavy swell, average length
8 Heavy swell, long
9 Confused swell

SEA SLED, a box-like craft possessing an inverted V underbody. With high power these boats show great speed and seaworthiness.

SEA TURN, a change of wind to one from the sea bringing a refreshing change in temperature.

SEA WATER, weighs 64 lbs. to the cubic foot and 35 cubic feet equal a ton, while fresh water is 62½ lbs. and river water about 63 lbs. See Salinity.

SEA WRACK. Kelp, debris, etc., floating or washed up by the sea.

SEAGOING, worthy and prepared to go to sea.

SEAMAN, one versed in the ways of the sea and ships. In the eyes of the law every man on the articles is a seaman, except the master who does not sign them. In these days there are two grades of seamen—*able-bodied* and *ordinary.* The former are supposed to understand all regular ship duties required of seamen, while of the *ordinary* little is expected in the way of skillful ship work.

SEAMAN'S DISGRACE, a fouled anchor.

SEAMS, the space between a ship's planks, which are caulked to prevent the entrance of sea water. In sewing seams of sail cloth or canvas the round seam and flat seam are used—which see.

SEAPLANE, an airplane supporting a pontoon or boat-like device beneath it which allows taking off from and alighting upon the water.

SEARCHLIGHT, a powerful electric lamp placed at the focus of a mirror, which projects the light in a beam of parallel rays. The apparatus consists essentially of a base and turntable fitted with arms carrying trunnion bearings, in which is mounted the barrel or drum containing the mirror and lamp with its operating mechanism. The drum may be elevated and depressed and turned in azimuth by means of handles at the back, or by either mechanical or electrical distant control gear. Of the various types of searchlights now in use, the principle differences consist in type of lamp used and in the lamp control mechanism.

SEAWAY, the motion of the sea when clear of shoal water.

SEAWEED, a marine plant which grows in long narrow ribbons.

SEAWORTHY, said of a vessel properly designed, constructed, equipped, manned and in good condition.

SECOND DIFFERENCES, the term applied to the differences between the comparisons of the same chronometer for two successive days. The term is also applied to the difference between quantities in the Nautical Almanac. The differences between the tabulated values are called the *first differences* and are sufficiently refined for navigational purposes, but the differences between successive first differences are known as *second differences*.

SECONDARY MERIDIANS, those that have been connected and established by telegraphic exchange of time signals with the prime meridian.

SECRET BLOCK, one whose shell encloses the entire sheave, allowing two holes the size of the rope which works through it. The purpose of the construction is to protect against such fouling aloft as is liable to occur with topsail clewlines.

SECURE, a signal consisting of several complete oscillations of the engine-room telegraph to signify that the engines are needed no longer, and may be secured.

SECURE FOR SEA, to lash all movable objects for sea—gripes on all boats, lashings on all furniture, etc.

SEE YOU IN LIVERPOOL, formerly a traditional parting hail of a pilot as he went over the rail of an outward bound vessel. Its origin is not clear, but in the opinion of many mariners it has some connection with the feeling in the sailing ship days that all sailors would sooner or later meet again in Liverpool. It used to be heard as a sailor's farewell to another.

SEEL, the sudden roll of a ship in a seaway.

SEICHE, a rise of water on a lake

probably due to a difference of atmospheric pressure.

SEINER, a fisherman using the seining method of fishing. Particularly applied to a mackerel seining schooner in American waters.

SEIZE, to bind with small stuff, as, one rope to another, a rope to a spar, etc. Seizings take their names from their appearance or the functions they are serving as *throat seizing, flat* or *round seizing, middle, racking,* etc. The terms *cross* or *frapping turns* apply to those several last turns which are at right angles with the main turns of the seizing: the *riding turns* are those of the second tier. A seaman is ordered to *clap on* a seizing. See Racking Seizing and Throat Seizing.

SELVAGEE, small stuff marled together, to serve as a strop.

SEMAPHORE SIGNALS, a daylight means of communicating between vessels and shore. Signals are sent by hand flags or by mechanical arms, each letter calling for a particular position of the arms.

SEMI-CIRCULAR DEVIATION, a compass error caused by two factors. The vertical iron causes a transient or changing error, and the ship's subpermanent magnetism induces a constant error, both of which are semi-circular in character. It is called semi-circular because the changes of deviation from W. to E. or vice versa occur 180° apart.

SEMI-DIAMETER, the angular distance from the edge of the sun or moon to the center. As the altitudes of these bodies are measured with the sextant by bringing the lower edge to the horizon, it is necessary to add the semi-diameter (S.D.) to the altitude so measured. It is done by the combined correction within the cover of the Nautical Almanac.

SENNIT (Sennet), braided small stuff. There are several varieties, viz: French, round, square, and flat.

SENSIBLE HORIZON, a circle of the celestial sphere indicated by a plane at right angles to a plumb line and tangent to the earth at the observer's position. See Rational Horizon.

SEPARATION CLOTHS, used to combat moisture in special types of cargo, principally sugar. The sheets of fabric are spread over and under the cargo to be protected.

SERVING, winding a rope or wire, after *worming* and *parceling* with small stuff, keeping the turns very close together, making it impervious to water after a treatment of tar. This is called *service.* The turns are made against the lay of the rope. "Worm and parcel with the lay, serve and marl the other way."

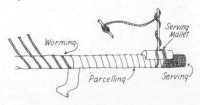

Serving

SERVING BOARD AND MALLET, each a simple device with a handle, scored to ride a rope while serving. They keep a convenient leverage on the serving material and keep the turns close together.

SET, the direction in which a current flows; also the direction in which a vessel is moved by the action of tide, wind or both. *Drift* is the amount that a current influences a vessel, but the word is often confused with *set*.

SET A COURSE, to give the course to the quartermaster with orders to steer it.

SET TAUT, an order to haul tight.

SET UP RIGGING, to take up all slack in the stays and shrouds with purchases. A tackle is clapped on the shroud and the end of the lanyard; when sufficiently set up, the lanyard is made fast with a lanyard hitch. When the purchase is applied, the lanyard is greased and the different parts are struck with the loom of an oar in order to make it *render*. With modern turnbuckles on each shroud there is no such trouble in setting up rigging.

SETTLE, to lower a yard by its halyards to a position that is "square by the lifts."

SETTLING TANKS, tanks into which fuel oil is pumped before using so that any water in it may settle to the bottom and drawn off.

SEVEN TENTHS RULE, a calculation giving the distance an object will be passed abeam, when .7 (⁷⁄₁₀) of the run between the bearings of 22½° and 45° on the bow is taken.

SEXTANT, an instrument for measuring angles. It is principally employed to measure the altitude of heavenly bodies, but is very useful in determining the horizontal angles between landmarks to fix position. The instrument consists of a triangular frame, one side of which is the graduated arc of a circle. At the opposite angle an arm is pivoted which swings across the surface of the frame and the graduated arc, and by a system of reflecting mirrors and images whose angle is desired are brought together and the angle read from the arc. The principal parts of a sextant are the *frame*, the *arc*, the *arm*, the *index glass*, *horizon glass*, *telescope*, and *vernier*. A sextant usually measures an angle of 120° to 150°.

Sextant

SEXTANT, ADJUSTMENT OF. See Index Glass, Horizon Glass, Index Correction and Sextant Telescope.

SEXTANT, PRINCIPLES OF. The sextant is based upon the law of optics that the angle of incidence is equal to the angle of reflection, and that when a ray of light is twice reflected by two mirrors lying in the same plane the angle between the first direction and last reflection is equal to twice the inclination of the mirrors with each other. The actual angle of the body's altitude is the difference between the first direction and last reflection. The actual angle through which the index arm is moved (not the reading) is the inclination of the mirrors with each other. The reading of the arc is twice the actual angle through which the arm has moved. The following explanation of the principle upon which the sextant is based uses the theorem that the external angle of a triangle is equal ot the sum of the two opposite interior angles.

Proof of optical principle:

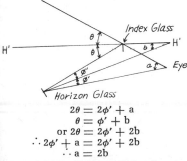

$$2\theta = 2\phi' + a$$
$$\theta = \phi' + b$$
$$\text{or } 2\theta = 2\phi' + 2b$$
$$\therefore 2\phi' + a = 2\phi' + 2b$$
$$\therefore a = 2b$$

b being the inclination of the glasses.
(Prof. David W. Reid)

SEXTANT TELESCOPE, a small telescope which screws into a collar, parallel to the plane of the instrument and in line with the horizon glass. The telescope collar is adjusted by bringing two stars together on the inner line of a double cross-haired telescope, then moving the instrument so as to bring the stars on the outer hair line; if the stars remain in conjunction, the telescope is parallel with the plane of the instrument. There is a telescope for star work called an inverting telescope, in using which the horizon is brought to the star.

SHACK LOCKER, a compartment on a fishing schooner where food is available at all hours.

SHACKLE, a U-shaped iron with a pin across the open ends. The shackles used about the rigging have the pin threaded, but where used for joining lengths of anchor chains, the pin is very heavy and is held in place by a small wooden or iron pin. Shackles are measured for working load at the sides of the shackle.

SHADE DECK, one of light construction above the main deck of a cargo steamer. There are usually openings or ports in the sides.

SHADE-DECKED VESSEL, a type having a continuous upper deck of light construction with openings in the sides.

SHADOW, a spinnaker, rectangular in shape, requiring a light temporary gaff to set it.

SHADOW PIN, a device for finding the sun's bearing. It is a pin 3 or 4 inches high, fitted to stand in the center of the compass and throws its shadow upon the rim of the compass card, thereby indicating the sun's bearing.

SHAFFLE, a split band or collar which receives the goose-neck of a boom.

SHAFT, the great rod which transmits the power from the engines to the propeller.

SHAFT ALLEY, the long compartment within which the shaft operates.

SHAFT BLOCKS. See Plummer Blocks.

SHAFT BRACKET, a strut to support the propeller shaft.

SHAFT TUBE, the water-tight tube where the shaft emerges from the hull.

SHAKE, a crack in a spar. *Shake out a reef* is to cast off reef points and set the sail. To take to pieces.

SHAKEDOWN CRUISE, one for the purpose of adjusting machinery and instruments, and familiarizing a crew with a new vessel.

SHAKES, the parts of casks or barrels knocked down.

SHAKINGS, waste rope, canvas and small stuff.

SHAMAL, a northwesterly wind which prevails in the Persian Gulf.

SHANGHAIED, to be taken against one's will aboard an outward bound ship, either under the influence of drugs, or liquor, or false representations.

SHANK, the principal part of an anchor that connects the flukes and the stock.

SHANK PAINTER, the chain holding the fluke of an anchor upon the rail or billboard.

SHANTY. See Chanty.

SHAPING A COURSE, the process of determining upon a course by calculation, or by taking it from the chart with parallel rulers, allowing for deviation, and giving it to the quartermaster to steer.

SHARK'S MOUTH, the opening in the forward or after side of an awning to receive a mast.

SHARP UP, the yards of a square-rigger braced as nearly fore and aft as the lee rigging will allow.

SHARPIE, a flat-bottomed shoal-draft boat with straight sides. This type draws its maximum at mid-length with the stem and stern post almost at the water's surface. Sharpies step two masts, unstayed, one well forward; the rig is jib-headed ketch. They sail well, especially off the wind and are seaworthy; have been extensively used in the oyster fishery. Very easy and economical to build.

SHEAR, to cut; a rivet is said to shear when the movement of two plates cuts it off. Also, the difference between the sum of all upward and downward forces acting on any section of a vessel. (Cook's Handbook.)

SHEARING PUNCH, a tool for driving out a forelock pin in an anchor shackle.

SHEARS (SHEERS), two or three spars called *shear legs* standing nearly on end and lashed together aloft. They serve as a derrick or tripod to lift heavy weights, step lower-masts, stacks, etc.

SHEARWATER, a sea bird about 20 inches long, head and back dark brownish, with light breast and lower body. They are seen in great numbers on the Grand Banks.

SHEATHING, the covering of copper sheets on a vessel's bottom to protect the wood from marine borers.

SHEAVE, the roller of a block. The *sheave hole* is the space between the cheeks.

SHEEPSHANK, a manipulation for shortening a rope. Greater security with the use of this knot may be obtained by tucking the ends through the eyes (Knotted Sheepshank) or by the use of toggles or by working a knot in the center.

SHEER, the curve of the deck line. A sudden change in course due to shoaling water, or the displacing of water by another vessel in close proximity. If this is violent, causing the temporary loss of control of the vessel, it is called a *rank sheer*. The angle a vessel takes with her anchor, or a quick turn to avoid another vessel or danger.

SHEER (SHEAR) HULK, an old vessel fitted with shear legs and used for lifting weights and removing masts. Also applied to a totally dismasted vessel—"reduced to a sheer hulk."

SHEER LEG DERRICK, similar to a *stiff leg derrick* which see.

SHEER (SHEAR) LEGS. See Shears.

SHEER POLE, an iron bar seized across the shrouds above the dead eyes, or turnbuckles, serving as the first ratline.

SHEER RATLINE, every fifth ratline that extends aft to the backstays.

SHEER STRAKE, the upper line of planking or plates.

SHEERHEAD LASHING, one used to secure the heads of two shear legs.

SHEERHEAD PURCHASE, a tackle made fast just below the sheerhead lashing, used to raise heavy weights.

SHEET, a rope used to control a sail. In a square sail the sheets are fast to the clews, in a jib to the clew, and in other fore and aft sails. Where there is a boom the sheet tackle works it and trims the sail.

SHEET ANCHOR was, in former days, carried in the waist and was the largest anchor aboard, being always ready for use in an emergency with cable bent. The term came to be used among seamen and others as a synonym for security.

SHEET BEND, a handy knot for making two ropes' ends fast, as it will not slip. One end is passed through the bight of the other, then carried around and tucked under its own part. Also called a *becket bend*.

SHEET BITTS, bitts near the mast. The topsail and often the topgallant sheets are made fast to them.

SHEET CLIPS, metal devices on the decks of small boats for quickly securing a sheet by jamming it instead of using cleats.

SHEETS, those planks below the waterline that end in the sternpost.

SHELL, the outside frame of a block in which the sheave revolves. A very light, long, narrow, rowing craft purely for racing and rowing exercise; seats are provided in the larger shells for eight oarsmen; the oars, owing to the small beam, work in outriggers. In certain localities the ocean floor is lined with broken shell. Its presence is indicated on the charts by the abbreviation *Sh.*, and it is often useful to a navigator in determining his approximate position.

SHELL LUGS, short pieces of angle iron riveted to the shell plating to support or help support stringer plates.

SHELL PLATING, the outside skin of a steel or iron vessel.

SHELLBACK, an old sailor.

SHELTER DECK SHIP, formerly a steamer having a very light upper deck in the sides of which are open ports to the second or main deck.

SHIIFT, to change in position.

SHIFTING BACKSTAYS, those which are set up only on the weather side and are slacked off to leeward. They are preventers and runners.

SHIFTING BEAMS, a portable support for hatchcovers; strongback.

SHIFTING BOARDS, temporary partitions extending fore and aft and down about six feet or more into a cargo that is liable to shift.

SHIM, a thin piece of metal or wood driven under a machine or other weight in order to square it up, or behind a frame to fair it up for planking, or between halves of a shaft bearing.

SHINGLE, the loose stones and gravel of a sea beach.

SHIP, strictly a vessel, square-rigged, on all masts from three up. The term is used loosely and applied quite generally to all vessels. A seaman speaks of his vessel as *the ship* regardless of rig or power.

When a sea is taken aboard it is said to be *shipped*. A man is *shipped for* duty on a vessel; anything that is put in place is *shipped*, like a boom or a boiler.

SHIP BROKER, a man who transacts a ship's business ashore, charters vessels, and buys and sells them on a commission basis.

SHIP CHANDLER, a dealer in ship supplies.

SHIP OF THE LINE, an armed vessel of the old Navy capable of taking a position in the first line of defense or offense. They were vessels usually carrying 74 or 86 guns. Sometimes they carried up to 120 guns, but never less than 60.

SHIP TIME, local apparent time. The clocks are set every day at 12 o'clock when the sun crosses the meridian. This is observed by its *dipping* in the sextant. In these days, the local time is deduced from the chronometer, and when the difference of longitude is considerable, the ship's clocks are set three times daily, viz: about 11 p.m. 3 a.m., and 5 a.m.

SHIPBOARD, on or within a vessel

SHIPENTINE, the name given by some people to a vessel square-rigged on three masts and fore and aft on the spanker or fourth mast. This rig, however, is more popularly called a four-masted bark.

SHIPMATE, a fellow seaman. Seamen also apply the term to things as, "I've never been shipmates with a rig like this before."

SHIPPING ARTICLES, the contracts entered into and signed by officers and men. The principal features of the voyage are enumerated, such as wages, character of the voyage, etc. The master only does not sign the articles.

SHIPS, A SHORT SKETCH OF. Man's attention was directed to ships back in the days of extreme antiquity; the raft, the hollowed log and the framework of saplings covered with skins were probably the first marine constructions. These boats grew in size and more seaworthy in model; paddles replaced poles and oars followed paddles; then the single square sail came to utilize the fair wind. Ships began to be constructed of various members—frames and planks—and the sizes grew rapidly.

There were two great centers of development in shipbuilding, quite separate from intercourse with each other, whose types of hull and propulsion were distinctive. The northern was that of Scandinavia and the other was the Mediterranean.

The Viking ships of the north employed the single square sail set about amidships on one mast; they had low freeboard with a remarkable upward extending stem and sternpost, often ornamented. In the extreme forward and after ends were sheltered compartments, but the waist was open.

The Mediterranean type ran to a sharp sheer which developed into high bow and stern erections, called castles, and comparatively high freeboard. The ships of these waters have clung tenaciously to the lateen sail until the present time, although a few types employed some square sails. The lateen sail was distinctly a development of Mediterranean peoples.

The voyagers of these two centers mingled but little until Richard I embarked on the Crusades to the Holy Land in the 13th century. From this time the advantages of the different types began to appear in the new models of each other's ships, and the merging of ideas has continued with extended intercourse until now a Japanese steamer cannot be distinguished from an American, except for minor characteristics only apparent to the practiced eye. The Spanish Armada in 1588 was a great practical lesson that was taken to heart by naval architects. The English ships excelled those cumbersome, slow-sailing, high-freeboarded vessels of the enemy in maneuvering ability and speed. It then became manifest that the high poops and forecastles were a hindrance to seaworthiness as well as the cause of excessive leeway, and they gradually, but with apparent reluctance, disappeared.

The demand for speed required more sails to be set, and from topsails, topgallants appeared during the reign of Queen Elizabeth I, and, later in time, the pressure pushed riggers to install royals, skysails, and even the lofty moonsail in the great clipper ship era. The lines of the hull at the same time were more and more refined until the peerless *Flying Cloud* was launched in the early fifties. It is noteworthy that fine graceful lines were not altogether of modern origin for those of the Gogstad ship, unearthed and preserved in Norway, would be hard to improve upon today. The excellence of this design seems to have been lost to many later generations. She is thought to have been built about A.D. 800, is of splendidly fastened clinker planks and measures 78 feet long and 16 feet beam. This ship is a valuable relic.

When sail reached its peak, in about 1850, steam propulsion was already cutting away its prestige, but steamers were in themselves crude of hull and machinery, while the clipper ship was in every line nothing but beauty. The steamers have passed through the refinements of progress: the developments of boilers, on to the turbine, the geared turbine, electric drive; fuel oil, diesel motor and nuclear power.

The size of ships has been marked by a steady increase from the one-man dugout to the great liners and cargo ships of today, but the small craft still traffic where there is a profit. It is shape and not size that has counted most in progress; size has never been a mark of seaworthiness; a Gloucester fishing schooner may come through safely where a large cargo steamer founders.

SHIP'S BELLS. The watches aboard ship change at 4, 8, and 12 o'clock, when eight bells are struck in double strokes. A watch contains four hours (eight half hours) and as each half hour passes an additional bell is struck. For instance:

12.30, one bell for the one half hour passed since 12; 1, two bells for the two half hours; 4, eight bells for eight half hours, and a new watch begins.

SHIP'S BUSINESS, the paper work of a ship, that is, the preparation of all documents, records of surveys, etc.

SHIP'S COUSIN, a favored person aboard ship who may be a relative of the owner.

SHIP'S HUSBAND, an agent of the owner who has charge of the expenses and receipts, while refitting.

SHIP'S OPTION, the privilege of accepting freight by measurement tons or weight.

SHIP'S PAPERS, the documents required by the authorities, such as a ship's register or enrollment, manifest, clearance papers, charter party, and bill of health.

SHIPSHAPE, in an orderly manner, as is the custom aboard ship.

SHIPWRIGHT, a builder of vessels.

SHIVER, to bring a vessel to the wind until the sails shake.

SHOAL, an area of relatively shallow water which usually breaks in heavy weather. A shoal, while usually thought of as sand or coral, may be composed of rock. Banks are deeper water. Depths of water are said to shoal when they decrease. A vessel steaming into shallowing depths, shoals her water.

SHOCK CORD, an elastic cord of many uses aboard a yacht. It is especially useful with parts of cord passing through eyes along each side of a boom. In securing a furled sail, bights of the cord are readily passed over the boom to hooks on the opposite side.

SHOD, a term applied to an anchor which has been broken out of its bed on the bottom, and lost its maximum resistance to cable strains. But the word *shod* also refers to an adaptation to an anchor. In the poor holding ground of very soft mud a triangular piece of wood or metal is bolted to the palm, which, by overlapping, increases the palm's area and hence its holding power.

SHOE, false keel; a plate for the fluke of an anchor to rest on. A plank for the heel of a sheer leg to rest on. The casting or timber projecting in the line of the keel and abaft the stern frame, upon which the rudder rests.

SHOE BLOCK, one containing two sheaves which, instead of setting parallel to each other, are at right angles.

SHOE PLATES, plates fitted around the keel to take wear and tear.

SHOLE, a piece of plank placed under a shore so as to increase its surface bearing on the ground or elsewhere.

SHOOT, to luff and make progress to windward. To observe the altitude of the sun is spoken of as *Shooting the sun.*

SHOOTING THE GULF, an expression used in Elizabethan times among the people who still thought the earth a plane, or two planes. To circumnavigate, a mariner was obliged to sail over the edge of the plane, or shoot the gulf.

SHOOTING THE SUN, to measure its altitude with a sextant.

SHORAN, a system of electronic short range navigation. Two transmitting stations are located ashore and a single indicator aboard ship to determine the distance to each beacon. With these two distances available the position of the ship is easily determined. The two beacons respond with a signal when triggered by the ship.

SHORE, a support; and, as a verb, to support. To set a stanchion or place blocking beneath an overloaded deck, for example, is to *shore up.* Also, coast line or land adjacent to a body of water.

SHORE BOAT, a term used to differentiate from the ship's boats a boat belonging to someone ashore.

SHORT BOARD, a short tack.

SHORT CAUSE ACTION, an action under a law which permits the prompt trial of cases in chancery (which includes admiralty) on documentary evidence. The decision is final and no appeal can be had. England and some of the states employ this method of saving time.

SHORT ENDED, an expression used to describe a vessel with a small amount of overhang at the bow and stern.

SHORT HANDED, without sufficient men.

SHORT LANDED, a consignment being short by tally at port of discharge.

SHORT SEA, a sea whose distance between two crests is shorter than is usual with their height.

SHORT SPLICE, a means employed to join two pieces of rope. It merely consists of tucking the parts over and under. It will not pass through a block as a long splice will.

SHORT STAY, the condition of the anchor chain when the anchor is nearly underfoot but not broken out—it is still effective in holding the vessel.

SHORTEN SAIL, to reduce canvas.

SHOT, a shot of chain is usually a 15-fathom length of a chain cable, but in the naval service, the first shot is 5 fathoms and the second, 40 fathoms. The British Admiralty uses shots of 12½ fathoms.

SHOVE OFF, to leave; go away from.

SHOVE IN YOUR OAR, to break into a conversation without invitation.

SHOW A LEG, a shout of a bo's'n in breaking the crew out of their hammocks.

SHROUD KNOT, a method of joining two parts of a rope.

SHROUD-LAID ROPE, four stranded, laid from left to right.

SHROUD PLATES, chain plates.

SHROUD RING, a washer between the propeller and the stern bearing.

SHROUDED PROPELLER (Gill), a type in which a band of bronze surrounds the periphery of the wheel. It has a somewhat greater diameter on the forward side than on the after side, in other words forms a section of a cone. Among the advantages claimed for this type are those that follow: the water is driven directly astern; there is less vibration and less slip; the danger of fouling is diminished; the wheel is strengthened structurally; it works more efficiently with small submergence, breaks water less than the open wheel; and is safer when encountering logs or ice.

SHROUDS, pieces of wire rope well served and fitted over the mastheads. They are made fast to turnbuckles or deadeyes and lanyards to the chain plates at the vessel's sides. They stay a mast at the sides.

SHUT IN. An object is said to be shut in by a point of land when the latter bears outside of it, and open when the object is outside of the point.

SHUTTER, the last plank or strake in planking up a carvel-built vessel or boat. The planks having been fastened to the frames from the sheer srtake down and from the garboard up, the shutter closes the gap.

SICK BAY, a room set apart for the sick.

SIDE BOYS, men standing at the gangway of a naval vessel to salute visiting officers of rank. The rank of the visitor determines the number of boys.

SIDE LADDER, a gangway ladder.

SIDE LIGHT CASTLES, features of foreign vessels. They are small towers erected at each side of the forecastle in which the side lights are installed. They are also called *bow lighthouses.*

SIDE LIGHTS, lanterns or electric lamps located on each side of a vessel, red light to port and green to starboard, and so screened as to show from ahead to two points abaft the beam. A screen projects well ahead of the light on the inner side to prevent its being seen across the bow. These are known as *running lights.*

SIDE STEPS, narrow steps located up and down the ship's sides at the gangway.

SIDE WHEELER, a steamer propelled by a large paddle wheel on each side of the vessel.

SIDEREAL, of or pertaining to the stars.

SIDEREAL CLOCK, an instrument geared to show sidereal time. It is 0 hrs. 00 m. 00 s., or sidereal noon, when the First Point of Aries crosses the meridian. The face is divided into 24 hours.

SIDEREAL DAY, the interval between two crossings of the meridian by the First Point of Aries. It is twenty-four sidereal hours long which is about three minutes, fifty-five and nine-tenths seconds less than a solar day. *Sidereal noon* is the moment the First Point of Aries crosses the meridian.

SIDEREAL TIME, star time; the hour angle of the First Point of Aries. Sidereal time for a given interval contains more hours than if measured in solar time. A solar day of 24 hours contains 24 hours, 3 m., 56.6 s. sidereal time and likewise in a sidereal day of 24 side-real hours, there are 23 hrs., 56 m., and 4.1 s. solar time.

SIDEREAL TIME OF MEAN NOON, an expression met with occasionally, which is the same as the right ascension of the mean sun. At mean noon, the mean sun is on the meridian and at that moment the number of sidereal hours that have elapsed since the First Point of Aries passed the meridian is the Sidereal Time of Mean Noon.

SIDING, the width of a frame; it is measured fore and aft at the stem, sternpost, and athwartships at the keel.

SIGHT, a navigator's expression for taking the altitude of a heavenly body.

SIGHT REDUCTION, the process of establishing a position line from a sextant altitude and time of sight.

SIGNAL HALYARD, halyard used for hoisting flags and signals. It is made of three-stranded plain laid hemp, also of hard-laid cotton, like window cord, called Samson cord, leading usually to a yard arm, peak of a gaff or a masthead. Braided or woven dacron is also used.

SIGNAL LETTERS. Four letters assigned to a vessel. When desiring to make her identity known, the vessel hoists the flags corresponding to these letters. If G tops the signal, it signifies a government vessel. Also called *number.*

SILL OF A DOCK, the timber at the foot of the entrance gate; a vessel must be light enough to pass over the sill in order to enter the dock.

SILT, mud brought in suspension and deposited in a harbor or river.

SIMOOM (SIMOON), a hot, dry, dust-laden wind of the Red Sea coming off the deserts.

SIMPSON'S RULES. There are three rules used to find the areas of figures bounded by a curve (such as a parabola) on one side, and a straight line on the other (such as a one-half plan view of the deck of a ship). These rules are for an approximate form of integration and can be found in almost any handbook on Naval Architecture or Marine Engineering. The first rule is often called the $\frac{1}{3}$ Rule, the second rule the $\frac{3}{8}$ Rule, and third rule the $\frac{1}{12}$ Rule, due to the fact that the common intervals between the ordinates to the curve is multiplied by these fractions in calculating the areas of the figures. (Courtesy of Mr. J. L. Bates.)

SINGLE-BANKED, one man with one oar to a thwart, as in a whale-boat or gig.

SINGLE BLOCK, one with a single sheave.

SINGLE BOTTOM. While this term is used to differentiate from a double bottom, it especially refers to a wooden vessel going without copper sheathing, which is then referred to as, "sailing on a single bottom."

SINGLE STICKER, a one-masted vessel; a sloop or cutter.

SINGLE TOPSAIL, a sail set above the course and below the topgallant sail. When divided so as to reduce the size, making an upper and lower topsail, they are called *double topsails.*

SINGLE UP, an order referring to the lines out at a pier securing a vessel. To single up is to reduce the number of lines to, perhaps, only one forward and one aft, preparatory to sailing.

SIREN, a device consisting of perforated rotating discs operated by steam or compressed air. It produces a rapidly rising tone as the pressure is applied. Sirens are used principally for emergency and fire signals.

SIROCCO (Scirocco), a hot south wind of a temperature much above normal, usually the wind in front of a cyclonic disturbance; it is quite characteristic of the Mediterranean.

SISAL ROPE, cordage made of the fiber of the henequin plant which grows abundantly in Yucatan. Its tensile strength is estimated to be about 20% less than Manila hemp.

SISTER BLOCK, one in which the shell is longer than usual and there

Sister Block

are two sheaves one above the other tandem fashion.

SISTER CLIP or **CLOVE HOOKS,** those comprising two twin hooks flattened on one side so that they lie together and form an eye when in use, and are then moused with a piece of marline. They differ from clip hooks (which see) in that the plane of the eye is at right angles to the plane of the hooks.

SISTER KEELSON, longitudinal stringers bolted to the sides of the keelson in order to give strength.

SISTER SHIPS, those built on the same lines.

SKATE, besides being a flat fish, is a long length of line consisting of about 8 halibut lines of 225 feet each fastened end to end. Fast to this is a line with a hook every 13 feet. The skate is payed over the stern and lies on the bottom buoyed at each end.

SKEET, a long-handled dipper.

SKEG, additional timbers added to deepen the keel in the after part of the vessel or small boat; an extension of the deadwood, which protects the propeller from the ground.

SKERRY, a rocky ledge, so named particularly around the British Isles.

SKIDS, timbers upon which weights or casks are hauled up or lowered from one height to another, or upon which they or a boat may rest. Also an elevated framework aboard a whaling vessel, upon which spare boats and gear are secured.

SKIFF, a small light rowing boat, a wherry.

SKILLYGALEE, oatmeal water once used by firemen working in a high temperature. It was believed to prevent cramp in the stomach.

SKIN, the inside or outside of a ship's planking or plating. It is a smooth surface made on a furled sail.

SKIN BOATS. See Bidarra.

SKIN RESISTANCE, the friction due to the water contact with the ship's side. This is reduced with the smoothness of the underbody.

SKIPJACK, a boat whose primary feature is straight frames—that is, unbent. The frames of the bottom and sides set in a chine log at the turn of the bilge. The skipjack may be sloop, schooner or ketch rigged. This type is easy to construct, hence economical; it is seaworthy.

The type is also called Deadrise, and V-bottom. Harry Pidgeon's Islander was a V-bottom boat.

SKIPPER, a name given to the master of a vessel, especially applying to the captain of a small sailing vessel.

SKY HOOK, an imaginary tool which many a green hand has sought in vain alow and aloft.

SKY PILOT, a minister of the gospel.

SKY WAVE, a radio wave that has been returned to the earth from the ionosphere.

SKYLIGHT, a window sash protected by brass rods usually set in pairs at an angle over a hatch for the purpose of giving light and air below. They are fitted with hinges and raised by screw gear devices from below.

SKYSAIL, a sail set above the royal.

SKYSAIL POLE, the upper extremities of the mast above the eyes of the rigging over the skysail yards.

SKYSAIL YARD, the yard above the royal yard.

SKYSCRAPER, a triangular sail set from the truck and the skysail yardarms.

SLABLINE or **SLAPLINE,** a rope which hauls up the bunt of a course passing around the sail through a bull's eye in the foot.

SLACK, the period between the flood and ebb or ebb and flood when no current exists. Slack in a line is the opposite condition from taut; to ease up a tension on a line.

SLACK AWAY, to pay out.

SLACK CLOTH, bagginess in a sail; spare canvas that should be taken up to make the sail set properly.

SLANT, a favorable wind.

SLAVE STATION. See Loran.

SLAVER, a vessel carrying slaves.

SLEEPER, a log or heavy piece of wreckage which floats almost entirely submerged.

SLEEPERS, the first tier of casks stowed in the hold. Also called the ground tier.

SLEET, frozen rain.

SLEWLINE, a rope used mainly in clearing hawse when a line is used to slew or rotate an anchor when clearing the chain of the other anchor.

SLIDING GUNTER, a sliding topmast for a leg-of-mutton rig in a small boat.

SLIDING WAYS. See Launch.

SLING, to pass a rope around a cask, barrel or piece of freight in a manner safe for hoisting. An arrangement of short pieces of rope or chain to sling a draft of cargo. The *rope sling,* or *strap,* is the most common, which is merely the two ends of a short rope spliced together. It is passed around a spar,

for instance, and one bight, the *rove,* is passed through the other bight, known as the *bite.* Slings are also made of flexible wire. See Cargo Slings.

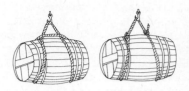

Butt Slings   Bale Slings

SLINGS of wire rope are made either of twisted or braided rope and are used in handling cargo. Braided slings are woven with an endless weave and opposite lays. They have the advantage of requiring no splicing and are flexible. There are two designs, flat and round weave. Slings are also short chains that take the weight of a yard at the mast. The *slings yoke* is the fixture on the yard to which the slings are shackled.

SLIP. See Slip of the Wheel.

SLIP, a foundation laid for the construction of a vessel; a berth for a ship between two piers. A *slip rope* consists of an end passed around a bollard or through a ring bolt, making two parts to bear the strain. When desired the end can be let go and the line recovered. It is used in letting the anchor chain go in clearing hawse, or in cases where a strain is to be released suddenly, and it serves convenience in other ways.

SLIP HOOK. See Pelican Hook.

SLIP KNOT, one in which an eye runs along the main part.

SLIP OF THE WHEEL, the difference between the distance a vessel actually goes forward in a given time, and the distance the propeller would go forward were it turning in the plane of the pitch of its blades through cold grease. It is the percentage of distance lost through the mobility of water. To get the slip, ascertain the distance run by the engines, that is, pitch $\times$ revolutions per minute $\times$ the minutes run (60), and dividing by 6080 feet. The result will be the miles made by the engines. Subtract from the actual distance made by a corrected log. This mileage represents the slip for this particular run. To express it in percentage (as it should be), divide it by the distance run by the engines. By using the distance by log the current is eliminated, which in no way must enter into the calculation of slip.

SLIP STOPPER, a short piece of chain with a slip or pelican hook. The end is fast to a ring-bolt in the deck and the hook to the anchor chain. The anchor is released by casting off the hook.

SLIPPERY HITCH, one so made fast to a spar or ring that by a pull on the rope it is released.

SLIPWAY, a term used in some places for a paved declivity extending eight or ten feet under water upon which small boats are hauled out for scraping and painting, and repairs. Also called a "Hard," which see.

SLIVER, a term in rope making: the parallel fibers of hemp lying in a pack just prior to being twisted into yarns.

SLOB ICE, a field broken up to such an extent that it takes up the motion of the waves and slowly grinds itself into slush.

SLOOP, a one-masted vessel carrying a large mainsail and one headsail. They traditionally had shoaler draft and broader beam than a cutter. See Cutter. A *sloop of war* was a light cruiser ranking below a frigate and carrying guns on one deck—18 to 32 in number. A *knockabout sloop* is one having no bowsprit.

SLOP CHEST, a compartment set apart for the storage of the clothing and other necessities provided for use of the crew. The law requires that the owner of a vessel provide her with a complete equipment of clothing for all the crew to be sold at a ten per cent advance over the wholesale value in the port of departure. The merchandise of a slop chest is called slops.

SLOPE OAR, an oarsman who, apparently pulling, is only dipping his oar.

SLOPS, the clothing and other necessities of the slop chest.

SLOT, the name given the course down from Japanese bases to Guadalcanal between the New Georgia Island Group and Choiseul. During the critical days of the Guadalcanal Campaign the enemy runs down the Slot became known as the *Tokyo Express.*

SLOT EFFECT. The improvement in speed derived from an overlapping headsail is due to the effect of accelerated air flowing past the lee side of the mainsail.

SLUDGE, a residuum or sediment in fuel oil tanks or boilers. Small floating pieces of soft or rotten ice or masses of saturated snow (snow ice).

SLUE or **SLOUGH,** a side channel. To turn quickly about and slide unexpectedly.

SLUICE GATES, valvular openings in the foot of bulkheads for the passage of bilge water from the different compartments to the bilge pumps. They are controlled from the main deck by long stems. In the newer ships pipes are run from the bilge pump to each compartment, doing away with the necessity of sluice gates. Sluice gates also empty canal locks.

SLUMGULLION, fish offal (and refuse) blubber, derisively applied to certain ship's stews.

SLUSH, a grease rubbed on masts after scraping; the skimmings from the galley, which are accumulated in the *slush bucket.*

SLUSH FUND, small sums of money derived from various sources, such as the sale of galley grease; it is usually used for the good of the ship or crew in meeting trifling expenses, for athletics, music or prizes in target practice.

SMACK (from Dutch Smak), a small fishing schooner or sloop engaged in the fresh fishery, formerly having a well to preserve fish alive.

Sometimes, but erroneously, applied to a small coaster.

SMALL STORES, personal necessities for a sea voyage such as tobacco, razors, soap, needles and thread, etc.

SMALL STUFF, marline, houseline, spunyarn, hamberline and roundline.

SMELLING THE BOTTOM, the action of a vessel when she sheers through the shoaling of the water beneath her. Also called *"Feeling the Bottom."*

SMITING LINE, one used to break out a sail sent aloft in stops.

SMOKE BOXES, receptacles containing phosphorous which were carried by merchant ships with which to make a smoke screen in the hope of escaping from an attacking submarine.

SMOKE COVER, canvas used to protect the sails abaft the stack in an auxiliary vessel.

SMOKE PIPE LINES, piping leading from each compartment to a glass-fronted cabinet in the wheelhouse. The slightest trace of fire is detected by smoke emerging from the particular pipe leading from the point of combustion.

SMOKE SAIL, a canvas protection for a forge being used on deck; and in sailing vessels a canvas screen at the galley smoke pipe to prevent smoke and sparks from blowing into the foresail. Also a canvas cover once used in auxiliary vessels to protect the mainsail, yard and mast from funnel smoke.

SMOKE SCREEN, a cloud of smoke laid by destroyers to screen the movements of a fleet or convoy.

SMOKING LAMP, of the old Navy was a brass receptacle in which was an oil lamp; whenever this lamp was lighted smoking was permitted and it served for lighting pipes.

SMOOTH, an area of comparatively smooth water in a gale following usually after two or three heavy seas.

SMOTHERING LINES, pipe lines for carrying steam or CO_2 gas to a compartment in order to smother combustion.

SNAFFLE. See Shaffle.

SNAKE, to worm, which is to lay small stuff between the strands of a rope.

SNATCH BLOCK, one having an opening into which the bight of a rope can be placed to save hauling the whole length through the block.

SNOTTER, a rope fast to the ring to which the lift and brace of a light yard are made fast. The snotter pulls the lift and brace clear as the yard is sent down. The becket holding the heel of a sprit in a small spritsail-rigged boat.

SNOW, a brig with a trysail mast close abaft the mainmast on which a boom trysail is set. Originally a snow had other hull characteristics, especially in the form of the bow.

SNUB, to check a chain or hawser quickly. To snub a ship is to let

go the anchor and bring her up quickly. To snub a line by tension around the bitts or pin.

SNUG DOWN, to reduce sail to a point where the anticipated or prevailing weather conditions leave a margin of safety.

SNY, a small toggle used on a flag. The curving of the edges of ship's planking where it curves upward at the bow.

SO, an order signifying that things are to be left as they are.

SOCKETS. See Patent Eye.

SOD-BANK, a phenomenon of refraction causing the appearance of many images of the same object.

SOGER, a seaman who is always hanging back when work is going on. One who dodges work by various subterfuges. Verb—to pretend or to dodge work, etc. Also Soldier.

SOLANO, an easterly wind on the eastern coast of Spain, usually a forerunner of rain.

SOLAR, of or pertaining to the sun.

SOLAR SYSTEM, the sun and all the heavenly bodies that revolve around it. It includes the earth, other planets, comets and the moon.

SOLAR TIME, indicated by the movement of the sun.

SOLDIER'S WIND, one which serves vessels sailing in opposite directions, say East and West.

SOLE, a plank bolted to the foot of a rudder to carry it down to the level of the false keel. The cabin floor of a small yacht.

SOLSTICES, the positions of the earth in its orbit where the inclination of the axis is directly towards or away from the sun, making at that time the sun's greatest declination. The 21st of June is called the *Summer Solstice* and the 21st of December, the *Winter Solstice.*

SOLSTITIAL POINTS, points on the ecliptic which are farthest from the equator. The sun is at these points about the 21st of June and December with a declination of about 23½°. The hour circle passing through these points is called the *Solstitial Colure.*

SONAR, a system of transmitting electronic pulses in supersonic frequencies in order to measure horizontal distances through water as sonic depth finders measure vertical distances.

SONIC DEPTH FINDER, an invention very valuable in charting ocean depths. They are determined by means of vibrations sent out from a moving vessel by an oscillator located on the under body, and the echo received through microphones placed at some known distance from the oscillator. "On Soundings" the depth is determined by the angle of reflection at the bottom of the sea, formed between the line of sound and that of the echo. But in greater depths the time interval occupied by the sound in traveling to the bottom and its return, is utilized. This is divided by two and multiplied by the velocity of sound in salt water, 4,800 feet per second.

This figure is used as on the safe side; the actual velocity being a little more. When high frequencies are used the instrument is called an *ultrasonic depth finder.* These are more satisfactory due to less interference by ship's noises. There are several forms by which the depth is recorded. One is using a recording tape.

SOUL AND BODY LASHING, a rough fastening sufficient to hold two objects together under great stress.

SOUND, to measure the depth of water with a lead. A *sounding* is the depth measured or the number indicating the depth on the chart. A whale *sounds* when it sinks in the sea. A vessel crossing a bar may *sound* 6 to 8 feet as she is lowered in the trough between the swells or seas. Sound travels about 4,800 feet per second in water, and 1,117 feet per second in dry air. Radio impulses travel with the speed of light 186,230 statute miles per second.

SOUNDING MACHINE, an instrument formerly valuable to the navigator for the purpose of taking soundings in deep water without stopping the vessel. It consists principally of a drum set in a case or standard upon which is wound some 200 fathoms of piano wire. The deep sea lead is attached to the wire when sounding. Just above it is also attached a metallic cylindrical tube with holes in the bottom. A glass tube coated with a chemical substance (chromate of silver), and sealed at the upper end, is inserted in the cylinder before the lead is cast. The drum is disengaged when the sounding is taken and, when the lead reaches the bottom, cranks are thrown in and the sounding wire reeled up. The chemical on the glass tube will be discolored, and almost obliterated just as far as the pressure has forced the water up the tube, and the depth is indicated by applying the discolored portion to a scale. Electronic instruments have now largely superseded the sounding machine.

SOUNDING POLE, a pole graduated for the purpose of obtaining the depth in shallow water, where it is handier than a leadline.

SOUNDING ROD, a rod used by the ship's carpenter to sound the bilges. It is usually of iron with a small line attached. The rod is chalked before sounding to show the water level.

SOUNDINGS. A vessel is said to be *on soundings* when the bottom can be reached with the deep-sea lead, and *off soundings* when it cannot be reached. The 100-fathom curve is generally considered the dividing line between soundings and ocean depths.

SOUTHERLY BURSTER a cold wind from the south in the wake of a cyclone which visits New Zealand.

SOUTHWESTER (SOU'WESTER), an oilskin hat projecting considerably more to the rear than in front. A heavy wind from that quarter.

SPADE RUDDER. The name suggests the shape. This rudder swings freely on its bearing in the hull. without being attached to the rudder-post in the conventional manner.

SPALES, temporary light supports acting as beams for the erected frames of a vessel under construction.

SPAN, a piece of wire or rope fast at each end of two fixtures such as davit heads; sometimes a tackle is hooked to it. The wire rope, called the *peak span,* suspends a standing gaff. The distance from the turnbuckles or deadeyes over the masthead to those on the other side is the *span of the rigging.*

SPANISH BURTON, a convenient purchase of single blocks. It is used by fishermen in removing baskets of fish at Gloucester and Boston and often in heavier work.

Spanish Burton

SPANISH FOX, an untwisted rope yarn retwisted the opposite way.

SPANISH REEF, a knot tied in the head of a jib. In square-rigged vessels, the lowering of a yard to the cap.

SPANISH WINDLASS, a wooden roller revolved by marline spikes and around which a rope is taken for the purpose of heaving two parts of a rope together, or like use.

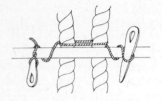

Spanish Windlass

SPANK, the heavy slap of a boat as she drops over a sea, usually in flat-bottomed craft.

SPANKER, the fore and aft sail set from the after mast of a sailing vessel. It was developed from the lateen mizzen by first cutting the sail vertically at the mast, lacing

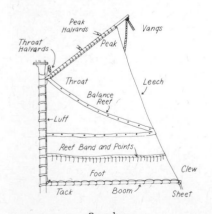

Spanker

its forward edge thereto, and discarding the forward part of the sail. Later the part of the lateen yard forward of the mast was cut off.

SPANNER, a tool for coupling hose to a fire plug, operating screw covers and similar uses.

SPAR AND BOOM GEAR, an arrangement generally used in handling cargo. A boom is guyed over the hatch, a second boom over the side. The hatch (or stay) tackle hoists the sling load of cargo while the boom (or yard arm) tackle, which is also hooked to the sling, sets taut and carries the sling load across the deck to the pier without swinging the booms.

SPAR BUOY, a painted spar moored by a mushroom anchor or block of concrete so as to float in an oblique or perpendicular manner.

SPAR DECK, the upper deck of a flush decked ship, usually a naval vessel.

SPAR DECKED STEAMER, a type having a continuous upper deck much heavier in construction than an awning deck. Not, however, equal to a three-decked vessel.

SPAR VARNISH, a varnish of superior quality for outside work on shipboard. It resists the destructive action of salt water, heat or cold.

SPARK SET, one in which electrical jump sparks were formerly used, which, when received in a telephone receiver are musical tones, short or long, according as dots or dashes were sent. A message sent by a spark set was heard by all stations within its radius regardless of the wave length to which it was tuned.

SPARKS, a nickname given the radio operator.

SPARRING DOWN, lashing small spars or oars across the rigging to stand on when rattling down.

SPARS, a term applied to all masts, yards, gaffs, booms, etc.

SPEAK, to communicate with a vessel at sea. Even though only with flags a vessel "speaks" another. She later would report "We spoke the ship *Ocean Pearl,*" giving date and position. In the column of maritime intelligence used to appear the heading: SPOKEN.

SPEAKING TRUMPET, a tapering hollow tube through which orders are given.

SPECIAL CARGO, that which has unusual value for its measurement, as specie or that which requires special attention. There is an extra charge for special cargo.

SPECIFIC GRAVITY, the ratio between the weight of a cubic foot of a substance and that of a cubic foot of water.

SPECTACLE or **CLEW IRON,** a contrivance made up of two or three rings cast together at different angles so that two or three ropes can be hooked into it and lead in the desired direction. They are used at the clews of square sails, courses especially. A *spectacle eye* is attached to a davit

head to receive the span and the guy.

SPECTACLE FRAME, the casting that supports the propeller shaft of a twin-screw steamer, where the shell plating swells outboard to enclose the shafts.

SPEED CONES, conical shapes exhibited by naval vessels to indicate their speed to those in formation astern.

SPEED LIGHTS, lights which serve the same purpose as speed cones in the nighttime. They are shown from the masthead.

SPENCER, a trysail carried on the fore or mainmast of a ship. It was usually set on a standing gaff, loose-footed and brailed in to the mast. A storm trysail is not a spencer.

SPERMACETI, fine oil from the upper forehead of a sperm whale.

SPHERICAL SAILING, that method whereby the courses and distances sailed take the spherical shape of the earth into account, in contradistinction to plane sailing.

SPIDER, a metal outrigger to keep a block clear, as of a mast.

SPIDER BAND, the band below the "top" having many eyes to which the lower ends of the futtock shrouds are bolted.

SPILE, a pile.

SPILING, shaping the edges of the bow and stern planks of a ship's side to take care of the rapid change in sheer.

SPILL, to throw the wind out of

the sails by use of the helm, the sheets or the braces.

SPILL PIPE, the fixture through which the anchor chain passes through the deck to the chain locker. Also called the *spurling gate.*

SPILLING LINES, those fitted to square sails to spill the wind and aid in getting the sail secured. They serve somewhat as buntlines to control the sail, and reeve down through bull's eyes abaft the sail to the leeches.

SPINDLE, a kind of beacon—pole set in the bottom and usually carries a cage as a topmark.

SPINDRIFT, the fine mist driven from the wave crests by the wind.

SPINNAKER, a large jib-headed sail used with a fair wind and set from a boom that swings out to the opposite side from the main or fore boom. Its head hoists to, or nearly to, the masthead. The derivation of spinnaker is a good example of how the sailor can twist a term to his satisfaction. The yacht *Sphinx* is said to have been the first to spread that three-cornered sail. It then appeared of great size and was derisively called Sphinx's acre, which has been weirdly corrupted to spinnaker. See Parachute spinnaker.

SPINNAKER NET, consists of spaced lines that parallel between the mast and the head stay for the purpose of preventing the sail from wrapping around the stay.

SPIRIT COMPASS, one in which the card floats in a solution of 45% alcohol and 55% distilled water.

SPIRKETTING, a heavy strake of ceiling either on the beam ends or next above the waterways. The *spirketting plate* is a vertical stringer plate riveted to the frames at the lower hold beams.

SPIT KID, a cuspidor.

SPITFIRE, a storm jib.

SPLASHBOARD, a guard to prevent discharged water from flooding a low pier. In a small yacht splashboards on the foreward deck help keep water from running into the cockpit.

SPLICE, to join two ropes by tucking the strands in different ways according to the purpose, whether *short, long, chain* or *sailmakers* splice.

SPLICE THE MAIN BRACE, means to take a drink or in the days of the old Navy when an extra tot of rum was served in celebration of some moving event.

SPLIT FALLS METHOD of cargo handling consists of the hatch and burton tackles, each with separate hooks; when the draft of cargo reaches the coaming the man tending the burton throws his hook around the hatch fall and the burton tackle assists the draft to the pier. In loading the operation is reversed, the burton man unhooking his tackle when the draft is over the hatch.

SPLIT TACKS, when two vessels beating to windward take opposite tacks.

SPOIL GROUND, an assigned area for dumping scow loads of dredged material. Such areas are usually marked by buoys.

SPOKES, of the steering wheel which extend out beyond the "rim" to form handles, are referred to as a measure of helm, viz: "Port two spokes." Now the order would be "Left two spokes."

SPONSON, a bulging part of a vessel's side either to support heavy machinery or mount a gun. Sponsons are also used to add to stability. The overhanging structure supporting the wheels of a side-wheel steamer are sponsons, or *sponson beams.*

SPONSOR, one who christens a vessel at launching.

SPONTANEOUS COMBUSTION, first started in coal or in paint, rags, etc., by the generation of heat within.

SPOON DRIFT (Spindrift), the mist blown from the tops of crested waves.

SPOON OARS, those which are curved near the outer part of the blade. They are used only in very light boats.

SPOT DOCKING, is so docking a ship as to line up the hatches with pier doors. A "bridge sign" on the loading platform aids in placing the ship at the desired spot.

SPOT SHIP, a term applied to a laid up vessel which has at least a skeleton crew aboard and is ready to sail on short notice.

SPREAD, the distance out from the central fore and aft line of a vessel.

SPREAD EAGLE, to tie a man in the rigging, arms and legs apart, for the purpose of lashing his back with a rope's end. See *Two Years Before the Mast,* Dana, Chapter XV.

SPREADERS, spar-like bars of iron, projecting from the bow of a narrow square-rigged vessel to give more spread for the tacks. Sometimes called *Tack Bumpkins.* Extensions of the cross-trees to spread the backstays. They are also used in yachts to spread the shrouds in staying a mast athwartships.

SPRING BUFFER, a heavy coil spring set in the wheel chains to take up the shock of the seas against the rudder. Also used at each end of a deck horse, on which travels a sheet block, to relieve the shock when jibing a fore and aft sail.

SPRING LINE, one leading from the forward part of a vessel aft to the pier or from the after part forward, to keep her from moving ahead or astern. A spring is a line used particularly to aid in maneuvering a vessel around a dock or made fast to a sea anchor or a kedge. A vessel can be put on another tack or made to lie closer or more off the wind by a proper placing of the spring line in a gale. *Cross springs* are sometimes used further to secure a vessel to a pier. The two lines cross, one leading forward, the other aft.

SPRING LOG, a device by which the resistance of a chip (see Chip Log) in the water is recorded on a spring balance in such a way as to indicate the speed of a vessel.

SPRING STAY, the horizontal piece of wire rope running between the mastheads of a schooner. Also a piece of gear used to assist a regular stay—a preventer.

SPRING TIDES, those tides that occur near the time of full and new moon. They have a greater range at this time, the high water being higher and the low water lower than the average. This condition is due to the fact that the attractive influence of the sun and moon upon the water are combined and working together. It is the opposite condition from neap tides.

SPRIT, a light spar that holds aloft the peak of a small fore and aft sail that has no gaff. The lower end fits into a becket or snotter secured to the mast several feet above the rail.

SPRIT TOPMAST, a small upright spar stepped on the end of a bowsprit or jib-boom in ancient ships; the sail set from it was usually called the sprit-topsail.

SPRITSAIL YARD, a spar formerly carried across the bowsprit; sometimes when a jib-boom was carried two of these spritsail yards were used. In former days a square sail that hung beneath the bowsprit was called a spritsail, and later a watersail. The spritsail yard later descended into the more modern whisker booms.

SPRITSAIL YARDING A SHARK, was a cruel practice of putting a double pointed stick in a shark's mouth so as to prevent his shutting it. In this condition he was set adrift.

SPRUNG, to be split or warped out of shape, especially applying to a spar.

SPUDS, vertical timbers with armored points at lower ends used at the corners of a dredge which when dropped to the bottom hold the vessel in place. Potatoes.

SPUN YARN, two or three-stranded stuff twisted loosely together. It has many uses about the rigging and sails of a vessel, especially where a smooth service is desired.

SPUNYARN SUNDAY, a day given over to boat races or games. See Ropeyarn Sunday.

SPUR, a short projection of a pier usually extending at right angles; a side track of railroad running down a pier or to a warehouse.

SPUR BEAM, the timber which fairs into the side of a sidewheel steamer at the ends of the sponson beams.

SPUR GROMMET, is one with a movable spur at right angles to the plane of its base and which fits through an ordinary grommet, turns and locks the two together.

SPURLING GATE, the iron casting set in the deck through which the anchor chain passes.

SPURLING LINE, the connecting wire, or chain, between the tiller and the telltale by the steering wheel; by this device the position of the helm is readily indicated to the quartermaster.

SPURSHORE, a spar used to hold a vessel off a dock.

SPY GLASS, an optical instrument used by the old shipmasters for bringing nearer the images of distant objects. It consists of a brass tube having a concentric extension tube within; an object glass is inserted at the outer end and an eye glass at the inner end of the extension tube.

SQUALL, a sudden and violent burst of wind. It may be just wind or a rain, snow or thunder squall. Squalls break during light airs or calms and also during gales of wind. The wind may be blowing with a force of 7, Beaufort Scale, when terrific squalls repeatedly burst with a hurricane force of 12.

SQUARE, a term applied to the yards when they are at right angles to the fore and aft line of the vessel. They are then *square by the braces.* When horizontal, they are *square by the lifts. Square Marks* are pieces of twine whipped on these lines to show when they are square.

SQUARE KNOT (Reef Knot), two overhand knots. It is a most useful knot and is used in a great variety of purposes.

SQUARE-RIGGED, a mast carrying yards.

SQUARE RIGGER, a vessel carrying square sails.

SQUARE SAILS, those set from yards and rectangular in shape.

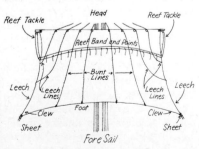

Square Sail

SQUARE UP, to arrange all gear in an orderly fashion.

SQUATTING, the settling of a vessel's stern due to speed of onward motion.

SQUILGEE (pronounced squeegee by seamen), a small, flat board with a piece of rubber set in its edge. A handle is inserted and the implement is used for drying water from a deck.

STABILITY, the moment of force which keeps a vessel upright, and if heeled over, returns her to an even keel. If weights are placed in the lower holds the center of gravity is lowered and the stability is increased. If heavy weights are placed on the upper decks the center of gravity is raised and there is a loss of stability. A vessel is said to be *stiff* or *tender* according as there is much or little stability.

STABILIZERS, are used to dampen the roll and are found as gyroscopes within vessels; as bilge keels outside at the bilges; as keel plates attached to the keel and as *fishermen's stabilizers.* Which see.

STACK, the smoke pipe of the furnaces, also called the *funnel.*

STADIA, a graduated rod which when used in conjunction with a telemeter offers a reliable means of measuring short distances.

STADIMETER, an instrument for measuring the distance of an object when its height is known.

STAGGERED RIVETING, two rows of rivets with alternate spacing.

STAGING OFF, a term applied to the method of holding a vessel off the bank of a river or off a pier. A rough timbered structure is put together between the ship and the shore to prevent her working in and grounding. High up the Plata River at less frequented ports steamers resort to staging off. Up rivers at some convenient spot for the mooring of a small yacht, posts are driven off the bank to keep the boat in deeper water; a platform connects with the shore.

STANCHIONS, upright pillars either of wood or steel. They are used to support the various decks. They are also set on deck for the purpose of spreading awnings and are known as *awning stanchions.*

STAND, to sail a course; *Stand in,* to sail inshore.

STAND BY, an order to be prepared to execute an order or a maneuver. To remain in the vicinity in order to render assistance if necessary. The seaman who stands by during the night watches subject to the whistle of the bridge officer. He is ready to do any duty required during his watch of two hours. A seaman is usually on lookout two hours and stand-by two hours.

STAND ON, to hold the course.

STAND-ON VESSEL, the craft that has the right of way.

STAND OF THE TIDE, the period when no vertical motion can be detected.

STAND UP, to steer up a channel or bay.

STANDARD COMPASS, an instrument similar to other compasses but placed in a location as remote from magnetic influence as practical. It is adjusted with great care and all courses are referred to its readings.

STANDING BACKSTAYS, those set up for permanence, not shifted on each tack. Also called Permanent Backstays.

STANDING BOWSPRIT, one not capable of being run in.

STANDING GAFF, one that remains aloft. Supported by a peak span and steadied by vangs.

STANDING LUG, a small boat rig. The sail is set from a small yard and the tack makes fast to the mast. It is with or without a boom.

STANDING PART, the fixed part of a rope, the part made fast; of rigging, that which is set up to turnbuckles or lanyards; of a tackle that which is made fast to the block.

STANDING RIGGING, the heavy wire ropes which support the spars, and which are not altered with the ordinary working of the vessel.

STAPLING, angle bar collars fitted around longitudinals where they pass through bulkheads.

STARBOARD, the right side of a vessel, looking forward. It dates back to the time when a steering board was used on the right side of a vessel and became corrupted into starboard.

STARBOARD TACK, sailing with

the wind coming over the right or starboard side.

STARBOWLINES, the men of the starboard watch.

START, to ease off a piece of gear, as a sheet or brace; to open a cask; a plank worked loose has *started.*

STATION BILL, a published list of the stations of a crew for abandon ship, or drills, fire, etc. This list must be posted in conspicuous parts of the ship, especially in the crew's quarters.

STATION BUOY, one of lower class moored close by a lighted buoy or lightship to mark the station should the main aid break adrift.

STATION POINTER, is another name for a Three-arm Protractor.

STATIONS FOR STAYS, an order for men to take respective places for tacking ship.

STATUTE MILE, equal to 5,280 feet.

STAUNCH, seaworthy; sound.

STAVE, to break in the planking of a boat, although seamen usually say *stove;* a vessel with her side broken is said to be stove.

STAY, a piece of rigging, usually wire rope, serving to stay a mast from forward. See Backstays. Strengthening pieces forming the frame of a rudder. As a verb, stay means to tack. Also to support a mast in a vertical position. A vessel is *in stays* when heading into the wind in tacking. She *misses stays* when failing to go about to

other tack. An anchor chain is at *short stay* when it leads forward at a sharp angle—nearly "up and down."

STAY TACKLES, those made fast to a stay for use in hoisting weights in a midship position over a hatch.

STAYSAIL, a triangular fore and aft sail set from the various stays and named accordingly, as the *foretopmast staysail.*

STAYSAIL RIG, is used to obviate the shifting of the foretopsail sheet over the spring stay when tacking a schooner. This would require a man to go aloft. With the staysail rig, in the place of the foresail and gaff topsail, a narrow sail hoists to the head of the marconi foremast (the mainsail of a ketch). The sheet, at about mid-height, is led to the end of a *wishbone gaff.* There is a main-staysail and a main-topmast-staysail that fill the remaining space between the fore and mainmasts. There are other arrangements of sails in a staysail schooner or ketch.

STEADY, an order to a quartermaster to hold the ship's head as she goes.

STEADYING SAILS, used on motor craft to dampen the roll in a beam or following sea. They are usually jib-headed and of small area. In case of engine failure they can give the boat headway before the wind.

STEALER, a special ship's plate worked into her structure at the stem and stern. It is placed at the end of the *drop plate* which does not quite reach the stem or sternpost and fills the space.

STEAM LIGHTER, a bulky craft used in the transferring of cargo about harbors with its own power.

STEAM SCHOONER, formerly an important factor in the transportation of lumber on the West Coast. Their engines were aft.

STEAM STEERING GEAR, machinery by which the lines leading from the steering wheel open and close valves on an engine which in turn moves the helm by steam power. The lines may be hydraulic.

STEAMBOAT, a light draft vessel employed on inland waters. The construction is lighter than used in sea-going steamers.

STEAMBOATING, the transfer of cargo on the backs of 'longshoremen.

STEEP TO, a bold shore; a coast rising quickly from deep·water.

STEERAGE, the lower compartments where third or fourth class passengers are accommodated. A compartment in the older naval vessels used as the quarters of the junior officers.

STEERAGEWAY, headway sufficient for the rudder to act.

STEERING COMPASS, the instrument used by the quartermaster in steering a course.

STEERING GEAR, the wheel, wheel ropes, steering engine, helm and rudder.

STEERING OAR, a long oar used as a rudder especially in whale-boats and lifeboats where the rudder becomes ineffective in a seaway. See Oar.

STEERING POLE. Where the wheelhouse of a steamer is very far forward the jack staff is often hinged at the foot, allowing it to take a position similar to a bowsprit. It aids in holding a course or in maneuvering ship. A very small dimmed electric light is set in its end to guide the helmsman and officer on watch.

STEERING SAILS, an old term for studding sails.

STEERSMAN, the man at the helm or wheel holding the vessel's course.

STEEVE, the angle the bowsprit takes with the horizontal.

STEM, the foremost timber or steel bar in a vessel. It is joined to the keel, and all the planks, or plates, are rabbeted or riveted to it. To *stem a current* is to proceed and make way against it.

STEM FENDER, a very heavy mat made of Manila carried on the stem of a tug in order that she may do pushing duty without damage.

STEM LIGHT, a white light carried on the stem of inland steamers.

STEM WINDERS, a name often given by coast sailors to the lake steamers that have their engines located aft.

STEMMING LIST, a precedence list in loading coal in English ports. A master applies to the dockmaster and enters the name of his vessel and her tonnage on the list. A *free stem* exists when vessels are allowed to enter the docks without the restriction of a list.

STEMSON, an inner stem for additional strength.

STEP, a frame structure prepared either on the keelson or a lower deck to receive the heel of the mast. To step a mast is to set it in position.

STEP OFF, to measure a course or distance on a chart.

STERN, the after part of a vessel.

STERN ALL, an order to oarsmen to back water. There is much romance connected with this order, for in days past, as a whale-boat was boldly brought in contact with a whale the order "starn all" (corrupted into a Nantucket and New Bedford localism), was given, precisely timed to miss the destructive sweeps of the great mammal's flukes in its flurry.

STERN ANCHOR, a convenience for anchoring by the stern. A hawse pipe is provided at the stern and fitted with a stockless anchor.

STERN FAST, a stern line to moor ship to a pier or buoy. A pile or buried post to which stern lines are made fast.

STERN FRAME, a large casting erected at the after end of keel to form the ship's stern. It includes the stern post, the rudder post, and the shaft hole. The stern frames are those which form the stern and determine its shape.

STERN POST, a perpendicular timber or steel bar joined to and erected on the after part of the keel.

STERN SHEETS, the space abaft the thwarts of a small boat.

STERN TRAWLER, is a modern automated fishing vessel, in which the trawl net is hoisted in over the stern, the catch dumped and the net reeled over a drum amidships. This is done by two winches located at the foot of the boom trimmed amidships. In fishing the trawl is operated by two other winches, port and starboard, carrying, in large vessels, 700 fathoms of wire. The trawl boards when hoisted are hung from gallows frames at the stern, port and starboard. The fishing operations and the maneuvering of the vessel are controlled from one station. As the vessel can recover her net readily by heading into the sea, this type can operate in weather not possible in the older trawlers.

STERN TUBE. See Shaft Tube.

STERN WHEELER, a steamer propelled by a paddle wheel at the stern. Such vessels are used only on sounds and rivers and now are few in number.

STERNBOARD, sternway; particularly applied, however, to a sailing vessel in stays and making sternway. The term is sometimes applied when a vessel, beating with a long leg and a short one, loses ground towards her objective on the short leg.

STERNSON, an inner sternpost for additional support.

STEVEDORE, a man in charge of the stowage of cargo and the boss of 'longshoremen. The stevedores are the foremen and the 'longshoremen are the laborers.

STEVEDORE'S KNOT, one used to prevent the unreeving of a rope through a block.

STEVEDORING, the loading and discharging of cargo.

STEWARD, the commissary of a vessel and the man who has charge of cooks, waiters, and other personal service men and women.

STICKS, masts.

STIFF, a quality of stability where a vessel returns quickly to an upright position. Although not a desirable condition for seaworthiness, a certain degree of stiffness is essential. A strong breeze is a *stiff breeze, Cape Stiff,* Cape Horn.

STIFF LEG DERRICK, a type in which the mast is stayed by two pieces of timber (or steel) which lead from the masthead down to the outer end of two ground timbers, upon whose inner ends the mast is stepped. The boom is topped in a general opposite direction from the ground timbers. The boom is capable of a swing through about 250°. Sometimes it is mounted in such a way as to be movable on tracks.

STERN LINE, a mooring hawser leading from a docked vessel's quarter to the pier.

It is also a term used in yacht racing; the stern line, in imagination, extends out at right angles to the fore and aft line, from the aftermost part of the boat.

STIFFENER, an angle bar, T bar, or channel iron, used to stiffen plating of a bulkhead, etc.

STILE, a shadow pin erected on a compass. The shadow cast indicates the azimuth or bearing of the sun.

STIRRUPS, short ropes suspended from a yard and fast to the foot-ropes which they support.

STOCK, the cross piece of an anchor. The stock being set at right angles with the shank, the strain on the cable causes the anchor to cant and take a biting hold on the bottom. The balls at the ends of the stock prevent its sinking too deep in the bottom before it is in its proper position.

STOCK AND BILL TACKLE, a purchase used to handle the stock type of anchor on the bows of a ship.

STOCKS, blocks forming the foundation upon which the keel is laid in building a vessel.

STOKE-HOLE, the fire-room.

STOKER, a man who transfers coal from the bunkers and feeds the furnaces.

STOMACH-PIECE, a piece set in at the after side of the stem to reinforce it. It is also called the *apron.*

STONEWALL, a term given by old seamen to that area off Cape Horn which was made difficult for square-rigged vessels to pass westward due to the prevailing head winds, current and persistent gales.

STOOLS, channels to which the backstays are sometimes set up. They are abaft the channels of the shrouds.

STOP-WATER, a treenail driven

through the stem and keel where they join at the forefoot. A packing of felt set in lead between two plates to make a watertight joint.

STOPPER, a short rope usually laid up in a soft pliable manner made fast in various convenient places where it is used for temporarily holding a piece of running rigging or cable by making a rolling hitch around it or better, a stopper hitch in which the second turn rides the first.

STOPPER KNOT, a wall knot with the parts followed around, making a double wall.

STOPS, pieces of small stuff or narrow bands of canvas used in securing a sail or awning.

STORM, a wind perhaps accompanied by rain, snow, hail, or lightning, which reaches a velocity of 56 to 65 knots, force 11, Beaufort Scale.

STORM CANVAS, staysails or trysails of extra heavy canvas for heavy weather use. Also called *storm sails.*

STORM CENTER. Storms that are cyclonic in character blow in spirally to a vortex where the air passes upward. The conditions (reversed) very much resemble the movement of water in a wash bowl when the plug is removed. Within the vortex or center, the wind is very erratic in direction, coming in heavy gusts from almost any quarter, interspersed by light air and short periods of calm. The seas are heavy and erratic, coming from any and every quarter. This center is called the *eye* of the storm. When one faces the wind (in north-

ern latitude) the center of the agitation will be about ten points on the right hand. The conditions are reversed in the southern hemisphere.

STORM OIL, oil used for spreading on the sea in heavy weather to prevent, or reduce the breaking crests. Vegetable or fish oils are better than mineral oils for this purpose.

STORM SAILS. See Storm Canvas.

STORM SIGNALS. *Small craft warning:* A red pennant is shown when winds up to 33 knots are forecast and/or sea dangerous; night signal is a red over a white light.

Gale warning: When winds of 34 to 47 knots are expected—two red pennants; night signal, a white over a red light.

Storm warning: When winds from 48 to 63 knots are forecast, a red square flag with black square at the center is shown; at night two red vertical lights.

Hurricane warning: When winds of 64 knots or over are expected, two red square flags, with black square at the center, are exhibited; at night, three vertical lights, two red with a white between them.

STORM TRACK. A cyclonic storm in the northern hemisphere usually moves bodily in a right-hand curve (left-hand in southern hemisphere). The line of this progressive motion is called the storm track. A vessel located on this track will not experience a shift of wind but the barometer will continue to fall. Such a vessel should put the wind on the starboard quarter (northern hemisphere) and run for the navigable semi-circle.

STORM VALVE, a check valve in a pipe leading outboard just above the water line.

STORMY PETRELS, Mother Carey's Chickens.

STOVE, a cask, case, or vessel broken in from outside is said to be stove. Seamen use the word *stove* for all the inflections of the verb, good grammar to the contrary notwithstanding.

STOW, to put anything away for sea; to put gear in its proper place.

STOWAGE, the proper packing away of cargo. This work has many angles requiring knowledge, skill and judgment. Weight must be so distributed that no undue stresses will be set up in a seaway; weight must also be distributed with regard to the center of gravity in relation to the metacenter to insure desired stability; the cargo must be protected from damage by sea water, sweat or other cargo; the cubic space must be utilized to gain the greatest amount of freight; cargo must be stowed with the thought of speed in loading and discharge; if calling at several ports cargo for each must be accessible.

STOWAGE FACTOR, the number of cubic feet of a certain merchandise necessary to weigh a long ton; pig iron has a low factor and crated furniture has a high factor. A cargo with a factor of over 40 is called *measurement freight;* that less is *dead weight* cargo. When the clause "ship's option" enters a rate it may be calculated either by weight or measurement.

STOWAWAY, a person secreting himself on a departing vessel for the purpose of getting a free passage.

STRAIGHT-LINE CRANE, one which travels usually on the roof of a warehouse. A boom is supported from the traveling structure at a point between the ends which allows it to be topped satisfactorily over a hatch, while its inner end extends within the shed. The carriage from which the cargo pendant is suspended travels in and out on the under side of the boom, which does not revolve.

STRAIK. See Strake.

STRAIN, a distortion due to an excessive stress.

STRAKE *(streak),* a line of planks or plates running the length of a vessel.

STRAKE BOOK, a list of all the plates of a vessel, their sizes and marks.

STRAND, a part of a rope. It is made up of yarns, the twist being opposite from the twist of the fibres. See Rope. A vessel *strands* when she takes bottom on a beach, because a beach is, in some countries, called a *strand.* A rope is *stranded* when a strand parts.

STRANDED, the condition of a vessel that has run on a strand or, with us, a beach.

STRAP, a piece of rope spliced into a circle and used for slinging cargo or gear. Sometimes called a *strop.* A *permanent strap* is spliced into the thimble with the hook of the block. It is used by passing it over the spar, or other object, to the hook. A *sail strap* is one where an eye is made by a seizing, and the bight tucked through the eye instead of the strap itself.

STRAPPED DOWN, a sailing yacht close on the wind with hardened sheets.

STRATO-CUMULUS (S.-Cu.), clouds which differ from nimbus by their globular or rolled appearance. They are not rain clouds. They are dark in color and are most often seen in the winter. The blue sky is often seen through them.

STRATUS (S), a uniform gray cloud sheet. May be blown into broken patches and become fractostratus clouds.

STRAY LINE. See Chip Log.

STREAK, a line of planking or plating, more often called a *strake*.

STREAM, to run out or launch the log, a sea anchor, or mine sweeping gear. *Out in the stream* is that part of the fairway where the strength of the current runs. A vessel anchored in the deep water off the wharves, is said to be *in the stream*. A current in the ocean. Also a brook or small river.

STREAM ANCHOR, a warping or working anchor. It ranks in weight between a kedge and a bower.

STREAM CHAIN, one that is close-linked with no studs.

STREAMLINED, a design of all parts of a vessel offering air resistance which conforms as nearly as practicable to the flow of air.

STRESS, an equivalent to a force applied to a body which tends to change its shape, whether by compression, pull, thrust, twist or shearing stress.

STRETCHERS, thwartship pieces of wood for oarsmen to brace their feet against.

STRIKE, to lower a mast, yard, or sail. To *strike soundings* is to come inshore sufficiently to reach bottom with the lead.

STRING PIECE, the timber forming the edge of a wharf.

STRINGER, a fore and aft member of a ship's structure. There are *bilge stringers, hold stringers* and *deck stringers*. The latter are named for the particular deck they help to strengthen, such as the *boat deck stringer*, etc. An *intercostal stringer* is composed of plates fitted between the frames, usually flush with the inner face of the frames, allowing a continuous angle iron to support its inner edge; a *side stringer* is riveted to the frames (or intercostals) along the bottom between the turn of the bilge and the keelson; *stringer plates* are the outermost strakes of plating forming a deck.

STRIP, to remove all rigging.

STRIP FOR ACTION, stow or get rid of all impedimenta and be ready for battle.

STRIPPING LINES, the pipe lines of a tanker which clear the tanks. They remove the residual oil after the main suction ceases to be effective.

STROKE, the sweep of the oars, as a *long stroke* or a *short stroke*. In the captain's gig an interrupted stroke was used, that is, a pause after-power stroke. The oarsman farthest aft and pulling the starboard oar *sets the stroke* and is known as the *stroke oar.*

STRONGBACK, a steel (or wood) beam placed across a hatch to support the sections of the hatch covers. See Fore and Afters. A spar lashed to and running between the old style davits to steady them and to aid in controlling and securing the boat.

STROP, a name synonymous with strap, a circle of rope used to sling a peice of freight or for use about the rigging. Perhaps the word *strop* is more frequently used in connection with the circle or grommet that encircles a block. To do this is to *strop a block.*

STRUM BOX, a rose box; a strainer at the end of a bilge pump.

STRUT, the heavy bracket at the stern of a twin-screw steamer which supports the end of the propeller shafts.

STUD LINKED CHAIN, that which has a bar of iron across the middle of each link. The bar, called a stud, keeps the chain from kinking.

STUD SAIL, an extension on the leech of a fore and aft sail.

STUDDING SAILS (Stun'sa'ls), light sails formerly set from studding-sail booms which were portable extensions of the yardarms. These sails were controlled by halyards, outhauls, downhauls and sheets. The clipper ships carried these sails from the so-called *lower studding sail* up to a *royal studding*

sail. The knots used with these sails are still in use for many purposes. These are the *studding-sail halyard bend* and the *studding-sail sheet bend.* A studding-sail yard was a short club or flying yard which was bent to the outer part of the head of the sail. It was set and taken in with the sail. The booms were run out through a ring in the yardarm, rigged with lift, halyard and tack line (for outer sheet). The sail, except lower stun's'l, was sent up in stops around the short yard. A seaman on the end of the yardarm received the sail, cut the stops and made fast the sheet (inner). On the weather side the stun'sa'ls were set abaft, and on the lee side forward, of the regular sails. The lower stun'sa'ls were set from a boom on the lower yard and sheeted to a lower boom at the ship's side like a boat boom.

STUFFING BOX, a device so designed as to prevent the entrance of sea water around the propeller shaft where it enters a ship's hull or passes through a bulkhead. A gland is forced upon packing which is laid between it and the stuffing box, making a close contact with the shaft.

STUNNER KNOT, a double Blackwall hitch.

SUB-SOLAR POINT, the point directly beneath the sun.

SUBMARINE, an under-sea boat. It is propelled by internal combustion engines when on the surface and by storage batteries when submerged. Its buoyancy is controlled by tanks into which water is admitted and expelled according to the desired buoyancy. The most modern submarines are powered by nuclear energy.

SUBMARINE BELL, a device for safeguarding navigation.

SUBMARINE CHASER, a small fast patrol vessel. The shallow draft offers some protection against torpedoes.

SUBMARINE CURRENTS, those that flow beneath the surface and irrespective of those on the surface.

SUBMARINE PRESSURE. As the depth increases the pressure increases consistently and is approximately as follows: At 1,000 fathoms 2,700 pounds to the square inch; at 2,000, 5,400; at 3,000, 8,100 and at 5,000 fathoms the pressure is 13,500 pounds.

SUBMARINE SIGNALS, electric or electronic oscillators attached to the under bodies of lightvessels or buoys and which give characteristic signals in foggy weather. A ship fitted with detectors can pick up these signals and be guided to them. There are two of these detectors or microphones, one on each bow. If the signal comes in on the port bow the helm is put a little to starboard. As soon as the signal is heard in the starboard detector the ship is steadied in this direction, keeping it ahead by bringing the signal alternately louder in one ear and then the other. Bells were formerly used.

SUBSIDY, a grant or subvention given by a nation to its merchant vessels in order to afford them an advantage in commerce on the seas or to remove a disadvantage.

SUDD, floating vegetable matter that obstructs navigation in or near the mouths of rivers.

SUE, to be left high and dry.

SUEGEE, caustic soda, soft soap and water for scrubbing paintwork. Also suegee-wugee, or suji-wuji.

SUEZ CANAL RUDDER, an additional plate increasing the power of the rudder for use in maneuvering in close quarters. See Salmon-Tail.

SUGAR STROP, a piece of canvas about 18 inches wide roped and tapering to ends where eyes are provided to receive the tackle hook. This strop will not cut bags of sugar, beans, etc.

SUGG, to roll heavily on the bottom when aground.

SUMATRA, a heavy squall in the China Sea coming up suddenly with a flash of lightning. It is almost a daily occurrence in December.

SUMMER TANKS, those along the sides of a tanker only filled at good seasons when less freeboard can be carried.

SUMNER LINE, first practised by Capt. Thos. H. Sumner in the ship *Cabot.* It is an arc of a circle of equal altitude, which for a comparatively short distance is considered a straight line. It is a position line, for when once established, the ship's position is somewhere upon it. An intersection of two such lines definitely locates the vessel. These lines are now largely established by tables of altitude, and are called *position lines.*

SUN DOGS. See Parhelia.

SUN OVER THE FOREYARD, an expression to indicate that it is time for a drink.

SUNDOWNER, a sea going expression for a sea officer who is a bully. The term was originally applied to those captains who gave liberty up to sunset only.

SUN'S BACKSTAYS, the bands of sunlight seen against a dark cloud when the sun itself is obscured from the observer—commonly spoken of as the sun drawing water; it has been poetically referred to as the "Ropes of Maui," a South Sea Island god.

SUPERCARGO, a representative of the owner on board a ship. He was authorized to attend to all business to do with cargo, and to manage ship's business. The authority of a supercargo varied much, depending upon his special work.

SUPPLEMENT OF AN ANGLE, what an angle lacks of 180°.

SURF, the sea breaking on the shore.

SURGE, to slack off a line. The swell of the sea.

SURVEY. A ship is surveyed on completion to determine her tonnage and measurements for official documents. A board may be appointed to survey a quantity of merchandise, cargo or a ship; the board examines for condition, extent of damage and determines its disposition.

Captain Howard Patterson in his Nautical Dictionary states well the procedure of a survey of a damaged vessel: "In the event of putting into port with masts or bulwarks gone, or the vessel leaking, the master reports to the port authorities, also to his consul, if in a foreign port, and after *noting a protest,* calls for an examination upon his vessel and cargo in order that the damages may be appraised; and this examination is known as a *survey.* Two shipmasters or other experienced persons are called to examine the rigging, hull and hatches, and in the event of damaged cargo, two merchants acquainted with the kind of cargo carried, are called to examine and report whether the cargo was properly stowed and dunnaged. Upon receiving the report the master immediately *extends his protest.* Should the vessel be a steamer and the machinery or boilers be injured, then a shipmaster and an engineer would be called."

SWAB, a rope or twine mop for cleaning paintwork. A sailor.

SWAGING, the process of fusing stainless steel wire rope to a terminal or fitting by using a cold rolled application under great pressure.

SWALLOW (of a Block), the space between the sides of the shell where the rope passes.

SWALLOW THE ANCHOR, to leave the sea for good and all and live ashore.

SWAMPED, overwhelmed by water, or an open boat so filled as to sink or be hopelessly awash.

SWASH PLATE. See Baffle Plate.

SWAY AWAY, to hoist away on a line or halyard. Swaying away carries the meaning of hoisting as in sending a spar or sail aloft, rather than of pulling as in warping a vessel.

SWEAL, to burn off barnacles and weed from wooden ships. Sometimes used for the process of wire brushing and scraping copper sheathing and hulls.

SWEAT, to haul anything, especially sails, as taut as possible; to get every appearance of slackness from a sail by a heavy pull on the sheets or halyards. The condensation appearing on the iron structure of the interior. *Cork paint* is used to prevent this moisture.

SWEEPING, dragging for rocks, anchors or anything searched for on the bottom. A horizontal wire drag is used in surveying to reveal any isolated rocks or coral heads.

SWEEPS, long oars used in early colonial vessels and later in harbor lighters; the oars of ancient galleys.

SWELL, undulations of the sea, having greater length than ordinary sea waves, caused by a disturbance at some distant point. Swell is often the forerunner of a hurricane. See Sea Scale.

SWIFT, to bring two pieces of gear together side by side with ropes.

SWIFTER, the foremost shrouds of each mast. The swifter at the time of the Spanish Armada consisted of a pendant with a double block and fall and served as a preventer for the mast forward of the shrouds.

The rope once used to hold capstan bars in place.

SWIG, to get a little more on a tackle by taking a turn around a cleat, swaying out on the hauling part and giving in to the cleat.

SWIMS, moves along over or under the water. As a line of guns swims but four feet above the sea or a vessel swims by the head—an obsolete expression.

SWINGING, the turning of a vessel from one direction to another under influence of tide or wind.

SWINGING BOOMS, boat booms.

SWINGING SHIP, the process of finding the deviation of a compass on every or every other compass point of the ship's head. With these, a *deviaiton table* is prepared. The procedure is to set a watch to local apparent time, head the ship on north and take an azimuth of the sun, repeating this on the different compass points. If especial accuracy is desired, the whole swing can be repeated backwards. The deviations are obtained in the usual manner as with true and compass azimuths. In swinging ship, bearings can be taken of the sun, of a range, a distant object, or by reciprocal bearings.

SWINGING THE 'TWEEN DECKS, a term used in loading cargo. It is a double operation through same hatch—while a sling load is being removed in the hold another is being swung into the 'tween decks.

SWIVEL, a hook or link joined to another by a longitudinal pin around which each part revolves, thereby taking the turns out of the block or chain.

SWORD MAT, a fabric made by weaving some selected stuff like cloth into a mat for chafing purposes. A piece of wood called a sword assists in alternately raising and depressing alternate parts, allowing the warp of marline or house-line to be passed through.

SYNCHRONISM, a condition where the period of ship's oscillation and that of the waves are in time with each other; when the waves and a ship reach their greatest angle of inclination at the same moment and at regular intervals a greater pitch or roll is caused with each succeeding wave. The result is an excessive motion. It is the ship keeping time with the waves. It is broken up by changing the course or speed.

SYNOPTIC CHART, one showing the weather as prevailing simultaneously in many places.

SYPHERING, forming a bulkhead by lapping the edges of the planking.

SYZYGY, the moon is *in* syzygy when it is in range with the sun and earth. This occurs twice each month.

T

TABERNACLE, a boxlike step, or socket, on deck, for a mast that does not pass through to a lower deck, sometimes having the after side open so that the mast can be lowered. It is sometimes seen in tugboats and yachts to facilitate passage under bridges. See Mast Tabernacle.

TABLE CLOTH, a remarkable cloud that hangs over Table Mountain, Cape Town, South Africa, before a southeaster.

TABLING, a reinforcing border of canvas around a sail to which the bolt rope is sewed. At the head the tabling is on the after side of a square sail, but around the rest of a sail it is on the forward side.

TACHOMETER, a device recording and showing the revolutions of propeller or engine.

TACK, a leg sailed with the wind on one side of a vessel. To go about by going into the wind is to *tack* or *tack ship*. A vessel is on the *port tack* if the wind comes over the port side. The rope holding down the weather clew of a course is a *tack*. The lower forward corner of a fore and aft sail is known as the *tack*.

TACK BUMPKIN, an iron bracket extending a few feet from the bow of a square-rigged sailing craft, to the end of which the tack of the foresail is hauled down.

TACK CRINGLE, a ring in the tack of a fore and aft sail, which is used for reefing. The *tack earing* is a short line that holds the reefed part of a sail down on the boom.

TACKLE (Tay-kle), a purchase composed of blocks and ropes. See Luff Tackle and Jeers. The theoretical power of a tackle is equal to the number of parts of rope entering the moving block (or blocks). In order to obtain the working power of the tackle, a deduction ranging from 10 per cent to 50 per cent is necessary for friction, depending on the type of tackle and of the sheaves. The rope used in reeving off a tackle is called the *fall;* the free end is the *hauling part.* See Rope.

TACKLINE, a 6-foot length of signal halyard used to separate groups of signals. A line to haul down the tack of a gaff topsail, jib, or staysail.

TACTICAL DIAMETER, the distance a vesesl departs from her original course in swinging through 180°.

TAFFRAIL LOG. See Patent Log.

TAIL, the direction in which the stern swings when at anchor, as for instance, she *tails inshore* or *downstream.* The short rope of a tail block.

TAIL ON, to take hold of a rope and haul away.

TAIL BLOCK, one with a rope stropped about it and an end several feet long hanging from it.

TAIL ROPE, is fastened to the end of the *jumbo boom* of a schooner and used to back the fore staysail (jumbo) and she will lie-to with sail so trimmed. It is, or was, especially so used by fishermen.

TAIL SHAFT, that section of the shaft passing outboard through the stuffing box and to which the propeller is keyed.

TAKE THE BOTTOM (or Ground), to become grounded.

TAKE A DEPARTURE. See Departure.

TAKEN ABACK, to be taken unprepared with the wind on the forward side of a square or other sail.

TALL SHIP, a term used in the old days to distinguish the large lofty vessels.

TALLY STICK, a short piece of bamboo used by the Chinese in tallying cargo, each Chinese giving the mate or quartermaster a stick for each piece of freight discharged.

TANGENT. A trigonometric function. A line of bearing on the edge of an island is said to be its right or left tangent.

TANGENT SCREW, a device attached to the index arm of a sextant, by the use of which a very refined contact can be made by the sun, or star, with the horizon.

TANGS, upturned pad hooks, or mast bands aloft with broad-based hooks, to receive the eyes of the rigging and take the downward thrust in the staying of a mast.

TANK, a water, oil, or airtight compartment, or container. There are ballast, peak, deep, settling, and bunker oil tanks.

TANK GAUGE, a gauge to measure ullage. It is in the shape of a cross with a butterfly bolt by which the cross piece can be set at the desired measurement. The technique in using the gauge is to place the longer end down through the ullage plate in the tank; when the oil rises to the bottom of the gauge, it is valved off the next tank to slow the flow. The gauge is then turned end for end to measure the desired ullage which has been set on the gauge. Sometimes called a Tank Stick.

TANK SHIP, one whose interior is divided into compartments for the carrying of liquids.

TANK TOP, the plating of the upper side of the double bottom.

TANKERMAN, a certificated rating serving in tankers. The man must be familiar with the whole process of loading and discharging of oil cargoes.

TAP RIVET, a screw, or threaded, rivet.

TAPS, a bugle call to douse lights and maintain quiet about the decks.

TAR, a protection given to standing rigging. It is the residue of the gum of a pine after distillation. A sailor.

TARPAULIN, a painted or treated canvas covering for a hatch. Also a waterproof hat worn by seamen. There should be three tarpaulins over the hatch of a sea-going vessel. They are secured to the sides of the hatch coaming by means of battens driven tight with wedges.

TARPAULIN MUSTER, a term applied to the pooling of all the financial resources of a group of sailors.

TARTANE, a vessel of the Mediterranean having a predominating mast, square-rigged, set well aft, large jib; there is also a lateen jigger sheeting to a long bumpkin extending directly astern. Small tartanes may have only one mast, lateen-rigged with bowsprit and jib.

TATTOO, a bugle call to pipe down in the evening preparatory to taps.

TAUNT MASTS, lofty spars and all-a-taunt-o is a term applied when a vessel's masts are all rigged, taut, and shipshape.

TAURUS, the second sign of the zodiac.

TAUT, hauled tight; the opposite condition of slack.

TAUT BOWLINE. To be sailing on a taut bowline is to be close-hauled on the wind.

TELEMETER, a telescope fitted with two cross hairs. It may be the telescope of a theodolite, a transit or a plane table. If used in conjunction with a stadia rod it offers a reliable method of measuring short distances.

TEHUANTEPECER, a violent northerly wind, mostly associated with the west coast of Mexico, in the Gulf of Tehuantepec.

TELEMOTOR, a steering apparatus operated by hydraulic pressure applied by the wheel as it is turned in the usual manner. The pressure is transmitted by means of oil in two small pipe lines leading aft to the steering engine. The oil moves forward in one pipe while it moves aft in the other, through the movement of a pump driven by the steering wheel. The movement of the oil operates the valves of the steering engine, which are opened and closed as the desired action on the rudder is indicated by the steering wheel.

There are also electric telemotors operated by a horizontal lever or wheel in the wheelhouse. The telemotor is aft, close by the steering engine. A movement of the wheel closes a circuit through a relay located aft; the operation of the relay closes a circuit through the main generators and the telemotor. A system of gears from the telemotor actuates the valve arm of the steering engine. The extent of wheel given in the wheelhouse is regulated on the steering engine by an electric, so-called, follow-up device consisting of a set of gears also leading from the telemotor to the valve arm, which when the position of the wheel is reached breaks the circuit and stops the motor.

TELESCOPE. See Spy Glass.

TELESCOPE MAST, one in which the topmast is capable of being lowered inside the lower mast.

TELLTALE COMPASS, one usually found in the cabin for the convenience of the master. It is usually suspended from the deck above and is, when so used, of an inverted type. Some old masters used to have one over their bunks.

TEMPERATURE CHIMNEYS, pipes leading down into a bulk cargo into which thermometers are lowered to ascertain the degree of heat in the holds. It is an aid in forestalling spontaneous combustion.

TEMPLATE, a mould; a pattern of a member of a ship's structure usually made on heavy paper, the exact size and shape desired.

TENDER, an attendant vessel to lighthouses, buoys, submarines, etc. She supplies them with needed stores. A dory or dinghy used by a boat or vessel anchored off to keep contact with the shore. A vessel is said to be *tender* when her center of gravity is too high and she lacks stability.

TENDING SHIP, using the helm, a little sail even, to preserve the sheer of a vessel at anchor and prevent her, if possible, from *breaking her sheer*—dragging the chain in a bight over the anchor and fouling it. See Break Her Sheer.

TENON, the projecting member of a mortise; the prepared part of the foot of a mast that fits into the step.

TENSILE STRENGTH, the capacity to withstand a pulling stress. It is usually measured in tons or pounds per square inch of cross-section.

TENTING AN AWNING, casting off the stops from the jack-stay and making them fast to ring-bolts in the deck. This is done either, or both, to catch fresh water or to keep the wind out of the awning during a squall.

TEREDO, a ship worm which does immense damage to unprotected hulls of wooden ships and piles of wharves.

TERN SCHOONER, a three-masted schooner.

TERRESTRIAL, of or pertaining to the earth.

TETRAPODS, multi-legged obstructions of reenforced concrete used in the construction of jetties that are exposed to the full force of the sea. They were used by the Germans to obstruct the landings on the Normandy beaches.

TEXAS DECK, that of a river steamer adjacent ot the wheelhouse and officers' quarters.

TEXAS TOWERS, are structures built offshore with legs set deep in the bottom. They were originally developed to support underwater oil drilling rigs. Later as reporting stations for passing planes. Now they have largely replaced lightships as aids to navigation.

THALASSA, the sea (Greek).

THERMOCLINE, the demarcation between the surface layers of the sea at which the temperatures are the same and the layer where the temperatures rapidly decrease to those of the ocean depths.

THERMOMETER, an instrument used for the purpose of measuring temperature. In the Fahrenheit thermometer 32° is freezing and 212° represents the boiling point. In a centigrade, now called celsius, thermometer 0° is freezing and 100° the boiling point. These points in a Reaumer instrument are respectively 0° and 80°.

THERMOMETER, MAXIMUM and MINIMUM, an instrument consisting of a U-shaped thermometer tube so arranged that the temperature is shown on each side. A marker or index is left at the maximum temperature in one side, while a similar index is left at the minimum on the other. It is used in chronometer cases and magazines to detect extremes of temperature.

THERMOSTATIC ALARM, one which operates upon an abnormal rise in temperature.

THICK AND THIN BLOCK, one in which the sheaves are of different thicknesses.

THIMBLE, a heart-shaped (or round) ring, grooved on the outside to receive the eye of a rope.

THIS IS A LONG SHIP, a hint that it is time for another drink.

THOLE PINS, wooden pins that fit up in the rail of a boat to hold the oars in place while rowing.

THOROFARE, a passage or channel connecting two bodies of water; used as a short cut to avoid a longer outside route.

THOROUGHFOOT (or Put), the condition of a tackle when one of the blocks capsizes through its parts. A more common expression is that the tackle has a dip in it. To *thoroughfoot* a rope, coil down contrary to the lay and bring the end up through the center; this will clear the rope of turns.

THREE-ARM PROTRACTOR, an instrument designed to plot a position when two horizontal angles are given between three known objects. It consists of a graduated metallic circle, pivoted at the center of which are three arms. The two outside arms are moveable, and are set to the given angles. In setting the angles the operator is assisted by a clamp screw, tangent screw, magnifying glass, and vernier, as in the ordinary sextant. When all three arms are on their respective landmarks, the hole in the very center of the instrument indicates the vessel's position. This instrument is also called a *station pointer.*

THREE-DECKED VESSEL, the highest type of cargo carrier. There are three decks, all of heavy steel construction.

THREE ISLAND STEAMER, one with three deck erections—forecastle, poop and midship house.

THREE-POINT PROBLEM, a method of locating position by two horizontal sextant angles between three known objects. By transferring these two angles to a three-arm protractor, the position is easily plotted on a chart. This is a very accurate method and has the advantage of requiring no correction for variation or deviation. The positions of soundings of the charts are located by this method. See Three-arm Protractor and Revolver.

THREE SHEETS IN THE WIND, a term applied to a man with too much liquor aboard, especially when of unsteady gait.

THREE SKYSAIL YARDER, a sailing ship carrying skysails on the fore, main and mizzen masts.

THREE STAR PROBLEM, a method of plotting a ship's position by the use of three position lines derived from the observations of three stars.

THREEFOLD BLOCK, one having three sheaves. A threefold purchase consists of two threefold blocks with the rope rove off.

THROAT, that part of the gaff near the mast. The bolt passing through the gaff by which it is hoisted is the *throat bolt,* and the halyards the *throat halyards.* That part of the anchor shank which is close up to the arms is also called the throat.

THROAT SEIZING, fastenings used to lash an eye in a rope or hold it around a thimble; also used to seize two parts of a rope together that cross.

THROTTLE WATCH, an engineer's watch when a steamer is pitching so much that he must constantly operate the throttle to prevent racing of the propeller.

THROUGH THE CABIN WINDOWS, said of a man who reaches a command without serving time as a seaman in the forecastle.

THROUGH FASTENING, bolting clear through planks and frames.

THROUGH THE HAWSE HOLES, said of a master who has come up through all the grades.

THRUMS, pieces of rope yarns sewed by their bights to a piece of canvas for chafing gear or for a collision mat. The verb is *to thrum.* *Thrum mats* are placed between the oars and rowlocks to prevent noise in pulling; hence the term *muffled oars*.

THRUST BLOCK, a fixture located in the lines of the shaft securely fastened to the ship's structure. A flange of the shaft on the after side of the block transmits the thrust or onward push of the screw to the block and ship. This is taken up in a recess in the block by collar bearings running in oil, called the *thrust bearings*.

THRUST BOW PROPELLER, an aid in docking a steamer. It is recessed in the underwater bow section and is operated from the bridge to cant the ship's head as desired.

THUMB CLEATS, cleats formed near the end of a yardarm to prevent the reef earing from slipping in.

THWARTS, seats in a small boat.

THWARTSHIP TACKLES, purchases used for rigging in boat davits that swing out.

THWARTSHIPS, crosswise of the decks; from side to side.

TIDAL CURRENTS, those horizontal movements of water occurring periodically as a result of the attraction of the moon and sun.

TIDE and HALF TIDE (and QUARTER TIDE), is that tidal condition in a river or channel where the flood runs for 3 hours after high water and the ebb, 3 hours after low water. When the tide runs 1½ hours after high or low water the term Tide and Quarter Tide is applied.

TIDE GAUGE, a graduated staff erected usually at the end of a wharf from which the rise and fall of the tide is recorded. There is a self-registering tide gauge, in which a float actuates a pencil resting lightly on a revolving cylinder covered by paper. The cylinder turns by clockwork.

TIDE RIPS, patches of broken water caused by rapid tidal currents. See Rips.

TIDE RODE, a vessel riding to the tide and not the wind.

TIDE WALKER, a dangerous log floating perpendicular. Also called a propeller inspector. See Sleeper.

TIDES are the inflow and outflow of the sea in coastal harbors and bays. This phenomenon is primarily due to the attractive influence of the moon and sun. There are two tide-creating forces, one that tends to produce one high and one low water a day and is called the *diurnal tide;* it prevails in the Gulf of Mexico. The other force produces two high and two low waters a day, about 12 hours apart. This type is known as the *semi-diurnal tide* and prevails on the Atlantic coast. The a.m. and p.m. tides of this type are about the same height. When in some localities, as on the Pacific coast, these two types are combined, a so-called *mixed tide* results. There are then two high waters a day, but there is much difference in their heights; the sequence is a higher high followed by a lower low, a lower high and a higher low. The difference in the heights of the high water is known as the *diurnal inequality*.

The moon's influence is 2¼ times that of the sun, but when these two bodies are acting together, as at full and new moon, a greater range results which are called the *spring tides;* when the sun is opposing the moon, as at the first and last quarters, there is a smaller range called the *neaps.* When the moon is in perigee (nearest the earth) the range of tide is markedly increased over that when the moon is in apogee. At the times when the moon is full or new and at the same time is in perigee, the tidal range is greatest.

TIDEWAY, where the tidal currents are running.

TIE (Tye), the single part of a halyard which hoists a yard. It passes up from the yard through a sheave in the masthead where the tackle of the halyard is made fast to it.

TIE BLOCK, a single block sometimes used in lieu of a sheave in the mast. See Tie.

TIE PLATE, a single fore-and-aft course of plating attached to deck beams under wood deck to give extra strength.

TIER, a layer or range of casks. To tier an anchor chain is to stow it in even layers in the chain locker.

TIERCE, a wine cask of 42 gallons capacity.

TILLER, a bar of iron or wood connected with the rudder head and leading, usually forward. By the tiller, the rudder is moved as desired. The quadrant is the most

frequent form of a tiller in steamers.

TILLER HEAD, the part of the tiller farthest away from the rudder head and the point of greatest leverage.

TILLER ROPES, lines leading from the tiller to the steering wheel.

TILLER TELLTALE, an indicator which moves as the tiller moves and shows its position to the helmsman.

TIMBER HEADS, projecting timbers above the deck which serve as bitts.

TIMBER HITCH, a turn around a spar, around the standing part and then several around its own part.

TIMBERS, large pieces of wood used in a vessel's construction, especially the frames.

TIME AZIMUTH, a method of obtaining the sun's bearing by solving the astronomical triangle with the time angle, the polar distance, and co-latitude, given to find the azimuth angle or angle at the zenith. Tables are available giving the time azimuths.

TIME BALL, a black sphere-shaped signal formerly dropped usually at noon from the flag-staff of a prominent building for the purpose of correcting chronometers.

TIME COURSES, a method of navigating a steamer by steering a certain course for a given number of minutes before changing to another course.

TIME SIGHT, the longitude sight taken in the morning or afternoon in which the astronomical triangle is used to calculate the time or polar angle. Position lines have replaced this time-honored longitude sight.

TIMENOGUY, a light rope fast in the mizzen rigging and leading down to a bull's eye passing through which is the hauling part of the main brace. The bull's eye is also made fast to the block of the standing part of the brace. The purpose of the timenoguy is to prevent the brace when slack from fouling the boat davits. Also a line used to keep the fore tacks and sheets clear of the anchor stocks when tacking.

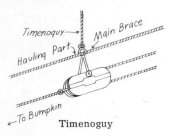

Timenoguy

TIP CLEARANCE, the distance that the tips of a propeller clear the hull.

TJALK, a small Dutch sailing vessel of about 60 tons used for sea and river navigation; usually with but one mast.

TOE AND HEEL WATCHES, watch and watch, viz: 4 on and 4 off, or 2 on and 2 off, particularly applied to the Officer of the Deck.

TOE RAIL, a moulding similar to quarter round, set at the edge of the deck of a small yacht to offer a degree of safety on slanting decks.

TOGGLE, a small piece of lignum vitae scored about its center, with a small rope spliced around it. The function of the toggle is to receive the becket or eye of another rope and join them together. They are used among other things on bunt whips and life buoys, being easy to cast adrift.

TOM COX'S TRAVERSE, the course taken by a sogering sailor to kill time, such as frequent trips to the scuttle butt. "Three turns around the galley and a pull at the scuttle butt."

TOMFOOL KNOT, a kind of slipknot with two loops.

TOMMING DOWN, the opposite of shoring up. A piece of timber is braced under a deck beam and on a plank on the cargo to hold the cases or bales down.

TOMPION, a plug fitted in the muzzle of a gun for protection against weather.

TON, a long ton is 2,240 lbs.; a short-ton, 2,000 lbs. A ton of fuel oil equals about 6.7 bbls. A measurement ton is 40 cubic feet and a cargo ton 100 cubic feet.

TONGKANG, a Malayan junk.

TONGUE, a vertically placed piece of wood between the jaws of a gaff. It pivots on a bolt passing through the jaws. Its function is to facilitate the passing of the spar up and down the mast.

TONNAGE. "A ton is really a measure of weight, and legally is 2,240 pounds. But in ship work, on account of the varied bulk of the material dealt with and the desire to rate cargoes, etc., on a weight basis when only the volumetric capacity was known, there were evolved various volumetric equivalents, such as 44 cubic feet = 1 ton, for coal; 35 cubic feet = 1 ton, for sea water, etc., and later it was proposed to accept 100 cubic feet as the equivalent of 1 ton of general merchandise. The tonnage given on certificates of registration, legal documents, etc., is generally called *registered tonnage*, and simply means the cubical contents of the vessel divided by 100, and has no bearing whatsoever upon the *weight of the vessel and cargo*, which is *displacement*. The registered tonnage has three forms: *Gross*, *net* and *underdeck*, all depending upon the spaces included in the measurement. For example, underdeck tonnage comprises all space below the tonnage deck; gross tonnage is 'all spaces below the upper deck, as well as permanently closed in spaces on that deck' and net tonnage is gross tonnage, less certain allowed deductions, supposed not to be available for carrying cargo. These are all simply cubical contents divided by 100, on the basis of 100 cubic feet = 1 ton. Displacement (sometimes called displacement tonnage) is the actual weight in tons (2,240 pounds) the ship displaces when floating at the draft under consideration. It is a true weight measurement and is derived by figuring the volume of the submerged body of the ship and dividing by 35, on the basis of 35 cubic feet sea water = 1 ton. Deadweight, or dead-weight tonnage, is the carrying capacity of the ship in actual tons of 2,240 pounds and is the difference in displacement of the ship light, but with stores and fuel, and loaded, but with the same stores and fuel. As registered tonnage was evolved to obtain a fair estimate for the payment of port charges and taxes, only commercial craft use it. When war vessels use facilities for which they have to pay, their rate is determined usually upon their *displacement*, as they have no registered tonnage, and this has given rise to the use of the word 'displacement-tonnage' which is really a misnomer." (*Marine Engineering*.)

The gross tonnage in a modern freighter is roughly half again as much as the net tonnage, and the deadweight carrying capacity 2½ times the net; approximately 2¼ times the gross gives the loaded displacement.

TONNAGE DECK, the upper deck in one- and two-deck steamers, and the second continuous deck from below in other steamers.

TONS PER INCH IMMERSION or **TONS PER INCH,** the amount of weight a vessel will take aboard to increase her mean draft one inch. By dividing the square feet in the waterplane at a certain draft by 420 the tons per inch at that draft will be approximately at hand.

TOP, a platform supported by the trestle-trees of a lower mast. It serves as a spreader for the topmast rigging, futtock shrouds, and often has a chest with boatswain's gear in it. *To top* a boom or gaff is to elevate its end; to top a yard is to cockbill it.

TOP-BURTONS, usually luff tackles which lead from the topmast pendant to the deck. They are used to handle heavy weights, set up rigging or act as topping-lifts when hoisting heavy weights with the lower yards.

TOP-HAMPER, all spars and gear above the ship's deck.

TOP LINING, extra canvas sewed to a sail where it chafes against the top.

TOP MARK, a characteristic object on a staff at the top of a buoy, beacon, or perch, like a cage, arrow, ball, diamond, cone, broom, etc. Each mark indicates the channel or a danger.

TOP-ROPE, the one used in sending up topmasts.

TOP SAWYER, a member of a crew who is ambitious to work and be useful.

TOP-TIMBERS, the highest part of a vessel's frames.

TOPGALLANT FORECASTLE, an elevated deck in the bow of a ship, while the similar one aft is the topgallant poop. However, seamen nowadays drop the topgallant.

TOPGALLANT MAST (pronounced t'gallant or t'gal'n), the next above the topmast; its shrouds and stays form the *topgallant rigging*. It is secured in a manner similar to that of a topmast described below.

TOPGALLANT SAIL (pronounced t'gansul), a square sail set from the topgallant yard which is next above the topsail yard.

TOPMAST, next above any lowermast. The shrouds and stays which support it form the *topmast rigging*. It overlaps the lower masthead on the forward side by some feet; it is supported by bands and rests on a fid or pin which passes through holes in the trestle-trees and heel of the topmast.

TOPOGRAPHY, the physical features of the land shown by symbols on a chart or map, such as the contours of elevation, woods, fields, rocks, cliffs, and conspicuous objects. The same name applies to the process of surveying by which this data is collected.

TOPPING-LIFT, a tackle by which the after or outer end of a boom is topped (hoisted) or supported. *Topipng-lifts* find various uses suspending spars from above. There are *boom topping-lifts, boat davit, boat boom topping-lifts* and *cargo boom topping-lifts.*

TOPPING OFF, a term used where a steamer loads oil to a draft sufficient to cross the bar of her port of departure. She then proceeds to a nearby port to complete her cargo. To fill tanks to their capacity when partly full is to *top off* the tanks.

TOPSAIL, the sail next above the course. It is usually in two sections called upper and lower topsail *(double topsails),* a *single topsail* being too large for a small crew to handle conveniently. In a fore and aft rigged vessel, a topsail is triangular in shape and sets above the gaff, being called a *gaff-topsail.*

Topsails to the mast indicates that these square sails are aback.

TOPSAIL SCHOONER, one having a square topsail and sometimes a top-gallant sail on the fore. The lower mast is higher than in a brigantine. See Two-Topsail Schooner.

TOPSAIL TYE, a wire rope leading from the yard up through a sheave under the trestle-trees, down abaft the mast where a gin-block is spliced in the end. Through this gin a wire whip is rove with the topsail halyards fast to the end of this whip, while the other end is fast to the deck.

TOPSIDES, lie between the waterline and the ship's rail.

TORCH OIL, kerosene or coal oil.

TOSS, an order given to oarsmen in a cutter in obedience to which the oars are placed in a perpendicular position, blades fore and aft, preparatory to *letting fall* and *giving away together.*

TOT, a drink of rum.

TOUCH, the slight shiver of the leech of a sail when a little too close to the wind.

TOW, to haul another vessel through the water by a hawser or tied up alongside. A *tow* is a tug towing one or more barges, or other floating property, but the word particularly refers to the vessels towed. The short ends of manila fibre in rope making.

TOWAGE, the charge made for towing. Also the service of towing.

TOWER CRANE, a steel tower mounting a derrick. There is usually a house aloft for the machinery and the operator. If it is capable of swinging in a circle it is a *revolving tower crane;* and if the whole is on tracks it becomes a *traveling revolving tower crane.*

TOWER MAST, one consisting of four steel uprights supported by latticework braces with no stays.

TOWING BUOY. See Towing Spar.

TOWING HOOK, a casting resembling a hook in a horizontal position made fast to the top of the low substantial house of a British or Continental tug boat. As wire is generally used in Europe, the eye is readily thrown over the hook. The hooks are fitted usually with compression springs to save shock on the hawser.

TOWING LIGHTS, three white masthead lights carried by a towing vessel, if the tow exceeds 600 feet, and two white lights if under that distance.

TOWING LINES, are of heavy wire rope. Formerly, and now with lighter tows of cordage. The best bolt rope was and is used; 200 fathoms to the coil. The rope used to tow another vessel is called the *hawser.*

TOWING SPAR (Fog Buoy), used in naval vessels when it is desired to maintain formation in a fog or at night. It was much used in the first war but little in World War II. It is a spar or shape that is easily seen, is towed astern by the leading vessel at a given distance, usually about 490 yards, and the next vessel in line keeps it close under her bow.

TRACK, the path of a vessel on a voyage. To tow a vessel by a tow line led ashore.

TRADE CLOUDS, light fleecy clouds near the horizon in the reions of the Trade Winds.

TRADE WINDS, movements of the atmosphere caused by the rising of the heated air of the equatorial region and the resulting indraft from the adjacent temperate zones. Were it not for the rotation of the earth, these winds would be from the north in the northern hemisphere and from the south in the southern hemisphere, but owing to the more rapid rotary speed of the equatorial region, the winds are diverted towards the west on the equatorial side, making northeast and southeast trade winds for the northern and southern hemispheres respectively. These winds blow with great regularity, moving their limits northward and southward a few degrees with the change of the sun's declination. The area or belt of calms lying between the trade winds is known as the *doldrums.*

TRADER, a vessel which barters one cargo for another in moving from port to port.

TRAIL, to let go the oars of a whale boat or gig (single-banked) allowing them to swing in the rowlocks until the blades trail aft with the onward motion of the boat. *Trailing lines* are made fast to the loom of the oars to prevent them going overboard entirely.

TRAIL BOARDS, carved, and sometimes, gilded boards that lead aft from the stem formerly helped to support the figurehead in old ships. They are sometimes seen decorating the bows of sailing yachts.

TRAIL TABS, small plates secured to the extreme after part of the underbody. They extend out beyond the bottom of the transom to stabilize the boat's performance.

TRAIN, the supporting force of the fleet consisting of the supply vessels, tankers, ammunition and repair ships. To aim a gun or a searchlight horizontally, as "*Train* right thirty degrees."

TRAIN TACKLES, formerly used to handle guns in an armed vessel.

TRAJECTORY, the course followed by a shell from a gun.

TRAMONTANA, a wind on the Adriatic coast of Italy having the characteristics of the bora. See Bora.

TRAMP, a steamer which proceeds wherever freight is offered and never on established and regular runs.

TRANSIRE, an official paper issued by the Government of the Bahama Islands allowing a yacht to cruise those waters.

TRANSIT, the passage of a body across the meridian. If the passage is across the meridian above the observer, it is known as the *superior* or *upper transit;* if across the meridian below us, as the sun's passage at midnight, it is called the *inferior* or *lower transit.*

TRANSOM STERN, a flat vertical type of stern popular in motor boat design.

TRANSOMS, the athwartship timbers of a vessel bolted to the sternpost. The floor, frame and beam that comprise the transverse member at the sternpost are designated the *transom floor, transom frame* and *transom beam.* They are usually of heavier dimensions owing to the overhang which they in part support. Also, stationary couches built into a ship.

TRANSVERSE, running at right angles with the keel.

TRANSVERSE FRAMING, the structural parts of a vessel that contribute to the athwartship strength.

TRAVELER, the ring of a sheet block that travels along the deck horse or boom. See Deck or Boom Horses.

TRAVERSE SAILING, a number of plane sailing courses and distances, as the track of a vessel beating to windward.

TRAVERSE TABLE, used to find the sides and course angle of a right triangle in plane or middle latitude sailing. It is Table 3, Bowditch, 1958.

TRAWL, a contrivance used by fishermen on the Banks. It consists of a long, good-sized line, anchored and buoyed at each end; hanging from which at short distances are pieces of small line about two feet long with a hook at the end. This gear is kept in half barrel tubs when not set. The trawls are set from dories, which are cast adrift from the schooner one after another. The fisherman manning the dory (sometimes two) puts the boat directly before the wind and flicks out the trawl with a short stick. After a certain time the trawl is hauled and the catch thrown into a compartment temporarily made by the portable bulkheads. Should the catch load the dory before the trawl is completely hauled, an oar held upright brings the schooner alongside. Sometimes a trawl is *under run,* which means it is left set and the dory passes under it, as it were, taking off the catch and rebaiting. Schooners of the larger size carry eighteen dories. This type of trawling is largely superseded by the powered beam and otter trawlers and draggers.

TRAWLER, applied especially to a steamer or power vessel equipped with a large drag net and the machinery for handling it. These vessels are very seaworthy with a pronounced sheer and heavy construction. Under-running the long line trawl is now also done by medium-sized motor vessels provided with a power winch. These vessels can tend a dozen miles of trawl. See Stern trawler, Dragger and Otter Trawl.

TRAY. See Cargo Slings.

TREACLE, molasses.

TREBLE BLOCK, one with three sheaves.

TREENAIL, a wooden pin, usually of locust, for securing timbers together. Pronounced trunnel.

TREND, the general direction, as of a coast; the direction a chain takes from the hawse pipe. The lower part of the shank of an anchor.

TRESTLETREES, two short fore and aft pieces of timber which rest on the hounds and support the top or crosstrees of the mast.

TRIANGULATION, a system of triangles between all prominent landmarks which definitely locates them on the survey sheets. Such a system is started with two well-established points and a base-line very carefully measured between them. By setting up a theodolite on each of these points and measuring the angle between the signal at the opposite end of the base line and a third prominent object, a side and two angles are obtained. These data open the way to compute any other elements of the triangle. The position of the third object is then occupied and a fourth is observed, and in this way the triangulation is carried along a coast, establishing the position of all prominent marks.

TRIATIC STAY, the arrangement of gear by which cargo is hoisted or lowered through a hatch, consisting of a pendant from each masthead shackled at their ends over the hatch where the hatch tackle is hooked. The name is also sometimes given to the stay leading from the fore-topmast head of a schooner back and down to the main-crosstrees. Among the applications of the term is the support given to a jury mast when a single hawser is so utilized as to serve as forestay and shrouds without cutting, but this is probably a corruption of the term *sciatic stay* found in Falconer and used for this purpose. The term *triatic stay* was applied in a naval vessel to the combination of two pendants, one from each lower or topmasthead, and a span between their lower ends. This stay was used in hoisting boats. The so-called stay tackles for hoisting the boat were hooked into the lower ends of the pendants. The span was the same length as the boat. If the boat was heavy the yards were braced abox and yard tackles used to assist the stay tackles. A stay between fore and main masts of a steamer to which the signal halyard block is made fast.

TRICE, to haul up.

TRICK, a period of duty at the steering wheel.

TRIGGER BAR, a short rod set horizontally on the deck. It is fitted with two short projections set at right angles to the bar over which are placed the rings of the short chains (shank painter and ring stopper) that hold the anchor on the bill-board. By giving the trigger bar a half turn its fixtures release the shank painter and ring stopper and the anchor is let go.

TRIM, the manner in which a vessel floats on the water, whether on an even keel, or *trimmed* by the head or stern. To *trim ship* the ballast or cargo, or both, are rearranged to bring the vessel to desired trim. Seamen usually leave the word *trimmed* from the phrase, simply saying a vessel is *by the head*.

TRIM SAILS, to set them properly by using the sheets and braces.

TRIM TABS, are attached plates at the stern that extend the planing surface of a boat's bottom. The purpose is to prevent excessive squatting and a high riding bow, hence a smoother ride. For boats around 20 feet the tabs are about 8 inches. They have also been called *afterplanes* or *squat boards*.

TRIMMING TANKS, tanks at the bow and stern of a vessel to alter her trim by the head or the stern.

TRIP, to break an anchor from its bed in the bottom either by the chain with capstan as usual or by hauling on a line previously made fast to its crown. A yard is *tripped* when it is swung by the lifts to a perpendicular position; a topmast or topgallant mast is *tripped* when hoisted sufficiently to allow the fid to be knocked out preparatory to housing or lowering. A trip is a catch of fish in the fisheries.

TRIPPING LINE, a rather general term: It is the line fast to a sea anchor by which it is hauled aboard. See Becueing. It is the line fast to the lower end of a yard when it is sent either down or aloft.

TRIREME, a warship of the Phoenicians (and others) having three tiers, groups or banks of oars. There were also biremes, quadriremes, and quinqueremes. The arrangement of these banks of oars (or men) is a point in controversy. The term later became applied to warships in general regardless of whether they were triremes or biremes.

TROCHOIDAL WAVE, the mathematical wave which very closely resembles the shape of a sea wave in deep water. It is the curve traced by a particle of water located in the radius of a circle which is assumed to be rolling with its center in the sea level line.

TROPIC OF CANCER, the parallel latitude corresponding to approximately 23° 27′ North. This parallel is the one reached by the sun when in its greatest northern declination at the summer solstice—about the 21st of June. It is the northern limit of the Torrid Zone.

TROPIC OF CAPRICORN, the parallel of latitude corresponding approximately to 23° 27′ South. It is the farthest point the sun attains in southern declination, and is the southern limit of the Torrid Zone.

TROPIC TIDES, are those occurring at moon's highest declination. The difference between the higher high water and lower low water at the time of tropic tides when the moon is full is the Great Tropic Range.

TROT, a line of mooring buoys and moorings.

TROUGH OF THE SEA, the hollow between the crests of two seas.

TRUCK, the top of a mast; often with a gilded ball with holes for flag or signal halyards. Or a small circular piece of wood topping the mast. Signal halyards reeve through holes or sheaves in it.

TRUE COURSE. A course steered by a ship's compass is in error for variation and deviation; corrected for these errors it becomes a true course based on the true compass whose north and south line is one with the meridian, and whose east and west line lies in the direction of the parallels of latitude.

TRUNDLE HEAD, that part of a capstan providing the holes for the capstan bars, especially applying to the capstan of the lower deck of ancient vessels in a double set up.

TRUNK, a vertical shaft.

TRUNK CABIN, one raised above the deck in order to get headroom below, leaving a narrow side deck for passage fore or aft.

TRUNK-DECKED VESSEL, a type where a longitudinal trunk runs the full length of the vessel and is of heavy construction, the deck erections extending out flush with the sides.

TRUNNEL, a treenail.

TRUSS, an iron bracket which aids in supporting a lower yard and lower topsail yard. The *truss yoke* is the fixture on the yard to which the bracket is bolted. The truss is hinged in such a way as to allow the yard to move in either a vertical or a horizontal plane, that is, capable of being topped or braced.

TRYSAILS, fore and aft sails set from the fore or main or other mast. They are supported by gaffs but are without booms. *Trysail* is also a triangular sail used in heaving to in a gale of wind. This is a *storm trysail.* The sail regardless of shape is primarily one to heave to under. In early days ships were said to *"lie at trye."*

TSUNAMI, an abnormal wave,

caused by some seismic disturbance, that inundates low coasts.

TUB OARSMAN, the second oar from aft of a whaleboat. He is beside the tub and tends the line.

TUCK, that part of a vessel's bottom where the sides come in.

TUCK PLATE, a flat plate fitted over the bridge piece of the stern frame, when the body of the hull is some distance above the arch. *(Standard Seamanship.)*

TUCKER, food.

TUG, a small vessel for towing and docking purposes equipped with an engine whose great power is wholly out of proportion with her size. Tugs vary in size according to the duty required.

TUG BOAT SIGNAL, the ensign placed in the main rigging, or YA International Code.

TULE FOG, spreads over the low plains of the lower Sacramento and San Joaquin Rivers of California. The name comes from the abundant tule grass of the region.

TUMBLE or **FALLING HOME,** the amount the sides of a vessel come in from the perpendicular.

TUMBLER PIN, one which prevents the trigger bar from turning when the anchor is on the billboard.

TUNNEL STERN, a motor boat so designed below the waterline that the propeller works in a partial tunnel of water. With such a stern a boat can take the bottom without injury to her propeller.

TURK'S HEAD, an ornamental knot or plaited ring used on grab ropes, jib-boom foot ropes, manropes and for purposes to give a fancy appearance.

TURN, a common word aboard ship. Seagoers turn in at night and turn out in the morning. The tide turns after flowing in one direction for (usually) six hours. To give a turn ahead or astern is to turn the propellers over several times. And, of course, to take a turn is to wind a rope once around a bitt, spar or anything. Turn turtle is to capsize. Turn to is to commence work. To turn out a reef, we now say shake out a reef and set a whole sail. Turn about, the time consumed between a vessel's arrival and her departure. A short turn about is essential to efficient management.

TURN AROUND, the interval between a vessel's arrival and sailing.

TURN OF THE BILGE, where the frames turn from the vertical to form the bottom of the vessel.

TURNBUCKLE, a contrivance made of metal, cylindrical in shape, with an inside thread (one left-handed, the other right-handed) in each end. Into each of these ends screws a threaded eye bolt. A turnbuckle spliced into shrouds, stays, backropes, etc., can be screwed up with great facility and keep a satisfactory tension on the rigging.

TURNING CIRCLE (of a steamer), that circle described when steaming under a hard-over rudder.

TURRET-DECKED VESSEL, a type where the sides turn inboard above the main deck to a longitudinal superstructure.

TURTLE DECK, one with very pronounced camber or crown like a turtle's back.

'TWEEN, between decks, particularly between the main deck and the one below it.

TWIN-SCREW, a vessel propelled by two shafts and propellers. There are also triple-screw and quadruple-screw vessels. Twin screws usually turn out at the upper point of revolution, viewed from aft.

TWO BEARINGS AND RUN BETWEEN, a method of obtaining a ship's position. A bearing of a known object is taken and the log is read; a straight course is steered until the bearing of the object has changed considerably, when the log is again read, and a second bearing taken simultaneously. Both bearings are plotted on the chart, and with the distance run on the dividers, the dividers are advanced towards the object with the points kept in the direction of the course steered. At length, the position will be found where the legs of the dividers will rest in the lines of

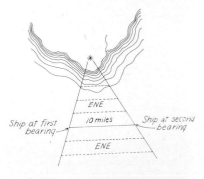

Two Bearings and Run Between

bearing. These points represent the first and second positions of the ship.

TWO BLOCKS, the condition when the two blocks of a purchase have come together by hauling on the fall.

TWO HALF HITCHES, a very useful way of making a line fast.

TWO POINT BEARING, a method of obtaining the distance of a vessel from a lighthouse or other landmark. It is accomplished by multiplying the distance run between the times when the light bears two points forward of the beam, and when it is abeam, by 2½. This term is also often applied to the method of locating a vessel by noting the distance she runs while changing the bearing of an object from two points (22½°) on the bow to four points (45°) on the bow. The distance run is the distance the vessel is off the light at the time of the second bearing. Furthermore, seven-tenths (⁷⁄₁₀) of this distance will be the distance the light, or object, will be passed when abeam. This is valuable information when a reef or rock lies off the object.

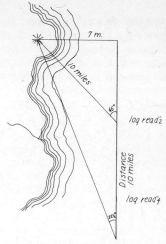

Two-point Bearing

TWO TOPSAIL SCHOONER, one in which there is a square topsail on the main as well as the foremast.

TYE. See Tie or Topsail Tie.

TYE BLOCK. See Tie Block.

TYPHOONS, the violent cyclonic gales of the East Indies and China Seas which correspond to the hurricanes of the West Indies. See Laws of Storms. The word comes from tai fung—tai meaning veering and fung a wind.

U

U., unwatched.

U-BOLT CLIPS, are used in lieu of an eye splice in wire rope. The end of the rope should be against the closed side of the U.

UDOMETER, a rain gauge.

ULLAGE, what a partially filled tank or cask lacks of being full.

ULLAGE PLATE, a small round plate (about 9″) set in the deck of a tanker through which ullage is measured. It is closed by a locking bar across it and is equipped with a firescreen.

UMBRA. That conical space of shadow in the wake of the moon (in a solar eclipse) within which the eclipse is total. The penumbra is that conical space (umbra excluded) within which the eclipse is partial. It follows that a certain position on the earth about to experience a total eclipse of the sun will enter penumbra as the first shadow appears, will enter umbra, as it becomes total, will leave umbra and enter penumbra as the first light appears, and leave penumbra as the last arc of shadow passes. See Eclipse.

UMBRELLA, a conical shield riveted to the casing of the smokestack to protect the air casing from the weather.

UMIAK, a large open Esquimo boat made of skins.

UNA BOAT, a type of small craft in England having a rig similar to a cat boat.

UNDULATING LIGHT, one so designed that the illuminating apparatus rises and lowers, giving an occulting effect to observers in the horizontal plane and raises the beam for the benefit of air craft.

UNBEND, to cast adrift. To remove sails from their spars, or chain from anchor.

UNDER BELOW, a warning call to those beneath of a danger.

UNDER CANVAS, under sail.

UNDER HACK, said of an officer who is confined to his stateroom as a result of a minor infraction of naval discipline.

UNDER THE LEE, off the lee side.

UNDER RUN, to take a line in on one side of a boat and pay it out on the other side. A fisherman *under runs* a trawl, taking the fish off and rebaiting. A log is said to *under run* when the ship goes farther than the log indicates.

UNDER SAIL, to be underway without other power than the wind on the sails.

UNDER WEIGH. See Underway.

UNDERCURRENT, a movement of the water below the surface which may be contrary to the movement of surface water.

UNDERFOOT, the condition when an anchor is under the forefoot but still on the bottom. Also a term applied to the current when it is running fair with the vessel's course.

UNDERHAUL, a term sometimes used when a vessel at anchor rides at an angle to her normal heading due to a subsurface current.

UNDERTOW, a seaward current near the bottom on a beach where there is a surf.

UNDERWAY, a term applied when the anchor has been weighed, or lines cast off from a wharf. A vessel can still be underway even though stopped, provided she has no connection with the land. The term *under weigh* is synonymous, but underway is now given the preference among seamen, way referring to progress while weighing is the raising of the anchor preparatory to making way.

UNDERWRITER, an insurer of vessels and cargoes. When a vessel is offered for insurance various underwriters *underwrite* for a certain portion which they will assume.

UNION DOWN, a distress signal made by hoisting the ensign upside down.

UNION JACK. See Jack.

UNITED STATES COAST AND GEODETIC SURVEY. See National Oceanographic Survey.

UNMOOR, to heave up one anchor—a vessel is moored when more than one anchor is out; to cast off mooring lines.

UNREEVE, to haul a line or rope out of a block, fairlead, etc.

UNRIG, to take down the rigging; to lower a derrick boom and remove its gear, or to send down a topgallant mast and its rigging, etc.

UNSHIP, to detach or remove anything from its proper place, as unship a mast, an oar, a capstan bar, etc.

UNWATCHED (U), a term employed in the lists of lights to designate an automatic light without a keeper.

UP ANCHOR, an order given to heave up and get underway.

UP BEHIND, an order given when the haul on a halyard or other line is complete and slack is needed from the seamen on the line to make fast.

UP AND DOWN, in a vertical position. The chain leads up and down when the anchor is about to come off the bottom.

UP AND DOWN TACKLE, is the one which lifts or lowers a draft of cargo through a hatch.

UPPER DECK. See Deck.

UPPER TOPSAIL, the upper sail of a double topsail square-rigged vessel. It sets by hoisting the upper topsail yard. The lower topsail yard does not hoist, the sail being set by hauling the clews out to the lower yard arms by the sheets. Double top-gallant yards are similarly operated.

UPPER TRANSIT. The passage of a body across the meridian in the visible heavens, in distinction from lower transit below as the body crosses the lower meridian at midnight in case of the sun.

UPPER WORKS, superstructures on the weather deck.

UPSETTING LEVER. See Righting Lever.

UPSETTING MOMENT, the displacement (tons) multiplied by the upsetting lever (in feet). It is expressed in foot-tons.

UPTAKE, the breaching in the smoke flue connecting the boiler with the funnel.

USEFUL LOAD, a vessel's weight tonnage.

V

V-BOTTOM, a type of boat building with a sharp angle at the turn between the sides and the bottom planking instead of the carvel's round side. The boat is sharp forward, but the bottom flattens toward the stern. The chine is very pronounced forward.

V-DEPRESSION, an area within which the isobars are v-shaped. The circulating winds blow according to the usual law down one side of a central line, and up the other. In the vicinity of the point the shift of wind is sudden. One side is usually clear while the other is overcast with rain.

VANE, a streamer of bunting at the mast-head whose head is attached to a vertical axis around which it revolves and shows the direction of the wind. A peep and slot sight of an azimuth compass and pelorus.

VANGS, whips leading from the peak of a gaff to the rails to steady it in a desired position. The tackle in modern yachts leading forward from the end of the boom of a fore and aft sail when running is also called a vang.

VAPS, naval slang for the evaporating tanks.

VARIATION CHART, shows the lines of equal magnetic variation. Variation chart 1706 of the Naval Oceanographic Office covers the world. It is also called an isogonic chart.

'VAST, to stop heaving hauling or pulling.

VEER, to pay out chain or a line. When the wind changes direction to the right—with the hands of a watch, for instance from west to north, it is said to *veer;* otherwise it *backs.* This holds in both hemispheres, North and South.

VEER AND HAUL, to slack and haul alternately.

VELOCITY OF SOUND, in air is 1,117 feet per second at 60°F at sea level standard pressure; in sea water at 60°F, 4,945 feet per second.

VENDAVAL, a stormy period on the coast of Mexico with heavy rain, thunder and lightning. It occurs in the autumn.

VENDAVALES, a southwest wind of the western Mediterranean accompanied by much rain. Frequent in winter.

VENTILATORS cylindrical tubes leading from below to above the decks where cowls catch the wind and force it below. A *ventilating trunk* is the space between two frames when closed to form an air duct to ventilate the bilges. When a system of ducts is built in the stack where the hot air forms a draft it is called a *ventilating fun-*

nel. A *goose-neck* or *swan-neck ventilator* is curved downward at its upper end—that is, through an arc of 180°. A *mushroom ventilator* is one in which the top of the pipe is protected from the entrance of water by a mushroom top but is inefficient as a conductor of air.

VENTURI EFFECT. The weather cloths of the old open bridges and the later solid constructions of wood, metal or glass that now protect the watch standing personnel of all types of craft, deflect the wind upwards over the heads providing the advantage of relatively calm air.

VERNAL EQUINOX, the point in the heavens where the equator and ecliptic intersect (about March 21st), also known as the First Point of Aries. The declination of the sun is 0° at the equator, bound north. The First Point of Aries is in range with the sun and sidereal clocks are in agreement with solar clocks at this time.

VERNIER a small graduated arc which is attached to the index arm of a sextant or other instrument for the purpose of refining the readings of its angles. The length of the vernier scale being equal to a certain number of divisions of the main scale, it is divided into parts numbering one more or one less than the divisions of the main scale. The zero of the vernier indicates the angle on the main arc. If a little to the left of the smallest graduation, this amount can be obtained by noting the graduation of the vernier scale which precisely coincides with a division of the main scale. This vernier reading added to the original amount indicated by the zero of vernier on the main scale will be the angle desired.

VERTEX OF GREAT CIRCLE, the point nearest the pole. The sun is at the northern vertex of the ecliptic on the 21st of June.

VERTICAL CIRCLES, great circles which pass from the zenith to nadir, square with the horizon.

VERY GOOD, the customary acknowledgment of a superior to an acceptable report by a subordinate.

VERY SYSTEM, a method of signaling consisting of a pistol which shoots green or red stars. The dot and dash code is employed, a red star signifying a dot, and a green star a dash. The cartridge is so corrugated that the colors may be distinguished by touch at night. This system is now out of use at sea, but a similar pistol is used to shoot a distress signal by yachts.

VESSEL, a general term for a floating structure that carries passengers or cargo, or both.

VIGIA, an illusion at sea giving the appearance of a shoal or other danger. The report of its existence not being conclusive, perhaps being based on discolored or broken water, it is put on the chart with a reservation as to its authenticity. Shoals and even islets have been reported to hydrographic offices which, through the curious deception of appearances at sea, have been only some form of animalculae, vegetable matter, floating whales, or derelicts. It is from the Spanish word meaning to watch or lookout.

VIKING SHIPS. These ships were characteristically double-ended, of low freeboard with high projecting stem and sternposts; the rails were lined with shields which in a way increased the freeboard. They had sheltered cabin compartments, forward and aft, but the waist was open. The cruising of the Vikings was largely confined to the summer season and the men slept with what shelter a fabric cover afforded; cooking was done ashore when possible. They were rigged with one square sail and a single bank of oars; with these modes of propulsion they made some truly remarkable voyages to Iceland and America.

Among the types of craft used by these people were the *dragon*, a large and very elaborate war vessel; the *snekkja*, a speedy, handsome craft; the *skuta*, small but fast; the *longship* (langskip), a fighting ship; and the *skeid*, a large longship with no figurehead.

VIRGO, the sixth sign of the zodiac.

VISIBLE HORIZON, the line indicated by the meeting of the sky and water.

VOLUNTARY STRANDING, purposely beaching a vessel to escape the greater danger of foundering. This is a case of general average, a loss to be made good by contribution from all parties interested.

VOYAGE, an outward and homeward passage; although the passage from one port to another is often referred to in insurance policies as a voyage.

VOYAGE CHARTER, the agreement to hire a vessel for a voyage, the conditions being stipulated.

VOYAL or **VIOL,** a line formerly made fast to the anchor cable and brought to the capstan (in fact, a messenger) the cable being awkwardly large to make the turns around the capstan. A *voyal block* was used in the lead of the voyal.

VULGAR ESTABLISHMENT, the interval between the time of the moon's passage and the succeeding high water on the days of full and new moon. This interval added to the time of the moon's passage on any day gives a reasonably accurate time of high water.

W

W-C, the difference between the navigator's watch and the chronometer. W-C applied to watch time equals chronometer time. In East longitude the watch, which is set near ship time, is fast of Greenwich time.

W/M, weight or measurement at ship's option, in accepting cargo.

WACK (or Whack), a sailor's share of food—his ration.

WAFT, a flag tied in the center or to a mast. Also called a *wheft.*

WAIF, a term applied to the buoy or signal made fast to the end of a whale line the harpoon of which is fast to a whale. The waif is attached when the whale is temporarily abandoned in order to give pursuit to others and retain title. Some times a drag or *drugg* was attached to hinder the mammal's progress.

WAIST, that part of a vessel's deck between the forecastle and the quarterdeck; the middle part of the fore and aft line. The planking from the covering boards down to the bends.

WAIST ANCHOR, a sheet anchor.

WAISTER, an incompetent or worn out seaman.

WAKE, the track of a vessel left astern. The effect upon the efficiency of the propeller due to its revolving in the forward moving water of the wake current is known as the *wake. Wake of a hatch* is that part directly beneath the opening.

WAKE CURRENT, the motion of water following a vessel set up by the skin friction of the hull. See Skin Resistance.

WALE, a heavy strake running fore and aft below the gunwale, sometimes called the *rubbing strake.* Those strakes of planking between the waterline and topsides. The *wale-piece* is a horizontal timber spiked to a wharf acting as a fender.

WALE SHORES, timbers which hold a vessel upright in a dry dock.

WALK AWAY. See Haul.

WALKING, a peculiar vibration in a steamer when she is "feeling the bottom."

WALKING BEAM, the oscillating beam of a beam engine conspicuous on many of the older side-wheel steamers.

WALL KNOT, a knot made in the end of a rope.

WALL-SIDED, a straight-sided vessel.

WARDROOM, the officers' compartment aboard ship.

WARM FRONT, a mass of warm air riding on a "wedge" of retreating cold air. As the warm air cools, clouds are formed several hundred miles ahead; first high cirrus, stratus and nimbus with precipitation over and just ahead of the actual front.

WARP, a light hawser used for warping; to haul a vessel by an anchor (kedge) carried ahead or by a line (a warp) carried to a buoy or wharf. A line for hauling a vessel with the power of the capstan or man-power, not a towline. The distortion in the shape of timbers due to weather.

WARPING WINCHES, are located on the poop for warping purposes.

WARSAW RULES, intended to facilitate the establishment of uniform rules to govern the terms of C.I.F. contracts.

WASH BOARDS or **STRAKES,** comparatively thin oak boards secured so as to project above the edge of a cockpit of boats and small vessels. They are coamings.

WASH PLATE (or Bulkhead), a baffle plate.

WASH PORT, an opening in the bulwark protected by bars for the freeing of sea water.

WASTE, disused cotton yarn; it is used for brass work and about machinery.

WATCH, a period of time on duty. A watch is usually four hours long, changing at 12, 4 and 8 o'clock. In order that a man will not get the same watch each day, the 4 to 8 p.m. period is divided and called the *dog watches*. The persons off watch are said to be in the *watch below. Watch and watch* is the term applied when there is a routine of four hours on and four hours off. Sometimes called "toe and heel" watches. A facetious interpretation of the term *watch and watch* given among deepwater mates was: "I'll watch you and you watch me." The watches are named as follows:

4 a.m. to 8 a.m., Morning watch
8 a.m. to 12 noon, Forenoon watch
12 noon to 4p.m., Afternoon watch
4 p.m. to 6 p.m., First dog watch
6 p.m. to 8 p.m., Second dog watch
8 p.m. to 12 mid., First watch
12 mid. to 4 a.m., Middle (mid) watch

A buoy floating is said to *watch* in distinction from being dragged under.

WATCH BUOY, a station buoy, auxiliary to the main navigational aid.

WATCH CAP, the canvas cover over the funnel of a naval vessel whose boilers are not in use. A blue woolen cap worn by enlisted men of the Navy.

WATCH HO WATCH, a warning call given by the men along the rail as the line leaves their hands when sounding by hand with a deep-sea lead. It is seldom heard these days.

WATCH TACKLE, one comprising a single and double block, also known as a luff tackle and sometimes called a clew jigger, a jigger, and a handy billy.

WATCH TIME. See C-W or W-C.

WATER BALLAST, that carried in the double bottoms or low flat tanks. It is pumped out, or flooded by sea cocks, properly to trim the ship.

WATER BOAT, a tank boat which serves with fresh water vessels lying in the stream.

WATER BOTTOMS, the flat water ballast tanks in the bottom of a steamer; double bottoms.

WATER BUTT, a water cask.

WATER COURSES, limber holes and gutters in the lower compartments.

WATER FINDER, a device for measuring the water that may exist in the bottom of an oil tank when full.

WATER-LAID ROPE, left-handed. Also that made by wetting the fibers before spinning instead of using grease.

WATER-LINE, the line indicated along the side of a vessel by the plane of the surface of the water. The line separating the bottom paint from that of the topsides. There are *load* and *light water-lines.*

WATER-LOGGED, the condition of a vessel kept afloat only by the buoyancy of her cargo. To be so saturated with water as to lose buoyancy.

WATER MONKEY, a globular (usually) piece of pottery made of porous clay. The evaporation of the water seeping to the outside keeps the contents cool. They are used aboard vessels in tropic waters.

WATER PAN BRACKET, the fixture often found fitted beneath an air port to catch leakage and to support the open port.

WATER SAIL or **SAVE ALL,** a small sail formerly set under the lower studding-sails.

WATER SKY, the reflection of the blue sea water upon the sky in polar regions.

WATER SPAR, a spar used to hoist water aboard a vessel at sea for washing purposes. It is rigged derrick-fashion with a snatch block at its head with a whip through it and with bag or bucket attached.

WATER SPOUT, a phenomenon at sea of the same character as a whirlwind or tornado on the land. The upward rushing air takes on a gyratory motion becoming so violent as to carry up spray and actual water in a great hour-glass-shaped column. They are often very threatening in appearance. They can be very destructive to a sailing vessel; less to powered vessels.

WATER WHIPS, purchases used from yards to take aboard moderate weights. They are usually gun tackles.

WATERBORNE, to lie in sufficient water to float freely.

WATERLITE, a trade name for the small containers of a chemical which upon coming in contact with salt water burns as a brilliant torch for the assistance of a man overboard. They are usually attached to a life preserver. An electric light for the same purpose is a later development, but an electronic device now gives the life buoy its most brilliant light.

WATERPLANE, the plane of a saw-cut (if it can be imagined) of a ship severed from her underbody along her waterline. It is the plane of her waterline. There are *load waterplanes* and *light waterplanes.*

WATERTIGHT COMPARTMENTS, spaces protected by watertight bulkheads and doors. Water gaining entrance to one compartment is excluded from others.

WATERWAY, the channel iron serving as a gutter at the side of a ship's deck; the last outboard plank of a wooden deck usually heavier than others and so hollowed as to carry off the water by way of the scuppers. The *waterway bar* is the angle iron forming the inner side of the waterways against which the deck planking lies.

WAVE PROFILE, the actual waterline in still water while underway at a certain speed.

WAVES, undulations of the sea. The *period of waves* is the time between two successive crests while the *length* is the distance between them. The *height* is the distance from trough to crest. A wave *breaks* when its crest topples forward. This occurs in heavy weather or when tripped by shoal water.

WAX, the moon is said to wax when growing after new moon.

WAY, a vessel's movement through the water. *Way over the bottom* is the actual distance made good in position whether aided or retarded by current.

WAY ENOUGH, a boat order, when there is sufficient motion to reach the landing point.

WAYS. A ship is built on a foundation upon which are laid two long inclined timbers leading beneath the water. These are stationary and are called *ground ways*. Upon these are laid the *sliding* or *launching ways*, upon which the partially completed vessel slides down the incline to the water. A cradle is built on the sliding way to support the ship and launching tallow is used generously between the ground and sliding ways. A vessel hauls out on the *ways* (Marine Railway) to be examined and repaired. These comprise a movable cradle on a foundation which extends out beneath the water. The cradle runs beneath and receives the vessel and she is hauled out by mechanical power.

WEAR, a maneuver by which a vessel is brought on the other tack by going around before the wind. Some vessels will not tack and are shifted from one tack to the other by wearing. This is sometimes a thrilling maneuver when a ship is suddenly found on a lee shore.

WEATHER, towards the point from which the wind blows. The side towards the wind is the *weather side*, as is the *weather bow, weather quarter, weather yardarm*, etc. The condition of coming through, as, *she weathered the cape*, that is, got around, a ship may, when riding easily in a gale, be said to be *making good weather of it*; or, if laboring dangerously, to be *making heavy weather of it*.

WEATHER BITT, an extra turn of the chain around the windlass.

WEATHER BOARDS, planks placed above the rail of an open boat to keep out the water coming over the bow.

WEATHER-BOUND, to be detained by weather conditions.

WEATHER-BREEDER, a fair day which seems to presage foul weather.

WEATHER CLOTHS, canvas spread around a bridge to afford protection from the wind.

WEATHER DECK, a deck without overhead protection; the uppermost deck.

WEATHER EYE OPEN, to be on one's guard.

WEATHER GAGE, the windward position.

WEATHER GALL, the bright edge of a cloud from which rain can be seen falling.

WEATHER GLEAM, the clearing to windward of a storm cloud.

WEATHER HELM, the tendency of a vessel to come to the wind, requiring the helm up a little to maintain the course.

WEATHER MAIN and **LEE CROJIK BRACES,** an order in a square-rigged ship when wearing. It is a phrase identified in many a sailor's memory with some close call on a lee shore. This order manned the gear of the after yards whenever the helm was put up.

WEATHER ROLL, the lateral oscillation of a vessel towards the wind and sea. When a vessel rolls to windward she invites a boarding sea.

WEATHER SHORE, the coast lying in the direction from which the wind is coming.

WEATHER SIDE, that upon which the wind is blowing. It is good sea usage to speak of moving to windward, or an object is to windward, while all parts of the vessel on the side towards the wind are spoken of for instance, as the *weather yardarm,* the *weather rigging, weather brace,* etc. The old sailors differentiated the use of weather and windward thus: It is the weather side of a vessel, but another ship was to windward of them.

WEATHER SIGNALS, flags shown at most seaports in anticipation of coming meteorological conditions. See Storm Signals.

WEATHER SYMBOLS,

CLR ... Clear
SCT ... Scattered clouds
BKN ... Broken clouds
OVC ... Overcast
T ...... Thunder storm
R ...... Rain
L ...... Drizzle
E ...... Sleet
F ...... Fog
S ...... Snow
A ...... Hail
H ...... Haze
K ...... Smoke
D ...... Dust.

WEATHER TIDE, one that sets to windward.

WEATHERLY, a seaworthy vessel with especially good qualities in working to windward.

WEAVER'S KNOT, a sheet bend.

WEB, the vertical portion or depth of a beam, the athwartship dimension of a frame, etc.

WEB FRAME, a frame with a deep web, composed of web plates. The *web frame system* provides greater strength by making every sixth frame of extra heavy construction.

WEB SLING, a flat woven strap for handling bag cargo liable to be ruptured by a rope sling.

WEDDING KNOT, a crossed seizing that is placed between two eyes.

WEEPING, a very slow leak; seepage.

WEFT. See Wheft.

WEIGH, to raise the anchor.

WEIGHING LINE, usually of wire; it is made fast to the crown of an anchor for the purpose of recovering it should the cable part or be slipped.

WELD, to join two pieces of metal, leaving no joints. It is accomplished by applying a high degree of heat necessary to fuse and unite the parts as they are held in the position desired. This is done by an electric arc; by a torch burning acetylene gas and oxygen; and by the thermit process.

WELDED SHIP, one in which all joints are made by the electric process of welding, no rivets being used in the construction. Such a ship is estimated to take 15 per cent less steel, 40 per cent less labor and to have 5 per cent greater capacity.

WELIN DAVIT, one whose lower end is in the form of a cogged arc, swinging out and in with great facility by the use of cranks which operate the gears.

WELL, the space on the main deck of a steamer lying between the topgallant forecastle and the so-called midship house, also between the latter and the topgallant poop. Such type is called a *well-deck steamer.* A cylindrical chamber about the pumps, or the rectangular space in which a center board is hoisted.

WEST COUNTRY WHIPPING. See Whipping.

WESTERLIES, an area in which westerly winds prevail, notably in the southern latitudes of the Atlantic, Pacific, and Indian Oceans, where the westerlies blow consistently around the world.

WESTERN OCEAN, North Atlantic.

WET COMPASS, a spirit compass.

WET DOCK, a basin made necessary in harbors of great tidal range in order that vessels may remain afloat. They enter at high water and the gates are then closed retaining the water.

WET NURSE, an officer acting as an instructor to a man taking over the duties of a bridge watch.

WHACK, a seaman's allowance of food; a share.

WHALE. In zoology whales are classed as cetacea. This classification embraces whales and dolphins which are warm-blooded mammals and suckle their young. These mammals are divided into two great families: those which have teeth, and those which are provided with whalebone, so-called, or baleen.

The family of toothed whales is led by the great *sperm whale* (cachalot), which is from 60 to 70 feet long, reaching 80 feet in some instances. It is an inhabitant of warm seas and is made conspicuous by its large head with an abrupt forehead. Within its head is a curious fatty substance from which the highly prized spermaceti oil is obtained. Sperm whales are met in groups or singly; when cruising singly the mammal is invariably a bull, for in the breeding season terrific fights occur between bulls for the custody of a pod of cow whales. A vanquished bull is forced to become an outcast on the sea.

Then there are *beaked whales* of moderate size, among which are the *bottle-nosed* species. They are very active, being able to leap clear of the water. The toothed whale family merges into that of the *dolphins* of which the largest is the *grampus* or *killer whale* reaching 25 or 30 feet in length. It is marked by bands of white and yellow and is a very rapacious creature, even attacking larger whales. The *caaing whale* is more commonly called *blackfish.* It is taken, when no other whales are in sight, but yields a lower grade of oil. The *beluga* is a small whale, only about 12 feet long, and is found particularly off the coasts of Newfoundland and Labrador. It is whitish in color. The *narwhal,* a native of the Arctic, is a curious creature having a long horn or tusk projecting straight forward. It grows to be about 20 feet in length. These small whales come under the head of the dolphinidae family of dolphins. The *porpoise* of this family differs little from other dolphins except in the teeth—porpoise teeth being wedge-shaped, and those of the dolphin pointed. The jaws of the porpoise do not form a beak as is the case with other dolphins. The common dolphin of the coryphaena family, also known as the *dorado,* changes with brilliant colors as it dies in the sun on deck.

The whalebone family consists of *right whales (bowhead* and *biscayan)* which have very large heads and long whalebone (see baleen), and *rorquals (finback* and *humpbacks)* which have short whalebone. They have, respectively, a conspicuous fin and a hump, whence their names. A right whale sounds with flukes of the tail upward, while the rorquals disappear gradually. The bowhead or Greenland whale is found near the ice, while the biscayan whale or a very similar type, is (or was) found in the temperate waters of almost all the world. The largest whale of the sea is the *blue whale* or *sulphur bottom* of the rorquals, whose length averages 80 feet. It is bluish gray on the upper parts with a white and yellowish underbody. The largest whale on record was stranded in the Australian Bight in 1918 and measured 87 feet 4 inches in a straight line. Other greater lengths have been reported.

WHALE SHARK, the largest of the sharks having rows of spots over the body. This fish reaches 40 feet in length.

WHALEBACK, a type of steamer formerly much used on the Great Lakes. Its topsides round in like a whale's back and its machinery is aft.

WHALEBOAT, a very seaworthy double-ended single-banked pulling boat. It is commonly a *whaler,* which latter term is sometimes applied to vessels engaged in the whaling industry, but whaleship is better. The whaleboat was carried at davits, called cranes, and was used to pursue the whale. It was equipped with a sail and five oars; the aftermost (starboard) was the stroke *oar,* the next forward was the *tub oar,* next the *middle* or *midships,* second from the bow the *bow oar* and forward the *harpoon oar.* The latter was pulled by the harpooner, or *boatsteerer,* until nearing a whale when he laid aside the oar for the harpoon. Naval vessels carry a whaleboat; it is used as a lifeboat.

WHARF, a projecting structure extending off to a depth of water sufficient to accommodate vessels alongside, where they are discharged, loaded and repaired. The term has been somewhat superseded by the word *pier* when applied to the great solid structures of the larger municipalities.

WHARFAGE (usually), the charge made against a vessel for the use of a wharf for loading, discharging or storing cargo.

WHARFINGER, a man in charge of a wharf. Now on larger wharves called the pier superintendent.

WHEEL, the part of the steering apparatus where the power is controlled or applied. There are wheels operating hand gear, steam and electric engines or motors. The propeller is often called the wheel.

WHEEL CHAINS, those which connect the steering wheel with the tiller.

WHEEL RODS, iron rods forming part of the line of the wheel ropes or chains.

WHEEL ROPES. See Wheel Chains.

WHEELHOUSE, the deckhouse within which the steering wheel is located. In many steamers the officer stands his watch here.

WHEELSMAN, the man at the wheel, especially applied to those on lakes, rivers and sometimes tugboats.

WHEFT, any flag tied in the center, or with fly tied to the staff. Also spelled *waft* and *weft.* Originally used as a distress signal.

WHELPS, corrugated parts of a capstan barrel or iron strips bolted to the barrel of a windlass to give the chain or rope a better hold, and to prevent chafing the wood.

WHERE AWAY, a question directed to a lookout reporting a sail, light or object. He is expected to answer, giving the bearing.

WHERRY, a small light rowboat; a small cargo boat of the coast of England which has one large mast stepped well forward and sets a large sail with a gaff but no boom.

WHIFFLING BREEZE, light and erratic.

WHIP, a single block with a rope rove through it. If there are two single blocks, it is a *double whip.* To *whip a rope* is to bind the strands of its end with yarn or cord.

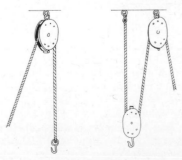

Whip   Double Whip

WHIP AND RUNNER, a whip in which the block is spliced in the end of a pendant.

WHIPPING. A rope is *whipped* by winding sail twine around the end of it to prevent fagging. If the twine is not tucked through the strands it is called a *west country whipping.*

WHIPSTAFF, a vertical lever extending upward from the end of the tiller by which ancient vessels were steered. The staff passed through a roller unit set in a cross beam at about the first third of its length. This allowed the steering, or whipstaff, to be moved athwartships activating the tiller.

WHIP-UPON-WHIP, where a whip is clapped upon the fall of another whip.

WHIRLWIND, a diminutive cyclone.

WHISKER POLE, an aluminum spar used when carrying a spinnaker. Its inner end is secured by a bale to the mast while the outer end engages the after spinnaker guy with a snap fitting. The pole extends a foot to 3 feet beyond the shroud and protects it from chafe when the guy leads far forward.

WHISKERS (Whisker Booms), horizontal spars, iron or wood, extending at right angles from the bowsprit to spread the jib-boom guys. They are used also to spread the jib nets.

WHISTLING BUOY, an aid to navigation having apparatus which causes a whistle to operate as it rises and falls on the waves. They serve as a warning of dangers and also in other places as fairway buoys.

WHITE HORSE, meat from the head of a sperm whale.

WHITE ROPE, untarred hemp.

WHITE SQUALL, a sudden and violent wind difficult to anticipate which covers the sea with spindrift. Some seamen claim that white squalls are unaccompanied by clouds, and hence dangerous by the lack of this warning.

WHITE WATER, breaking wave crests in coastal waters due to oceanic waves shortening and steepening by the shoaling depths. Also the light-colored water seen over shallow water with a white sand bottom.

WHITECAPS or **HORSES' MANES,** the crested foam seen on the tops of waves in a breeze. The term *white horses* is often seen, but refers more to the white crests of breakers than to the crests of seas on the open ocean.

WHOLE GALE, a wind moving with a velocity of 48 to 55 knots.

WIDE BERTH, a comfortable distance from a ship, a shoal or the shore.

WIDOW'S MEN, fictitious names carried on ships in the Elizabethan era. Their pay went to the benefit of naval widows.

WIGWAG, a system of distance hand signaling, using a flag or a light on a long staff to spell messages by Morse code—a dip to the right indicates a dot and to the left a dash.

WILD, applied to a vessel steering

badly, or to an oarsman without good control of his oars. Any of the ship's gear out of control.

WILDCAT, the part of a windlass around which the chain leads and which revolves when heaving in or out the chain. The wildcat is so recessed as to receive the chain links and prevent its slipping.

WILLIE-WILLIES, small violent cyclones on the northwest coast of Australia.

WILLIWAW (williwaus), a very violent burst of wind coming with great suddenness off the mountains of the Patagonian Channels and Magellan Strait. This term has been extended to other localities, notably Alaska.

WINCH, a piece of machinery which operates a horizontal or vertical shaft, upon its ends being fitted the drums by which lines and tackle, or whip falls are hove in. Winches are driven by either steam or electricity and are used for the loading and discharging of cargo, and the handling of spars and sails. There are various types of small yacht winches operated by removable handles. Some are geared on top, some at the bottom, some have built-in cleats. There is a type capable of unwinding to ease off a line. These winches serve to increase the capability of the crew of a racing yacht and to lighten manual labor in hoisting sail and hardening sheets.

WINCH PLATFORM, or **TABLE.** a raised structure, usually around a mast, upon which cargo winches are installed.

WINCHMAN, the operator of a cargo winch. He skillfully applies the power smoothly when there is slack in a fall, lifts without sudden surge and eases in the brake when the draft of cargo reaches the bottom of the loading hold or discharging pier.

WIND, air in motion, current of air.

WIND BOUND, a condition of idleness due to head winds.

WIND CATCHER, a scoop of sheet metal open forward which is thrust into an air port to force air into a stateroom.

WIND GALLS, portions of rainbows.

WIND RODE, the condition of a vessel riding to the wind, the dominating influence affecting her.

WIND ROSE, a diagram of wind averages found on the pilot charts.

WIND A VESSEL, to turn end for end at a pier or a tug to wind a tow by giving a sheer, casting off after line and using stem to assist stern of tow around.

WINDFALL. In England no trees (oak) could be cut in early days, except for the Navy, but when blown down they were exempted from the law and became a *windfall*. Hence, a bit of good fortune is called a windfall.

WINDJAMMER, a sailing vessel or a person who sailed in such craft. Orignially applied to those deep water square-rigged vessels, but is of relatively recent origin.

WINDLASS, a machine for hoisting an anchor. It is made in various forms, some working by hand with brakes, others by steam and electricity. In general it is a machine with a horizontal shaft on which the wildcat and winch head revolve. It is driven, in the case of steam, with an ordinary reversible engine working a worm gear. The hand windlass still found on some sailing vessels is a horizontal cylinder revolved by hand brakes and a ratchet.

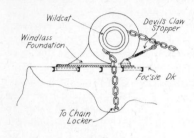

Windlass

WINDLASS BITTS, projecting timbers that support and rise above the old-fashioned windlass. They are also called *carrick-heads.*

WIND'S EYE, the direction from which the wind comes.

WINDSAIL. Fresh air is forced below by means of a canvas tube

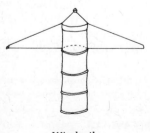

Windsail

which has an opening in the side near the top. On either side of the opening are canvas wings designed and set to catch the wind and force it down the tube to the holds below. It is suspended from a stay by a halyard and the wings are held by guys.

WINDSCOOP. See Wind Catcher.

WINDWARD, the general direction from which the wind blows. It is a point of reference in designating a movement or a location. See Weather.

WINDWARD FLOOD, the wind blowing out against a flood tide.

WINDWARD TIDE, a tide which sets to windward.

WING BOARDS, boards built at an angle extending down from a hatch in a coal bunker to prevent the coal from shifting into these corners (the wings) which might give the ship a dangerous list. (Cook's *Shipbuilder's Handbook.*)

WING AND WING, sail of a fore and aft vessel running before the wind with her booms on opposite sides. Also called by sailors "Wung out."

WINGERS, casks stowed in the wings of a hold.

WINGS, the parts of a hold or bridge deck out near the sides. *Winging* weights is to move them outboard, thereby increasing the period of roll.

WINTER LOAD LINE, one having extra freeboard for winter conditions.

WIRE DRAG, a device for ascertaining depth of water, the existence of pinnacle rocks, etc., more quickly and efficaciously than can be done with the sounding lead. It consists primarily of a wire hawser suspended from floats by stirrups which carry twenty-pound shots at the bottom to preserve steadiness. A tension is kept on the hawser by towing launches at which a spring balance is cut in to show the strain. If a pinnacle is caught or the shots take bottom, the strain immediately increases and the circular line of buoys become V-shaped. The stirrups can be set at any desired depth and the area swept accordingly. This method allows hydrographers to report an area clear of shoals and especially pinnacle rocks which formerly so often escaped detection when using the sounding lead.

WIRE ROPE. The durability and efficiency of wire rope has increased in late years. New processes of depositing zinc as a protective coating allows bending without flaking or chipping. Stainless steel rigging is a notable advance in durability. In wire rope a group of seven wires lend themselves conveniently to form a strand— six around a central wire. In standing rigging, not requiring flexibility, seven wires form a core, turned around which are twelve wires of the same gauge. Another type of standing rigging has a core of seven wires surrounded by six strands of seven wires each and is known as 7 x 7 rope. The fiber core formerly used in wire rope is largely superseded by wire. Where

flexibility is desired as in running rigging and tiller ropes, the strands are laid up around a core of nineteen wires with six 19-wire strands laid up around it; this is called 7 x 19 running rigging rope; it is stronger than 6 x 19 where a fiber core is used. Wire rope has, roughly, three times the strength of Manila.

WIRE ROPE CLIPS, metal devices which are designed to clamp two parts of a wire rope in lieu of a splice.

WIRES, a common name for wire rope gear.

WISHBONE GAFF, a spar used particularly in the staysail rig. The clew of the foresail is sheeted to the end of this gaff. It is sharply bowed on each side of the sail to prevent chafing.

WITH THE SUN, with the hands of a watch or sun's path from east to west.

WITHE (or Wythe), an iron ring at the end of a mast, boom or yard through which another spar can be run out; as for instance, the iron ring on a yardarm through which a studding-sail boom was run out.

WOODLOCK, a piece of wood bolted beneath the pintles of a rudder to hold it down and prevent unshipping.

WOOD PACK CLOUDS, those of cumulus type.

WOOLDING, a rope lashing around a fished spar to reenforce and support it.

WORKAWAYS, persons working for a passage; also homeward

bound men put on a ship by a consul.

WORKING LINES, those with which a vessel is made fast or worked around the docks.

WORKING POOL, an area of clear water amidst ice in which a vessel can maneuver.

WORKING SAILS, those used regularly, those not specially set like a studding sail or a balloon jib, etc. In a schooner this includes the lower sails. The so-called *four lowers* of a fisherman (schooner) comprise the jib, fore staysail (jumbo), foresail and mainsail.

WORKING TO WINDWARD, proceeding toward the direction of the wind by repeated tacks.

WORKS, a vessel *works* when her different members begin to have play where there is rigidity under normal conditions; a cargo *works* when the stowage ceases to be compact.

WORMING, to lay small stuff in between the strands of a rope.

WRACK, seaweed, kelp and flotsam in general cast up on a beach or floating. A bit of detached fast-moving cloud.

WRECK, a disabled or totally destroyed vessel.

WRECK MASTER, the man in charge of salvage operations.

WRECKER, a salvager of wrecks and wreckage. The term is applied to both legitimate and illegitimate salvage.

WRECKING CABLE, hawser laid cable, fourteen to sixteen inches in circumference.

WRECKING TUG, one equipped with powerful pumps and wrecking outfit.

WRIGGLE, a piece of iron over an air port like an eyebrow which diverts the water running down the vessel's side.

X

XEBEC, a vessel native to the Mediterranean Sea, formerly used chiefly by the Barbary corsairs. They were distinguished by an unusual overhang forward and aft, by low freeboard, and by the extreme crown of the decks. There appear to have been many hull forms of the Xebec, some with flat floors and hard bilges and flaring sides, while others had narrow floors and no tumble home. They employed an interchange of rig, comprising large square sails, for light favorable winds, large lateen sails for windward work, and small lateens for heavy weather.

Y

Y-GUN, a two-barreled Y-shaped mortar developed in World War I for the simultaneous discharge of two depth charges, one on each beam of a vessel.

YACHT, a sail, steam or motor vessel used for pleasure, and usually a fast, fine-lined craft. Yachts of sufficient tonnage to require documenting sail under a legal paper called a license.

The question may arise when a boat becomes a yacht? An answer might be: When the navigating and maneuvering of the craft becomes a task greater than the owner's capacity and the services of friends or hired hands are employed.

YANKEE JIB TOPSAIL, a British term for a large jib topsail first popularized by American yachtsmen who call it the Number 1 jib top.

YARD, a spar crossing a mast horizontally from which a square sail is set; a tract of ground on the waterfront used for the construction and repair of boats and vessels.

YARD BOOM, a derrick or cargo boom swung over the ship's side and guyed. The *yard whip* or tackle attached to this boom takes the draft of cargo from the *hatch whip* and swings it overside without shifting the booms. This is known as the yard or spar and boom gear.

YARD ROPE, that used for hoisting or lowering a yard.

YARD TACKLE, one attached to a lower yard where the latter is used as a derrick or a cargo boom.

YARD WHIP. See Yard Boom.

YARDARM, a yard is divided for easy designation into two parts, port and starboard; the outer quarter of each of these parts is the yardarm.

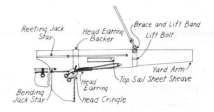

Yardarm Detail

YARN, a number of fibers twisted together; also called a thread. See Rope. A story.

YARROW STERN, is the design where the profile shows a strong rake forward or in simpler terms the stern is farther aft at the waterline than at the rail. In some designs the forward raking stem and yarrow stern bring the profile lines of the bow and stern parallel with pleasing results.

YAW, to steer badly, as of a ship, usually in running before the wind.

YAWL, a convenient rig consisting of two masts, the after one being much smaller and set abaft the sternpost.

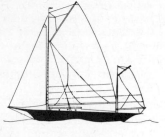

Yawl

YAWL BOAT, a heavily constructed, square-sterned, pulling, work boat, usually about 16-18 feet long. They used to be carried at the stern davits of our coasting schooners. Some were equipped with gasoline engines.

YELLOW JACK, yellow fever. The quarantine flag Q.

YEOMAN, a petty officer, clerk or storekeeper. But in the British Navy a *yeoman for signals* corresponds with the American signal quartermaster.

YOKE, a cross piece of wood or metal fitting on the rudderhead of a small boat to steer by using *yoke ropes* or *lanyards.*

YORK-ANTWERP RULES. 1924, a title given to rules drawn up or rather revised at Stockholm, Sweden, by an international conference, to aid in the adjustment of general average, and offering a uniform basis to follow. They were first formulated in Glasgow in 1860 and have been revised several times since.

Z

Z-FRAME, a reversed angle iron which in cross-section is z-shaped.

ZENITH DISTANCE, the angular distance from the zenith to a body. It is found by subtracting its corrected altitude from 90°.

ZIGZAG, a combination of courses used by a vessel or convoy to confuse an attack by a submarine.

ZINCS, plates of this metal placed at points where bronze comes in

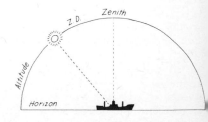

Zenith Distance

contact with steel in order to prevent electrolytic action.

ZODIAC, a belt around the heavens about 8° each side of the ecliptic. It is divided into twelve parts of 30° each and has signs of conventional characters to represent them. The names and signs are as follows:

Spring: Aries (♈), Taurus (♉), Gemini (♊); Summer: Cancer (♋), Leo (♌), Virgo (♍); Autumn: Libra (♎), Scorpio (♏), Sagittarius (♐); Winter: Capricornus (♑), Aquarius (♒), Pisces (♓).

ZODIACAL LIGHT, a phenomenon usually met in the tropics, a faint white light that appears in the wake of a setting sun and in advance of a rising sun.

ZONDA, a hot wind of the Argentine pampas.

ZONE TIME, standard time of the sea. The earth is divided into 15° bands of longitude, each carrying the time of its central meridian, that is, the band lying between 52° 30′ W., and 67° 30′ W., carries +4 zone time, because the 60th meridian is at its center. It is 4 hours earlier (by the watch face) than that of Greenwich at 0°. The sign plus is used because adding 4 to any hour of the day will convert that hour into Greenwich Mean Time (G.M.T.). Conversely −4 zone is 60° east of the prime meridian.

ZONES. The torrid zone lies between 23½° N. and 23½° S. The north and south temperate zones lie between 23½° and 66½° in the respective hemispheres. The frigid zones lie poleward of 66½°.

ZULU, a Scotch lug-rigged fishing boat.